Native Pragmatism

Native Pragmatism

RETHINKING THE ROOTS OF AMERICAN PHILOSOPHY

SCOTT L. PRATT

INDIANA
UNIVERSITY
PRESS

Bloomington and Indianapolis

Parts of chapters 2 and 9 were previously published as "Native American Thought and the Origins of Pragmatism," in *Ayaangwaamizin: The International Journal of Indigenous Philosophy* 1, no. 1 (1997): 55–80.

This book is a publication of
Indiana University Press
601 North Morton Street
Bloomington, IN 47404-3797 USA

http://iupress.indiana.edu

Telephone orders   800-842-6796
Fax orders   812-855-7931
Orders by e-mail   iuporder@indiana.edu

The paper used in this publication meets the minimum requirements of American National Standard for Information Sciences—Permanence of Paper for Printed Library Materials, ANSI Z39.48-1984.

Manufactured in the United States of America

Library of Congress Cataloging-in-Publication Data
Pratt, Scott L.
Native pragmatism : rethinking the roots of American philosophy / Scott L. Pratt.
p.   cm.
Includes bibliographical references and index.
ISBN 0-253-34078-0 (cloth : alk. paper) — ISBN 0-253-21519-6 (pbk. : alk. paper)
1. Pragmatism. 2. Philosophy, American. 3. Indians of North America—
Philosophy. I. Title.
B944.P72 P74 2002
144'.3—dc21
2001005662

1 2 3 4 5   07 06 05 04 03 02

FOR MARY

CONTENTS

ACKNOWLEDGMENTS

My sense of place and history begins in a stretch of prairie on the south edge of the flood plain of the Rock River in northern Illinois where I grew up. From my grandfather, who farmed this land, I gained a sense of the way a place makes a person; from my grandmother, a storyteller, I learned how history makes a place and how retelling the past makes new futures possible. This project began in the spirit of my grandparents as an attempt to give credit where it is due, to look at what had been left out of histories of European American thought, and to tell the story again with a different future implied.

I began this project under the guidance of Douglas Lewis, who, as my mentor and friend at the University of Minnesota, helped me to give form and direction to my work in philosophy. At the University of Oregon I was privileged to receive invaluable encouragement and criticism from Mark Johnson and Nancy Tuana. Much that is right about this book owes to our conversations; the mistakes, of course, are my own. I would also like to thank my other colleagues at Oregon who have been willing to engage in long conversations about early Native American literature, the philosophical commitments of colonialism, and alternative ways of understanding the growth of American pragmatism. In particular, I would like to thank Shari Huhndorf, John Lysaker, Sidner Larson, Lorraine Brundige, and Rob Proudfoot. I would also like to thank those who provided opportunities to discuss this work in the wider context of ongoing work in American philosophy: Erin McKenna, John McDermott, Charlene Haddock Seigfried, Viola Cordova, Thomas Alexander, and Leonard Harris. These philosophers are among the best examples of people whose work is tightly bound to the central strand of the pluralist American tradition that began along the border between Native and European peoples in the seventeenth century. I am also grateful for the formative influence of Scott Crom, Beloit College, on my own philosophical history and for the editorial assistance of Richard Breiter in preparing the final draft of this work.

Finally, I would like to thank my parents, Lawrence and Betty

Pratt, for decades of unfailing support and confidence that someday the book would be done. And for this last accomplishment, finishing this book, I owe my deepest thanks to Mary Breiter, my wife, and to our sons Alex and Aaron, whose patience, support, and love made all of this possible.

INTRODUCTION

Pragmatism is America's most distinctive philosophy. In the received history, it has been understood as a development of European thought in response to the "American wilderness." A closer examination, however, reveals that the roots and central commitments of pragmatism are grounded not just in European intellectual traditions, but also in ways of thinking indigenous to North America. In this book I will present a different history of pragmatism that traces its origins along the border between Native and European America in a context significantly conditioned by Native American thought.

It is common for critics of American thought and culture to argue that American history is fundamentally a story of conquest, dispossession, slavery, and destruction. American philosophy and history, from this perspective, is finally the philosophy and history of Europeans in America made distinct by their particular form of capitalism and imperialism. While one can view American thought as a kind of intellectual (or perhaps anti-intellectual) monolith, a broader reading of the past argues against a single "American way" and in favor of a complex story of interaction among Europeans, Native peoples, and other peoples and cultures as they came together in the Western hemisphere. Although it is rarely clear from the published histories, the immigrant Europeans were never alone in America and were never free of the diverse influences of those they encountered, enslaved, and dispossessed. While some held fast to particular ways of thinking that justified and rewarded the processes of colonization, others came to learn new ideas. Those who did the latter sought to structure American communities in ways compatible with the richness they found. When this complex history is recognized, the American intellectual tradition can be seen to have at least two lines of development, one largely dominated by a philosophical perspective exported to the Americas from Europe, and another informed by an indigenous philosophical perspective. That pragmatism is, in important ways, a product of European philosophy is already well-recognized. My purpose will be to examine the ways in which it is also a product of an indigenous philosophy.

Evidence for the claim that an indigenous philosophical perspective served as a crucial source of American pragmatism involves three general points. First, the central commitments of the later classical pragmatism of Charles S. Peirce, William James, and John Dewey are apparent much earlier in Native American thought, particularly within Northeastern Native traditions. These commitments, I will argue, are prefigured in indigenous thought at a time when European thought in America was marked by a set of contrary commitments. Second, there are at least some clear cases in the seventeenth, eighteenth, and early nineteenth centuries where one can reasonably trace the influence of these Native commitments on European American thinkers. I will argue that these figures, who are also important in the development of the recognized American philosophical tradition, were in a position to learn from the Native perspective and integrate aspects of indigenous philosophy into their own philosophical perspectives. Third, a genealogy can be given connecting these early European American thinkers to the philosophical context out of which classical pragmatism emerged. This genealogy is crucial because it helps to affirm that pragmatism is not simply a further development of modern European thought faced with the conditions of a "wilderness." Rather, it develops as a philosophy of resistance, to challenge the European perspective. The genealogy also suggests that pragmatism is not only a critical perspective but one that tries to respond to the problems faced by those who find themselves in a place where radically different peoples meet and seek to coexist.

The reconstructed history brings two significant results. First, by locating the origins of American pragmatism in Native thought and tracing its development as a resistance movement, it converts the limited canon of well-known academic philosophers into a broad philosophical tradition. This expanded tradition requires a place for the philosophical voices of Native people, women, and others within American philosophy and provides a means to frame their points of agreement and divergence in an ongoing dialogue with both the classical pragmatist and European philosophical traditions. Second, the reconstruction of the history of American philosophy can ground a new interpretation of the ideas of pragmatism both as a philosophy of resistance but also as a viable framework for reconstructing American society in a new pluralist era. By reconsidering the history of American philosophy in this way, new interpretations of American thought take shape and have the potential to provide a philosophical perspective for life in a pluralistic world.

This strategy of reexamining the American past as a resource for sustaining a pluralistic community and the importance of Native American traditions in this effort have been suggested before. In 1952, Felix S.

Cohen published an essay entitled "Americanizing the White Man." Cohen, then a professor of philosophy at the City University of New York, described a meeting in which the commissioner-elect of the Bureau of Indian Affairs asked a group of Native people how the bureau could best "Americanize the Indian." A Native American man in the audience arose and replied this way:

> You will forgive me if I tell you that my people were Americans thousands of years before your people were. The question is not how you can Americanize us but how we can Americanize you. We have been working at that for a long time. Sometimes we are discouraged at the results. But we will keep trying. And the first thing we want to teach you is that, in the American way of life, each man has respect for his brother's vision. Because each of us respected his brother's dream, we enjoyed freedom here in America while your people were busy killing and enslaving each other across the water. The relatives you left behind are still trying to kill each other and enslave each other because they have not learned that freedom is built on my respect for my brother's vision and his respect for mine. We have a hard trail ahead of us in trying to Americanize you and your white brothers. But we are not afraid of hard trails. (Cohen 1952, 177–178)

For Cohen, the American tradition is ultimately grounded in the ideas, practices, and material culture of Native American peoples. Equally significant, however, is Cohen's commitment to the idea that the future of North America depends not on the reduction of difference to a common culture, but on the presence of diverse cultures in a process of respectful interaction. The possibility of this diversity depends upon the ability of the dominant culture to reengage the American intellectual traditions grounded in Native thought. These traditions, he thinks, can provide the resources for a flourishing American community.

The American tradition, from this perspective, offers a kind of meta-level viewpoint or, better, a methodological framework that can support a diversity of particular viewpoints. The process of learning this perspective is a process of adopting a philosophical attitude, well established in Native traditions, that will sustain diversity and growth. The result of the process of reengaging the American tradition will be a transformation of those who are part of the dominant culture. For those who take up the process from the dominant culture, Cohen concludes that "we" ought to stop trying to make "them" more like "us": "we might do better to concentrate on the real job of the New World, the job of Americanizing the white man" (Cohen 1952, 191). This does not mean overthrowing one's own heritage, however, but rather the adoption of a philosophical perspective that recognizes the value of difference and the goal of respectful coexistence in a diverse and growing community.

I argue that American pragmatism begins along the border between Native and European America as an attitude of resistance against the dominant attitudes of European colonialism. The first chapter sets the stage for a new history of American pragmatism by considering the problems of accounting for its origins. In order to clarify what constitutes pragmatism in this discussion, the second chapter presents four commitments or interests that can serve as a starting point. These commitments, what I call the principles of interaction, pluralism, community, and growth, mark lines of thought that ultimately connect Native American philosophy with the emergence of classical pragmatism.

Chapters 3 and 4 develop the character of the attitude of colonialism as it emerged along the border, framing both the dominant European American conceptions of America and establishing practices of exclusion and dispossession in the name of progress. As examples of the colonial attitude, I examine the influential work of the Puritan historian and philosopher Cotton Mather, the work of Thomas Jefferson, and the work of the Jacksonian historian and philosopher George Bancroft. Despite the radical differences between their views and in how historians of philosophy have viewed their work, the three nevertheless share a philosophical perspective grounded in the dispositions of the colonial attitude. The attitude, reminiscent of what Dewey called the "quest for certainty," amounts to a particular way of understanding the world which seeks to reduce meaning to a single set of truths and a single hierarchy of value. Although each version of the attitude is grounded in a different philosophical language, each is led in practice to exclusion, intolerance, and attempts to eliminate difference. Against this logic of domination an indigenous attitude characterized by commitments to interaction, pluralism, community, and growth emerged in Native responses to the growing European society in America. This attitude came to be adopted by some non-Native people who also rejected the colonial attitude and became part of a long intellectual tradition that includes classical pragmatism, anti-racism, and feminism.

In the fifth and sixth chapters, I show that the commitments of pragmatism were already well-established aspects of Northeastern Native culture and were expressed as the practices of *wunnégin*, welcome or hospitality, a way of understanding and acting consistent with the coexistence of cultural differences. I illustrate the priority of Native ideas in the new European American philosophical perspective through the work of the Puritan minister and philosopher Roger Williams. I show that Williams developed a distinctive version of the indigenous attitude through his friendship with the Narragansett leader, Miantonomi, and other Native Americans along the northeast American coast in the mid-seventeenth century. Through a close analysis of the Narragansett response to outsiders developed in a range of *Mohowaúgsuck* (cannibal) stories and Williams's own discussions of Native thought, I argue that his conception of a pluralist community and the philosophical attitude that supports it is grounded in Native thought. Williams's work provides a crucial instance of how Native American thought could be transmitted to European Americans and come to influence their views. It also helps to lay the groundwork for the adoption of the indigenous attitude as a mode of resistance to colonial ways of thinking in later generations of American thinkers.

The seventh chapter traces the development of the broadening influence of the indigenous attitude through the "Native Prophetic movement" of the eighteenth and nineteenth centuries. This movement of Native American orators and political and military leaders focused on establishing Native land rights and cultural autonomy. While interactions between Native and European peoples in America continued in places to be framed by the practices of *wunnégin,* changing circumstances led to the expression of another version of the indigenous attitude as a standpoint of resistance to the colonial attitude—what I will call the logic of place. I look in particular at the speeches of Teedyuscung and Neolin of the Delaware people, Tenskwatawa of the Shawnee, and Sagoyewatha of the Seneca. These speakers at once demonstrate a commitment to the four principles that are central to pragmatism and make explicit the ways that these commitments lead to an alternative way to organize and value things and events. The result is a logic of place that locates meaning in situations that are framed by culture and environment. This attitude, from the perspective of many European Americans, provided both a means of resistance and a model for an alternative way to understand and act in the world.

In the eighth and ninth chapters I consider the impact of the Prophetic movement, in particular on the seminal work of Benjamin Franklin. In crucial ways, Franklin represents the central intellectual tradition that led to Peirce's and James's initial formulations of pragmatism. His work in Pennsylvania brought him in close contact with the Delaware leader Teedyuscung and others. At the same time, in his work as a scientist and writer, he brought the practice of science and the interests of community together through an attitude and logic remarkably similar to that of the Native Prophetic movement. In chapter eight, I examine Teedyuscung's version of the logic of place as it emerged in peace conferences between his people and the Pennsylvania government. In chapter nine, I consider the development of Franklin's own philosophical perspective, both in his experimental science and in his writings on Native Americans. Taken together, these perspectives, grounded in his interactions with Native thought, helped to frame both a distinctive approach to American science and a distinctive conception of a pluralist democratic society.

In the tenth and eleventh chapters I examine the influence of a new generation of Native thinkers on the development of the women's movement of the first half of the nineteenth century. By the 1820s, the logic of place that emerged from the Native Prophetic movement was enhanced with new attention to the problems of differences within communities as well as between them. The result was a new version of the logic of place—what I call the logic of home—that was developed both in Native narratives and in Native activism. Native author Jane Johnston Schoolcraft, in particular, helped to develop this logic in her stories, first published in 1826. At the same time, the logic of home was also developed by Native leaders such as John Ross as a means to understand and resist the policy of Indian removal formalized by Congress and President Andrew Jackson in 1830. While the logic of place provided a way to understand interactions between peoples, the logic of home provided a way to see the effects of differences within a place. In response to the triple crises of Indian removal, slavery, and the demand for women's suffrage, some European American women followed the lead of Native people and adopted both the indigenous attitude and its logic of home as a way of carrying out their own challenge to the dominant colonial attitude. At the center of this development in European American thinking is the work of Lydia Maria Child. For Child and others, the logic of home served not only as a means of attacking laws that permitted slavery and denied women rights, it also became a framework for a new form of feminism and a new approach to social inquiry.

In the final chapter, I outline the ways in which the lines of pragmatic development in the work of Franklin and Child reunite in the philosophical work of the classical pragmatists. From Franklin and his successors the pragmatists learned one version of the indigenous attitude, framed by a conception of experimental science grounded in community and a community grounded in the practices of freedom and democracy. The classical pragmatists, and Dewey in particular, learned from Child and her successors to apply the abstract conceptions of science and democracy to the lived experience of a pluralistic society in which a diversity of groups, interests, and ideas could coexist. In the end, classical pragmatism and its four commitments emerge from a complex environment characterized by both the colonial and indigenous attitudes. What is generally recognized as distinctively American philosophy arises from the influences of both European and Native thought on key figures and movements throughout the seventeenth, eighteenth, and nineteenth centuries. In the end, the genealogy of pragmatism becomes more than the development of a particular philosophy. It becomes a genealogy of a rich American philosophical tradition—diverse in its thinkers, plural in its traditions, and potentially valuable in its implications for life in a multicultural world.

North America in the twenty-first century will be an increasingly diverse place. Long-established principles of equality and national unity will be disrupted by the demands of difference. Any adequate response to this pluralist environment will require changes in established ways of thinking. It will call up, in fact, a philosophical crisis, whether or not it is so named, in which options will be narrow. People can ignore difference, suppress it with escalating violence, or they can search for other principles, alternative ways of understanding and acting in the world, that will promote coexistence. This work is a response to the crisis in favor of coexistence. I argue that a philosophical perspective already exists within the American tradition that offers an alternative to a violent response to cultural pluralism. This perspective provides a logic that helps to defuse conflict while fostering both differences and connections. Such an attitude has long been part of American thought, but it has been hidden or misunderstood for much of its career by a dominant attitude more interested in promoting unity and the progress of civilization than in diversity and the growth of communities. The value of reconstructing the history of American pragmatism is in its contribution to the recovery of this alternative attitude.

When W. E. B. Du Bois sought a way to promote the coexistence of different races early in the twentieth century, he proposed to begin by presenting a "plain unvarnished tale," a study that could find in lived human experience models that would serve as a vision and critical standard for life beyond the colorline (Du Bois 1989, 115). Unlike the "plain unvarnished truth" often sought to settle hard questions, Du Bois aimed for a reconstructive examination of historical traditions and present circumstances, with the goal of undermining the colorline and building a diverse community. It is a "tale" because it is to be responsive and transformative, not final. It is "plain" and "unvarnished" like "truth" because it is not fiction but a retelling grounded in a recognizably common history and experience. The problems of the twenty-first century call for a similar strategy, a plain unvarnished tale that can provide the resources for the coexistence of a diversity of groups, interests, and ideas. Following Du Bois, my reconstruction of the history of pragmatism is a plain unvarnished tale that reconstructs the American philosophical past in order to support an American community that supports, and perhaps even cherishes, differences as a basis for growth.

Native Pragmatism

CHAPTER ONE

The Problem of Origins

IN MOST HISTORIES OF American thought in general and in histories of American philosophy in particular, people indigenous to America are viewed as having made no contribution to the intellectual, moral, and social progress of immigrant European peoples. From this perspective, the immigrants invariably viewed America as an obstacle to be overcome, a resource to be used, or even an opportunity to be exploited as part of the progress of a European vision of humankind. One version of this story sees American thought as the development of distinctive conceptual responses of European science, religion, and philosophy to the wilderness of North America. America makes no intellectual contribution, only a material one. As Frederick Jackson Turner put it in his famous 1893 address "The Significance of The Frontier," "Our early history is the study of European germs developing in an American environment" (Turner 1996, 3). Another version sees American thought as a combination of European ideas with ideas that emerged spontaneously from the minds of European-descended thinkers in America. In either version, America's native inhabitants matter little. While America's plants, animals, water, and minerals all are viewed as the raw material for humanity's future, Native American peoples are taken as an insignificant group of primitive people who are neither raw materials (except as slaves) nor possible contributors to the rich intellectual life of immigrant Europeans.

Histories of American philosophy, in fact, face a problem of origins. Although most provide good reasons to see American thought as dependent upon and as a further development of European philosophical resources, they are significantly less clear about what makes American philosophy something more than just European philosophy in America. As a result, histories of American philosophy tend to tell either a version

1

of the frontier story in which ideas from Europe adapt to the trials of the wilderness or a story of genius in which what is American springs from the minds of talented European Americans. The first leaves the source of recognizably different American thought a mystery, and so the story of origins remains incomplete. The frontier story focuses on why different aspects of European thought might have been called up by the very non-European circumstances faced in America, but it still leaves apparently "new" ways of understanding and acting in the world unexplained. The second strategy locates the origins of distinctive aspects of American philosophy in the remarkable insights of extraordinary men breaking free of age-old limitations. In this case, the problem of the origins of distinctively American thought is explained, but only by converting the problem into a mystery of human genius. Both approaches have value, but there is another alternative. I will argue that the problem of origin can also be addressed by recognizing the origin of distinctive aspects of American philosophy in Native American thought.

When American philosophers in the late nineteenth century first began to reflect on the history of philosophy, they boldly declared their dependence on European ideas alone. Noah Porter, president of Yale College and one of the first American philosophers to describe the history of American philosophy, identifies the major influences: English, French, and German philosophy. The American tradition as he presents it "followed the lead of England, her mother country . . . and has, in some cases, outrun the scholars of England in a readiness to follow the processes and to appropriate results of speculation on the continent" (Porter 1894, 443). Absent from Porter's assessment is recognition of any distinctly American influences, and indeed he rejects the idea of an American genius. "America," he concludes, "cannot boast of many writers of pre-eminent philosophical ability or achievements, [though] it can show a record of honorable interest on the part of not a few of its scholars" (Porter 1894, 443). In this case, American philosophy is European philosophy in a wilderness America.

Herbert Schneider, the great historian of American philosophy, seems to agree with Porter. He prefaces his 1946 history with the flat assessment that "in America . . . it is useless to seek a 'native' tradition, for even our most genteel traditions are saturated with foreign inspirations." The list of inspirations he provides is not brief. Immigrants came laden with ideas from their homelands, and America was an ideal stage for these developments. Schneider concludes, "America was intellectually colonial long after it gained political independence and has been intellectually provincial long after it ceased being intellectually colonial.

We still live intellectually on the fringe of European culture" (Schneider 1946, vii–viii).

This story of American philosophy echoes the story of American progress told by Turner. "The wilderness masters the colonist. It finds him a European in dress, industries, tools, modes of travel, and thought." At first the wilderness "strips off the garments of civilization and arrays him in the hunting shirt and moccasin. . . . [because at] the frontier the environment is at first too strong for the man." Using his imported resources, however, European man is able to "transform" the wilderness, "but the outcome is not the old Europe, not simply the development of Germanic germs. . . . The fact is, that here is a new product that is American" (Turner 1996, 4). While the material contribution of America is made clear, America's intellectual contribution is obscure. Turner asserts that "from the conditions of frontier life came intellectual traits," but it remains unclear how distinctive American "traits" could emerge in the intellectually closed society he portrays.

The alternative history, the story of genius, is proposed by Vernon Parrington in his seminal *Main Currents of American Thought.*[1] Parrington affirms the European origins of American thought but suggests its distinctive qualities are not merely a product of encountering difficulties and opportunities in the process of colonizing North America. Instead, the difference is found in ideas created *ex nihilo.* Distinctive American thought—here American liberalism—was the product of three kinds of "materials." The first was "the plentiful liberalisms" of seventeenth-century Europe; the second, British natural rights philosophy and French Romanticism; and the third, "the native liberalisms that had *emerged spontaneously* from a decentralized [immigrant] society" (emphasis added, Parrington 1927, 1: xii). The thesis of the spontaneous originality of European American thinkers is held by a variety of commentators. Lewis Mumford, in his 1926 book *The Golden Day,* helped to refocus interest

---

1. One of the earliest academic philosophers to discuss an American philosophical tradition was James McCosh, an Edinburgh-trained philosopher and president of Princeton University. Despite American dependence on European sources, McCosh shared Parrington's commitment to the idea of an American genius. In an 1887 paper, "What an American Philosophy Should Be," McCosh declares, "The time has come, I believe, for America to declare her independence in philosophy" (McCosh 1887, 3). Such a philosophy must, like other national philosophies (e.g., German, French, and English), somehow reflect the "national character." "If a genuine American philosophy arises, it must reflect the genius of the people. Now, Yankees are distinguished from most others by their practical observation and invention. They have a pretty clear notion of what a thing is, and, if it is of value, they take steps to secure it." The result, according to McCosh, is that an American philosophy will be "Realistic" (McCosh 1887, 4).

on nineteenth-century American literature and philosophy in part by declaring its originality. Affirming European descent, Mumford declares unambiguously that, "The settlement of America had its origins in the unsettlement of Europe. . . . The dissociation, displacement, and finally, the disintegration of European culture became most apparent in the New World: but the process began in Europe, and the interests that eventually dominated the American scene had their origin in the Old World" (Mumford 1926, 11). At the same time, the distinctiveness of the "New World" was the product of spontaneous creation exemplified in the work of Ralph Waldo Emerson. He was, says Mumford, "the first American philosopher with a fresh doctrine. . . . He was an original, in the sense that he was a source . . . a sort of living essence" (Mumford 1926, 94–95). American thought in general and American philosophy in particular, Mumford argues, are to be viewed as a new stage of human development, standing on the ruins of a disintegrated medieval culture and free of its alter ego European industrialism. For Mumford, American thought at its best stands with Emerson, Henry David Thoreau, Nathaniel Hawthorne, Herman Melville, and Walt Whitman as adolescent sons of European immigrants bright with potential but still trying to overcome their dependence.

In an important way, historians of American philosophy were simply stating conclusions already implied in the conception of America dominant in nineteenth-century European philosophy. When, in 1857, G. W. F. Hegel's *Lectures on the Philosophy of History* was published in English, his conclusions reaffirmed a well-established expectation. "What has taken place in [America] up to now is but an echo of the Old World and the expression of an alien life; and as a country of the future, [America] is of no interest to us here, for prophecy is not the business of philosophy" (Hegel 1975, 171; also see 1861, 90). When American philosophers and historians framed the story of American intellectual development as progress from Europe westward to the American colonies and across North America they followed Hegel, who set the stage for such histories by framing the history of human consciousness in similar geographical terms. As American philosophers established strong ties with German philosophy in the early and middle nineteenth century, Hegel became a crucial influence. Lacking other ways to conceptualize their own history within the recognized tradition, American philosophers seemed willing to accept his.

For Hegel, human history is the process of *geist* or spirit becoming aware of itself by manifesting itself in the real world. Since this concrete actualization occurs in actual locations, geography plays a crucial role in the process (Hegel 1975, 152ff.). The physical environments that provide the context for the development of *geist* are of three types: mountains, valleys, and coasts. These environments are distributed in such a way that the three continents of the pre-Columbian tripartite world play particular roles in the process. African geography and its particular climate, viewed as mountainous and hostile, provides a physical environment for "natural" human beings. According to Hegel, indigenous Africans have not yet "reached an awareness of any substantial objectivity —for example, of God or the law—in which the will of man could participate and in which he could become aware of his own being" (Hegel 1975, 177). Since native Africans lack self-consciousness, they also lack history. Africa thus serves as a fixed point against which the progress of *geist* can be seen. Asia, on the other hand, provides a geography of mountains and wide river valleys where human beings begin to become conscious of themselves. Transactions between people of the mountains and people of the valleys provide the first thesis and antithesis necessary to generate the synthesis of consciousness. And with consciousness, history begins. Just as "the sun rises in the Orient," Hegel observes, "world history travels from east to west." (Hegel 1975, 196–197). Yet, while the native people of Asia are the beginning of history and consciousness, they are nevertheless hampered by a kind of "self-oblivion" which comes with the first moments of awareness. Hegel compares these first moments with the experience of "someone watching the moment of daybreak, the spreading of the light, and the rise of the sun in all its majesty. Descriptions of this kind tend to emphasize the rapture, astonishment, and infinite self-oblivion which accompany this moment of clarity" (Hegel 1975, 196).

As history and consciousness move westward toward Europe, the "astonishment" diminishes, and human beings progress from "passive contemplation to activity, to independent creation" (Hegel 1975, 196). Europe, then, becomes the place where *geist* achieves self-consciousness. Here the land is characterized by mountains, valleys, and coast and forms a rich interactive environment—here the physical potential of the European continent combines with the potential of *geist* to generate the endpoint of progress. The progress of humankind, then, is at once geographical, moving with the sun from east to west, and spiritual, moving from the unconscious, animal-like native African to the self-aware, intellectual European. "Europe," Hegel concludes, "is the absolute end of history, just as Asia is its beginning" (Hegel 1975, 197).

America's place in Hegel's scheme is necessarily less clear. Given that the logic of the development of *geist* was already exhausted by the three-part Old World and its people, he was forced to conclude that "the only principle left over for America would be that of incompleteness or constant non-fulfillment" (Hegel 1975, 172). It is no surprise then that America is viewed by Hegel and many of his successors as having no important intellectual contribution of its own to make to the development of humanity. Without giving Native Americans a role in the dialectical story of the progress of *geist* of the sort granted the native people of the tripartite world, Hegel simply concludes that the American peoples "were destroyed" through contact with the Europeans. At best, the Americans could be thought of as "a purely natural culture that had to perish as soon as the spirit approached it." He summarizes, "America has always shown itself physically and spiritually impotent, and it does so to this day" (Hegel 1975, 162). Despite this sweeping conclusion, America as a land does find a place in the three-part story of the development of *geist* whose "absolute end" is Europe. "Since the original American nation has vanished—or as good as vanished—the effective population comes for the most part from Europe, and everything that happens in America has its origin [in Europe]" (Hegel 1975, 165). In short, America is an all but empty land ready to serve as a resource for the further development of humankind whose most advanced stage is found in European peoples.

The story of American intellectual dependence on Europe was reasserted after World War II by a new generation of historians of American thought. Philosophers such as Joseph Blau and Morris Cohen retold the old story of the origin of American philosophy in English and French thought, its distinctive qualities largely a matter of the peculiarities of conquest and colonization.[2] In 1972, Morton White took up the task of recovering the origins of American philosophy in his *Science and Sentiment in America*. Although critical in the end of the American tradition's reliance on "sentiment" and its resulting anti-intellectualism, White traces the origins of such thinking directly to European sources. "In the beginning," he intones, "American philosophy was a colonial philosophy—as derivative and unoriginal as one might expect it to be in an outpost of civilization" (White 1972, 9). Literally sustained by philosophical development in Europe, America's "philosophical subservience" continued after the Civil War when the work of Charles Darwin and J. S. Mill set the boundaries for philosophical investigation. "From the beginning then," White concludes, "American philosophy was dominated by transatlantic philosophy, until pragmatism, the first original American philosophy, emerged in the writing of Charles Peirce and William James" (White 1972, 9–10). Pragmatism, when it finally entered

2. See Blau 1952 and Cohen 1962.

the scene, was a product of intellectual resources descended from John Locke, the Scottish Enlightenment, and the ingenuity of Peirce and James as they attempted to "clarify language in which claims to knowledge are made and to hasten the day when scientific and philosophical disputes would be settled by the use of a more rational method" (White 1972, 150).[3]

While White recalls the vision of European thought in America, John Smith, in *The Spirit of American Philosophy*, follows Parrington and Mumford by recalling the story of original genius. "American philosophical thinking in the past three-quarters of a century," he says, "has exhibited its own original and unmistakable spirit" (Smith 1963, xi). As for Mumford a generation before, the promise of originality has more often surrendered to the parent thinking of British and continental philosophy, but such surrender, like the adolescent afraid to strike out on her own, is merely a stage to be overcome. For Smith, American dependence will be overcome by recovering the spontaneous genius of an earlier generation of European American philosophers.

Neither the story of dependence told by White and his predecessors nor the story of genius told by Smith and his predecessors provides an adequate account of the origin of American thought. The former, while it denies a distinctive intellectual origin, nevertheless affirms a distinctive intellectual outcome, American pragmatism. The mystery of origin is made more perplexing when the basic commitments of pragmatism emerge in the work of philosophers such as Roger Williams, Benjamin Franklin, Cadwallader Colden, Lydia Maria Child, and others more than a century before the classical pragmatists began to present their views. The latter story attempts to fill the gap by explaining how European philosophy could become so transformed. But even this story has difficulties. First, while stories of spontaneous emergence may satisfy those who seek a kind of American exceptionalism, when the emergence of a distinctive tradition is considered in its rich historical context, it is at least as possible that what appears to be spontaneous emergence could be the product of a well-funded collaboration. While it is possible that ideas emerge from nothing, such an account is also a way to overlook a much more complex origin as well as a way to avoid giving credit where it may be due. It is unlikely that such an approach would be acceptable in a history of European thought. To claim, for example, that John Locke's empiricism was solely a product of Locke's genius, or perhaps his genius in the face of the troubles of civil war, would at once be far

---

3. Flower and Murphy's *A History of American Philosophy* (1977) shares similar expectations.

too simple and would disconnect Locke's work from its significant relationship to the development of modern science and continental rationalism. Our understanding would be diminished, as would the value of Locke's thought as a way to think of human knowledge that attempts to be consistent with Newtonian physics and that tries to serve as an alternative to other philosophical approaches.

The second problem with both the frontier story and the story of American genius is that they lead to a narrow and exclusive history. Committed in advance to a tale of European descent, those aspects of American thought which do not fit the story can easily be set aside as unimportant or anomalous. In European philosophy, if one is convinced of Locke's originality and value, other philosophical alternatives could easily be set aside as inconsequential or mistaken. Rather than being seen as a viable alternative and catalyst, rationalism could be dismissed, its arguments lost, and its countervailing insights overlooked. If one believes that modern European philosophy descended solely from the Greeks, then a philosopher like Spinoza, whose work was strongly influenced by Jewish thought, must be viewed as an anomaly without precedent. While historians of philosophy are necessarily selective in their accounts, such selectivity can also be tested. The apparently unimportant and anomalous can sometimes be the key to generating a better, or at least a potentially more useful, account. Years of one sort of approach to the history of philosophy can make trying alternatives difficult, but the difficulty diminishes neither the possibility nor the value of the alternatives. In this case, opening the question of the origin of American philosophy to the possibility of Native American influence will allow a more general reconsideration of American thought and its potential to help address new problems.

The response I propose to the received history of American pragmatism is not intended as a comprehensive history, but rather as an additional perspective. For example, H. S. Thayer's history of pragmatism, *Meaning and Action* (1981), develops in detail many of the connections between classical pragmatism and the European philosophical tradition. For Thayer, pragmatism is a distinctive answer to the long-standing questions that motivated eighteenth- and nineteenth-century philosophy in Europe. An account of the development of pragmatism that locates it relative to another tradition does not invalidate alternatives like Thayer's but provides new angles of vision on American thought, some of which lead to tensions and critique and some of which lead to new connections and possibilities. My account of the beginnings of pragmatism joins two other reexaminations of the tradition, one by Cornel West, *The American Evasion of Philosophy* (1989), and another by Charlene Haddock Seigfried, *Pragmatism and Feminism* (1996). West rereads a significant portion of the American tradition as a philosophy of social transformation relevant to the issues of culture, gender, and class difference. Seigfried examines the connections between feminist philosophy and pragmatism both to raise critical concerns about the classical pragmatists and to provide a way to enrich both feminism and pragmatism by understanding their points of convergence. Similarly, my reconstruction of the early history of American philosophy also shows pragmatism in a different light and, at the same time, opens a door to a broader American philosophical tradition.

Rather than seeing Native American thought as irrelevant, I propose that we see it as the starting place of some of the distinctive aspects of the American philosophical tradition, as a way to answer the problem of origin. By tracing the career of the central commitments of pragmatism beginning in Native American thought, through their use in resisting exclusion, racism, and sexism, to their emergence in the work of the classical pragmatists, these ways of understanding and acting in the world can become renewed resources. While alternative stories of the origins of American pragmatism can and will be told, this story of origin serves as both a history and a response to the ongoing problem of the coexistence of different cultures in American society.

The classical American pragmatists, Peirce, James, and Dewey, provide a useful perspective from which to begin this reconsideration of the history of American philosophy. As historians of their own tradition, they appear to be troubled by the same problem of origin that later historians display. At the same time, they suggest a strategy for the reconstruction of this history beginning with recognition of what is distinctive about pragmatism and recognition that its intellectual influence is not only a product of abstract discourse, but also a product of ordinary lived experience. William James presents a version of the frontier story in the best-known account of the origins of pragmatism. In his 1898 address to the Philosophical Union of the University of California at Berkeley, James credits Charles S. Peirce with originating the central idea of pragmatism, the so-called pragmatic maxim, in the 1870s. In this case, James makes Hegel's general discounting of indigenous America more precise when he suggests that Peirce's innovation developed from the empirical commitments of "English-speaking philosophy." "Mr. Peirce," he says, "has only expressed in the form of an explicit maxim what [the English philosophers'] sense for reality led them all instinctively to do. The great English way of investigating a conception is to ask yourself right off ' . . . What is its *cash-value* . . . ?'" (James 1967, 360). Peirce disagrees with the account. Despite James's claims of an empiricist origin, Peirce himself reports that pragmatism came out of his reflections on methods of inquiry, particularly in his study of Kant. The term pragmatism itself, he says, derives from Kant's distinction between *praktisch* and *pragmatisch*, "the former belonging in a region of thought where no mind of the experimentalist type can ever make sure of solid ground under his feet, the latter expressing relation to some definite human purpose" (Peirce 1955, 252). Although they disagree in the details, Peirce and James agree with the general historical perspective proposed by Hegel and conclude that pragmatism is a further development of European thought.

Dewey, in his 1925 summary of the origins of pragmatism, restates Peirce's version of the story and argues explicitly for the European roots of pragmatism. According to Dewey, pragmatism is what happens to European philosophy when it encounters the "distinctive traits of the environment of American life" (Dewey 1925a, 19). Dewey concludes, "American thought continues European thought. We have imported our language, our laws, our institutions, our morals, and our religion from Europe, and we have adapted them to the new conditions of our life. The same is true of our ideas" (Dewey 1925a, 19).

Despite his apparent commitment to the European origins of American thought, however, in an article written in 1922 Dewey suggests that his account of the origins of pragmatism is not complete. Here he restates James's conviction that pragmatism follows the empirical philosophy initiated by Bacon, Locke, and Hume, but he follows the claim with the observation that the empirical tradition was "revived and then made central by Peirce and James" as a philosophical response to a disposition peculiar to the American tradition. This disposition may be, he says, "as obnoxious to ultimate philosophic truth as it is repellent to certain temperaments." Dewey describes the disposition this way:

> It discourages dogmatism and its child, intolerance. It arouses and heartens an experimental spirit which wants to know how systems and theories work before giving complete adhesion. It militates against too sweeping and easy generalizations, even against those which would indict a nation. . . . It fosters a sense of the worth of communication of what is known. (Dewey 1922, 308)

This disposition, he suggests, has its origins outside the confines of European thought and in lived experience. In his 1904 commencement address at the University of Vermont, Dewey distinguishes between conceptions of philosophy which are interested in system-building and those which aim "at a philosophy which shall be instrumental rather than final, and instrumental not to establishing and warranting any particular set of truths, but instrumental in furnishing points of view and working ideas which may clarify and illuminate the actual and concrete course of life" (Dewey 1905, 77). The conception that takes philosophy as a method is the one appropriate to "the logic inherent in our America." From this perspective,

> Philosophers are not to be a separate and monopolistic priesthood set apart to guard, and, under certain conditions, to reveal an isolated treasury of truths. It is theirs to organize—such organization involving, of course, criticism, rejection, transformation—the highest and wisest ideas of humanity, past and present, in such fashion that they may become most effective in the interpretation of certain recurrent and fundamental problems, which humanity, collectively and individually, has to face. (Dewey 1905, 77)

For Dewey, then, despite the importance of the intellectual resources gleaned from European philosophy, there remains a clear but unexplained disposition or attitude which forms the ground for American philosophy in general and pragmatism in particular.

This unexplained disposition and commitment to philosophical method was apparent to other commentators, including Alexis de Tocqueville in his 1835 commentary *Democracy in America*. Tocqueville, in terms more unequivocal than Dewey's, suggests that American philosophy ought to be sought outside the European tradition. In his discussion of "the philosophical approach of the Americans," he writes:

> Less attention is paid to philosophy in the United States than in any other country of the civilized world. The Americans have no school of philosophy peculiar to themselves, and they pay very little attention to the rival European schools. Nevertheless, it is noticeable that the people of the United States almost all have a uniform method and rules for the conduct of intellectual inquiries. So, though they have not taken the trouble to define the rules, they have a philosophical method after all. (Tocqueville 1969, 429)

According to Tocqueville, despite a lack of attention to European thought, Americans nevertheless developed a distinctive philosophical method which, he finds, is characterized by opposition to dogma, an interest in the past and present as resources, and strong individualism. This last characteristic, Tocqueville suggests, contributes to developing other "mental habits," including a commitment to find meaning in present experience, not in a supernatural world nor a remote past nor even a distant future. "So the Americans," he concludes, "have needed no books to teach them philosophic method, having found it in themselves" (Tocqueville 1969, 429). The implicit question is, of course, from whence, if not Europe, did this distinctive philosophical method arise. Where Hegel and others saw an American intellectual life drawn solely from European roots, Tocqueville saw a distinctive, though perhaps mysterious, perspective well worth the attention of his European audience. Ironically, while Tocqueville suggests that the experience of Americans was crucial to the development of their way of thinking, even to the exclusion of systematic European influence, he never considers the possibility that important sources of American thought were already flourishing when the Europeans came ashore.

Tocqueville's conclusion and Dewey's suggestions are echoed by John E. Smith in the 1992 introduction to his collection of essays, *America's Philosophical Vision*. Although this assessment recalls his earlier claim for the spontaneous emergence of American philosophy, his wording ironically recasts its meaning. He observes that "pragmatism clearly represents an indigenous and original philosophical outlook" (Smith 1992, 2). Originality here seems reassigned, implicitly taken away from thinkers descended from Europe and assigned to those indigenous to America. Just how pragmatism is "indigenous" remains unexplored by Smith, but pragmatism, and what he takes to be a still broader philosophical vision, are nevertheless deeply connected with "American experience." "These ideas and ideals," he says, "to be sure, show the influence of past thinkers from Plato and Aristotle to the philosophers of the nineteenth century; the important point, however, is that they were reshaped in the light of the experience of American life aimed at the resolution of problems that arose within that experience" (Smith 1992, 2; also see Dewey 1905, 76). In short, while one kind of American thought descended from European forebears, another kind may be indigenous to America. It is this second way of thinking that is at the center of what is distinctive about American philosophy.

In fact, the central commitments of American philosophy, especially as represented by the work of the classical pragmatists, can also be found in the philosophical perspective of Northeastern Native peoples and can be traced through a history of cross-cultural contact to the work of important European American thinkers. The problem of the origins of a distinctly American philosophy can be addressed in a significant way by reconsidering the influence of Native thought. But such reconsideration will not be easy, since that influence is not explicit in the classical pragmatists or the already well-known histories. Following the suggestions of Tocqueville and Dewey, we need to look again at the moments of cultural contact in the lived experience of those who served as examples and resources for the philosophers who came later. In effect, this alternative history will be grounded in the possibilities of lived experience.

John McDermott, whose work has gone far to expand the range of what is recognized as American philosophy, helps to frame this approach. What he finds distinctive about American philosophy, and especially its manifestation in classical pragmatism, is its notion of experience. It is, McDermott argues, the deep and consistent commitment in the American tradition to learn from and enrich experience that sets the American philosophical perspective outside the European. Even though one can find an interest in the things of experience in European empiricism, it is only in America and in the unique conditions prevailing there that experience is taken seriously as the source and product of human action. McDermott cites Santayana, among others, as recognizing but failing to develop this distinctive American conception of experience. In his survey of the "Genteel Tradition in American Philosophy," for example, Santayana describes the earliest New England colonists this way:

> As much as clearing the land and fighting the Indians they were occupied, as they expressed it, in wrestling with the Lord. The country was new; the race was tried, chastened, and full of solemn memories. It was an old wine in new bottles, and America did not have to wait for its present universities, with their departments of academic philosophy, in order to possess a living philosophy—to have a distinct vision of the universe and definite convictions about human destiny. (Santayana 1912, 171)

For McDermott's purposes, Santayana properly focuses on the particular character of the experiences of the earliest European immigrants, but further points are worth noting in Santayana's description.

First, Santayana views early American experience as aggressively colonial. The immigrants cleared the land, evidently converting it from a useless wilderness to productive farms and cities, and fought Indians— presumably to defend against, Christianize, civilize, and finally eliminate from the rapidly diminishing wilderness. While this is clearly the received impression of the early European American experience, it is perhaps too quickly accepted by Santayana and McDermott. In fact, when we consider the records left from the earliest period of European American history, we find that the experience was far less clearly focused. The land was surely being cleared, but to an extent little different from the clearing that had routinely taken place for centuries in clearing places for the fields of the Haudenosaunee, Pequot, Narragansett, and other

Native peoples of the Northeast. The immigrants fought the Indians, but they also ate with them, hunted with them, laughed and joked with them, made love with them, bore children with them, and learned with them. Second, while Santayana's European "race" is "tried, chastened, and full of solemn memories," the European immigrants, in their lived experience, came to join with another "race" also tried, chastened, and as full of solemn memories. To focus on experience as the ground and product of American thought as McDermott suggests is to focus in the right place, but going beyond Santayana's proposed borders to an experience which includes both European immigrants and Native Americans and all the dimensions of that interaction seems a more honest starting point.

If one is serious about looking toward American experiences for the sources of American thought, then it makes sense to consider even these early experiences as comprehensively as possible. If one is serious about a conception of experience which is not abstract but rather rooted in present difficulties and joys, concerns, and surprises, then to understand the American experience as it bears on philosophy is to examine also the variety of viewpoints and voices that played a role in its ongoing character. Such an approach is consistent with McDermott's view of the importance of located experience in the development of American thought. While he accepts that "philosophy was all but nonexistent" in early European American history, he nevertheless concludes that

> reflection was intense and self-conscious, primarily as a response to a pressing and omnipresent collective experience of a situation that was novel at every turn. And although that period in American history offered no articulation of the notion of experience as such, there was a correspondingly rich awareness of the significance of the situation over against inherited "wisdom." It was a period that dealt with philosophical themes without recourse to a formal philosophical language. In effect, the American seventeenth century realized a broadly based cultural "experience of experience." (McDermott 1976, 3)

From this perspective, one can explore the possible origins of the ways of thinking suggested by Tocqueville and the philosophical method described by Dewey.

McDermott's account of the origins of American thought shares a language common to other received accounts that identify the frontier as the central fact of American development, the central resource, and the central image. "What is crucial here," McDermott says, "from the philosophical side, is that the press of environment as a decisive formulator of thought about the basic structures of the world became the outstanding characteristic of the American temperament" (McDermott

1976, 4). Following the story of European dependence, English colonists responded to their circumstances by transforming the inherited ways of thinking to cope with the "New World." This transformation became a new sort of philosophy grounded in experience. McDermott concludes, "Openness to experience [is a product of] an anthropocentric view of nature and a sense of frontier as human imaginative horizon" (McDermott 1976, 17). At first, it appears that this account differs little from the received view of American intellectual dependence on Europe and the exploitation of America itself as a resource. But the conclusion is undermined by his implicit reconstruction of the "frontier" along pragmatic lines.

In his chapter on art, "To be Human Is to Humanize," McDermott reminds us, following James, that experience includes both ends and "transitions." These transitions are the primary sources of meaning and are a matter of relations, not just objects. In trying to describe this Jamesian notion of experience in relations, McDermott talks about the aesthetics of jazz. What is significant is that the meaning or aesthetic quality of a work is not found in the efforts of single performers, nor in the composer's vision, nor in the audience, but in the complex interaction of individual performances, composer, instruments, and audience. "Outside of a relational setting, jazz is meaningless, for it proceeds by a series of interwoven tensions" (McDermott 1976, 38). In effect, the jazz performance is not a "thing" or something passively beheld, but an open-ended, dynamic interaction which brings together diverse elements, a shared purpose, and a sense of responsibility. When McDermott talks about the frontier it is not as a thing to be used or admired or crossed, but rather, like jazz, as an interaction. Just as jazz is not usually a performance carried out according to a fixed plan, as though the players were following a detailed score, the frontier is not a part of manifest destiny or some inevitable stage of human development. McDermott's frontier, understood as an interaction, is better viewed as a borderland and a region of complex relations that manifest new and changing meaning. If "life is in the transitions" as James and McDermott suggest, then the life of American thought is to be sought along borders, including the one between European immigrants and their descendants and America's Native peoples. This suggestion applied to a critique of received histories directs one to look not only at the composition being played out by the recognized figures in well-known events, but also to the experience of the borderlands, geographical and intellectual, where American thought gains its character and complexity.

In short, to account for the development of American thought, we may refigure the frontiers as borders, as regions of interaction, exchange, and transformation. Some aspects of the border are surely aspects of conquest, that is, "frontiers" of European expansion and the accompanying destruction of Native life and culture. But this does not exhaust the character of the border. If we take McDermott seriously, experience is a matter of relations, and relations involve the potential for mutual influence and resistance as well as for assimilation and destruction. Borderlands are regions of colonization, but they are also regions of decolonization. Things are learned and resisted as well as forgotten and overwhelmed. Following McDermott and the suggestion implicit in the assessments of Tocqueville, Dewey, Smith, and others, I will argue that much of what American philosophy is known for can be traced to its origins in the borderlands between Europe and America and its "originality" to well-established aspects of Native American thought.

This approach to the history of philosophy, grounded in lived experience even as it challenges established histories, is nevertheless consistent with a central commitment in the history of American philosophy. For example, while Herbert Schneider views American thought primarily as a descendant of European thought, he does not view influence as a process of the abstract exchange of ideas, but rather as the by-product of the very human, lived experience of immigration. The development of a distinctive American philosophical tradition is neither the product of historical necessity nor spontaneous emergence on this account, but the product of influence at particular times and places. Schneider explains, "But the imported goods are not being swallowed raw; they must be blended with those homegrown ideas, for which an established taste and preference exists" (Schneider 1946, viii). Philosophical history in this sense is just the ongoing process of doing philosophy in the American tradition. As a process, it is context-dependent, but there is no single context in which to establish final answers or a single authoritative history. "The variety of contexts at our disposal gives us many handles by which to take hold of novelties. But we do take hold of them as much as they get a hold on us" (Schneider 1946, ix). In the light of new contexts at the beginning of the twenty-first century, this work recalls the past in order to bring it to bear on present problems and to help frame future possibilities. In a sense, this very project of reconstructing the origins of American philosophy is itself the practice of American philosophy. Schneider concludes, "the many ways we resist, distort, adapt, revise new importations is the best evidence that an American tradition lives" (Schneider 1946, ix).[4]

---

4. Also see Randall 1958 for another version of pragmatist philosophy of history.

CHAPTER TWO

American Pragmatism

THE PROBLEM OF THE ORIGINS OF American pragmatism provides reasons for reconsidering its history through an approach that focuses on the process of influence in lived experience. In order to take up the history, however, it is necessary at the outset to shift one's usual expectations of what counts as philosophy. An alternative conception can be found within the pragmatist tradition itself. In the introduction to the 1948 edition of *Reconstruction in Philosophy,* Dewey summarizes his conception of philosophy, saying that "the distinctive office, problems and subject matter of philosophy grow out of stresses and strains in the community life in which a given form of philosophy arises, and that, accordingly, its specific problems vary with the changes in human life that are always going on and that at times constitute a crisis and a turning point in human history" (Dewey 1948, 256). Rather than supposing that philosophy consists in attempts to answer ultimate questions as is often supposed within the recognized European tradition, Dewey's conception reorients what counts as philosophical practice by reconnecting it with experience. When philosophers ask about the nature of being or truth, the question is asked from a particular time and place in a particular community, and the answer, even a most abstract one, responds finally to that place. "In other words," Dewey says, "whatever else philosophies are or are not, they are at least significant cultural phenomena and demand treatment from that point of view" (Dewey 1934, 29). Taken this way, philosophy can be defined as "a critique of basic and widely shared beliefs." When the beliefs and commitments of a community or culture are challenged, philosophy emerges as a critical response helping to transform how the community understands the challenge and how it might respond. Philosophies become distinctive less in terms of the general questions they ask and more in terms of the situations that frame them, the conceptual resources they call upon, and the attitudes and practices with which the criticisms and transformations are carried out. From this perspective, a history of a philosophical tradition becomes the story of the problems, resources, methods, and attitudes as they are received, changed, transmitted, and used over time and in particular places.

Dewey's conception of philosophy has the further virtue of widening the range of what can be recognized as philosophy. If philosophy is a culturally located critique of widely held beliefs using resources, methods, and attitudes present in the culture, it follows that the practice of philosophy may take radically different forms.[1] In some cultures, storytelling and ceremony might serve the function of critique and reconstruction, while in others, philosophy may be a matter of treatise-writing and formal discussion. In some cases, philosophy might be a practice accessible to most, while in others it may be confined to an elite class of specialists. In either range of cases, though, the critical function remains central. The practice of philosophy that occurs in the borderlands between different cultures will necessarily be even more complex in that it will involve a still wider range of resources and attitudes. In these cases, philosophy may start in the process of overt embodied practices such as diplomatic ceremonies and trade negotiations and continue in a transformation of language, interests, and the beliefs that lead to new meaning. Implicit in the give and take of diplomacy and exchange are critiques, replies, rejections, and acceptances that can raise questions and possibilities. While such interactions are ordinary features of borderlands, when they are engaged reflectively and responsively they can themselves be both moments of philosophy and moments of influence.

A particular philosophy, from this perspective, is a particular "point of view" or standpoint that serves to frame the common responses to problems and routine ways of understanding the world for communities and cultures. A standpoint is then a matter of how things are done as well as how they are conceived. Actions in response to problems are practical manifestations of dispositions or attitudes that serve to frame both understanding and action. These dispositions amount to commitments to value things in certain ways, some things as true and others as false; to treat some things as real and others as mere appearance; or, in fact, to adopt some other less dualistic stance. As a result, philosophies in this sense pervade our experience and interactions, ground how we are

---

1. Dewey recognized this diversity of philosophical practice within the European and Asian philosophical traditions and also within indigenous cultures in America. See his foreword to Paul Radin's *Primitive Man as Philosopher* (Dewey 1927).

known and how we know. As practices, as well as stated principles and preferences, philosophies can be learned, challenged, undermined, and reinforced. In effect, philosophies in this sense are habits and attitudes as well as ideas, and so philosophy is not unlike other forms of reflective practice. To be a carpenter or a farmer requires certain dispositions to act and attitudes about oneself and the world as well as ideas that frame plans and possibilities. To be a carpenter is a process of learning practices and ideas. Similarly, to have a philosophy of a certain sort, one adopts a range of practices and ideas. One has a philosophy when one responds to crises in particular ways. One already, in a sense, has an idea of the value of human life when one rushes into a fire to save another. One has a sense of the role of experimentation when one tries a variety of answers when solving a problem. Such behaviors are at once part of one's embodied responses to the world and at the same time representative of particular ideas about the world.

In contrast to having a philosophy, philosophical investigation is a process of reflecting on habits, established beliefs, and ways of understanding and interacting with the world when well-established ways become blocked, or come into conflict with each other. Philosophical investigation, in this sense, is the process of trying to make clear what ideas and practices are in conflict and to propose alternatives that will get things going again, fostering new experience and action. The story of the Native origins of American pragmatism is the story of cross-cultural contact and learning, the sharing of philosophy. It is not a sharing that proceeds unimpeded or unchallenged, and it is not a sharing that emerges only with respect to mutual interest. The story of the origins of American pragmatism is the story of a struggle among radically different people, and the character of the struggle, when it involves reflection on differences, practices, and ideas, is in part philosophical. Some participants will choose a response that aims to reduce differences and make more uniform the basic ways of engaging each other and the world. Others will stand in resistance to attempts at reduction and will work to create an alternative American philosophy that, in one form, will become classical pragmatism.

At the center of classical pragmatism are at least four common commitments. These commitments, expressed here in philosophical fashion as "principles," amount to the acceptance of certain ideas and their implications, but more importantly reflect a collection of attitudes or dispositions to engage the world in certain ways. There is, on this account, not a significant break between the affirmation of the "principles" on one hand and ways of acting on the other. In fact, this continuity of action and thought is itself part of what the pragmatic philosophical perspective involves. These commitments will be key elements in the process of reconstructing the history of American philosophy. I will argue that these commitments are part of a particular Native American philosophical perspective that is evident well before the emergence of classical pragmatism. The history of American philosophy from this angle will be a history of how these commitments in Native American thought might have come to form the central commitments of pragmatism and a distinctive American philosophical point of view.[2] The four commitments that characterize a common core of classical pragmatism are the principles of interaction, pluralism, community, and growth.[3]

The first principle, interaction, is the most recognized aspect of classical pragmatism. In Peirce's famous paper "How to Make Our Ideas Clear," he proposes what became known as the pragmatic maxim: "Consider what effects which might conceivably have practical bearings, we conceive the object of our conception to have. Then, our conception of these effects is the whole of our conception of the object" (Peirce 1992, 132). Our conception of a thing understood pragmatically is what "practical bearings" a thing will have, that is, what it will do. James echoes Peirce's principle but adds to it an explicit value component, the role of a thing's "cash value." When the thing is an idea, for example, James concludes that its merits turn on "what definite difference it will make to you and me" (James 1967, 349). In this case, conceptions go beyond reports of conceivable effects to include what constitutes preferred effects. By considering a thing in terms of its "cash value," James thinks one gets a measure of relative worth. Things with greater "cash value,"

---

2. In this discussion, I will primarily consider the work of Peirce, James, and Dewey as representative of "classical pragmatism." The work of George Herbert Mead and Josiah Royce could also be included both as committed to the four pragmatic principles and as important to the broader development of American thought. In addition to his contributions to philosophy, Mead was also instrumental in the development of American sociology and was for a time closely connected with the pragmatist work of Jane Addams's Hull House. Royce, though often viewed as an idealist whose work was in tension with the pragmatists, drew heavily from the work of Peirce and James and was an important influence in the development of twentieth-century African American thought, particularly the work of Martin Luther King Jr. and Alain Locke. I nevertheless focus on Peirce, James, and Dewey because they are generally regarded as central to any discussion of American pragmatism and because their work is comprehensive enough to provide a framework for the reconstruction of the history of pragmatism that I will propose.

3. There are many ways to characterize American philosophy in general and pragmatism in particular. I will not discuss alternative characterizations in detail but rather here propose what I take to be a reasonably unproblematic gloss of some of the common commitments of the three philosophers generally recognized as central to both pragmatism and American philosophy. Also see Smith 1963 and Stuhr 1997, especially chapter 3. See Lovejoy 1963 for a challenge to the idea that there is a common core of commitments in pragmatism.

that is, things that have more valuable effects, become things preferred in choosing actions and seeking possibilities. These preferred effects then become normative aspects of our conceptions of things and events. To accept this view of knowledge, however, appears to accept a kind of sophistry where human interests become the measure of what constitutes knowledge. The view is bound to run into trouble if desire-controlled "knowledge" encounters an indifferent world. "Knowledge" would have no reliable connection to things and events as they pleased or failed to please human beings. What we know would be only a matter of wishful thinking, with little relation to what is "real" or "true."[4]

James addresses the difficulty of the potential disconnection between knowledge and the world by making what human beings think continuous with what things are. As a result, the pragmatic maxim is not merely a method for examining ideas, it is both an epistemological principle and an ontological one. It is epistemological because it provides a way of thinking about the meaning of ideas, that is, what it is we know when we know. If we know that the sun shines brightly, then we have some ideas about what effects the sun will have on us. At the same time, James takes the principle as an ontological one. Just as our knowledge of the sun shining brightly is an anticipation of the effects it will have, what the sun shining brightly *is* is also a matter of what it does. As he puts it in the 1898 address, "Grossness is what grossness *does*" (James 1967, 354), that is, a thing known, or in this case a quality known, literally *is* the effects it has or, to animate the example, the way it acts or interacts.[5]

Dewey follows Peirce and James and affirms the pragmatic maxim and its epistemological and ontological implications. He also reinforces a further implication (also recognized by Peirce and James) that if a thing is what it does, then knowledge can reliably proceed experimentally. In order to know something, we proceed by reflecting on what happens when we interact with it. This process can be done casually or carefully, but in any case it *can* be done in order to know about the world. As Dewey defines pragmatism in his 1938 *Logic: The Theory of Inquiry,* "the proper interpretation of 'pragmatic' [is that consequences] function . . . as necessary tests of the validity of propositions, *provided* these

---

4. This was part of Bertrand Russell's criticism of James's theory of truth and later his criticism of Dewey's theory of inquiry. See Russell 1919, 1939, and 1945.

5. It is in this way that James makes the pragmatic method, that is, an epistemology of action, continuous with radical empiricism, that is, an ontology of action. See James 1996a, pp. 12–14, "Does Consciousness Exist?" and James 1996a, p. 52ff, "World of Pure Experience."

consequences are operationally instituted and are such as to resolve the specific problem evoking the operations" (Dewey 1938, 4). For Dewey, as for Peirce and James, a pragmatic approach will consistently look toward experience in general, but toward "testing" experience in particular, as the key to knowledge.

The principle of interaction and the consequent importance of experimentation in the process of engaging the world also points to the role of the investigator or "knower" in structuring experiments and interpreting their results. This role is understood in part as a matter of the attitudes brought to the process by the investigator, and all three classical pragmatists explicitly recognize attitudes as important both in hindering and advancing the process of knowing and engaging the world. Peirce's account of the history of theories of knowledge as given in his paper "The Fixation of Belief" turns not on explicit epistemological or ontological principles, but on operative attitudes. Peirce identifies four attitudes or methods of fixing belief (Peirce 1992, 115–23). The first, the method of *tenacity*, amounts to the simple process of rigidly clinging to a belief or set of beliefs regardless of what happens in experience. In this case, the range of consequences which are the meaning of a proposition are viewed as already set, inflexible, and independent of experienced change. The fixation of belief is conditioned by a disposition of rigidity and an unwillingness to consider consequences. The second method, the method of *authority*, conceives the meaning of a proposition as a matter settled by consulting recognized authorities. Here again, meaning proceeds from independent sources that may or may not respond to consequences as experienced. The disposition that conditions the process is a readiness to defer to authority or an unwillingness to question it. Peirce identifies the third method, the *a priori* method, with the approach taken by much of the European philosophical tradition. In this case, meanings are deduced from already established principles. As in the other cases, the disposition that conditions the fixation of belief is one that is closed to experienced consequences and expects meanings to be fixed and independent of the process of understanding.

While each of these methods can be understood as ways of conceiving consequences and so of determining the meaning of objects or events, Peirce argues that each is inadequate once one adopts the view that meaning is a matter of consequences. In each case, believers fail in some way to consider the full range of consequences and so prematurely cut off the process of understanding. In contrast to these methods, Peirce proposes a fourth. This method, the method of *science*, is characterized by a disposition open to change and interested in consequences, including those that verify the concepts at issue. Past results serve to

suggest ways of proceeding, according to this approach, and present experience provides a means to confirm or refute these concepts. Traditional methods of fixing belief are marked by rigid dispositions prone
to look to the past or to already established authority. The method of
science marks a new disposition as well as a new direction. To adopt
Peirce's method is to adopt a disposition of openness and experimentation consonant with the idea that meaning is a matter of consequences.

While Peirce focuses on the role of attitudes in scientific investigation, James presents pragmatism as a critical method concerned with the
practice of philosophy as conditioned by particular dispositions. In his
1907 volume *Pragmatism*, James begins by identifying two philosophical
attitudes: the tender-minded and the tough-minded. The history of European philosophy, he says, is a history of these two attitudes. Pragmatism,
the American alternative, amounts to a philosophical method controlled
by an attitude that has elements of both the tough and the tender. If
tough-minded philosophers focus on the facts and tender-minded philosophers focus on principles, the pragmatist, he concludes, "preserves
a cordial relation" with both (James 1975, 26). The attitudes one adopts
control one's expectations about what will count as knowledge and truth,
and so the attitudes are also ontological in their import. For James, the
general commitment to the principle of interaction means that being,
knowledge, human attitudes, and the world in which human beings live
are all connected and together form the starting place for the possibilities of human life.

Dewey, following James and Peirce, also identifies dispositions as a
defining feature of the process of determining meaning. In his paper
"Context and Thought," Dewey makes the connection explicit. Interest
is always present in thought, he says. "Every particular case of thinking
is what it is because of some attitude, some bias if you will" (Dewey 1931,
14). The role of attitudes, he concludes, cannot be eliminated. "No re-
gress will eliminate the attitude of interest that is as much involved in
thinking about attitudes as it is in thinking about other things." The
traditional conflict between subjectivity and objectivity is only a conflict
between alternative dispositions, not their presence or absence (Dewey
1931, 14–15). For Dewey, as for Peirce and James, dispositions significantly condition the process and outcomes of understanding, and he
favors a particular disposition in this connection.[6] In *Democracy and Education*, Dewey argues that in light of a pragmatic conception of meaning,
understanding is best conditioned by the attitudes of "directness, open-

6. Also see Dewey's discussion of dispositions in *Experience and Nature* (1925, 182–86).

mindedness, single-mindedness (or whole-heartedness), and responsibility" (Dewey 1916, 173).[7] Significant in Dewey's description is the idea that the best disposition for the process of inquiry is one which proceeds with a sense of responsibility to others. At the heart of classical pragmatism is the idea that human beings live in a reciprocal relationship with the world.

As the principle of interaction has implications for the role of the knower or inquirer, it also has implications for the objects of knowledge. Just as action determines what a thing is known as, it also frames what a thing is expected to be beyond the process of knowing. A tree, we might expect, is a tree whether or not anyone knows it. Such ontological claims seem to argue for a separation of subjects from objects, knowing from the known; but from the pragmatist perspective this is a mistake. Things are what they are in the context of action and interaction. That something is a tree is not independent from its tree-like actions in and on the world. To be a tree, one can say, is to have certain interactions with human beings, with the soil, with the air, and so on. If a thing is a matter of interaction, then attempts to make permanent separations between things are misguided. Trees are trees in their connections with their environments. Any separation can only be hypothetical in service of some purpose. Although continuity is often argued for by the classical pragmatists on somewhat different grounds, it also follows from the general commitment to the role of interaction. Things are and are known in and through their actions in the world. Actions, however, are not isolated moments but rather have beginnings and consequences. Continuity naturally emerges in the process of knowing and, in fact, knowing depends on being able to take advantage of such continuity to connect retrospective knowledge to prospective understanding. The principle of interaction, in short, demands recognition of continuity. From this perspective, organisms such as trees and people are not independent things that occasionally act on others, they are rather constituted by their interactions and so are at once continuous with their environment. Dewey makes this explicit on a number of levels, but in particular with respect to organisms and environments. "The processes of living," he says, "are enacted by the environment as truly as by the organism; for they *are* an integration" (Dewey 1938, 32).

From a pragmatic perspective, the principle of interaction and the resulting commitment to continuity undermine all manners of dualisms. The alleged distinctions between organisms and environments, for ex-

---

7. Dewey presents a similar view in *Ethics* (1932, 256–57). Also see Dewey 1938, 273.

ample, are at best resources for investigation rather than ontological categories. Similarly, individuals and society are not separate in any absolute sense. When they are taken separately it is generally in order to better understand and even promote their continuity. And, for purposes of the processes of knowing, valuing, and action in the world, ends are continuous with means. This is not to say that one cannot view the world from an alternative standpoint, where dualism and separations abound; it is rather to say that the pragmatic standpoint adopts an alternative stance toward and in the world. The resulting differences in ways of thinking and acting are, at least from the pragmatist perspective, strikingly different. As Dewey explains in *The Quest for Certainty,* the quest that characterizes much of European thought is replaced from the pragmatic perspective by a quest for practical security. To adopt the principle of interaction as part of a philosophical attitude is not only to recognize the role of attitude in understanding and acting in the world, it is also to be wary of dualisms which claim fundamental standing and instead to focus on what happens in experience.

With the commitment to the principle of interaction and its corollaries comes a commitment to a pervasive principle of pluralism: ontological, epistemological, and cultural. Even as interaction implies the continuity of things, the experience of interaction also implies an equally important pluralism. As James observes, despite a long-standing philosophical prejudice toward noticing the connections between things, that is, recognition of continuity, it is also possible to attend to the disunity or separation as well. "If our intellect had been as much interested in disjunctive as it is in conjunctive relations, philosophy would have equally successfully celebrated the world's disunion." The point is not that diversity is to be viewed as more fundamental than unity, but that "neither is primordial or more essential or excellent than the other" (James 1975, 68). The commitment to pluralism makes clear both a break from what James viewed as the philosophical tradition, and an explicit interest in noticing and even promoting difference. James summarizes, "Just as with space, whose separating of things seems exactly on a par with its uniting of them, but sometimes one function and sometimes the other is what comes home to us most, so, in our general dealings with the world of influences, we now need conductors and now need non-conductors, and wisdom lies in knowing which is which at the appropriate moment." Using the metaphor of space, which provides both a means of marking difference and a ground for connection, James argues that we need to recognize both connections and differences in experience and be ready to focus on one or the other or both, depending on circumstances.

For James, the commitment to the principle of interaction necessarily

brings a commitment to epistemic pluralism. In this case, pluralism implies "a world of additive constitution," that is, a world that is incomplete
(James 1975, 82). The principle of interaction reveals the possibility of
other knowledge from the start. "The very fact," he says in *Pragmatism*,
"that we debate this question shows that *our knowledge* is incomplete at
the present and subject to addition." This character of knowledge, however, makes demands as well on our expectations about the world. "In
respect of the knowledge it contains the world does genuinely change
and grow," so that pragmatic epistemological pluralism implies an ontological one as well (James 1975, 82). The status of this ontology, however, remains itself "pragmatic" and subject to changing effects. "Pragmatism," James concludes, "pending the final empirical ascertainment
of just what the balance of union and disunion among things may be,
must obviously range herself upon the pluralistic side" (James 1975, 79).
As he says at the beginning of his collection *The Will to Believe*, "*Prima
facie* the world is a pluralism; as we find it, its unity seems to be that of
any collection; and our higher thinking consists chiefly of an effort to
redeem it from that first crude form" (James 1956, viii). And later, in
his posthumously published work *Some Problems of Philosophy*, he concludes, "To sum up, the world is 'one' in some respects, and 'many' in
others" (James 1996, 133).

Although Peirce was less willing to affirm a commitment to pluralism, at least of the radical sort proposed by James (see, for example,
Peirce 1998, 457), he nevertheless affirms a pervasive and necessary pluralism in the world of human experience. As he remarks in a paper challenging the doctrine of absolute necessity, variety is "beyond comparison
the most obtrusive character of the universe" (Peirce 1992, 310). Peirce's
general view is a kind of monism, what he calls "objective idealism"
(Peirce 1992, 293), where the "stuff" of the universe is at its beginning
only "mind." Such monism, however, gives way to pluralism with the ad-
vent of life. He writes, "what we call matter is not completely dead, but
is merely mind hide-bound with habits. It still retains the element of
diversification; and in that diversification there is life" (Peirce 1992,
331). In the end, diversity is essential to life, to reflective thought, and
to the possibility of community. Such diversity is not the absolute pluralism of an atomist or a skeptic like David Hume, but is rather an essential
feature of the phase of the universe characterized by life.[8]

Dewey, on the other hand, affirmed pluralism in more concrete
terms. "That 'knowledge' has many different meanings," Dewey con-

---

8. For a useful reinterpretation of Peirce's approach to pluralism see Rosenthal 1994.

cludes, "follows from the operational definition of conceptions. There are as many conceptions of knowledge as there are distinctive operations by which problematic situations are resolved" (Dewey 1929, 176–77). In short, the principle of interaction, here expressed as the "operational definition of conceptions," demands a radical epistemological pluralism. Different ways of interaction with the world lead to different ways of knowing the world. Modern science structures one way of interaction, controlled experimentation, and it leads to a particular form of knowledge. Aristotelian science, "non-Western" approaches to healing, religious traditions, all lead to alternative forms of knowledge. Such epistemological diversity directly relates to an ontological diversity as well. "If we see that knowing is not the act of an outside spectator but of a participator inside the natural and social scene, then the true object of knowledge resides in the consequences of directed action. . . . For on this basis there will be as many kinds of known objects as there are kinds of effectively conducted operations of inquiry which result in the consequences intended" (Dewey 1929, 157). In effect, the requirements of the principle of interaction and its corollary of continuity lead to parallel epistemological and ontological pluralisms.

At the same time, Dewey's pluralism explicitly goes beyond traditional philosophical categories and sets expectations for social and cultural pluralism as well. Just as diverse methods of inquiry lead to diverse objects of knowledge, diverse methods of inquiry affirm that there are also diverse cultural contexts from which to inquire. "[E]very inquiry," he claims, "grows out of a background of culture and takes effect in greater or less modification of the conditions out of which it arises" (Dewey 1938, 27). While logic texts often "observe that science itself is culturally conditioned and then dismiss the fact from further consideration," Dewey finds that diverse cultural contexts are continuous with the resources available for inquiry on one hand and productive of distinctive and diverse results on the other. At the center of the demand for cultural pluralism is recognition that knowing proceeds by means of language, which serves as its frame and resource. Continuity locates that language in a wider context involving the speakers and history of the language and the world in which it is used. But different histories, peoples, and contexts naturally lead to different languages, where language is understood in "its widest sense—that is, including all means of communication such as, for example, monuments, rituals, and formalized arts —[as] the medium in which culture exists and through which it is transmitted. . . . Neither inquiry nor the most abstractly formal set of symbols can escape from the cultural matrix in which they live, move and have their being" (Dewey 1938, 27–28). As a result, epistemological, ontological, and cultural pluralisms are all connected, framing human practices and setting human expectations for reflection and action. It is a view Dewey labels "cultural naturalism."

The principle of community follows from the first two commitments and marks an explicit recognition by the classical pragmatists of the constitutive role of human communities in knowledge and ontology. The principle, most simply stated, is the expectation that human communities will serve as ground and limit for human experience. From this perspective, human communities play a key role in framing knowledge and reality. Early in his work, Peirce drew together the epistemological and ontological implications of the principle of interaction in the role of human community. He concludes in his paper "Some Consequences of Four Incapacities" that "what anything really is, is what it may finally come to be known to be in the ideal state of complete information, so that reality depends on the ultimate decision of the community" (Peirce 1992, 54). At the same time, even as the community "in the ideal state of complete information" determines what a thing really is, what counts as knowledge is similarly framed by an anticipation of this future state of community knowledge. "[T]he existence of thought now," he says, "depends on what is to be hereafter; so that it has only a potential existence, dependent on the future thought of the community" (Peirce 1992, 54–55). The possibility of an unlimited community is both an "indispensable" condition for knowledge and the limit of what is real and true. It is, Peirce argues, only when individual inquirers identify their own interests with those of an unlimited human community that they are rightly disposed to discern truth (Peirce 1992, 150). This is so, Peirce thinks, because the interests and inquiries of the human community ultimately frame truth and reality. In "How to Make Our Ideas Clear," he concludes, "The opinion which is fated to be ultimately agreed to by all who investigate, is what we mean by truth, and the object represented in this opinion is the real" (Peirce 1992, 139).[9]

For Peirce, the principle of community is largely a matter of the role of communities in framing knowledge and its objects. James, however, makes communities inseparable from and partly constitutive of human identity. In his 1890 *Principles of Psychology*, James argues that human selves as known can be understood as having at least three aspects: the material self, the social self, and the spiritual self. The first, the material

---

9. While Peirce adopts a realist position that appears more rigid than those of his colleagues James and Dewey, Dewey himself recalls this definition of truth in his 1938 *Logic*. What is most significant for Dewey is Peirce's attempt to locate the meaning of truth in a community of inquirers.

self, includes one's body but extends beyond it to include one's clothes and material possessions, as well as one's family and friends. To the extent that the material self is a product of socio-economic structures, cultural notions of kinship, and so on, the material self is an embodied self in community. The social self deepens the locatedness of human individuals in community by attending to the construction and imposition of social roles. "*A man's Social Self* is," as he puts it, "the recognition which he gets from his mates."[10] In this case, what others think about each other, how they know each other, and so on form part of each person's self. He continues, "Properly speaking, *a man has as many social selves as there are individuals who recognize him* and carry an image of him in their mind. . . . But as the individuals who carry the images fall naturally into classes, we may practically say that he has as many different social selves as there are distinct *groups* of persons about whose opinion he cares" (James 1950, 294). Both the material and social selves commit James to locating human individuals in and continuous with their communities. On this view, the community constitutes key parts of each human self, for better and for worse. To be materially poor in a society plays a concrete role in who a person is, as does wealth, physical differences, and clothing. Similarly, the social self is an explicit product of interactions in communities. Human beings are, in this sense, what they do. The pluralist commitment is revealed here in the sense that communities will produce a diversity of selves relative to their complex structures and opportunities, and individuals themselves will be irreducibly plural as selves in community.

James's idea of the spiritual self at first appears to be an aspect of self independent of community. It is, he says, "a man's inner or subjective being, his psychic faculties or dispositions, taken concretely" (James 1950, 296). It is, in short, how we know ourselves, as something "felt." Keeping in mind James's commitment to the principle of interaction and its corollaries, it follows that rather than being an independent self, the spiritual self is a self framed in community but where the self is taken as a subject rather than as an object, as an agent rather than a patient. As an agent, the spiritual self is how a person finds herself disposed to act. Such a disposition is not something separate either from the other selves or from one's community, but rather is a disposition to act in a certain

10. James's discussion consistently uses the masculine pronoun to identify the ideal person. The use is significant in that his discussion often seems to leave out significant aspects of selves that might be identified by women or non-white men, particularly the role of power in constituting identity. See Charlene Haddock Seigfried's discussion of James in *Pragmatism and Feminism* (1996), especially chapter 6.

way as a member of a particular community, with a particular material location and under the aspects of one's "mates." In short, while Peirce makes the community of inquirers partly constitutive of knowledge and reality in general, James takes up the question of self-knowledge and identity and concludes in similar fashion that human individuals are selves in living communities.

Dewey is also committed to the principle of community but shifts focus to better understand how communities ground inquiry and how they come to be organized. Dewey rejects Peirce's strong determinism with respect to communities of inquiry. The truth is not fated nor singular, but dependent upon the diversity of cultures and problems that frame inquiries. Most important, for Dewey, it is human sociality that marks the beginning of language and so the beginning of the possibility of inquiry. Peirce argues in general that a shared interest is necessary for inquiry. Dewey argues less grandly that it is the human ability "to take the standpoint of other individuals and to see and inquire from a standpoint that is not strictly personal but is common to them as participants or 'parties' in a conjoint undertaking" that is necessary for language and what follows from it (Dewey 1938, 52). The possibility of shared interests, shared language, and shared consequences in a common environment together form the starting point for all distinctively human endeavors.

The result of the commitment to the principle of community, combined with the principles of interaction and pluralism, is a further corollary that suggests a model for the process of organizing human interactions in and between communities—what can be called the practices of hospitality. In the liberal philosophies of Locke and Mill, communities are best organized around practices of toleration. From this perspective, individuals are permitted their differences while the integrity of the community is maintained by a commitment to non-interference. The pragmatist commitments lead to a different set of expectations in James and Dewey. Rather than adopting the practices of toleration as central, they adopt a view that mandates a context of openness that both respects the differences of individuals and their communities and at the same time recognizes value in interaction with those differences. Hospitality in its ordinary sense suggests practices of welcoming guests into an environment that is sustaining. Going beyond tolerance, hospitality suggests that hosts and guests look to each other's interests and needs. Just as Dewey finds that inquiry depends upon seeing things from others' perspectives, hospitality is a comparable social principle that requires participants to promote each other's well-being by seeing to their distinctive needs.

Dewey himself uses the term "hospitality" to describe how one ought to proceed with respect to different views in the process of inquiry. Hospitality, in this case, is taken to mean "open-mindedness," that is, "an attitude of mind which actively welcomes suggestions and relevant information from all sides" (Dewey 1916, 182). It does not, however, mean complete openness. "Open-mindedness is not the same as empty-mindedness. To hang out a sign saying 'Come right in; there is no one at home' is not the equivalent of hospitality. But there is a kind of passivity, willingness to let experiences accumulate and sink in and ripen, which is an essential of development" (Dewey 1916,183). This same principle becomes a central principle for Dewey's conception of democracy. In an address given in 1944, he concludes that "toleration in democracy is more than merely putting up with or 'standing' diversity of belief, while permitting experimentation with ideas" (Dewey 1944, 460). Democracy, on the contrary, demands a process of openness and mutual support. In a 1938 pamphlet, "Democracy and Education in the World Today," Dewey concludes, "Through mutual respect, mutual toleration, give and take, the pooling of experiences, it is ultimately the only method by which human beings can succeed in carrying on this experiment in which we are all engaged, whether we want to be or not, the greatest experiment of humanity—that of living together in ways in which the life of each of us is at once profitable in the deepest sense of the word, profitable to himself and helpful in the building up of the individuality of others" (Dewey 1938a, 303). Taken together, then, the principles of interaction, pluralism, and community form a philosophical standpoint that also supports a vision of human communities characterized by diversity and hospitality.

The pragmatist perspective is not, however, without its strong challenges, one of which helps to show the importance of the fourth principle: growth. One of the strongest reactions against the classical pragmatists was a response to the kind of relativism their perspective seemed to demand. In his history of "Western" philosophy, Bertrand Russell called pragmatism a "cosmic impiety." By affirming the unreliable principle of interaction, where knowledge and being are a matter of what may or may not happen, pragmatists appear to reduce the world to a matter of human interests and desires. The commitment to pluralism in all its forms seems to have the result of undermining even reliable principles since they stand on equal footing with other ways of understanding and responding to the world. If the principle of interaction makes things a matter of human preference, then the principle of pluralism guarantees that there would be no stopping human preference. The principle of community, then, either became grandiose as it appeared to become in Peirce, a kind of monolithic human absolute, or it became, as people like

Randolph Bourne argued, a kind of permission for dominant groups to have their way. The latter criticism, surrounding Dewey's belated support for the United States's entry into World War I, was particularly harsh because all of the apparent commitments to democracy and equality seemed, in light of the principle of community, to work exclusively for those who managed to obtain and hold power.[11] The criticisms, striking as they are, took pragmatism as if it were committed only to the first three principles without the fourth. In fact, the classical pragmatists also remained committed to the principle of growth, which serves as a standard for and limit on the community.[12]

In 1906, in the process of offering a case in favor of his own version of pragmatism, Peirce introduced the idea of growth as a key element. Pragmatism, at its center, is an approach to thinking about what is most common, what Jeremy Bentham had called "cenoscopy." Such a study, Peirce observes, faced the difficult problem of being already embedded in the common. "In commencing it we are confronted with the fact that we already believe a great many things," Peirce says (Peirce 1998, 373). In order to proceed, it is crucial that one take a critical stance, but to do so requires a framework that is adequately general to provide perspective. The key proposed by Aristotle, in Peirce's interpretation, is the idea of growth. "This idea of Aristotle's has proved marvelously fecund; and in truth it is the only idea covering quite the whole area of cenoscopy that has shown any marked uberosity" (Peirce 1998, 373). Aristotle's idea of growth brings together potentiality and action, matter and form, or, Peirce suggests, "τύπος," "the blow." In effect, growth is the process of interaction between what Peirce calls the "female function" or the seed, and the "male function," which "executes a hunch" as a "principle of unrest." The two functions, however, are not complete for they require a "third, not implied in either of them, nor in both together." This third, on Peirce's account, is "the congress of those two . . . something demonstrably additional to them" (Peirce 1998, 374). It is an "urge" which provides purpose and direction to the particular union and provides "the blow" necessary to overcome the inertia of habit and the disruption of chance. The "urge," however, is not simply a random direction, but one framed in relation to others, a process of what he calls "creative love" (Peirce 1992, 362). Commenting on the Apostle John's proclamation that God is love, Peirce makes the link between growth and love explicit. "Everybody can see that the statement of St. John is the formula of an

11. See Bourne 1999.
12. Charlene Haddock Seigfried also makes growth an explicit commitment of pragmatism (1996, 7).

evolutionary philosophy, which teaches that growth comes only from love . . . from the ardent impulse to fulfil another's highest impulse" (Peirce 1992, 354). For Peirce, the only principle broad enough to provide a context for the study of what is common is the principle of growth. This principle brings together subject and object, knower and known, potential and actual over a motivational and directional "urge," creative love, that is also a normative principle governing human knowledge and community.

In his *Varieties of the Religious Experience,* James mirrors Peirce by concluding that the shared element of human religious experience is not a particular doctrine or even belief in a supreme being, singular or plural, but rather a search for something more. What is common, James concludes, is that religions consist of two parts: "an uneasiness; and . . . its solution" (James 1902, 508). In a way that suggests Peirce's description of growth, James goes on. "The uneasiness, reduced to its simplest terms, is a sense that there is *something wrong about us* as we naturally stand." The seed of one's self, following Peirce, is unsettled. "The solution is a sense that *we are saved from the wrongness* by making proper connection with the higher powers." Setting aside the hierarchy implied, the solution, like the resolution of the union of seed and unrest, is a directed connection. A person *"becomes conscious that this higher part is coterminous and continuous with a MORE of the same quality, which is operative in the universe outside of him, and which he can keep in working touch with"* (James 1902, 508). Salvation, in a word, is a matter of connections with "the 'more' " (James 1902, 511).

The idea that connections are the ground for salvation not only recalls Peirce's notion of "creative love" and the idea of growth as an explanatory framework, it also points to James's further development of pragmatism in his lectures published in 1907. The book, and especially its chapter "The Pragmatic Theory of Truth," was criticized for its apparent radical relativism, made all the more pernicious because it seemed to make truth simply a matter of what one wants. In fact, one of the ways that James might have responded to the critics would have been to remind them to take seriously the final chapter.[13] In this chapter, "Pragmatism and Religion," James returned to the themes of *Varieties of the Religious Experience,* but here proposes growth as a standard as well as a way of understanding the diversity of human religious experience.

He begins the discussion by quoting Walt Whitman's poem "To You,"

---

13. Charlene Haddock Seigfried makes a similar point in more general terms in *William James's Radical Reconstruction of Philosophy* (1990, 306ff.).

in which Whitman proclaims, "O I could sing such grandeurs and glories about you!" (quoted in James 1975, 132). James proposes that there are two interpretations of Whitman's verse. The first—he calls it the "monistic" interpretation—imagines that Whitman has a kind of God's eye view of the reader, the "you" in the poem, and can see the reader's "true soul and body" (as Whitman says in a stanza not quoted by James). Such a view of human nature at once makes one "inwardly safe" and at the same time amounts to a kind of "quietism" and "indifference." The alternative interpretation is pragmatic. James explains, "the you so glorified, to which the hymn is sung, may mean your better possibilities phenomenally taken, or the specific redemptive effects even of your failures" (James 1975, 133). The alternatives are both legitimate. "But the background of the first way is the static One, while in the second way it means possibles in the plural, genuine possibles, and it has all the restlessness of that conception."

Just as Peirce affirms the legitimacy of alternative notions of evolution, James affirms that those committed to "monism" and "pluralism" each have legitimate views of themselves and the world. While they stand as philosophical poles, it is a third way that seems to James the most general and the most valuable. He calls the alternative the "doctrine of meliorism." The point of the doctrine is to recognize the value of the two extremes, but that to live in accord with only one or the other leads to limited alternatives. It is meliorism that explains both the process of growth and the standards that growth imposes on living beings. Such a view does not lead to necessity because, in an important way, growth is not a necessary function of the world. Growth is as contingent as life itself. Rather, as he puts it, in light of the realization we can ask: Why not adopt the view as the guide for living and knowing? "Our acts, our turning-places, where we seem to ourselves to make ourselves and grow, are the parts of the world to which we are closest, the parts of which our knowledge is the most intimate and complete. Why should we not take them at their face-value?" (James 1975, 138). For James, one could adopt a view that sees the world as fixed and determinate, but such a view does not promote growth but rather "the slumber of nonentity" (James 1975, 139). If growth is adopted as a standard consistent with pragmatic truth and the experience of human life, then there is also a standard that bounds the relativism of a view that makes truth "what works." The standard of growth is the standard of maximizing possibilities and promoting further growth. Such a view does not arrive of necessity, since the stance taken resists the idea that there are fixed things. To leave behind the idea of fixed truths or relations which determine truth does not leave

one with nothing; that is, it does not leave one with radical relativism. Rather it leaves one with a view that is directed but open. One
chooses, in effect against a fixed universe and in favor of the possibility
of growth.[14]

Dewey is also explicit about affirming the principle of growth. In
his discussion in *Experience and Nature* of theories that divide human
beings into minds and bodies, adults and children, organisms and environments, he concludes that "[t]he reality *is* the growth-process itself"
(Dewey 1925, 210), in effect, that organisms are their growth process.
Following his claims about the unbreakable continuity between organisms and their environments, growth represents another axis of continuity—the continuity of a life. Rather than mere persistence, however,
growth is a contingent process of change in a particular direction, its
outcome indeterminate, but still dependent upon earlier phases, current circumstances, and future interests. That growth is growth of an
organism means that the continuity of life is a point of connection between the history of an organism and the history of the environment to
which it is bound. The result of such a view, as it is for both Peirce and
James, is an explanatory framework that begins by assuming that there
is change and that change takes place in a context. Flourishing life, in
this case, depends upon maintaining connections and in particular those
connections that promote the process of growth.

Dewey converts this explanatory notion of growth to a normative
one in two contexts. Most explicitly, the principle of growth becomes a
standard for the process of teaching. In *Experience and Education* growth
is an implicit product of continuity. Should continuity stand as a guiding
principle for education, then so too should growth. However, Dewey observes, someone might object that "growth might take many different
directions: a man, for example, who starts out on a career of burglary,
may grow in that direction, and by practice grow into a highly expert
burglar" (Dewey 1938, 19). From this perspective, growth seems to be
a principle open to any kind of development; for teachers, it amounts to
a risky, open-ended relativism. Dewey's reply reaffirms what Peirce and
James already concluded. "[F]rom the standpoint of growth as education and education as growth the question is whether growth in this
direction promotes or retards growth in general. Does this form of

14. Of course, one could also choose a universe in which nothing was ever stable, even
the commonality of growth. Such a view is not an alternative to the idea of fixed world.
In this case what is fixed is the lack of continuity and cohesion. Meliorism avoids both
pitfalls by emphasizing the process of growth.

growth create conditions for further growth, or does it set up conditions that shut off the person who has grown in this particular direction from the occasions, stimuli, and opportunity for continuing growth in new directions?" (Dewey 1938, 19). If growth is adopted as an explanation for the process of human life, then it may be used as a guideline for understanding the relative value of alternative ideas, processes, and actions. When it is taken as a way to understand education, it follows that those things—actions, conditions, expectations—that promote further growth are to be favored over those which do not. Dewey makes the same point in more detail in *Democracy and Education* in the chapter "Education as Growth." Growth as a standard has two dimensions. In general, "there is nothing to which growth is relative save more growth" (Dewey 1916, 51) and so a general attitude is established. What growth means in any given case, however, is a matter for further consideration. Commenting on the differences between adults and children, Dewey concludes that "the difference between them is not the difference between growth and no growth, but between the modes of growth appropriate to different conditions" (Dewey 1916, 50). Just as good and bad, for Peirce, could be understood in terms of their fostering growth or undermining it, so Dewey affirms that growth can serve as a standard of evaluation.

From this perspective, growth frames both freedom and principles of social organization. "Freedom," Dewey concludes in the 1932 *Ethics*, "in its practical and moral sense . . . is connected with possibility of growth" (Dewey 1932, 305). The principle of growth, while active in ongoing human life, emerges with the developing awareness of its importance as a way of understanding human life. "Potentiality of freedom is a native gift or part of our constitution in that we have *capacity* for growth and for being actively concerned in the process and the direction it takes" (Dewey 1932, 306). We can live in the direction of growth or not, but once we identify the possibility, it can become the frame for further reflection and action. Drawing together implicitly both Peirce's and James's commitment to growth, Dewey says, "In the degree in which we become aware of possibilities of development and actively concerned to keep the avenues of growth open, in the degree in which we fight against induration and fixity, and thereby realize the possibilities of recreation of our selves, we are actually free." At the same time that growth focuses on the "re-creation" or transformation of individual selves, the principle also serves as an organizing principle for human interaction. Dewey asserts in *The Quest for Certainty* that "the stable and expanding institution of all things that make life worthwhile throughout all human relationships is the real object of *all* intelligent conduct" (Dewey 1929, 25). The "stable and expanding institution" of goods for Dewey becomes the ground for the "democratic ideal," which is predicated on the notion that while growth provides a framework to understand goods, the content of what constitutes the good in a given case is a matter of the particulars of the circumstances. A democracy based on growth is a community that both affirms the value of individual growth and construes the growth of the community as a matter of promoting opportunities for growth among its people. Jane Addams calls this notion of growth "lateral progress" in that it redistributes the direction of progress from vertical, with its commitments to "improvements and civilization," to one committed to widening and deepening connections among its members and along its borders with other communities.[15]

The central commitments of pragmatism, here taken as representative of a distinctive American philosophical tradition, are commitments to the principles of interaction, pluralism, community, and growth. There are other similarities among the three classical pragmatists I have considered, as well as many significant differences. Nevertheless, the four principles identified are both pervasive elements of their philosophical perspectives and recognizably distinct from much of the European philosophical tradition. This is not to say that some European philosophy does not share these principles. Rather, it is to say that these principles, taken together, form a coherent philosophical ground in American thought whose genealogy can be traced from indigenous traditions of America, through other American traditions of resistance, and into classical pragmatism.

The pragmatic commitments together make for an approach to understanding and acting in the world that Dewey called "the quest for security." The process of meaning-making, from this perspective, focuses on things and events in context and as changing. Knowledge, that is, meaning that can serve to guide action, will be fallible, and knowers must be prepared to try new meanings and reject old ones as circumstances change. This approach stands in sharp contrast with the "quest for certainty," an approach, born in reaction to the insecurities of the world, that seeks meaning outside contexts and in truths that transcend particularity. In this tradition, despite a wide variety of accounts about where things get their meaning, they all nevertheless share an interest in certainty. This certainty, representing both confidence and permanence, requires that meaning in general and knowledge in particular be guaranteed by an unchanging reality. Some versions of the approach

15. See Addams 1912.

claim that the unchanging reality is ideal, some versions that it is material, and some versions that it is a combination of both. Such views nevertheless hold in common the expectation that the things of experience
will at best be a starting point for the discovery of meaning that will go
outside the shifting terrain of the interactive world and find its answers
in something fixed and permanent. When the quest for certainty is imported to the Americas, it becomes part of the philosophical inheritance
of American philosophy—what I will call the colonial attitude. The alternative attitude advocated by Dewey is comparable to the "American"
attitudes he and Tocqueville identify as a distinctive American philosophical approach. This second attitude constitutes another crucial part
of the inheritance of American philosophy and the center of American
pragmatism—what I will call the indigenous attitude. In the next two
chapters, I will examine the character of the colonial attitude as it developed along the border between Native and European America. This attitude provides a part of the context into which the indigenous attitude
emerged for some European American thinkers. I turn to the indigenous
attitude and its commitments to interaction, pluralism, community, and
growth in the remaining chapters.

CHAPTER THREE

The Colonial Attitude

COTTON MATHER, a Puritan preacher and descendant of two of New England's founding families, was renowned as a religious leader, historian, and philosopher. His works were widely read, and his 1702 history of New England, *Magnalia Christi Americana,* was an important reference for later historians. The opening lines indicate the tenor of Mather's approach to the meaning of New England.

> I WRITE the *Wonders* of the CHRISTIAN RELIGION, flying from the Depravations of *Europe,* to the *American Strand:* And, assisted by the Holy Author of the *Religion,* I do, with all Conscience of *Truth,* required therein by Him, who is *Truth* it self, Report the *Wonderful Displays* of His Infinite Power, Wisdom, Goodness, and Faithfulness, wherewith His Divine Providence hath *Irradiated* an *Indian Wilderness.* (Mather 1977, 89)

The meaning of New England, in short, will be a matter of its place in the story of the progress of "Divine Providence." Even as he will tell the story of the movement away from Europe geographically, Mather nevertheless preserves a European framework for making the move meaningful. The distinction between Europe and America is primarily geographical, a displacement in location, but not in conceptual framework or context, a distinction he suggests in his reference to the Puritan flight from Europe to "the American Strand." Strictly speaking, the "strand" to which the Europeans fled is the American coast, and for Mather the northeast coast in particular, where a series of English colonies formed New England. The flight Mather describes unambiguously reinforces a key element in his approach to New England's history. While his story will be a story of Europeans, it is nevertheless the story of a movement away, a flight from Europe toward America, from a sinful world of depravity to a promised land of salvation.

In 1678, when John Bunyan described this sort of flight he called it progress. Anticipating Mather's tale of the Puritan immigrants, Bunyan describes the flight of a young man named Christian, who sets out from his home in the "City of Destruction" encouraged by a character called Evangelist. When Evangelist hears Christian is in fear for his life in the city, he gives Christian a parchment roll on which is written the advice, "Fly from the wrath to come." Christian takes the advice and, leaving his family behind, begins to run toward the distant light of the Celestial City. When they see him running away, his wife and children call for him to come back, but "the man put his fingers in his ears and ran on crying, 'Life, life, eternal life.' So that he looked not behind him" (Bunyan 1965, 41). Later in his journey when another character, Prudence, asks if he ever thinks about his home, Christian replies, "Truly, if I had been mindful of that country from whence I came out, I might have had opportunity to have returned; but now I desire a better country; that is, an heavenly [one]" (Bunyan 1965, 82). In Mather's *Magnalia*, the figure of the American Strand is the "heavenly country" and marks both the direction and destination of the Puritan flight.

Even as Mather presents a story of a flight from Europe, it is also a story about Europe. Just as histories of American thought have made America the raw material for the development of European thought, so Mather begins his history by making America part of the story of European and Christian progress. The flight to America is necessarily a flight from depravity, but it is not a flight from European ideas or progress. Quite the contrary: Mather's history is an effort to shape the meaning of America in terms of the already ongoing story of European and human development. In this sense, Mather begins his narrative exhibiting an attitude in tension with the commitments at the center of pragmatism. His work represents, in fact, a first version of the colonial attitude manifested in the language of the Calvinist tradition and framed in the context of the Puritan "errand into the wilderness."[1] From its particular expression of the colonial attitude, Mather's approach also represents a particular way of making the world meaningful, of understanding it and acting in it. The figure of the "American Strand" orients Mather's effort to make his world meaningful, but it also provides a direction for his story.

At the same time, the "American Strand" is also a reference to a concrete place of contact between the American native inhabitants and

---

1. See Mather's reference to the "errand" (Mather 1977, 144), the analysis of the idea by Perry Miller (1956, 1–15), and the critique of Miller's analysis by Sacvan Bercovitch (1978, 3–30).

the English immigrants. In cartographical terms, the American strand is represented as a series of English villages spread along the bays and rivers connected with the North Atlantic. In Mather's experience, however, it was a series of English settlements interspersed with villages of Native American people, bands of people of "mixed blood" and mixed culture, and large tracts of forests and wetlands backed by a low mountain range. This was no stretch of beach and it was no empty wilderness. The Puritan remove to America was also an arrival at a borderland, at a place of contact between America and Europe. Mather's opening lines lead the reader to expect that his story will reflect this arrival and the need to make it meaningful. The irony is that although Mather lived on the American Strand, he ultimately viewed it as continuous with Europe and not a point of contact with a radically different world. As a result, his experience was framed and circumscribed by the colonial attitude and consequently was not the experience of a borderland at all.

The figure of the American Strand suggests a third sense that would not have escaped Mather's attention. A strand may mean a coast or a shore, but it may also mean a length of yarn or thread. Strung between the American inland terrain and the North Atlantic, the metaphor of a thread suggests that the American Strand was also a means of connection, a way to link the so-called Old and New Worlds, a thread tied to each. Such a thread would have been a long one, literally binding together what had been viewed as opposites. Until Columbus's voyage, any people imagined to live outside the world of Europe, Asia, and Africa were called "antipodes," literally those who stand on diametrically opposite sides of the globe and, figuratively, those who have opposing ideas. Before 1492, writers were regularly excommunicated for positing the existence of such people, and the name itself suggested that, whatever they might be, the antipodes would necessarily be as different from Europeans (and Asians and Africans) as night from day. Mather himself recognizes the irony of the Medieval view and declares, "I can assert the Existence of the *American Antipodes:* And I can Report unto the *European* Churches great Occurrences among these *Americans*" (Mather 1977, 117). In the end, Mather uses the "strand," the connection between Europe and America, as a means to make the antipodes, both the Natives and the immigrants, part of Europe and so the American Strand (as the other senses of the figure suggest) is both the place and the means by which America becomes continuous with Europe.

Despite Mather's efforts to use the strand literally and figuratively as a means of connection, New England was nevertheless on a real strand between the Atlantic and the "wilderness" populated by antipodal "wild men." How the Europeans stood in relation to their neighbors is suggested in the figure of God's "*irradiat[ion of]* an *Indian Wilderness.*" The figure is significant because it calls up at least three levels of contact between the newly arrived Europeans and Native America. First, "irradiated" may be taken as synonymous with "illuminated," suggesting that God illuminated the "wilderness" so that the chosen people could find their way. In effect, God provided a means of clearly understanding the region, of mapping it and fixing it, in a sense, under the "aspect of eternity." Such irradiation would have been a crucial step both in practical survival and in Mather's own process of telling the American story; that is, irradiation was conceived as the way to make America meaningful to Mather and his people.

Irradiation also means "enlightenment." From Richard Hakluyt's 1584 report to Queen Elizabeth of the possibility of establishing English colonies in America, a central goal of "Western Planting" was the conversion of Native souls to Christianity. "It is necessary for the salvation of those poore people which have sitten so longe in darknes and in the shadowe of deathe," Hakluyt writes, "that preachers should be sent unto them . . . principally [for] the gayninge of the soules of millions of those wretched people, the reducinge of them from darkes to lighte." He concludes, "the people of America crye oute unto us, their nexte neighboures to come and helpe them, and bringe unto them the gladd tidinges of the gospell" (Hakluyt 1877, 8, 10–11).[2] While the English were less effective than the French or Spanish in the process of conversion, it remained a central concern for Mather and the other English colonial leaders that Native people would "see the light" of Christianity. But the interest in conversion was practical as well as spiritual. Along the American Strand the immigrants were novices in understanding the meaning of the land and people. Native converts who became fluent in English helped the immigrants learn how to adapt to the new place. Irradiation in this second sense meant the conversion of Native people to European ways of understanding the world, a figure that would reemerge in the work of the Great Awakening in the eighteenth century.

A third sense of irradiation lurks here as well. Although Mather could not have anticipated it, from the perspective of an early twenty-first–century commentator the figure of irradiation calls up terrible meanings. In our time, irradiation is no longer a term naming illumination and enlightenment, but rather contamination, sterility, illness, and

---

2. In the same spirit, the coat of arms for the Massachusetts Bay Colony included the image of a Native person uttering the words "Come over and help us."

death. In this case, objects irradiated are physically transformed, their vitality destroyed. It is a frightening turn of Mather's sense of the term in that, for him, irradiation meant that those concerned could "see" better and by analogy know better. In the tradition of European philosophy, to know is like seeing; the object affects the eye but remains itself unaffected. In this way knowers can know things without changing them and the things known become the solid foundations of meaning. From this perspective, irradiation recalls the spectator theory of knowledge and its ground in the attitude associated with the quest for certainty. Irradiation in a nuclear age reverses the process. While the source of radiation degrades in its own time, indifferent to its circumstances, its objects are changed and ultimately destroyed. The figure of an irradiated "Indian Wilderness" suggests an American terrain stripped of life without hope of restoration, of whole populations dying of unseen, unpreventable causes, of empty towns, of lost traditions. Mather's reference is unintentional, but its connections can call up a critical angle on the attitude of meaning Mather adopts for his history.

While the opening lines suggest the tone of Mather's approach to the history of New England, he is also explicit about the process he adopts to make New England's past meaningful. "*Reader!*," he calls in the general introduction, "I have done the part of an *Impartial Historian* . . . " and then immediately offers a caution from the Roman historian Polybius. "*Historici Legantur cum Moderatione & venia, & cogitetur fieri non posse ut in omnibus circumstantiis sint Lyncei*"[3] (Mather 1977, 97). The caution is important because it affirms the fallibility of the "impartial historian" but does so while also affirming the ideal historical perspective. The reference to Lynceus identifies the process of meaning as one ideally involving "sharp sight" or clear vision, recalling the figure of the irradiation of the Indian wilderness. At the same time, while clear vision is the ideal, Mather's notion of impartiality includes the idea that clear vision also involves correct judgment. He is not, he says, "of the Opinion, that one cannot merit the Name of an *Impartial Historian,* except he write bare Matters of Fact, without all *Reflection*" (Mather 1977, 98). Instead he offers an alternative definition of history: "*Historia est rerum gestarum, cum laude aut vituperatione, Narratio*" (Mather 1977, 98), "History is the story of events, with praise or blame" (Mather 1977, 98n6). As a story of events, a history will be, as he says earlier, "*testis temporum,*" a witness

---

3. "Let historians be read with moderation and indulgence, and let it be considered that it is impossible for them always to be like Lynceus." Kenneth Murdoch observes that Lynceus, in Greek mythology, was renowned for his "sharp sight" (Mather 1977, 97n1).

of a period of time. Taken together, all histories will present a story of all events, combining them into a single account of the world.[4] At the same time, impartiality weds the witnessing of events to the process of judgment. If one can see the "facts" clearly, one can also see their value. The judgments Mather has in mind are of two sorts. On one hand, judgments are of praiseworthiness and blameworthiness of the events witnessed by the impartial historian. It is the impartial historian's job to make those judgments clear. On the other hand, the historian will also judge people and events on the basis of their value to the narrative. Some crimes, Mather suggests, are too awful to be included, while some acts of beneficence are routine but serve a didactic purpose. The impartial historian is also an impartial teacher, presenting truth to foster truth. Impartiality, in this sense, is clear-sightedness with respect to both "facts" and "values." A history, then, will make a particular period of time meaningful by observing it as clearly as possible and presenting the resulting facts with judgment so that the narrative will be organized along two axes, one chronological and the other valuational.

With the general attitude of the historian established, Mather begins his presentation of the history of New England with an account of what he calls "the Antiquities," the period in American history before the arrival of the Mayflower in 1620. This account is useful because it provides hints about the chronological and valuational axes operative in the process of making New England meaningful. The general history that the *Magnalia* joins is the history of the world and, in particular, of God's people in the world, that is, church history. The flight by the Puritans to America was simply the latest chapter in the much longer story of the church beginning with Abraham and the still longer story of humanity beginning with Adam. From Mather's perspective, his history adds to histories already written. The addition of another chapter in church history in this case is challenging because on the surface it seems to contradict the histories written before Columbus returned from his first voyage, including those recorded in the Bible. According to biblical accounts, humankind had a single point of origin. This monogenetic story affirmed that the origin of all earthly life was in what is now called the Middle East, the point of connection between Europe, Asia, and Africa. Following the Great Flood, all life reemerged on the slopes of Ararat where Noah's ark came to rest. When Columbus reported a disconnected

---

4. See Mather's discussion linking histories of the "whole world" and "Church History" into a comprehensive story of creation (Mather 1977, 94–97).

but populated continent, reliable expectations were overturned and history faced a crisis.

Mather's history responds to the crisis by incorporating the process of the "discovery of America" and the required restatement of human history into his own story of New England. According to Mather, America was literally concealed from the writers of the Bible and their successors by God as part of His long-term plan for the development of the church. America's flora and fauna, including its people, did indeed come from Noah's restoration of life after the flood, and so America, although once known to the people of Europe, Asia, and Africa, had been forgotten (Mather 1977, 117). How America had come to be populated and forgotten, however, remained to be completely reported. Though Mather admits some doubt about the details, in order to "stay [the] Stomach" of his reader, he offers an account by a "very sensible *Russian*" and published by a Jesuit missionary, Phillippe Avril. The Russian proposes more or less what is later called the Bering Strait hypothesis. After describing a people who live along the Arctic Ocean and hunt "monsters" (perhaps whales), the Russian concludes, "I am perswaded that several of those Hunters have been carried upon . . . floating pieces of Ice . . . to the most Northern Parts of America, which is not far from that Part of Asia that jutts out into the Sea of Tartary" (Mather 1977, 121–122). Mather further speculates that the reason America became populated at all was because the devil seduced "the first inhabitants of *America* into it" in order to prevent them from hearing the gospel. In any case, for a great while, America was hidden from Europe and the church until God decided the time was right. The reintroduction of America, according to Mather, came as part of three crucial developments. The first was the *"Resurrection of Literature"* in the fifteenth century that involved the beginning of modern science, its technological developments, and the wide circulation of literature, including the Bible. Columbus's voyage in 1492 opened the "New World" or better, the "New Jerusalem," to God's developing church. Finally, in 1520, the Reformation overturned the constraints of the Roman church and provided a new direction for God's people. By the end of the sixteenth century the ground was laid for the next stage in history: the movement of the Reformed church out of Egypt, through the wilderness, and into the Promised Land.

The story illustrates the two axes of organization, in effect, the logic of the colonial attitude. On one hand, the events both in America and in Europe are tied together into a single chronology. New England is made meaningful in part because it can be joined seamlessly with the story of Christianity, the chosen people, and human genesis. The prob-

lem of Native American inhabitants standing outside the story is solved
by incorporating them into both the timeline and the purposive flow of
the narrative. Native people descended from the survivors of the flood,
but were led astray, "herded" as Mather says, by the devil and hidden
from those who became the chosen people. Eventually, the hidden
Americans reemerged into the history of the chosen people as the latter
arrived in the New Canaan, the land where God's kingdom would be
established. The result is a narrative that is not merely a *sequence* of
events, but rather a *progression* of events from a distinct origin toward a
distinct conclusion. Just as Bunyan charts Christian's progress from the
City of Destruction to the Celestial City, Mather charts the progress of
Christianity from depraved Europe, into a wilderness, on its way to the
New Jerusalem. His incorporation of America into the story reveals his
expectation that all "facts" can be organized into a single chronology.
In this case, Mather preserves past histories by making America meaningful in terms already established in the story of Christianity. America
is populated by descendants of Noah, governed by the devil, and like the
land of Canaan, given to the chosen people by God at the expense of
the Canaanites.

Put another way, Mather's *Magnalia* illustrates the expectation that
there is a single timeline ordering all things and events. For Mather, the
timeline is God's plan for earthly creation. Events in human experience
are finite periods in the timeline. While no human being can know the
entire timeline, that is, what happens everywhere moment to moment,
human beings can know their own moments and report them. This concept of time involves at least two expectations for those who will make
the reports. First, all accurate reports of moments in time will be consistent with all other accurate reports. One will expect, for example, a
single story of the origin of human beings and a single account of New
England's history. This is not to say that there may not be different histories of the same period, however. The Bible itself has both a general
account of creation and a detailed account of the origin of human beings. These are, from Mather's perspective, simply different stories of the
same event in history, or rather reports of different events going on at
the "same time" historically. Stories of American "pre-history" and European "pre-history" may be dramatically different in detail, but Mather
expects that they will necessarily be consistent. No story of America will
challenge any stories of Europe and vice versa. Should someone propose
that some human beings were created separately in America, Mather
would naturally reject the story in light of the story of creation in the
Middle East already accepted as accurate.

A second expectation connected with the chronological organization of meaning is that the ordering timeline will be independent of any particular point of view except God's. The course of earthly events proceeds in the order given by God. If one wants to know what has happened or will happen, one will try to settle the question by attending to the event's place in God's timeline or plan. Once its place is found, all the important questions have been answered, and the event's meaning apprehended. From Mather's perspective, the fixed character of chronological ordering provides more than meaning; it also provides certainty. In cases of dispute about when the world will end or when the Great Flood occurred, the disputants can turn to God's own timeline, as revealed in scripture and other accurate historical records, to settle the question.

Spatial location is similarly fixed in the expectations of chronological ordering. Things occur in order in part because they have locations. If God's timeline specifies an order, then it must also specify locations. If America becomes concealed from Europe at a certain point in history, it does so occupying the location God deems it to occupy and its "discovery" by Europeans involves a chronological development and spatial movement. The exodus of the Jews and the exodus of the Puritans represent a temporal and spatial process. There is, from this perspective, no relative location except secondarily. Each event occurs in its space and time, and discovered relationships among things are at best useful relations that can assist limited human minds in apprehending the meaning of things and events in God's plan. The spatial relationship between Jerusalem and Plymouth colony, the temporal relationship between the Jewish exodus and the Puritan one, the relationship between celestial signs and important events are all significant, that is, they all gain their meaning because they bring attention to relationships between events and God. Chronological ordering of events, then, amounts to an expectation that events will occur in fixed locations and moments in God's timeline. As a feature of Mather's attitude of meaning, it prescribes an approach to making things meaningful by seeing them with respect to the development of God's plan for creation.

The other axis of the attitude, the axis of valuation, connects the chronology with a hierarchical structure of value. In general, things earlier in the chronology are of less value, relatively speaking, than things later because, in general, value recapitulates chronology. If events move from an evil past to a good future, things further from the beginning and closer to the end will be better, just as things which facilitate progress toward the end will be better than those which obstruct it. This is not to say that America prior to Columbus is not important from Mather's perspective; it is rather that, relatively speaking, America before Columbus was both further away from the end of the chronology than Mather's own time, and closer to the beginning of the story, the fall of human-kind.[5]

At the same time, Mather's own demand that Christians return to an earlier form of Christian community seems to cut against the chronological organization of value. In *Bonifacius: An Essay Upon The Good, that is to be Devised and Designed by those Who Desire to Answer the Great End of Life and to Do Good While They Live,* Mather demands that New England return to a primitive form of Christianity. He writes, "I take the *works of our day* to be. . . . The *reviving of primitive Christianity;* to study and restore everything, of the *primitive* character" (Mather 1966, 142). If these are really the true "works of our day," Mather seems to value things in reverse of the chronological development. Yet to see Mather as valuing the past over the future is to miss the function of the primitive in the colonial attitude. Primitive Christianity is not valuable in its own right, but only as it contributes to achieving the future state by readying the world for God's inevitable return. In his call for the restoration of primitive Christianity, Mather makes the link more explicit. "The *apostasy* is going off. The time for *cleansing the Temple* comes on" (Mather 1966, 142). The restoration here compares with the other parallels important to Mather's narrative. The Puritans are participating in an exodus, for example. The exodus is not a return to the old Jerusalem, but rather a new process that recalls past actions but is a new stage of history. The restoration of primitive Christianity likewise recalls the institution of Christianity after the chosen people were established in Jerusalem and awaiting the return of the Messiah. Rather than gaining its value relative to the past, the past provides an interpretive context that points to the value of Puritan Christianity as another step closer to the end.

Native people and Catholics, like others who are not saved, are treated as less valuable or even as evil both because they are correlated with obstacles to achieving the end and because they themselves represent a stage of the chronology that is past. Native people are Canaanites and obstacles to the New Jerusalem, while Catholics are Romans and

---

5. This notion of hierarchical value is different from Arthur O. Lovejoy's famous notion of the "Great Chain of Being." Lovejoy defines the chain of being as the "conception of the universe as a 'great Chain of Being,' composed of an . . . infinite number of links ranking in hierarchical order from the meagerest kind of existents, which barely escape non-existence, through 'every possible' grade up to *the ens perfectissimum*" (Lovejoy 1936, 59). Rather than making an ontological claim, I suggest that explanatory ideas like the chain of being illustrate the operation of an attitude of meaning. In Lovejoy's case, the use of the idea of the chain of being illustrates a general approach to making things meaningful, one which expects a fixed valuational axis.

Pharisees, obstacles to establishing the church among the gentiles. They are to be overcome and converted, not "studied and restored." The resulting complicated attitude shared by Mather and his contemporaries helps us to understand the so-called Jeremiads, the political sermons, of the time. These sermons condemned the evils of New England in the second half of the seventeenth century and demanded a return to the original vision of New England's founders. Some, including Perry Miller, have argued that these sermons marked the end of the Puritan approach to America because they appear to declare that the original mission of the Puritans had failed. However, from the perspective I suggest, the Jeremiads did not mark the end of the Puritan way of thinking, but rather were consistent with the attitude that framed it. The fire-and-brimstone sermons against the then-present state of New England were simultaneously a positive claim of progress toward the millennium, an assertion that time will continue to advance to a new stage anticipated by the early church and the Old Testament.[6]

Taken together, the organizational axes in Mather's *Magnalia* illustrate an attitude which makes things and events meaningful in terms of their connections with a progressive chronology and in terms of the value of their determined place with respect to the chronology's beginning and end. Mather adds to this "logic" of history two other crucial expectations that underlie his efforts to tell the story of New England. First, he holds that humankind, though at different stages with respect to salvation, nevertheless shares a common origin and a common relationship with its creator, and second, that America's Native inhabitants will make no contribution to the progress of humankind except as obstacles or dangers that will serve as trials for the chosen people. The first expectation, the unity of humanity, is consistent with expectations associated with the chronological ordering of events and the presumed truth of the accepted accounts of creation, but it is also a crucial component of the way Mather viewed difference along the American Strand. Given an attitude of meaning characterized in part by a commitment to the unity of humanity, one will expect that differences will be epiphenomenal and, even if contingently important, cannot be essential to what people really are. Pluralism, as it is experienced, is only an appearance that obscures the more real and valuable unity below. This expected commonality is

---

6. Bercovitch makes a similar point in his book *The American Jeremiad*. He grounds his interpretation in his view that Puritan theology focused largely on the coming of the millennium. The conclusion is consistent with my proposal, but I wish to argue that the Puritan view is more generally grounded in an attitude that goes beyond particular doctrinal commitments. See Bercovitch 1978, 61.

well-illustrated in Mather's discussion of the life of the missionary John Eliot.

Eliot exemplified for Mather the ideal Christian response to the American Strand. Eliot came to New England in 1631 and shortly thereafter began to serve as a missionary to the neighboring Indian nations. Sharing Mather's view that Native people were common descendants of Adam, he also held that they "had been forlorn and wretched Heathen ever since their first herding here" by the "Divil" (Mather 1691, 74). Despite their common roots, Mather observes, their fallen state made them susceptible to special punishment. "Just before the first arrival of the English in these parts a prodigious Mortality had swept away vast numbers of the poor Indians, and those Pagans who being told by a Shipwrack'd Frenchman which dy'd in their hands, *that God would shortly extirpate them; and introduce a more civil and worthy people into their place* blasphemously reply'd *that God could not kill them;* were quickly kill'd with such a raging and wasting pestilence, as left the very earth covered with their carcasses" (Mather 1691, 74). But some survived, and Eliot, Mather concludes, "was willing to rescue as many of them as he could" (Mather 1691, 75). While others took "the Salvation of the Heathen as an article of their *Creed,*" as a matter of God's grace and not a matter of conversion, Eliot "thought men to be lost if our Gospel be hidden from them." Even as others concluded that "the *Heathen* might be saved without the knowledge of the Lord," Eliot held otherwise. "It very powerfully moved his holy Bowels, to hear the Thunderclaps of that Imprecation over the heads of our Naked Indians, . . . and thought [Eliot], *What should I do to rescue these Heathen from that all-devouring fury?*" (Mather 1691, 75). The answer, for Eliot, was to learn the local languages, translate the Bible, and establish Christian Indian communities. Behind his commitment, Mather observes, was the idea of a common humanity or rather common immortal soul that united Europeans and Americans as a single kind. The heart of the doctrine was repeated by Eliot's converts themselves as they became part of the new Christian communities by entering into a covenant which began "We are the Sons of *Adam;* we and our Forefathers have a long time been lost in our sins" (Mather 1691, 101). Such people were to be saved regardless of their own desire to be saved, and Eliot provided an aggressive example of how it could be done. At the end of his *Essay Upon the Good,* Mather returns to the theme of Native conversion when he reports on English reactions to newly formed Indian congregations. "To see such forlorn savages, and the most rueful ruins of mankind, not only *cicurated* into some civility, but also *elevated* unto so much knowledge and practice of *Christianity,* has to some appeared an amiable and admirable spectacle" (Mather 1966, 155). Mather's attitude and its element of conviction that humanity is one kind and potentially one people plays an important role in how he and his contemporaries make the American Strand meaningful.

The second expectation implicit in Mather's history is that America's Native inhabitants will make no positive contribution to the progress of the church. While the view at once seems to contradict the implication of a unified humanity, it is nevertheless important because it recasts Native peoples as part of the history of European progress and justifies leaving the voice and perspective of Native people out of the history he and his successors would write. Native people can be a part of the story only for their wars and their help when given, but these moments do not include the Native perspective on why or how these actions were taken. For example, while Europeans are viewed as exercising free will in their various roles in the progress (unless under the influence of the devil), Native people are viewed as having no such choice until they are converted. As a result, in his story of New England, Mather treats Native Americans, as well as American land and other inhabitants, as resources for the advancement of European and Christian interests. When Mather describes the help provided the new colonies by the Native people in the area and their apparent willingness to tolerate the presence of the upstart communities, Mather asks, "And who see not herein the special Providence of the God who disposeth all?" (Mather 1977, 135). In effect, the Indians did not decide to help, but rather were disposed to help by God. And what goes for Native people goes as well for American land and indigenous life. This element of Mather's attitude of meaning is important in part because it helps to explain the role of America in the *Magnalia,* but it also serves to introduce crucial elements of the dominant attitude of meaning and makes it more difficult to identify the alternative American attitude I have set out to recover. In the end, all four elements of Mather's approach, the organizational axes of chronology and value, the commitment to the unity of humankind, and the expectation that Native people could make no contribution to the story of progress, persist in framing the dominant view.

Mather's general philosophical attitude, while not the negation of the attitude of the classical pragmatists, nevertheless stands in sharp contrast to it. The disposition to understand events chronologically and hierarchically, for example, stands in tension with the principle of interaction. While the principle of interaction focuses on the context of things and events as interactions, Mather's approach focuses on the ways in which things and events are only understood from a perspective outside their context, that is, from the perspective of God's plan for the world. The epistemological commitment mirrors an ontological commit-

ment to the idea that what is understood is independent of and not affected by human understanding. Existence, like God's perspective, is
outside the particulars of human experience. Interactions may reveal
truths about the world from God's perspective, but they ground neither
the truth of knowledge nor the existence of its objects.

The same attitude that runs contrary to the principle of interaction
leads as well to a tension with pluralism. For Mather, even if there are
diverse things and people in the world, their diversity is only an appearance concealing the fundamental unity. Native people, for example, are
different from Europeans in general and the English Puritans in particular, but they are different only with respect to a single timeline of which
they are both a part. That they are different helps to confirm for Mather
that God does have a plan for the Puritan colonists and that they are
properly understood as God's chosen people. Even if the Native people
fail to recognize it, they are part of the creation of the God of the
Christians and in this sense are one with the Puritans. Their differences,
radical as they appear, are simply part of one divine plan. Mather's
chronological and hierarchical narrative sets aside both the principle of
interaction and the principle of pluralism.

Yet, even as he places differences under the aspect of Providence,
Mather does appear to assert a version of the principle of community.
Bonifacius is often cited as an example of the American commitment
to community, since it marks an explicit demand for individuals to attend to the needs of their communities. Despite appearances, however,
Mather has something unlike the pragmatic commitment to community
in mind. Mather's notion of good works in the community as presented
in *Bonifacius* is directed toward *"those Who Desire to Answer the Great End
of Life and to Do Good While They Live."* Even though Mather argues for
the necessity of good works on behalf of the community, he remains a
strict Calvinist. On this view, works, good or evil, have no bearing on
whether or not one receives God's grace and is saved. In opposition to
those like the Arminians, who argued that one's good works can aid
one's chances for salvation, Mather holds that salvation is a necessary
condition for good works. "Indeed," he says, "no *good works* can be done
by any man until he be *justified* [that is] united into the glorious Christ"
(Mather 1966, 27). When one receives the gift of grace, one accepts it
by entering the "Covenant of Grace" which is manifested in one's renewed faith. With the covenant and renewed faith, however, comes an
obligation to do good works. "A *workless faith* is a *worthless faith*," Mather
concludes (Mather 1966, 29).

The view has two important implications. First, those who have not
entered the covenant and do not share either God's grace or the atten-

dant faith are incapable of doing good. Mather is clear when he quotes Jerome, the early Christian theologian. "*Sine Christo omnis virtus est vitie*" —"Without Christ, all virtue is vice" (Mather 1966, 28, 28n). In the end, only those who have been saved by God's grace and who have the proper faith can contribute positively to a community. Second, what constitutes a "good" work is defined strictly in terms of Judeo-Christian doctrine. "The *rule*," he says, "by which we are to *glorify* God, is given us in the law of *good works,* which we *enjoy* (I will express it *so!*) in the *Ten Command-ments*" (Mather 1966, 28). Whatever a Christian might do in and for a community must itself be consistent with established doctrine and its "correct" interpretation. While neither of these conditions for good works undermines the importance of the community, they do suggest a principle of community different from the pragmatist notion. At least in part, the same bounds that frame the chronological and hierarchical nar-rative also frame Mather's understanding of human society and the role of individuals within it. In every case, the defining features are found outside the particulars of individuals, communities, and their circum-stances and histories. Mather's commitment to the unity of humankind and to the irrelevance of the Native American contribution to human development further reinforce the differences between the pragmatic principle of community and Mather's. The unity of humanity ensures that the standards that necessarily apply to Christians apply as well to all human beings regardless of their differences, historical, geographic, or morphological. The irrelevance of Native Americans reflects the impo-tence of those who fall outside the grace of the Christian God.

Mather's attitude also stands in contrast to the pragmatic principle of growth. At a minimum, the universal claims of his view and the ne-cessity of a transcendent ground for knowledge and existence under-mines the particularities implied by the notion of growth. In contrast, Mather affirms the principle of progress. Unlike growth, progress stands as a general process of development, where the process also provides a general standard against which particular events can be understood. Dif-ferences in circumstance, interest, resources, and so on amount to ele-ments that contribute to the general scheme of development. Earlier stages make their contribution, but their value is strictly a matter of their contribution to progress. At the same time, whereas growth marks an interest in increasing connections and the lateral expansion of goods, progress marks an interest in a narrowing of connections toward the determined end. Goods are shared vertically, handed from one genera-tion to the next and from lesser groups to chosen groups. In the end, progress organizes the world in an efficient assent to the establishment of God's kingdom, while growth, with considerably less efficiency, generates an increasingly complex world that alternates perpetually between risk and security.

Mather's *Magnalia* suggests another crucial theme in the discussion of the development of the indigenous philosophical attitude: the place of racial and cultural difference. Although Mather does not frame his history in terms of race, the hierarchical relations between cultural practices is a key feature of the presentation, both justifying European colonialism and undermining attempts at coexistence. The logic of the chronological and hierarchical narrative presented by Mather parallels the logic of racism as it emerges in the nineteenth century. Two important points need to be remembered. First, while the logic manifested by Mather and the logic of racism affirm relative value among "distinct" races, both are in tension with the principle of interaction because they find their meaning by reference to a fixed ideological point outside their world, and both reject the principle of pluralism. The former is easily seen when attributions of character are made according to what a Native person "really is." To be an Indian is to satisfy some standard outside the world. Mather frames the standard in terms of Providence; some race theorists frame it in terms of some necessary and sufficient condition for membership in a racial group. The latter point, the rejection of pluralism, is clear when no alternative conceptions of difference have standing within the theory. On this view, differences may be affirmed, thus fostering a kind of pluralism, but such differences are then made relative to a single view of the world and a single structure of relative value. The chronology Mather offers recognizes that the "divil's" servants in the Americas are different, but the difference for him does not admit of any other interpretation. One of the contrasts that will develop between the colonial and indigenous attitudes is that both affirm the idea of racial and cultural difference, but the colonial attitude views differences relative to a single valuational scheme. The indigenous attitude values such differences in a way that is both racialist and anti-racist. The presumption that race and racism are necessary correlates, from this perspective, is best seen as a product of a colonial attitude.

Mather's attitude of meaning, then, is a practice of ordering things and events chronologically and valuationally. The chronological ordering keys all things to a single timeline which is also a story of progress, of each event standing in relation to a necessary end. The chronological ordering implies a spatial ordering as well, so that the present relationships among things are understood in terms of the developing timeline. The progressive aspect of the timeline informs the valuational axis of meaning. Things and events are valued with respect to their relationship to chronological progress. Mather's attitude engages his experience and the experience of his community in a way that finds order and value expressed as the progress of European people through time and space toward the final fulfillment of God's purposes. The result of this attitude is that Native American people are necessarily made part of the unfolding history of Europe and that the American contribution to the history will be unimportant except as an element of what is provided, God's Providence. By organizing his history of New England the way he does, Mather illustrates one version of the colonial attitude.

CHAPTER FOUR

American Progress

WHILE MATHER'S WORK sets the stage for understanding the shape of the colonial attitude, his version of it was framed in terms of Puritan theology. A more influential version of the attitude, developed in the work of Thomas Jefferson, came to dominate American thought at the turn of the eighteenth century. Jefferson's version is particularly interesting because it is also a version of the colonial attitude that is often taken to be at the core of what is most distinctive about American thought.[1] From this perspective, some historians of philosophy trace a single intellectual tradition from the Puritans to Jefferson to the common-sense philosophers of the first half of the nineteenth century to the beginnings of pragmatism.[2] While this approach is especially helpful in tracing the ways in which European philosophical movements were influential in America, it also obscures a substantial conflict within the American philosophical tradition between the demands of the colonial attitude and the resistance of the indigenous attitude. Jefferson represents an aspect of American philosophy rightly associated with the dominant tradition from Europe and the colonial attitude as it came to be realized in America. Despite the dramatic difference between Mather's and Jefferson's views, they approach meaning in remarkably similar ways, and they

1. Even Dewey regarded Jefferson as anticipating pragmatism (Dewey 1940, 173–188). For Dewey, this anticipation is found particularly in Jefferson's experimental attitude toward democracy and his commitment to, among other things, a principle of growth. Dewey's interpretation focuses on what may better be understood as Benjamin Franklin's contribution to the thought of the revolutionary period. My discussion focuses in particular on Jefferson's liberalism that was foundational for both United States Indian policy of the nineteenth century and for the Jacksonian democracy movement and its attendant commitments to "manifest destiny." See Sheehan 1973.
2. See for example Blau 1952 and Flower and Murphey 1977.

mark the passing down from Mather to Jefferson of the colonial attitude as it was adapted to changing circumstances in North America.

Just as Mather organizes the history of New England chronologically and hierarchically, Jefferson organizes his philosophical anthropology the same way. For Jefferson, humankind must be progressively understood as moving from a "primitive" past to a "civilized" present toward an open-ended future. The value of ideas, technology, and people is determined by their place in the story of humanity's progress toward the future. Consider Jefferson's 1824 letter to William Ludlow on progress. In order to see proof of the progress of society, Jefferson recommends that "a philosophic observer commence a journey from the savages of the Rocky Mountains, eastwardly towards our sea-coast." Along the Rocky Mountains, Jefferson continues, the philosopher "would observe [people] in the earliest stage of association living under no law but that of nature, subscribing and covering themselves with the flesh and skins of wild beasts. He would next find those on our frontiers in the pastoral state, raising domestic animals to supply the defects of hunting." The land between the hunting and pastoral states marks the boundary between Native and European America. Moving east, "succeed our own semi-barbarous citizens, the pioneers of the advance of civilization, and so in his progress [the philosopher] would meet the gradual shades of improving man until he would reach [humankind's], as yet, most improved state in our seaport towns." The trip, Jefferson concludes, "is equivalent to a survey, in time, of the progress of man from the infancy of creation to the present day" (Jefferson 1984, 1496–1497). Jefferson continues the letter with a curious inversion. Having just brought his philosopher from the Rocky Mountains to the Atlantic coast, Jefferson directs Ludlow's attention back to the West in order to assert that the "shades" of humanity are ordered progressively, from west to east and past to present, and overturned, "improved," progressively from east to west and from present to future. "I have observed," he says, "this march of civilization advancing from the sea coast, passing over us like a cloud of light, increasing our knowledge and improving our condition. . . . And where this progress will stop no one can say. Barbarism has, in the meantime, been receding before the steady step of amelioration; and will in time, I trust, disappear from the earth" (Jefferson 1984, 1497). Parallel to Mather's approach, Jefferson proposes a timeline of human development that organizes the "facts" of experience and helps make them meaningful.

Jefferson and Mather also share a basic commitment to organizing things and events along a single timeline where the line is progressive and developments are cumulative. While Mather's timeline was taken to be a divine plan, Jefferson's timeline is more directly a timeline grounded in nature. Replacing Mather's doctrinal Christian center, Jefferson accepts the so-called "stage" theory of human development.[3] Implicit in the older story is the idea of progressive development of humankind to final salvation. Explicit in the stage theory is the idea that humankind progresses toward an open-ended future characterized by ever-improving civilization. Roughly, the stage theory asserts that human beings at their earliest stage are hunters and, after a time, "progress" to a pastoral stage where they maintain easy access to food by keeping domesticated animals. Still later, human beings develop agricultural skills and begin to establish a more diversified diet and the technologies necessary for growing food crops. The last stage is the development of commerce and the associated technologies of travel, communication, record-keeping, and increased production of goods. While they appear and are surpassed at different times in different places, the stages themselves are nevertheless made necessary by human nature. Just as God's plan makes human history meaningful for Mather, human nature and its stages of development makes history meaningful for Jefferson.

The new given timeline that serves to determine the time and place of each event is no longer God's directly, but is transferred into nature so that time and space become the rigid framework for determining the location and meaning of events.[4] Jefferson's reference to "the march of civilization" is a spatial and temporal development in nature according to "natural law." To explain human development is to explain things relative to the location on the new spatial and temporal grid inscribed in nature. There is still only one timeline, but it is no longer outside. The differences between Mather and Jefferson only serve to highlight the connection between their attitudes. In both cases, the chronological ordering will allow a variety of different but consistent histories, so that, after Jefferson's naturalistic turn, it is still the case that humankind shares a single point of origin, for example. The temporal and spatial origin of a thing cannot be at two different locations according to the expectations of chronological ordering. If humankind is one kind, as Jefferson held it to be, then it cannot originate in two places or at two times. To say otherwise would be to propose more than one independent

---

3. See Meek 1976 for a detailed discussion of the development of such theories.

4. Jefferson's transfer of the frame of meaning into nature is comparable to the general reconstruction afforded by Enlightenment science. Just as Newton established a fixed space/time continuum for physics, biologists worked to establish detailed climatographic contexts for species and species differences. Political theorists such as Montesquieu combined these natural frames in an attempt to establish a natural science of politics.

chronology that would fall outside the logic of the established attitude. Jefferson, like Mather before him, accepted the idea that indigenous American people originated in the Middle East. In this case, he followed the methodology of James Adair's elaborate argument that Native Americans were a lost tribe of Israel and focused on the possibility of early migrations to America and on linguistic evidence of American descent from European and Asian peoples.[5] Despite their radical differences in belief, Mather and Jefferson shared a common approach to chronologically ordering things and events.

That Jefferson adopted a valuational organization parallel to Mather's is clear from his treatment of the past and of the truth. Things in the past are at best candidates for continued value, not givens. Beliefs established in the past are to be presumed, but only in conjunction with recognition of human fallibility. The passage of time, in a sense, is a sign of increasing value; newfound truths overcome past beliefs and those truths that continue to endure are more likely "real" truths. Native people in this model, since they are marked by their ways of living as earlier along the timeline of human progress, and since their ways are in evident decline, are necessarily of less value than the ascendant ways of the life of the immigrant Europeans. In his second inaugural address, Jefferson puts it this way: "The aboriginal inhabitants of these countries I have regarded with the commiseration their history inspires. . . . But the endeavors to enlighten them on the fate which awaits their present course of life, to induce them to exercise their reason, follow its dictates, and change their pursuits with the change of circumstances, have powerful obstacles to encounter" (Jefferson 1984, 520). In effect, Native ways of life have been "overwhelmed by the current [of European progress], or driven before it" and their only remaining option is to take up the new ways of "agriculture and the domestic arts," that is, European ways of life. As in Mather's approach, salvation for surviving Native people requires the acceptance of the ways established in the story of European development; in Mather's case, this was acceptance of the gospel of Christianity, in Jefferson's the gospel of civilization.[6] Jefferson concludes

5. See Jefferson 1984, 226–227. Also see Adair 1775.
6. Jefferson's vision of civilization was of an agricultural society enhanced by science and technology. See St. John de Crèvecoeur 1981 for a classic description of the Jeffersonian ideal. Ironically, Native people had long been an agricultural people who used experimental farming methods to improve crops and yield. See Weatherford 1988. The difference between Jefferson's vision and the Native reality was in the different conceptions of land "ownership," the gendered character of the process, and the envisioned purpose of agriculture. Native people held land communally while Jefferson favored private ownership. Women were usually responsible for decision-making and much of the agricul-

in his 1805 inaugural address, "We have therefore liberally furnished them [Native people] with the implements of husbandry and household use; we have placed among them instructors in the arts of first necessity" (Jefferson 1984, 520).

Jefferson's version of the colonial attitude shares Mather's commitment to the unity of humankind and to the unimportance of Native Americans in human development. In the same inaugural address that condemned Native ways of life, for example, Jefferson also asserted the lack of essential differences between Europeans and Native Americans. He declares that Native people are "endowed with the faculties and the rights of men, breathing an ardent love of liberty and independence" (Jefferson 1984, 520). On Jefferson's view, the differences between Native people and the European immigrants was largely one of circumstance and learning, and such differences did not affect one's basic "human nature." In his *Notes on the State of Virginia,* Jefferson concludes that once the particular "circumstances of their situation" are taken into account, "we shall probably find that they are formed in mind as well as in body, on the same module with the 'Homo sapiens Europæus'" (Jefferson 1984, 187). He puts the same point another way in an address to the Choctaw nation in 1803. "Born in the same land, we ought to live as brothers, doing each other all the good we can, and not listening to wicked men who may endeavor to make us enemies" (Jefferson 1984, 558). Earlier that year, Jefferson described his "personal dispositions and opinions" regarding Native Americans:

> In truth, the ultimate point of rest & happiness for [Native Americans] is to let our settlements and theirs meet and blend together, to intermix, and become one people. Incorporating themselves with us as citizens of the U.S., this is what the natural progress of things will of course bring on, and it will be better to promote than to retard it. (Jefferson 1984, 1115)

Like Mather, Jefferson found differences of less importance than similarities, and, as a result, the best way to understand Native people was as part of the ongoing story of human development whose high point and present point was found in the flourishing European American republic between the Appalachians and the Atlantic.

Despite Jefferson's image as an advocate for American exceptional-

---

tural labor in Native communities along the east coast. See Jensen 1990. Jefferson believed that men ought to be responsible and women excluded. Finally, the purpose of agriculture in Native communities was to promote the well-being of the community, while Jefferson viewed the purpose as a matter of promoting the well-being of the individual farmer and his immediate family.

ism, however, his attitude of meaning in fact works against recognizing indigenous Americans as anything but unimportant contributors to human progress. Just as Mather held that America was to be valued as a place that could serve as a home for the further development of the Reformed church, Jefferson argued that America was a place for the next stage of development for European peoples, particularly the English. In his "Summary View of the Rights of British America," he gives a brief account of the origins of New England and argues that its founding was a natural step in the progress of Europe. "Before their emigration to America," Jefferson observes, "[New England's ancestors] possessed a right which nature has given to all men, of departing from the country in which chance, not choice, has placed them, of going in quest of new habitations, and of there establishing new societies under such laws and regulations as to them shall seem most likely to promote public happiness." In a way which recalls Mather's flight to the "American Strand," Jefferson points out that New England's "Saxon ancestors had, under this universal law, in like manner left their native wilds, and woods in the north of Europe, [and] had possessed themselves of the island of Britain." Jefferson holds that "no circumstance has occurred to distinguish materially the British from the Saxon emigration. America was conquered, her settlements made, and firmly established" (Jefferson 1984, 105–106). Although the focus of Jefferson's argument is to undermine the idea that Britain retained any claim on the American colonies, the argument also makes it clear that America, as "conquered," becomes a place for the development of European descendants. While setting aside Mather's explanation of America in terms of church history, Jefferson maintains the same framework and explains it now in terms of natural law and European development.

Further, as Mather identifies the European-descended Christian framework as the ground for his approach to meaning, Jefferson identifies European Enlightenment thought as the ground for his. His works reference John Locke, Jonathan Swift, Count de Buffon, Marquis de Condorcet, Jean-Jacques Rousseau, Baron de Montesquieu, and so on. More importantly, however, it appears that the European descent is expected to take precedence over American influence in each of the elements of the attitude Mather and Jefferson display. In chronology, the organizing timeline originates in a European framework, that of Christianity or of Enlightenment science. In valuation, value is assigned in such a way that European people, cultural forms, and ends have higher value than indigenous American people, culture, or ends. The unity of humankind serves to affiliate all people, regardless of their own ideas of origin and difference, to the expected chronological and valuational

framework of European descent. Finally, the association of America with
"earlier" points in the chronological ordering, that is, the association of
America and primitivism, the devaluation of indigenous America, and
its necessary assimilation into the single humankind, combine to support
an expectation that Native Americans will make no important contribution to the progress of humanity. Despite the dramatic differences in the
content of their views, the Puritan Mather and the naturalist Jefferson
manifest a common attitude.

As Jefferson's philosophical anthropology began to frame the policies of the new United States, a second generation of thinkers began to
reconstruct the colonial attitude into the framework for what would become American liberal democracy. The new version replaced Jefferson's
intellectual elitism and Enlightenment science with a populism that affirmed the necessity of progress through a process that aimed at the
virtual elimination of cultural and racial difference. This view is well-
represented by George Bancroft. Once a student of Hegel, Bancroft introduces his history of the United States in a way that recalls both the
attitude of Cotton Mather and Hegel's story of human development.
Writing about America before permanent settlement by Europeans, Bancroft summarizes:

> Before that time the whole territory was an unproductive waste. Through-
> out its wide extent the arts had not erected a monument. Its only inhabi-
> tants were a few scattered tribes of feeble barbarians, destitute of com-
> merce and of political connection. The axe and the ploughshare were
> unknown. The soil, which had been gathering fertility from the repose of
> centuries, was lavishing its strength in magnificent but useless vegetation.
> In the view of civilization the immense domain was solitude. (Bancroft
> 1878, 1: 3)

The story of America, for Bancroft, will be the story of how humankind,
in the form of European immigrants, transformed a wasteland into "its
present happiness and glory." If Hegel brings developing human spirit
within sight of the American Strand, Bancroft carries the story forward
toward its fulfillment on the American continent. "Our land," he says in
an 1854 address, "extends far into the wilderness, and beyond the wilderness; and while on this side [of] the great mountains it gives the
Western nations of Europe a theatre for the renewal of their youth, on
the transmontane side, the hoary civilization of the farthest antiquity
leans forward from Asia to receive the glad tidings of the messenger of
freedom" (Bancroft 1854, 508). In short, America provides a venue for

the completion of human history and the human spirit, linking humanity's past with its promise in the renewal of European civilization.

At the same time, Bancroft draws together figures from both Mather's Puritan story of American history and Jefferson's naturalist story. As Mather describes it, America is found a wasteland, the domain of Satan, which will be transformed by the work of Reformed religion into a New Jerusalem. Its people are weak and scattered and, as Mather remarked in his story of John Eliot, a "more civil and worthy people" will replace the original inhabitants. The place of America in Bancroft's story is little different. While Satan is the mechanism devaluing America in Mather's account, Bancroft, like Jefferson, connects the failure of Native people and the success of Europeans to a geographic story. Bancroft vividly draws together the geographic account of Jefferson and the transcendent story of progress in Hegel's work when he uses the figure of the Rocky Mountains to mark the boundary of development and a goal for improvement. Bancroft's innovation in the effort to make the recent American past meaningful is to restore a transcendent timeline to the environmental account of Jefferson without significantly altering the operative attitude. As in the cases of Mather and Jefferson, Bancroft continues to order his account chronologically and hierarchically, expecting both the unity of humankind and the impotence of indigenous America. Although the meaning of America is presented in different terms, he displays the same patterns of order.

Bancroft, born in 1800 in Massachusetts, entered Harvard at thirteen, and at eighteen joined the first wave of young American scholars studying in Germany.[7] From 1818 until 1820, Bancroft studied at the University of Göttingen where he received his doctoral degree in 1820. He spent the next two years studying at the University of Berlin where he heard Frederich Schleiermacher and Johann Gottfried Eichhorn lecture on religion and, in 1820 and 1821, where he heard Hegel lecture on the philosophy of history. In a letter to a friend written in 1820, Bancroft commented on his study with Hegel, "I took a philosophical course with Hegel. But I thought it lost time to listen to his display of unintelligible words" (Howe 1908, vol. I, 92n1). Despite his lack of enthusiasm for Hegel at the time, his later views closely parallel Hegel's later philosophy of history. After an unsuccessful lectureship at Harvard, Bancroft and his colleague Joseph Green Cogswell, also a Harvard alumnus recently returned from Germany, co-founded the Round Hill School, a college preparatory school combining the approach of New England acade-

7. See Handlin 1984 and Nye 1964.

mies and the expectations of a German university education. When he left Round Hill in 1830, he began work on a history of the United States[8] and became an activist in the Jacksonian Democratic movement. In 1845, he was appointed Secretary of the Navy under President James Polk and served briefly as the Acting Secretary of War at the beginning of the Mexican–American War in 1845. He resigned his post in 1846 to become the United States minister to England (until 1849). In 1865, he authored President Andrew Johnson's first message to Congress after Lincoln's assassination and, from 1867 until 1874, he served as the minister to Prussia and then to the German Empire. Even as he became active in politics, Bancroft remained a historian and a philosopher. His political activism depended upon a well-developed conception of the meaning of America and its history, grounded in a conception of human unity that could support both United States expansionist policies and the idea of a populist democracy.

Even as he lost interest in Round Hill, Bancroft became increasingly interested in the political movement begun by Andrew Jackson, who was elected president of the United States in 1828. Although conservative Democrats of Massachusetts avoided directly endorsing Jackson's popular movement, Bancroft found in it a concrete expression of his conception of human nature. Bancroft summarized this conception as the ground for a philosophy of history and a philosophy of politics in an address to Williamstown College in 1835. For Bancroft, the general project of Jacksonian democracy was to overturn the power of privilege and wealth represented by the long political and economic domination of the English colonies in America by wealthy families whose politics after the Revolution favored a strong central government. Jackson's movement represented an attack on privilege and the promise of broad popular government and economic opportunity, particularly for all Anglo-Saxon men. Jackson shared Jefferson's anti-Federalism and his vision of an agrarian republic, but he also advocated wider democratic involvement of the new rising class of farmers, merchants, and land speculators. For Bancroft, as for Jefferson, the key to the movement was the fundamental unity of humankind. Despite the differences among people that emerged through the interaction of mind and body in the balance of temperaments, human beings nevertheless share common intellectual functions. "The intellectual functions, by which relations are perceived, are the common endowments of the race. The differences are apparent,

---

8. The first volume of his history was published in 1834 and the tenth volume in 1874. In 1876, he published a heavily revised "Centenary Edition" of the *History* in six volumes.

not real" (Bancroft 1854, 410). The intellectual functions include both the process of knowing and the processes of judging.

As a result of the fundamental similarity among the minds of all human beings, truths, moral, scientific, aesthetic, and religious, are all in principle accessible to everyone. When the faculties of knowing and judging are interfered with by bias, perhaps generated by a love of wealth or power, the truth may be obscured in the same way that vision can be obscured by obstacles or myopia. "[Yet] the relations of the eye to light is in all men the same," Bancroft concludes, "just so judgment may be liable in individual minds to the bias of passion, and yet its relation to truth is immutable, and is universal." The reliable relationship of human minds to truth suggests that truth will best be found in a context where individual bias will be most suppressed, that is, in contexts where groups and not individuals make judgments. From this perspective, group viewpoints are always better for finding the truth than individual viewpoints and so

> there never was a school of philosophy, nor a clan in the realm of opinion, but carried along with it some important truth. And therefore every sect that has ever flourished has benefited Humanity; for the errors of a sect pass away and are forgotten; its truths are received into the common inheritance. To know the seminal thought of every prophet and leader of a sect, is to gather all the wisdom of mankind. (Bancroft 1854, 416)

In short, intersubjectivity is by degrees the most reliable means of gaining access to truth and thus serves as the ultimate justification for democracy. "If it be true," Bancroft concludes, "that the gifts of mind and heart are universally diffused, if the sentiment of truth, justice, love, and beauty exists in every one, then it follows, as a necessary consequence, that the common judgment in taste, politics, and religion, is the highest authority on earth, and the nearest possible approach to an infallible decision" (Bancroft 1854, 415). This is not to conclude that the judgment of the masses "makes" something true, but rather, the combined viewpoints of the widest possible range of people will provide judgments nearest the truth. "[T]he people can DISCERN right. Individuals are but shadows, too often engrossed by the pursuit of shadows; the race is immortal: individuals are of limited sagacity; the common mind is infinite in its experience: individuals are languid and blind; the many are ever wakeful: individuals are corrupt" (Bancroft 1854, 424–425).

Progress, from Bancroft's perspective, is no longer the progress of the Reformed church toward salvation as it was with Mather nor the vague improvements of technology and knowledge as it was with Jefferson. Progress is now the achievement of the perfection of the common mind. "The exact measure of progress of civilization is the degree in which the intelligence of the common mind has prevailed over wealth and brute force; in other words, the measure of the progress of civilization is the progress of the people" (Bancroft 1854, 427). Since human beings gathered into groups have no choice but to become aware of "new truths," "the irresistible tendency of the human race is . . . to advancement. . . . The movement of the species is upward, irresistibly upward" (Bancroft 1854, 434). In an address to the New York Historical Society in 1854, Bancroft restates his position from the earlier paper, but here explains the necessity of progress as following "from the fact that the great Author of all life has left truth in its immutability to be observed, and has endowed man with the power of observation and generalization" (Bancroft 1854, 488). The commonality of truth and the commonality of reason, Bancroft argues, not only make progress necessary but also determine the shape of progress. In the end, "All is nevertheless one whole; individuals, families, peoples, the race, march in accord with the Divine will" (Bancroft 1854, 491). Bancroft argues that the United States in particular has a special place with respect to the common mind and its progress. In light of its commitment to freedom and the expression of ideas in a democratic context, the people of the United States come nearest to the collective voice of humanity. In America, he says, "we have made Humanity our lawgiver and our oracle" (Bancroft 1854, 423). The people of the United States are to be understood as the leading edge of human progress.

Bancroft's general position helps to illustrate the colonial attitude that frames his history of the United States. While his story is radically different from Mather's, his approach is closely parallel. Like Mather, events are ordered along a single timeline. The result in Bancroft's work is a broad synthesizing narrative that draws together a vast assortment of historical sources, all re-presented as consistent elements of the same story. As in the case of both Mather and Jefferson, the story being told is a story of progress from a relatively disharmonious and impotent past to a harmonious and powerful end. The chronological axis of meaning anticipates the valuational. Again, what is past is less valuable than what is in the present or the future. Here again, the past is not without value, since the present state of humanity depends upon the past as a foundation or source, but the past has value only as something passed, not something sought except as it might contribute to attaining the future ideal. Both axes presume that humankind is one kind, unified in reason and history, but divided by differences in value. At the same time, both axes presume, for reasons inherent in the timeline, that America and its indigenous life can make no contribution to the great story of progress.

The tension between the last two presumptions that appear to be at work in the colonial attitude is apparent in the debates about U.S. Indian policy under Jackson. While the commitments of Jacksonian democracy, at least as presented by Bancroft, appear to affirm the equal value of all human beings, the practical policy of removing Native people from their traditional homelands appears to deny it. Bancroft himself is close to an explicit statement of this issue in the discussion of Native Americans in his *History of the United States*. Affirming his general position, he claims that "there is not a quality belonging to the white man, which did not also belong to the American savage. . . . The unity of the human race is established by the exact correspondence between their respective powers; the Indian has not one more, has not one less, than the white man; the map of the faculties is for both identical" (Bancroft 1878, 2: 449). Despite this fundamental equality, however, "when, from the general characteristics of humanity, we come to the comparison of powers, the existence of degrees immediately appears" (Bancroft 1878, 2: 448). The problem, according to Bancroft, is that Native people are fundamentally inflexible and unwilling to change their ways. This "determinateness," Bancroft concludes, is physiological as well as cultural and intellectual. "[An Indian] has little flexibility of features or transparency of skin; and therefore, if he depicts his passions, it is by strong contortions, or the kindling of the eye, that seems ready to burst from its socket. With rare exceptions, he cannot blush" (Bancroft 1878, 2: 449). Despite the apparent role of climate and geography in producing cultural difference, Native people, according to Bancroft, have an inflexibility of organization, that is, of physiology, that "will not even yield to climate" (Bancroft 1878, 2: 450). At the same time, the physiology "is not so absolute as to forbid hope." Color differs among tribes, he observes, "and some have been found of so fair a complexion that the blood could be seen as it mantled to the cheek" (Bancroft 1878, 2: 451). What applies to the body applies to the mind and culture as well in that "improvement . . . has pervaded every clan in North America [so that the] Indian of to-day excels his ancestors in skill, in power over nature, and in knowledge."

There is no paradox for Bancroft in claiming both fundamental sameness and intractable difference between those of European and Native American descent. His discussion of the origins of indigenous Americans helps to settle the question. Like Mather and Jefferson, Bancroft remains circumspect about which account of the origin of Native Americans to accept. Surveying the then-dominant theories, he rejects each as inadequately supported. At the same time, it is also the case, he argues, that the morphological features of Native Americans seem continuous with the morphological features of Asian peoples. The result is that there are no sharp differences either between Asians and Americans

or between different American nations. In light of the evident continuity, despite the obscurity of origins and the apparently unchangeable
physiological stubbornness, it is still clear, from Bancroft's perspective,
that "the indigenous population of America offers no new obstacle to
faith in the unity of the human race" (Bancroft 1878, 2: 461). At the
same time, American people remain problematically different from
every other people. "[A]lone of mankind," he says, "the American nations universally were ignorant of the pastoral state; that they neither
kept sheep nor kine; that they knew not the use of milk of animals for
food; that they had neither wax nor oil; that they made no iron,—it
becomes nearly certain that the imperfect civilization of America is its
own" (Bancroft 1878, 2: 458).[9] In short, Native American culture is
primitive in terms of the broader story of human development and as
such can only be seen as a remnant, part of humanity confined to a time
long passed. While European civilization advanced through the four
stages of progress, indigenous Americans became bogged down in the
first and so were living fossils of a lost European prehistory.

The apparent inconsistency of Bancroft's view of Native American
peoples can be lessened if it is supposed that Bancroft operates with an
attitude like that of Mather and Jefferson. There is no conflict between
a commitment to human equality and the inequality of Native Americans, because meaning must be understood in time as well as space. In
the context of the story of human progress, all human beings are part
of the same story, carrying the same possibilities and bearing the same
defects. When the story is considered in detail, however, it becomes clear
that different points along the timeline are of different value. Despite its
existence in the same place as European civilization, Native culture is
really located earlier in the timeline than every other surviving people.
As members of the same humanity, Native people might be brought
along with everyone else; as a people out of time, however, it is more
likely that they will vanish.

Some might argue that the view offered by Bancroft is best understood as motivated by the other apparent project of the Jacksonian period: westward expansion and its economic implications. While it is
surely true that Jackson's Indian policies directly and indirectly supported by Bancroft provided justification for European Americans to remove Native people from east of the Mississippi and to achieve extraordinary wealth in the long run, I suggest that accumulation of wealth is

9. Bancroft's reference is to the stage theory of human development. By denying "knowledge of the pastoral state," he is claiming that Native people are physiologically and culturally "stuck" in the second stage of development.

not the entire or even the best explanation for the removal. In his 1828 essay, "The Removal of the Indian," Jackson's Secretary of War, Lewis Cass, is straightforward:

> A barbarous people, depending for subsistence upon the scanty and precarious supplies furnished by the chase, cannot live in contact with a civilized community. . . . That the aboriginal population should decrease [as civilized communities increase] can excite no surprise. From an early period, their rapid declension and ultimate extinction were foreseen and lamented, and various plans for their preservation and improvement were projected and pursued. (Cass 1828, 64, 67)

The meaning of Native people for Cass is as much a product of an established attitude as it is of any overt interest in power, money, or land. That power, money, and land would be a product of Indian removal was clear to Cass, but it was expected at least in part because Cass ordered his understanding of Native people in such a way that they necessarily would be displaced in favor of the westward advance of European American society, regardless of efforts to halt the advance. Even before the particulars of economic advantage are clear, Cass has already accepted the idea that Native culture is doomed.

Cass and Bancroft, like Jackson, begin with an attitude that obscures and undermines the paradox of affirming human equality and accepting the genocide of indigenous Americans. In a crucial way, there is no contradiction in the meaning of the events. The attitude with which they interact with the world expects an order that is verified in events and dictates further action. The Indian Removal Act was passed in 1830 and enforced over the next decade. During the process of relocation, tens of thousands were killed by neglect, disease, and war. To a large number of European Americans, the removal and the violent exploitation and death that accompanied it were tragic but necessary. The end of indigenous culture and the burgeoning of North American wealth were not to be stopped, in part because of the benefits they brought (land and wealth) and in part because they were expected, that is, because people were disposed to interacting with each other and the world in a way that made genocide and European expansion inevitable. Cass put it simply in his appeal to the educated classes for their support of the Removal Act:

> It would be miserable affectation to regret the progress of civilization and improvement, the triumph of industry and art, by which these regions have been reclaimed, and over which freedom, religion, and science are extending their sway. But we may indulge the wish, that these blessings had been attained at a smaller sacrifice; that the aboriginal population had accom-

modated themselves to the inevitable change of their condition, produced
by the access and progress of the new race of men before whom the hunter
and his game were destined to disappear. But such a wish is vain. (Cass
1828, 64)

For Cass there was no other way to see America's past and present except
as a progressive development of human nature. European civilization
follows Native American culture as day follows night.

Cass's conclusion makes the operative attitude concrete: progress is
inevitable and it comes at the cost of Native American people and culture. While it is possible to understand the Removal Act in other terms,
the crucial disposition shared by Cass, Bancroft, and the others helped
to frame the meaning of European contact with Native Americans and
Native resistance to European ways of life. Native susceptibility to disease, Native structures of government, agriculture, and religion, and Native resistance to European ways of life all were taken to mean that Native life was an obsolete stage of humanity. From this point of view, to
be a human being meant having the potential to be "civilized," to recognize the advantages of "industry and art," while to be a Native American meant only extinction, figuratively in the sense of giving up Native
ways of life or, if this proved impossible, literal death. The Removal Act
itself was a clever economic strategy devised by land speculators to generate wealth, and at the same time it was a clever political strategy by the
Democratic leadership to satisfy the increasing demand for land by the
growing European American middle class. But these accounts cannot
be divorced from the disposition that made many European Americans
ready to accept the Act and its consequences. Wealthy landowners in
Virginia had a near monopoly on land that also would have met the
needs of the middle class, but if the Removal Act had specified the removal of these wealthy farmers from their land, it is doubtful that it
would have been so quickly approved. In fact, it is difficult to imagine
that such a policy would ever have been suggested, even though it would
have provided land to address the concerns of Jacksonian Democrats.
Why it was not considered can be explained as the effect of the framing
of attitudes that make alternatives plain and provide the grounds for
arguments in favor of one alternative over another. In this case, the
dominant disposition of those in power was one that viewed westward
expansion and not redistribution of already acquired lands as a necessary
part of human nature. Further, the wealthy landowners actually represented part of the ideal that made the western expansion meaningful in
the first place. Native people were not only obstacles to the acquisition
of necessary lands, but their way of life, especially its communal and

non-acquisitive structure, were incompatible with the ideal. Few suggested the overthrow of the Virginia planters and the redistribution of their land because that was not consistent with the established philosophical framework. Put another way, Virginia landowners and the expanding European American middle class meant progress along the timeline of human development. They were "advanced" and "civilized" and "valued." Native Americans meant a failure to progress, a "primitive" stage, and a way of life less valuable than that of the European immigrants. These meanings were not, as part of an attitude of meaning, reflective categories based on some objective assessment, but rather were based on the ways of thinking and dispositions of a wide range of European Americans. These attitudes were grounded in long-established patterns of thought and action that emerged in the experience of American life and became the starting points for examination of the issues. Attitudes, in this sense, make the reality. Europeans are "advanced" because they are expected to be advanced, and Native people are "primitive" because they are expected to be primitive.

One might object to the idea that, taken as a general claim about what things mean, it should follow that the sun rises each day because it is expected to. There is a sense in which this conclusion does follow. On the view suggested here, the sun indeed rises because it is expected to, since the thing that happens is just an unqualified happening until it fits into some framework which will give it meaning. The sun rises because it is expected to, though it may also be right to say that it does not rise, but rather that the Earth revolves. The difference between an event taken as the sun rising and as the earth revolving is the expectation that frames the event and gives it its meaning. At the same time, it does not follow that *not* expecting the sun to rise can cause it not to rise. Expectations are, in this sense, interactions in experience, not impositions on experience. While dramatically different actions may follow from differing expectations (rising suns versus revolving earths, for example), it does not follow that every expectation will be satisfied in experience. Expectations frame experience in important ways, but they do not exhaust it. The discussion of attitudes becomes important in that it helps to identify the ways in which experience is framed, what alternatives are viable, and what alternatives are excluded. To say that the sun rises because it is expected to is an explanation that will not go far to explain celestial phenomena. At the same time, the recognition of the role of attitudes does make it possible to consider the difficulties and opportunities that emerge in the context of divergent approaches to talking about things like sunrises and human nature. In short, to talk about attitudes provides a starting place for talking about the sorts of issues that emerge along the borders between radically different ways of interacting with the world.

The conception of attitude I use develops two ideas proposed by John Dewey within the classical pragmatist tradition and are consistent with the principle of interaction. First, Dewey argued that there are two sorts of meaning: immanent and referential.[10] Immanent meaning is found "in" experience. When something is experienced as a tree or a person, for example, the meaning of the experience, that is, its being of a tree or a person, is often had directly without reflection. We often think that such meanings are "really" independent of the experience, that is, they are an experience of what a thing "really" is. From the perspective proposed by Dewey, however, such "reality" is simply to assign to the world something that may also be understood as the product of an interaction. Once one is accustomed to trees and people, such immanent meanings become the stuff of our lives, the environment in which we live, and the frame of our thinking. As they are part of human reality, immanent meanings leave open the possibility of alternative meanings, even as they also serve as a starting point for new experience.

Referential meaning, on the other hand, is a product of reflection. Where one is unsure about what a thing is, that is, when an experience is characterized by doubt or confusion and not an experience of something which already has a settled meaning, one inquires and, if the inquiry is successful, the experience gains new meaning. The two ideas of meaning are related in the sense that immanent meanings generally begin as referential meanings, that is, as the product of attempts to make the world meaningful. Once meanings are established through inquiry and integrated into behavior, physical conditions, institutions, and so on, new referential meanings become immanent. In some cases, experiences are characterized primarily by confusion and seem to require that meanings be created anew. Other times, meanings become refined or transformed; trees become oaks and elms, people become friends and enemies. In each case, an established framework of meaning structures a mediating process of meaning-production which responds to particular experiences and leaves new resources for making future experience meaningful. Once immanent meanings become established, they persist, structure the process of experience, direct action and reaction, until they become inadequate to new situations. When this happens, experiences again become confused and uncertain, and reflection intervenes to establish new meaning.

10. See Pratt 1997.

These notions of meaning connect with Dewey's conception of habit. Habits are dispositions to act in particular ways. They serve as the reliable background that frames ordinary experience and are called on when new meanings need to be generated. Habits amount to characteristic or usual ways of living and acting and as such are to be understood as interactions between those agents and the world or between organisms and environment. In this sense, habits cannot be understood only in terms of physiological processes, since they are interactions. But they also cannot be reduced to behavior alone, since overt action also has deep roots in the organism. Examples of habits range from the expected "bad habits" of smoking and pencil tapping, to "thought-saving" habits of dressing in a certain order or taking a particular route to school. But habits can also be dispositions to act in particular ways when teaching or talking, in particular ways of reacting to the unexpected, when solving math problems, or when setting up a laboratory experiment. In this sense, habits are simply a readiness to act and interact in the world as circumstances develop and change. If, as I suggested a moment ago, meaning establishes a framework for action, then in an important way, habits as established ways of acting might also be seen as the interactive dimension of immanent meanings. As a result, my habits of responding to oaks or friends are in a crucial sense what oaks and friends mean. "Immanent meanings" provide a way to talk about "what" things and events "are," and habits are the concrete expressions of what being a particular thing amounts to.

At the same time, since habits are ways of acting, they also become part of the way individuals are experienced by others, and so the habits of a person taken together may be taken as the character of the person, the expression of who that person is. They are what make us distinct from one another and form the background according to which we respond to each other. In effect, habits display the meanings we find in the world as action, and, in so responding to the world, are a way to make ourselves meaningful as well. When characteristic ways of acting, including the processes of meaning-making, are shared by a group of individuals, then these common habits can be taken as a way to understand the character of the group. Attitudes, in the sense I am using the term, are complex arrangements of habits that at once mark the character of individuals and their connections with others who share similar complex ways of acting in the world. Habits of respect, subservience, authority, parenting, teaching, and so on all mark complex ways of engaging each other and the world. Just as habits are a way to talk about the character of individuals, attitudes are a way of talking about the character of groups. In this way, as habits provide the material with which to talk about individual selves, attitudes provide a way to talk about the "self" of a community or culture or tradition.

It is often thought that commonalities within a community are to be found in shared ideas, beliefs to which all will assent, or at least in a common language, that is, a common set of linguistic signs and structures. However, attitudes of meaning, as they mark an intersection between immanent meanings and habits, are not only beliefs or linguistic signs, but rather they are ways of producing and responding to beliefs and signs as well as ways of responding to ambiguities, confusion, doubt, and disaster. Mather, Jefferson, and Bancroft can be seen as part of the same culture or tradition in that they share an approach to making experience meaningful even as they diverge in the claims they accept as true. Just as Mather would reject Jefferson's claim that Native Americans are a natural stage of human development, Jefferson would reject Mather's conclusion that Native Americans are servants of Satan. Setting aside the content, however, they nevertheless share a common attitude of meaning that "finds" a kind of order in experience that leads to a common approach to the meaning of America.

When Cass experiences Native people, the experience already includes the immanent meanings of primitive and undesirable and the responses that such meanings call for. His attempts to explain Native life begins with these immanent meanings and is structured by the play of a range of habits which frame his experience and the experience of others along the chronological and valuational axes of his attitude of meaning. In the end, even as he wishes to end the slaughter, Cass is unable to do anything but express regret; in part because the framing attitude obscures or eliminates access to alternative attitudes that may provide a different approach. The constraints of his own attitude are ironically recalled in his observation that Native Americans are unable to see the benefits of civilization. "They are contented," he says, "not contented merely, but clinging with a death-grasp to their own institutions" (Cass 1828, 75). As though describing his own attitude, he continues, "this feeling, inculcated in youth, strengthened in manhood, and nourished in age, renders them inaccessible to argument or remonstrance." The focus on attitudes helps to make accessible the points of contact among different ways of thinking and the ways in which understanding is fostered or blocked. In the end, the attitude illustrated by Cass suggests both the need for and possibility of an alternative attitude that might approach the experience of the American border in another way.

The discussion of the attitude illustrated by Mather, Jefferson, and Bancroft leads to two general points. First, the focus on attitudes widens the possibilities for understanding meaning. While philosophical studies of meaning tend to focus on the meaning of language or of other particular objects, the illustrations here shift the focus to patterns or ways of interacting, encompassing ideas of propositional meaning but going further to look at the implications of belief for action and the implications of action for belief. As a result, actions become indicators of belief beyond what is said, and what is said is taken to suggest what is expected or what is believed about action. From this perspective, belief and action are drawn closely together to become a complex source of insight and a resource for critique and change.

Second, this discussion of attitudes provides an approach for thinking about intellectual influence and inheritance. Typical intellectual histories focus on identifying chains of explicit beliefs. Influence, in this case, is sought in documented moments of formal learning or reading of texts. Inheritance is taken to be the recurrence of terms and "ideas" over time and among people who are also properly related by the processes of influence. Attention to attitudes undermines both aspects of this sort of approach to intellectual history. Influences on attitudes are not to be found strictly in moments of formal study. If attitudes are ways of making things meaningful, or patterns of interaction, then influence on the development of attitudes can come from a vast variety of sources: friends and family, reading, conversation, and any other experience which leads to learning particular ways of making things meaningful and interacting with the world. Charting influence becomes a matter of seeking commonality and divergence in patterns of interaction among people and texts. Inheritance is not only verified through the presence of like terms but extends as well to similar approaches to making things meaningful. As suggested in the examination of Mather, Jefferson, and Bancroft, despite a great divergence of terms and accepted beliefs, their approaches to making American experience meaningful are remarkably similar.

This is not, of course, to make a grand claim. Most intellectual and philosophical histories already adopt a view much like the one I propose. Rather than making explicit their interest in attitudes, however, they tend to focus on what they take to be a common idea that is variously considered by a succession of philosophers. Strictly speaking, however, what philosophers in ancient Greece and philosophers in seventeenth-century England mean by truth or God is not related by a clearly identifiable reference to some fixed idea, but rather is related as a term used in certain contexts to make experience meaningful. That is, the terms and their use illustrate ways of engaging the world and making it meaningful. Claims to the direct relationship between earlier and later philosophers in histories of this sort are not well-supported, since there is often little certain evidence that the sources of the ideas of one period are the ideas of another. Even if there is documentation that Descartes, for example, read Plato, there is no more certainty that Descartes's ideas are a result of that reading than there is that they are a result of a long night of drinking and arguing in Germany during his youthful travels. This is not to say that other forms of intellectual history are mistaken, but rather to suggest that there are other ways of proceeding which have other advantages and disadvantages.

Even as attention to attitudes can reshape what counts as a process of influence and what counts as an inheritance, it also expands what might count as sources. The approach which focuses on common terms or ideas alone carries with it the implicit requirement that the relevant influences will necessarily already share a language, education, class, gender, and race. Those who encounter the world differently, who fail to have opportunities to participate in the requisite discourse, who may find that such discourse is inadequate to their experience, are not included in histories of thought or are included only when they properly enter the debate. Despite, for example, the dramatic influence one's friends might have on how one looks at the world, if those friends are not properly certified intellectuals, their influence might be ignored in the context of a history of ideas. An approach which draws attention to distinctive attitudes makes it possible to look for influence outside the narrow range of professional philosophers and self-identified intellectuals within the European tradition and to look to a wide range of people whose ways of making things meaningful displayed in other ways can also count as sources for intellectual development.

What I have called the colonial attitude illustrated by Mather, Jefferson, and Bancroft is one that organizes things and events chronologically and progressively, accepts the unity of humankind, and affirms the unimportance of indigenous Americans. At the same time, there is another attitude that persists as an undercurrent in American thought that appears to have influenced some in the recognized American philosophical tradition and may have served as a starting point for classical pragmatism. This attitude, I will argue, emerges for European Americans in their interactions with Native people as they struggled to find ways to coexist. The Native strategies for coexistence, that is, the practices of negotiating differences and the approaches to ordering and valuing in a multicultural environment, at times served as a model for European-descended people who also sought the possibility of peaceful coexistence.

In the earliest period of Native and European interaction, the model for coexistence grew out of the practices that the Massachusett and Narragansett people called *wunnégin* (welcome) that entered the European American tradition in part through the work of Roger Williams. In the first third of the eighteenth century, a new Native strategy for conceptualizing and preserving a pluralist America emerged along the border in the speeches of the Native Prophetic movement. These thinkers transformed the practices of welcome into a strategy of separation and cultural conservation based on a logic of place. This approach to ordering and valuing experience in terms of particular places provided a model for Benjamin Franklin and others, both as a way of thinking about science in the context of American communities and as a way of structuring a diverse American society. In the 1820s and 1830s the character of Native and white relations changed again, this time in response to the United States policy of Indian removal. Here, new Native voices began to talk about ways of understanding differences both within and between culturally distinct communities. This new logic, a deepening of the logic of place, emerged through Native narrative traditions as a "logic of home." This way of ordering and valuing came to influence the work of European American women thinkers of the period, especially Lydia Maria Child. In the end, these three Native-influenced traditions, the tradition grounded in *wunnégin,* the Native Prophetic movement's logic of place, and the anti-removal activists' logic of home became part of the intellectual context that brought the indigenous attitude to classical pragmatism at the end of the nineteenth century.

CHAPTER FIVE

The Indigenous Attitude

IN AUGUST 1682 a comet appeared in the night sky of New England. Two years earlier, preaching on the appearance of another comet, Increase Mather, Cotton's father, declared that "Such Sights are *Heaven's Alarm* to a sinful World, to give notice that God hath bent his Bow, and made his Arrows ready, and that if Sinners turn not, the Arrows of Pestilence and Death shall fall down upon them speedily" (Mather 1986, 20). In the face of such a warning, Mather gave two pieces of advice. First, expect war and not peace. "O let us beware of crying Peace, Peace, when the Day of Destruction is at hand" (Mather 1986, 25). Instead, the chosen people of the Americas needed to take action and in so doing hope to avert the evil events foreshadowed by the comet. Second, however, despite the danger, the results of the coming war were not yet settled. "This word of comfort, I may safely speak," Mather continued, *"The Lord's Threatenings are not absolute, but conditional"* (Mather 1986, 32). The hope of victory came at the high price of holy war against all who would block the pilgrims' progress.

Years later, Cotton recalled the important appearance of the comets in his volume *The Christian Philosopher.* From his perspective, the comet was at once a knowable astronomical phenomenon, describable under the given rules of nature, and something whose meaning was ultimately part of a larger scheme. Thus, even as the comet could be understood in terms of the new science of Newton, "from whom 'tis a difficult thing to dissent in any thing that belongs to *Philosophy,*" it also signified impending troubles to be faced by Mather's community in its progress toward the new Jerusalem. While his father had been wary of "natural" disasters, Cotton displayed a special fear of the more insidious challenge of human chaos and its potential for breaking the will of the community. "When I see a vast Comet, blazing and rolling about the unmeasurable

Æther," he says, "I will think: 'Who can tell, but I now see a wicked World *made a fiery Oven in this Time of the Anger of GOD! The Lord swallowing them up in his Wrath, and the Fire devouring them!* What prodigious Mischief and Ruin might such a *Ball of Confusion* bring upon our sinful Globe, if the Great GOD order its Approach to us!" (Mather 1994, 53–54). The coming of Halley's Comet in 1682, like the comet of 1680, marked the potential for destructive chaos in America. In this case, however, the chaos was averted. Among the deaths that followed the appearance of Halley's Comet early in the following year was that of Roger Williams, a Puritan preacher who, for Mather, embodied "Mischief and Ruin."

Cotton Mather addressed the problem of Roger Williams in the final book of his *Magnalia Christi Americana.* The book is the penultimate chapter in Mather's story of New England, and it recalls the elder Mather's tidings of war in its title, *Ecclesiarum Praelia,* "The Battles of the Church" (Mather 1967, 2: 489, 489n). Like much of the *Magnalia,* the book presents a series of loosely related accounts, in this case, of the challenges faced by the religious leadership of the New England colonies in the seventeenth century. The accounts are roughly divided into three sections. The first focuses on Roger Williams, the second on a series of "internal" challenges to the Puritan leadership, and the third is an account of the wars between the colonies and the Native American peoples of the region. Given the scope of the movements that challenged the leadership which gave rise to the American Baptist and Quaker movements, and given the damage wrought in the Indian wars, it is curious that Mather opens his discussion with the story of Roger Williams. Williams was neither the leader of a popular movement nor even a preacher of dissent. Unlike Metacom,[1] who led a confederacy of Native people in a devastating war against the colonies in 1675 and 1676, Williams led no armed attack on the colonies.

Williams merits special attention because, as Mather suggests, he bore the "special mark" of someone "eminent" in sinning and so rightly called "the chief of sinners" (Mather 1967, 2: 495). Mather identifies the nature of Williams's sin with the sins of Korah, described in the Old Testament, who led a rebellion against Moses and Aaron as they led the people of Israel into the wilderness.[2] Williams's particular rebellion was,

1. Metacom was known by the English as King Philip. See Lepore 1998 for a review of King Philip's War and its cultural implications.
2. See Book of Numbers (Nm. 16) for the biblical account of Korah's rebellion. In the end, Korah, two other leaders, Dathan and Abiram, their families, servants, and goods were swallowed alive by a fissure in the earth (Nm. 16: 31–33). It is interesting as well that the other famous Old Testament Korah was a son of Esau, whose children were thought to be the "darker peoples" of the Earth and the ancestors of Africans and Native Americans.

however, less overt than that of his famous predecessor. Mather introduces Williams this way:

> In the year 1654, a certain Windmill in the Low Countries, whirling round
> with extraordinary violence, by reason of a violent storm then blowing; the
> stone at length by its *rapid motion* became so intensely hot, as to fire the
> mill, from whence the flames, being dispersed by the high winds, did set
> the whole town on *fire*. But I can tell my reader that, about twenty years
> before this, there was a whole country in America like to be set on *fire* by
> the *rapid motion* of a windmill, in the head of one particular man. Know,
> then, that about the year 1630, arrived here one Mr. Roger Williams.
> (Mather 1967, 2: 495)

Williams represented the thing most dangerous to Mather, the potential
to burn down the Puritan Jerusalem in America. Williams was not, however, to be feared as a blatant arsonist but as one who unwittingly sets
the stage for disaster. Rather than taking action as the Day of Destruction approached, Williams unaccountably demanded peace. Williams
leads Mather's chronicle of the Battles of the Church because he sets the
stage for them. More dangerous than dissenter movements or armed
insurrections, he represented an attitude of acceptance.

Even as Mather sought the demise of the dissenter movements and
the necessary and violent extermination of the Native people who resisted colonial governance, Williams argued that dissenters and even
whole societies of outsiders ought to stand side by side with the community of saints as it pursued salvation. His dangerous rhetoric did not demand the renunciation of the beliefs of the Puritan leaders or of the
Quakers or of the Native peoples they joined in America. He argued
instead for their interactive coexistence. In a letter to the General Court
of Massachusetts Bay, written in October 1654 in an effort to avert a war
with the Narragansett Indians, he asked the colonial leadership whether
it was "not only possible but very easie for the English to live and die in
peace with all the Natives of this countrey" (LaFantasie 1988, 2: 408).
From the perspective of the colonial attitude, such a question could only
be answered negatively: Puritan conceptions of meaning and progress,
morality and knowledge depended on the reduction of difference to
sameness. The English could live in peace with Native peoples but only
if the Natives became sufficiently like the English, in particular, as Christian converts. To the extent they were unwilling or unable to do so, the
alternative was death.[3] Mather would have been even more confounded

---

3. In fact, even conversion was, in practice, insufficient to establish peaceful coexistence

had he read Williams's letter to Governor Winthrop written on December 18, 1675. In the midst of King Philip's War, called "the most fatal war in American history" (Lepore 1998, xiii), Williams nevertheless appealed for peace. Even as the Puritan leadership prepared to exterminate the Native people who resisted them, Williams sought a quick end to the fighting and a return to a state in which Native and European peoples could peacefully coexist. "[If] it please God to deliver them [the Native confederacy] into our hands," he said to Winthrop, "I know that you will Antiquim obtinere [hold to the old way], and still Endeavour that our Sword may make a difference and *Parcere Subjectis,* though We *debellare superbos* ['To spare the conquered (though we) strike down the proud']" (LaFantasie 1988, 2: 708, 710n). Against the demands of virtually the entire colonial leadership and in spite of significant English casualties, Williams called for a return to the "old way" and rejected the genocide expected in the wake of an English victory.

Mather opens his discussion of the Battles of the Church with the story of Roger Williams as if to say that the attitude evidenced by Williams leads to the flourishing of destructive dissent and difference. Unlike the biblical Korah, New England's "chief sinner" did not challenge the integrity of the colonial government. His sin was rather to demand recognition of the standing and value of other communities as well. This demand was a sin because it undermined the progress and hierarchy of values that Mather and others like him had come to expect in their ordered world. Williams was a danger because he threatened the very ground of the colonial vision—what I have called the colonial attitude. But the threat was only part of the price of success. While *Ecclesiarum Praelia* describes the threat, it is also an assertion of a confidence in the ultimate success of the colonial vision. Resistance, from this perspective, may be necessary, but it is always futile. *Ecclesiarum Praelia* marks both Mather's fear of the attitude manifested by Williams and his confidence that such challenges will be reduced to stages in the story of inevitable progress.

While Mather is willing to admit the danger inherent in Williams's response to the colonial leadership and its vision for New England, the origins of Williams's radical ideas remain largely a mystery, inconsistent as they are with Puritan theology. Mather's own suggestion about the sources of Williams's views comes in the epigraph to the chapter in which Williams is introduced. *"Hic se aperit Diabolus!"* that is, "Here the

---

from the colonial perspective. When King Philip's War began, the so-called "Praying Indians" of the coast were imprisoned on Deer Island where many starved to death during the long cold winter of 1675 and 1676. See Lepore 1998, 136–145.

devil shows himself" (Mather 1967, 2: 495, 495n). More recent discussions, however, have looked for less diabolical sources. Some argue, for example, that Williams's commitment to toleration was a view without direct intellectual antecedents, a product of his own original thinking. Vernon Parrington, one of Williams's most exuberant twentieth-century commentators, writes, for example, that "Roger Williams was the most provocative figure thrown upon the Massachusetts shores . . . , the one original thinker amongst a number of capable social architects" (Parrington 1927, 63). On this view, Williams was "primarily a political philosopher rather than a theologian" (Parrington 1927, 66) whose conception of tolerance is grounded in his commitment to individual rights in a way that anticipates John Locke's arguments published forty-five years after Williams published his own defense of toleration, *The Bloudy Tenent of Persecution*. Parrington concludes that Williams was a "confirmed individualist who carried to its logical conclusion the Reformation principle of the right of private inquiry" (Parrington 1927, 72). However, while it is possible that Williams was radically original and that he anticipated liberal individualism, his argument in favor of toleration is quite different from those of the recognized liberal tradition, and he uses a language more closely related to the dominant theological tradition of his time.

Perry Miller, by contrast, argues that Williams was not a political theorist but a theologian who grounded his insistence on toleration in an interpretation of the Bible which saw the Old Testament as representing a picture of the world overturned by Christ's resurrection. If David and Solomon were kings of both a secular and spiritual nation, the "antitype" nation in the post-resurrection world would have a complete separation between the secular and the spiritual (Miller 1953, 18–20). For Miller, Williams was not offering a general political theory, but rather advice to Christians that argued for tolerance on the grounds that spiritual matters and secular ones were absolutely separate. Edmund S. Morgan, who follows Miller's emphasis on theology, carries the argument further. On Morgan's interpretation, Williams held that "Christians had lost their church and there was no present way to recover it" (Morgan 1967, 53). Toleration, on Morgan's interpretation, follows from the fact that there is no legitimate earthly church and so no earthly authority for demanding a particular set of religious beliefs and practices over another. In both cases, however, while a clear case is made for the separation of secular and spiritual matters in Christianity, it is not clear why toleration is to be adopted in secular matters, that is, why societies both Christian and non-Christian should adopt toleration as a political philosophy. Morgan recognizes the problem when he observes that "Williams seems to have reached his conclusion in some intuitive way before he had fully articulated the premises that underlay it" (Morgan 1967, 90). The difficulty is that Miller and Morgan focus on sources and arguments within the established European and European American Christian traditions and do not take seriously Williams's own conclusions that a tolerant society will tolerate both religious and nonreligious beliefs and practices. Whatever argument is made for toleration in such a society, it must be one that works for both believers and nonbelievers.

In fact, the mystery of the origins of Williams's attitude can in part be addressed by considering not only his European roots, but what he could have learned from the Native people with whom he lived in America.[4] A case for the Native origins of Williams's attitude of meaning will follow the same kind of outline I used in setting out the development of the colonial attitude. Certain patterns of engaging the world are displayed through texts and action. A case for the continuity between thinkers can be made when earlier patterns of engagement reemerge in the work of later thinkers. That the reemergence is related to the earlier material is supported when the later thinkers can be shown to have had the opportunity to learn from the earlier. Little argument is needed to establish the relationship between the attitudes evidenced by Mather, Jefferson, and Bancroft. In general, they share a common language, related intellectual roots, common social practices, and a common geographical region. That Mather's work is at least indirectly influential for Jefferson and Jefferson's, in turn, for Bancroft is already recognized in American intellectual history.[5] Mather's work was widely influential among most American intellectuals of the colonial period.[6] Jefferson's *Notes* were similarly influential on succeeding generations of political and intellectual leaders.[7] The continuity of the colonial attitude across generations amounts to a story of similarity of attitudes and points of contact. The case for Native influence follows the same approach, but where the sources for marked similarities and points of contact are different in kind. Within the European American tradition, it is relatively easy to

4. Only Jack L. Davis, in his short paper "Roger Williams among the Narragansett Indians" (1970), investigates this aspect of Williams's intellectual development. Davis's development relies primarily on an examination of Williams's *Key into the Language of America*. I will take a significantly broader approach considering both Native sources and Williams's later work.

5. In addition to Bancroft's own citations of Mather and Jefferson and important sources for his *History,* see especially Sacvan Bercovitch, *The Rites of Assent.* Bercovitch provides a useful discussion of the connections between these figures, especially Mather and Bancroft.

6. See, for example, Miller 1953a, Mather 1977 (Kenneth B. Murdock's introduction), and Bercovitch 1978 for different treatments of Mather's importance.

7. See especially Sheehan 1973 for a discussion of Jefferson's influence especially with respect to Native people.

trace the relationship of thinkers through common content often expressed in a common language. When the influence to be examined is
across a border between dramatically different cultures lacking a long-
established common language and history, other sources are needed. I
will focus in particular on the ways in which attitudes are displayed and
shared through common stories and other kinds of interaction.

Attitudes, as I have argued, are best seen as ways of understanding
and acting in the world. The attitudes displayed in Mather's *Magnalia,*
Jefferson's *Notes,* and Bancroft's *History* are part of the process of making
experiences in America meaningful. The process examined in these
cases is not unlike the process involved in telling other sorts of stories
or even in well-established practices that illustrate the relationship between people and their world. Stories and the practices of cultural
interaction in Native traditions also ground distinctive attitudes that involve particular commitments. Those encountered by Williams in the
Narragansett tradition in particular involve commitments similar to
those involved in the principles of interaction, pluralism, community,
and growth.

Williams, I will argue, adopted a version of a Native attitude and
supported it using conceptual resources from his own Christian and
European background. The Native attitude for Williams, according to
his published works and letters, emerged in his daily experience with the
Narragansett and through his view of their interactions with the English
colonists. To illustrate this influence, I will focus in particular on the
attitudes that emerge in a range of stories common to the Narragansett
and other Eastern Algonquian peoples that stood in striking contrast to
comparable European stories. The Narragansett attitude, marked by its
commitments to interaction, pluralism, community, and growth that
emerges from these contrasting stories would have become apparent to
Williams at a crucial moment in his own history, and he appears to adopt
this model both philosophically in his own published work and practically in the organization of his own settlement, Providence. In order to
illustrate the Narragansett attitude and to show how it would have been
accessible to Williams, I frame this discussion around the alternative ways
of conceiving and responding to what the Narragansett people called
Mohowaúgsuck and what the English immigrants called cannibals.

The stage was set for Williams to learn a new attitude of meaning
when he sat across a fire from Miantonomi, a leader of the Narragansett
people, in the winter of 1636. Banished from the Massachusetts Bay
Colony for preaching against colonial policies, Williams was probably
a receptive listener as Miantonomi talked about the necessity of achiev-

ing peaceful coexistence with the European immigrants, a coexistence marked by tolerance and mutual support.[8] It probably struck Williams as an odd response to the growing European presence on the edges of Narragansett country; from Miantonomi's perspective the world could only have appeared to be on the brink of disaster. Just sixteen years earlier, the settlers of the Mayflower had established a colony in an abandoned Pawtuxet village whose residents had been killed in the epidemics of 1616 to 1618. When the Mayflower's company came ashore, the "wilderness" was "empty," because the plague had reduced the indigenous population of Cape Cod by ninety percent.[9] The new European settlement, called Plymouth by its residents, was located on the coast north of Narragansett lands. Since the Narragansett had not been dramatically affected by the epidemic, they replaced the once powerful Massachusetts and Pokanoket nations as the dominant group in the area. With his uncle Canonicus, Miantonomi shared responsibility for negotiating relationships between the Narragansett and their allied nations and the English. As a result, he often visited the English villages, and it was probably during one of his visits to Plymouth in 1632 or 1633 that he met Williams, a young minister who arrived in America in February 1631.[10] Miantonomi and Williams apparently enjoyed each other's company and talked much about their interests and differences. Miantonomi is often mentioned by Williams in his correspondence and is one of two Native people mentioned by name in Williams's *A Key into the Language of America*. In a 1637 letter to his friend John Winthrop, then governor of the Massachusetts Bay Colony, Williams wrote, "Yet if I mistake not I observe in Miantunnomu some sparkes of true Friendship" (LaFantasie 1988, 1: 101).[11]

8. See John Winthrop's report on Miantonomi's peace treaty with the English colonies later in 1636 (Winthrop 1996, 191–192).

9. See Salisbury 1982, 101–108. David Stannard, in his volume *The American Holocaust*, concludes, "Within no more than a handful of generations following their first encounters with Europeans, the vast majority of the Western Hemisphere's native peoples had been exterminated. The pace and magnitude of their obliteration varied from place to place and from time to time." Historical demographers generally agree that the post-Columbian depopulation rate was between 90 and 98 percent (Stannard 1992, x). Stannard estimates that the pre-Columbian population of the Americas was near one hundred million at a time when the European population was between sixty and seventy million (1992, 267–268).

10. Dates in this discussion of Williams are rendered in the present "New Style" (Gregorian calendar) rather than the "Old Style" (Julian calendar) often used in the seventeenth century.

11. In his letter, Williams leaves the object of Miantonomi's "true friendship" ambiguous, but the context implies that it is both Williams and his people. Also see Williams's letters of May 1, 1637 (LaFantasie 1988, 1: 72), and September 21, 1638 (LaFantasie 1988, 1: 182–183).

Several years before, when Williams first arrived in America as a Cambridge-educated Puritan preacher, he spent a brief time in Boston where he was one of only six clergymen in the colony. As a radical separatist, however, Williams refused to join the church at Boston on the grounds that it had not separated from the Church of England. Believing that the climate at Salem would be more hospitable, he relocated there, but when he did not receive an appointment to the separatist church there, he moved again, this time to Plymouth, where he came to know the character and interests of both the immigrants and the Native people living nearby. Among his acquaintances in Plymouth in addition to the colonial leadership was the Pokanoket leader, or "sachem," Ousamequin (also called Massasoit), as well as the Narragansett sachems. After only two years, however, Williams and the Plymouth congregation parted company, and Williams and his family moved to Salem where he was eventually appointed as a teacher in the Salem congregation. After leaving Plymouth, and perhaps in light of his conversations with Native leaders there, Williams published his first work, a pamphlet denouncing the English right to Native lands granted through the king's patent. According to John Winthrop, "mr Williams (then of Salem) . . . disputes [the Colony's] right to the landes they possessed heere: & concluded that claiminge by the kings grant they could have no title: nor otherwise except they compounded with the natiues" (Winthrop 1996, 107).[12] No copy of the pamphlet survives, and Williams concludes the incident, according to Winthrop, by responding to a request to renounce his views with a "verye modest & discreet answeare" and the profession that he had written the pamphlet "for the private satisfaction of the governor" (Winthrop 1996, 107). Despite the warning from the Colony's leadership about preaching against land patents, Williams continued his criticisms and extended them with an argument against the right of the colonial government to enforce the "first table," that is, the first four Old Testament commandments, which describe human duties toward God, demanding, among other things, belief in one god.

The risks of holding such a view and of the community that would follow from it led to a straightforward recommendation recorded by Winthrop in his notes. "It beinge professedly declared by the ministers (at the request for the Court to give their advise) that he who should obstinately maintaine suche opinions (whereby . . . a Churche might runne into Heresye, Apostacye or Tiranye, & yet the Civill magistrate

---

12. See Winthrop's recollections of Williams's argument (Winthrop 1996, 107) and Gaustad 1991.

could not entermeddle) were to be removed, & that the other Churches ought to request the magistrate so to do" (Winthrop 1996, 150). In November 1635, Williams was brought before the magistrate to be persuaded again to renounce his views. This time Williams refused and was sentenced to banishment from the colony. Since he had a newborn daughter, Williams was granted a stay of his sentence until spring. In the meantime, however, he continued to preach in his home despite the magistrate's order for silence, and in January 1636 the magistrate voted to enforce the sentence immediately. "When I was unkindly and unchristianly, as I believe, driven from my howse and land and wife and children (in the midst of N. Engl. Winter . . .)," Williams reports, "Govr Mr Wintrop, privately wrote me to steer my Course to the Nahigonset [Narragansett] Bay and Indians. . . . I took his . . . prudent motion as a Hint and voice from God, and (Waving all other Thoughts and Motions), I steerd my Course from Salem (though in Winter snow, wch I feele yet) unto these parts" (LaFantasie 1988, 2: 610). Now, exiled by his own people, Williams may have been quick to condemn the Massachusetts Bay Colony in purely negative terms. Miantonomi, by contrast, was probably more ambivalent and may have made his viewpoint clear by telling a story about an encounter with a *Mohowaúgsuck*—a cannibal[13]—to suggest a way of thinking about encounters with those with contrary "tastes" and whose presence seems disruptive and dangerous.[14]

While there may be other starting points for an investigation of the development of Williams's philosophical perspective in his experience with the Narragansett, the subject matter of cannibals is especially useful for two reasons. First, both Narragansett and European cultures told such stories. As a result they provide a reflective context in which to examine the difference between Narragansett and European responses to encounters with significantly different ways of life. Even as philosophical treatises present conceptions of human nature and human community in ways that help direct action, so do the stories of *Mohowaúgsuck* and their European cousins, witches and sorcerers. Second, the exchange of stories about cannibals was a common feature of the experience of living along the border between Europe and America and so

13. The term "Mohowaúgsuck," "*from* mohó *to eate,*" is mentioned by Williams in his *Key into the Language of America* (Williams 1973, 104). The term is related to the Natick and Massachusett term "móhwhaü," defined as "he eats what is alive, devours, as a beast of prey" (Trumbull 1903, 67), and the Delaware term "mhú.we," or "cannibal" (Voegelin 1945, 106, 108). All three languages are Eastern Algonquian.

14. Native American author Jack D. Forbes, in his book *Columbus and Other Cannibals,* argues that European and European American society can be understood in terms of "wétiko" disease, that is, uncontrollable cannibalism (Forbes 1992).

provides one plausible context in which Williams may have come to reflect on the differences between his own English culture and the Native
American culture that received him. In the end, the stories of both
the Narragansett and the Europeans would have provided Williams with
resources for a philosophical response to the conflicts generated within
his community.

There are few attempts to consider Native responses to the arrival
of the Europeans along the east coast of North America from a Native
point of view. Most attempts rely on English, French, and Dutch reports
of Native reactions. A common starting point is the Native account of
one of the first encounters with Europeans along the northeast coast
reported through William Wood in the 1630s. According to Wood, "they
[the Native people] took the first ship they saw for a walking island, the
mast to be a tree, the sail white clouds, and the discharging of ordnance
for lightening and thunder, which did much trouble them, but this thunder being over and this moving-island steadied with an anchor, they
manned out their canoes to go and pick strawberries there" (quoted in
Bragdon 1996, 29). Such an account, however, mediated through English translation and emphasizing metaphorical rather than practical interpretation, fails to take seriously the ways in which Native responses
were conceptualized and justified.[15] The difficulty, of course, is that there
appear to be no Native sources from the period of first encounters which
can be relied upon to present the "Native voice." This problem is in part
due to a set of assumptions about the "quality" of traditional stories and
reports that circulated largely in oral form, assumptions that exclude
them from consideration. Vine Deloria Jr. has argued extensively that
these assumptions are mistaken and that traditional stories are both remarkably stable through time and can serve as sources of both "factual"
information and Native ways of understanding the world.[16]

At the same time, there is a difference between texts and stories. A
story can be told in many different ways and, as a result, its meaning and
influence may be much more difficult to trace than that of a text, a distinct "telling" of a story. The issue strikes at the heart of the methodo-

15. Bragdon 1996 presents a comprehensive summary of archeological and ethno-
graphic information about Native people on the Massachusetts coast, given here the general name Ninnimissinuok. While Bragdon's "goal is to provide an account that is, as far
as possible, consistent with the Native point of view and with Native voice" (Bragdon 1996,
xi), it is not clear that she has been successful. In the body of the work nearly all of the
sources are European, both historical and contemporary, and even those sources most concerned with the "Native voice" and "world view" rely on recent secondary sources, some
of which have as their subject matter indigenous peoples outside North America.

16. See Deloria 1995 for a discussion of this view in some detail. Also see Deloria 1979.

logical problems faced by cross-cultural comparative philosophy. Paul Radin, for example, faced a similar challenge in his 1927 work *Primitive Man as Philosopher* (which includes a preface by John Dewey). Radin relied on unique texts by Native "informants" and framed their meaning in terms of well-established philosophical questions asked within the European philosophical tradition. In contrast, my strategy is to consider a variety of overlapping texts (Native and European American) with common "story" elements. Influence can be traced by examining the contexts, similarities, and differences among the "tellings." Strictly speaking, the stories are not influential except as they are concretely shared and retold. My approach is to focus on particular texts and their logic historically and philosophically situated. From this perspective, taking European and Native sources together will provide a ground for comparing and contrasting views of cultural contact and tracing the influence of Native thought.

Although no Narragansett *Mohowaúgsuck* stories are available, a brief version of one such story is recorded from the Penobscot tradition.[17] The Penobscot are a nation whose country is in the present-day state of Maine. Like most of the Native cultures in the Northeast at the time, they speak an Eastern Algonquian dialect and share a wide range of cultural resources: material, ceremonial, and narrative. In the Penobscot tradition, "man-eaters" are called *Ki.wá'kwe*[18] and, as in most Northeast traditions, are giants in human form.

A man, his wife, and little girl were living far from other people in the woods. They heard someone coming. Suddenly a noise was heard in the smoke hole of the wigwam and looking up they saw a *Ki.wá'kwe* peering down. The old woman of the wigwam said aloud, "Oh! Your grandfather has come," speaking to her husband. The monster was pleased at this and grew small. He came around and entered the camp. The woman tried to

17. The traditions of the Narragansett are closely related to a range of other Native traditions of the Northeast and north. The Narragansett share a language family, Algonquian, with the Delaware, Pequot, Massachusett, Penobscot, Abenaki, Micmac, and Ojibwe, among others. See Goddard 1978 for a general discussion of the range of Algonquian languages. These peoples share similar stories as well, including cannibal stories. They also have stories and ceremonies similar to those of the Iroquoian peoples that include the nations of the Haudenosaunee Confederacy (Mohawk, Onondaga, Seneca, Oneida, Cayuga, and Tuscarora). In this discussion, I will consider stories from this range of peoples who shared borders with the New England colonies in the seventeenth century.

18. In the traditions of the Micmac and Passamaquoddy, also Algonquian peoples, "man-eaters" are called "Cheenoo" or "Djenu" (Leland 1884, 233; Wallis and Wallis 1955, 343). Among the Cree and Ojibwe people, such beings are called *windigo* (Teicher 1960, 2).

feed him but he would not eat in spite of her coaxing. He said, "I shall meet somebody here and we will fight." Then he sent them away across a lake and he fought with the other *Ki.wá'kwe*. He had told them to leave the place if he got killed by the other. But he won the fight and when it was over he ate with them, becoming again an ordinary man. (Speck 1935, 14)

The Penobscot story suggests three significant aspects of the *Ki.wá'kwe*: they are outsiders who are dangerous and disruptive; some can be effectively responded to with hospitality and kindness; and in some cases they can be transformed from outsiders to insiders or members of the group and at other times to peaceful neighbors.

Williams himself recognizes the "outsider" character of the *Mohowaúgsuck* when he defines the term as naming "*The Canibals, or Men-Eaters, up into the west two, three or foure hundred miles from us*" (Williams 1973, 104). The meaning recalls two connections that reinforce the view of cannibals as outsiders. By the seventeenth century, the name "Mohowaúgsuck" had come to be applied to the easternmost nation of the Haudenosaunee Confederacy, the Mohawks, who were viewed as dangerous enemies by many coastal nations, including the Narragansett.[19] At the same time, the reference to "up into the west" recalls the idea that cannibals originated far away in the cold northwest outside lands of the coastal Algonquian peoples. The Micmac tradition confirms the northwest origin of cannibals and their danger. "In the summer," according to a description recorded in the nineteenth century, "the Djenu [Cannibal] goes north and remains there until the approach of winter, then goes south. Wherever he goes, he will sweep [i.e., destroy] everything. Such is the temper of his wildness" (Wallis and Wallis 1955, 344).[20]

The Iroquoian tradition, of which the neighboring Haudenosaunee nations are a part, similarly places the origin of a nation of cannibals in the north. Here, the *Genonsgwa* or "Stone Coats" (or "Stone Giants") are a race of evil giants who prey on the unsuspecting who wander too far

19. Williams identifies another nation of cannibals as well: "Mihtukméchakick. *Tree-eaters.* A people so called (living between three and foure hundred miles West into the land) from their eating only *Mihtúchquash,* that is, Trees: They are *Men-eaters,* they set no corne, but live on the *bark* of *Chesnut* and *Walnut,* and other fine trees: They dry and eat this *bark* with the fat of Beasts, and sometimes of men: this people are the *terrour* of the neighbor *Natives;* and yet these *Rebells,* the Sonne of God may in time subdue" (Williams 1973, 102).

20. A Delaware account told by a twentieth-century storyteller, Willie Longbone, also emphasizes the danger and the directional element of contact with cannibals. In the story, the hero, Wehixamokas, and his partner set out to go "clean around this earth." They "went east, then north, then west; they got northwest in the cold country. They ran into some giants." After the cannibal giants nearly kill Wehixamokas, his partner says, "Let's go back from here. We can't go around the earth. I see these giants will kill you" (Bierhorst 1995, 115). Wehixamokas and his partner abandoned their trek and escaped.

into the woods alone. According to one story from the Iroquoian tradition, in this case from the Wyandot, the *Genonsgwa* originated when a band of Wyandot ancestors became stranded in a blizzard. While some escaped, others remained trapped and were driven by hunger "to kill and devour some of their own neighbors and friends." Those who remained alive "became monsters—man-eaters, giants, stone coats, stone giants—and were very strong in body" (Curtin and Hewitt 1918, 806n). At some point later, several Haudenosaunee stories claim that the Stone Coats were all but destroyed—although *Genonsgwa* survivors still lurk in the north woods (Parker 1989, 340–341; Curtin and Hewitt 1918, 260–261, 682–686). The Algonquian tradition also speaks of distinct cannibal nations living apart from human beings, a relationship reprised practically in the Narragansett relationship with the Mohawks.[21]

While some stories emphasize the idea that cannibals are an external danger to communities, other stories recognize that the character of a cannibal can emerge within a community as well. Such cannibals are particularly dangerous to the existence of the community and must be isolated from the group. In one Haudenosaunee story, for example, a man-eater or Ongwe Ias[22] named De'o'niot "developed his man-flesh appetite early in his childhood . . . [and now] lived in a hidden place far away from other human habitations" (Parker 1989, 284). Although born a human being, he developed the character of someone dangerous to the community and was isolated from it. Both kinds of *Mohowaúgsuck*, the outsider and the insider, share a common taste for human flesh over which they have little control and, unless they are changed, must remain a threat to the life of the community.[23]

Even though cannibals are dangerous and disruptive, the response to them recommended in the stories often involves hospitality and kindness instead of violence, a stark contrast to Puritan modes of dealing with similar situations. In the Penobscot story quoted earlier, for example, the first reaction to the horrible face of the *Ki.wá'kwe* is to welcome him and call him "grandfather." In a parallel Micmac story, a cannibal giant, a *Cheenoo*, surprises a woman who is chopping wood. According to the storyteller "[s]he saw with horror something worse than the worst she feared. It was an awful face glaring at her—a something made of devil,

---

21. See Teicher 1960, 22–23, for example.

22. While "Genonsgwa" and "Ongwe Ias" both refer to man-eaters, "Genonsgwa" is more often used to refer to man-eaters from outside the Haudenosaunee and "Ongwe Ias" to those who originate within the community.

23. See Teicher 1960 for a discussion of "*windigo* psychosis" in the Algonquian tradition, where members of a community become cannibals by acquiring a taste for human flesh.

man, and beast in their most dreadful forms. It was like a haggard old man, with wolfish eyes; he was stark naked; his shoulders and lips were gnawed away, as if, when mad with hunger, he had eaten his own flesh." Instead of fear, however, the woman "ran up and addressed him with fair words, as 'My dear father,' pretending surprise and joy. . . . The *Cheenoo* was amazed beyond measure at such a greeting where he expected yells and prayers, and in mute wonder let himself be led into the wigwam." The storyteller concludes, "She was a wise and good woman" (Leland 1884, 233–234).[24] A very similar story in the Ojibwe tradition is recorded by William Jones and published in 1919. "Now there were abiding some people with only their children," the story begins, "Now it was winter." Again, while her husband is out hunting, the woman in the story sees a giant approaching and rushes out to meet him. "On her way to meet him as he came along on the ice, and while yet some distance away, she spoke to him, saying: 'O my father! Have you now returned home?'" The *windigo* is suspicious. "I don't know if you are a daughter of mine," he replies. But the woman persists. "Oh my father! Have you now come home?" The *windigo* concedes to the welcome and agrees to follow the woman home and is even concerned that he not frighten his "grandchildren." The narrator concludes, "Then truly he came crawling [into her house since he was so large] that father of hers. So thereupon he kissed her children. Truly gentle was he, and it was then all the while that he had those children of hers in his hands" (Jones in Teicher 1960, 27–28).

The Haudenosaunee story of De'o'niot makes a similar point about the importance of kindness as a means of responding to those who are dangerously different. While De'o'noit is a cannibal, his isolation is nevertheless made easier by the steadfast presence of his nephew. According to the storyteller, De'o'noit lived in a house divided by a partition, with his nephew on the other side "lest [De'o'niot's] appetite for flesh become too strong a temptation and leave him without a companion" (Parker 1989, 284). Even though his uncle was ostracized from the community and despite his uncle's continued cannibalism (eating his nephew's wives), the nephew continued to show his uncle kindness. G. E. Laidlaw reports a similar story from the Ojibwe tradition. Here, an Ojibwe man canoeing a lake encounters a storm and is forced ashore at the camp of a *windigo* man and his brother. The *windigo*, isolated from others, is a danger. He is, his brother says, "the one that kills all the Indians." The *windigo* is accompanied in his exile by his brother, "a kind-

---

24. There is a related story in the Ojibwe tradition related by G. E. Laidlaw in his 1918 work *Ojibwa Myths and Tales*, see Teicher 1960, 19–20.

hearted man," who helps free the stranded visitor while the *windigo* is away. Despite the *windigo*'s danger and disposition, his brother stays by his side (Laidlaw in Teicher 1960, 19).

Kindness in these stories, however, is not its own reward but is presented as an element of a process of interaction and transformation which can dramatically diminish the danger and disruption of the cannibal and restore peace within a community or between nations. In some cases, the transformation is complete. For example, in the *Mhú.we* (cannibal) story told by Delaware storyteller Willie Longbone, after the cannibal's human companions fed him deer meat instead of human flesh, he fell asleep. "When [the *Mhú.we*] woke up he said, 'You fellows have conclusively saved my life (providing me with proper food and thus breaking the spell of cannibalism)'" (Voegelin 1945, 109). The kindness of the people who welcomed the *Mhú.we* and the hospitality they offered transformed him into a human being.

In the story of De'o'niot, the cannibal is also transformed. Initially, however, despite his nephew's efforts, De'o'niot continued to practice cannibalism and so sent away his nephew and his nephew's wife for their own protection. Some time later, the children of his nephew's village began to disappear mysteriously. The nephew realized that De'o'niot was nearby. When he found him, the cannibal was sick from too much food. The nephew offered to cure him and "made him a soup of fish bones and skins and fed it to his uncle. He continued this treatment for three days until De'o'niot had disgorged. By this time he was ravenous and begged for food and new clothing. . . . The nephew bade him strip and plunge in the water and bathe himself. Then, after giving him some new clothing he fed him on a little corn pudding, gradually increasing the allowance at each meal and each time moving the camp nearer the village" (Parker 1989, 288). In this case, the cannibal is fully transformed and reenters village life pledging "never to touch the meat of mankind again."[25]

Significantly, however, some transformations are not instantaneous or complete. Nevertheless, in these cases, even partial transformations are presented as enough to restore peace within a community. In the Penobscot *Ki.wá'kwe* story quoted earlier, the *Ki.wá'kwe* is changed from a threat to the family who welcomed him to an ally even as he continued to maintain his taste for human flesh. Later, after he defeats another *Ki.wá'kwe* in combat, he manifests an inward change as well and has a

25. There is an Eastern Algonquian version of the story of De'o'niot repeated by Laidlaw (quoted in Teicher 1960, 19).

meal with his new friends. In another Haudenosaunee story, a child and her mother befriend a *Genonsgwa* woman. For a time she helps the woman and her family by hunting. Later, with the help of her human friends she defeats her husband, also a *Genonsgwa*, who has come to beat her. When her husband is dead, the *Genonsgwa* woman leaves her human family, transformed in her behavior toward human beings, but not explicitly changed in her tastes as a *Genonsgwa*.[26] Erminne Smith reports a similar story. In this case, when her husband is dead, "[the *Genonsgwa*] stayed a while quietly with the hunter and his wife, fetching in the game and being useful until they were ready to leave and return to the settlement. Then she said, 'Now I must go home to my people, for I need fear nothing.' So she bade them farewell" (Smith 1883, 63). Again, while the cannibal was transformed in her relations with her human friends, she retained the disposition of a *Genonsgwa*. Finally, in a Passamaquoddy *Ki.wá'kwe* story, the woman who shows kindness to the *Ki.wá'kwe* recalls that "a Kewahqu' had a piece of ice for a heart. If this can be taken out, the Kewahqu' can be tamed and cured" (Wallis and Wallis 1955, 248). She prepares a drink for her friend and, when he drinks it, he vomits up one icy heart and then another, both of which the woman quickly destroys in the fire. When he disgorges a third heart, he quickly takes it from the woman and swallows it again. "[H]e was," the storyteller concludes, "almost entirely cured." In this case, while the transformation of outward behavior was complete, the transformation of the *Ki.wá'kwe*'s attitudes and tastes were not completely changed.

While most often relevant to the restoration or inclusion of individuals, in several cases the transformation of a cannibal is also relevant to establishing peace among nations. In the Ojibwe story reported by Jones and mentioned earlier, the *windigo* who is transformed by kindness sets off to protect his new daughter and her family from the danger of the *windigo* nation across the "great sea." As he leaves, he tells his daughter to expect the sounds of battle with another *windigo*. For four days, the woman hears fighting across the sea, and on the fourth day she hears the sound of her *windigo* father winning the fight. Following his instructions to her, she proclaims, "Pray, never permit him to return again to this island! How can there be any more people than there are? . . . Would that you (and the rest of yours) would live over there (where you are)!" In this case, the transformed *windigo* helps to establish a kind of plural-

---

26. See Curtin and Hewitt 1918, 437–439. Curtin and Hewitt give another *Genonsgwa* story in which a human being and a Stone Coat remain on "friendly terms" though the Stone Coat is not changed in his tastes (Curtin and Hewitt 1918, 440).

ism that reinforces both the standing of the different nations as distinct and their peaceful ongoing relations.[27]

The peaceful relations established in the Ojibwe story are developed in another way in the famous Haudenosaunee founding story. In this story, the last barrier to peace among the Onondaga, Mohawk, Seneca, Oneida, and Cayuga was an Ongwe Ias of the Onondaga nation. This Ongwe Ias, named Adodarho, was a destructive force, killing his own people and refusing to join the peace process. Seth Newhouse, an Onondaga himself, describes Adodarho as "an evil-minded man. His lodge was in a swale and his nest was made of bulrushes. His body was distorted by seven crooks and his long tangled locks were adorned by writhing living serpents" (Parker 1968, 17). He was also a "master of wizardry and by his magic . . . destroyed men but could not be destroyed." Despite his character, he was nevertheless a leader of the Onondaga, who "obeyed his commands and though it cost many lives they satisfied his insane whims, so much did they fear his sorcery." After repeated attempts to destroy him by force, the cofounders of the confederacy, Dekanawida and Hiawatha, approached Adodarho with kindness and respect and sang the "Peace Hymn." When Dekanawida finished singing, "he walked toward Adodarho and held out his hand to rub it on his body and to know its inherent strength and life. Then Adodarho was made straight and his mind became healthy" (Parker 1968, 28). Dekanawida proclaimed, "We have now overcome a great obstacle. It has long stood in the way of peace. The mind of Adodarho is now made right and his crooked parts are made straight. Now indeed may we establish the Great Peace [the Haudenosaunee Confederacy]" (Parker 1968, 28–29).[28]

In each of these cases, cannibals are taken in as cannibals, are welcomed, made part of the group, and by degrees are transformed. Yet not all responses to cannibals are so peaceful. A wide range of stories describes times when cannibals must be fought and killed.[29] The use of kindness as a response to dangerous others is not to be understood as an absolute response mandated in every possible circumstance. Given

27. Laidlaw reports a similar story as well (in Teicher 1960, 22–23). Framed as an explanation of "why people don't kill to eat each other today," the story is resolved by establishing this same sort of cultural autonomy and separation.

28. Paul Wallace, in his version of the founding story, *White Roots of Peace,* says that Hiawatha also was a cannibal who, when he sees a reflection of Dekanawida's face in the kettle where he is boiling his meal, gives up his taste for human flesh. Mistaking Dekanawida's face for his own, he says, "it is not the face of a man who eats humans. I see that it is not like me to do that" (Wallace 1994, 43).

29. See Teicher 1960 for a variety of examples.

the range of stories in the Algonquian and Iroquoian traditions, it is better to see the practices of welcoming cannibals as a preferred response to be chosen based on the circumstances at hand. It is clear, for example, in their interactions with Williams that the Narragansett did not set out initially to convert or exterminate the Europeans. Rather they sought coexistence. What is important is that the Narragansett had alternative ways of responding to the encounter with dangerous differences, including a well-developed process of welcoming and coexisting with such diversity. In this case, the strategy of welcoming the cannibal English was chosen as the better response. Later, when the Narragansett became part of Metacom's (King Philip's) alliance and joined him in attacking the English, it might be seen as the adoption of an alternative model based on the apparent inability of the English colonies to understand and respond properly to the offer of peaceful coexistence.

Despite the alternatives, however, it was perhaps most apparent to Williams that with certain attitudes and practices, even dangerous outsiders could find a peaceful place in a pluralist community. When Williams introduces the term for cannibals, he offers the term "Cummóhucquock. *They will eat you.*" He follows the dictionary entry for "Cummóhucquock" with a general comment. "Whomsoever commeth in when they are eating, they offer them to eat of that which they have, though but little enough prepar'd for themselves" (Williams 1973, 104). The ambiguity of "they" and the openness of "whomsoever" suggests that Williams saw the ideal response to strangers, despite the danger of cannibals, as a process of hospitality or welcome. From the perspective implied, a community that frames its response to outsiders in terms of hospitality has the potential to support diverse viewpoints and ways of life united in a mutual interest in maintaining peace.

Williams's book, *A Key into the Language of America,* written in 1643, points at a variety of Native ideas and practices that support the vision of a peaceful and diverse American community compatible with the notions of tolerance found in these Native stories about encounters with cannibals. The volume begins and ends with metaphoric keys. At the beginning, referring to the purpose and possibilities of the volume, he writes that "a little *Key* can open a *Box,* wherein lies a *bunch* of *Keyes*" (Williams 1973, 83). At the end, he recalls the image, calling the volume a "poore KEY which may . . . open a Doore; yea, Doors of unknowne Mercies to us [the English] and them [the Native people]" (Williams 1973, 250). The metaphor is important because it focuses on the explicit purpose of the book, to offer a volume "*pleasant* and *profitable* for *All,*" but also on one of the central features of Narragansett culture: the open door. The *Key* is a unique volume in that it presents a series of phrase-book translations of the Narragansett language in the rough form of a dialogue, with the exchanges grouped under a range of broad subject headings such as "Of Salutation," "Of Eating and Entertainment," "Of Discourse and Newes." The translations are interspersed with observations and lessons which attempt to extract a variety of lessons from the language and culture he describes. As Williams's second work, following his lost pamphlet condemning the English Royal patent, the *Key* provides a glimpse into the origins of some of the ideas which would be reformulated in *The Bloudy Tenent of Persecution,* his treatise on "heathens," *Christening Make Not Christians,* his defense of "soul-freedom," *The Examiner Defended in a Fair and Sober Manner,* and his critique of Quakerism, *George Foxx Digged out of his Burrowes.*

That Williams knew many of the traditional Narragansett stories is clear from references in his *Key* to other material not included in the book. In the introduction, Williams provides a brief description of what he takes to be a common starting point for European efforts to interact with the Native people of the Americas. First, like Cotton Mather and most other seventeenth-century writers on America, he recapitulates part of the widely accepted case for the claim that Native Americans descended from a lost tribe of Israel. Unlike Mather and most other writers, however, he then goes on to suggest that, like Christian Europeans, Native people have a range of stories that serve both as histories and guides. "They have many strange relations," he says, "of one *Wétucks,* a man that wrought great *Miracles* amongst them, and *walking upon the waters, &c.* with some kind of broken Resemblance to the *Sonne of God*" (Williams 1973, 86). William Simmons, in his study of New England Native traditions, observes that "Wétucks" "might be the same word etymologically as the Ojibwa windigo [cannibal]," or it might be the name of the "culture hero" also known as Maushop by the Wampanoags, Glauskop among the Micmacs, Gluskabe among the Penobscot, and Wehixamokas among the Delaware. Whether "Wétucks" is taken as the name of a cannibal or the central figure in a range of "culture hero" stories like those of Maushop, Williams was clearly familiar with the Narragansett oral tradition. Significantly, he was willing to treat that tradition as more than a series of fictional tales. Rather, he saw them as stories that bear a "broken resemblance" to the stories that served as a ground for European thought and action. From this perspective, it seems that Williams both heard cannibal stories and could have understood them as providing crucial instructions for the proper response to *Mohowaúg-suck,* the practices of welcome, in Narragansett, *wunnégin.*

In general, the process of welcoming strangers serves as a central practice in the attitude of meaning Williams experienced in his contact with Miantonomi and the Narragansett and adopted to frame his own conception of a pluralist community. The practice, explicitly identified with what constituted good in Narragansett society, also points toward underlying commitments to something like the principles of interaction, pluralism, a moral standard focused on community, and a social ideal framed in terms of growth and not progress. Williams himself introduces the connection between the process of welcome and the Narragansett idea of goodness early in the *Key* in his chapter on "Sleeping and Lodging" with a brief dialogue.

Nsowwushkâwmen.	*I am weary.*
[. . .]	
Wunnégin, cówish.	*Welcome, sleepe here.*
Nummouaquômen.	*I will lodge abroad.*
Puckquátchick nickouêmen.	*I will sleepe without the doores,* Which I have knowne them contentedly doe, by a fire under a tree, when sometimes some *English* have (for want of familiaritie and language with them) been fearfulle to entertaine them.

In Summer-time, I have knowne them lye abroad often themselves, to make roome for strangers, *English* or others. (Williams 1973, 106)

What marks both the proper Narragansett response to strangers and the contrast with the English response is the practice of welcome. The centrality of the process in Williams's presentation suggests that *wunnégin* is not only good in Narragansett culture, but that it captures the character of things that indicate their value. This seems confirmed when Williams translates a form of the same word, "Wunêgin," as "*Well, or good.*"[30] Welcome is important in particular because, as a practice, it suggests the attitudes that frame the process of understanding and valuing things and events from a Narragansett perspective.[31] Williams's discussion of Narragansett culture in the *Key* helps to identify what he takes to be the key aspects of this attitude.

It is clear, for example, that the goodness of welcoming is to be un-

---

30. Trumbull spells the term "wunnegen" (Trumbull 1903, 202) and explicitly associates the term cited by Williams as meaning welcome to be a use of the term meaning "(it is) good" (Trumbull 1903, 202).

31. The term "wunnégin" itself may be a derivation of the third person pronominal prefix "wu-" and the root "-unnun-" used to form the terms for give. The combined roots would suggest that "wunnégin" may also carry the implication of "it gives."

derstood in terms of particular acts. Rather than having the character of an abstract good, welcoming has a concrete character that requires particular actions and results in order to be welcoming at all. In effect, an interaction with others gets its meaning from what actually happens in the process. James Trumbull, in his study of the Natick (or Massachusett) language, implies that this character of good extends to the general use of the terms for good: "Wunne," "Wunnegen," and their variants. Trumbull argues that "strictly regarded, *wunne* or *wunni* is applicable to the abstract, the possible or suppositive, or the subject, *wunnegen* to the concrete, the actual, or the object" (Trumbull 1903, 202). The distinction Trumbull draws, however, seems to miss the point of his own examples. Contrary to his conclusion about the abstract character of "wunne" in the words for good courage, good land, and good fruits, both terms appear to be used to identify the character of concrete objects or actions and the implications they have for what happens. The concrete character of what constitutes a good is confirmed by the need for missionaries such as John Eliot to change the meanings of the terms in order to accommodate the idea of a good whose meaning comes from outside experience. As Trumbull puts it, "Eliot was compelled to employ [*wunnégin*] to abstract good."[32] This shift in use effected by Eliot can be seen in part as a confirmation of the distinctive character of Native values and in part as an indication of the importance of the conflict between attitudes along the border between Native and European peoples. By incorporating "wunnégin" and its new meaning into the Natick translation of the Bible and using it in sermons and catechisms, the very notion of what constituted a good was transformed. Josiah Cotton, in his Massachusett grammar published to aid new missionaries to the Native people on Massachusetts Bay, illustrates this sort of transformation of meaning in one of the sample sentences missionaries were to use in instruction. "Samppoowash ne wanegkuk [*wunnégin*] uttiyeu adtumunnuman ne mat nehenwonche ken," Cotton begins. "Confess that the good which thou receivest is not for thine own sake." He continues, "nor for the good which thou doest, by thine own power; it is the mercy of God that moves him to do for us, and that inables us to do that which pleaseth him" (Cotton 1830, 237). What is valued, *wunnégin*, is no longer to find its meaning in what happens, but rather in the meaning it gets outside the concrete in terms of a transcendent god and a transcendent history of salvation.

The emphasis on particulars in the process of responding to strang-

---

32. See Trumbull's entry for "wunnegen."

ers relies in part on a range of other commitments that help to frame
the meaning of things and events. These commitments can be seen
as important to the philosophical position developed by Williams and
roughly parallel to those that emerge later in the work of the classical
pragmatists. The emphasis on the idea that the meaning of actions is
found in what actually happens is structured in part by a commitment
to something like the principle of interaction. The vision of a pluralist
community also brings with it practical strategies for interaction, including hospitality, reciprocity, and the formulation of explicit sustaining relations. Finally, embedded in both the ideas and practices associated with
the vision of pluralism is the expectation that what is valuable contributes to the ongoing development of both individuals and communities;
that is, value is a matter of relative growth.

The commitment to the principle of interaction emerges in a variety
of ways in Williams's *Key*. In addition to the overt demands placed on
the process of welcoming, the expectation that knowledge is a matter of
doing is suggested in Williams's discussion of honesty and truth. For example, "Wunnêtu nittà," Williams observes, means "*My heart is good*"
(Williams 1973, 132). "This speech," he says, "they use when ever they
professe their honestie; they naturally confessing that all goodness is first
in the heart." But goodness does not depend upon the heart alone. In
his discussion of "Discourse and Newes," Williams offers the following:

> Wunnaumwâunonck, Wunnaumwáyean. *If he say true*. . . . *Canonicus*, the old
> high *Sachim* of the *Nariganset Bay* (a wise and peaceable Prince) once in a
> solemne Oration to my self, in a solemne assembly, using this word, said, I
> have never suffered any wrong to be offered to the *English* since they
> landed; nor never will: he often repeated this word, *Wunnaumwáyean, En-
> glishman;* if the *Englishman* speake true, if hee meane truly, then shall I goe
> to my grave in peace, and hope that the *English* and my posteritie shall live
> in love and peace together. I replied, that he had no cause (as I hoped) to
> question *Englishmans, Wunnaumwáuonck,* that is, faithfulnesse, he having
> had long experience of their friendlinesse and trustinesse. He tooke a
> sticke, and broke it into ten pieces, and related ten instances (laying downe
> a sticke to every instance) which gave him cause thus to feare and say. (Wil-
> liams 1973, 136–137)

At issue in Canonicus's vision of the American community is the role of
faithfulness, *Wunnaumwáuonck,* as making a difference in the possibility
of a peaceful plural community. Faithfulness represents the connection
between word and action, and it is a way of making the meaning of one's
words apparent in action. Faithfulness is mirrored by a second notion,

Coanáumatous, which Williams translates "I believe you." "This word," he continues, "they use just as the *Greeke* tongue doth that verbe, pisein: for believing or obeying, as it is often used in the new *Testament*" (Williams 1973, 137). Here, what one comes to believe amounts to what one is willing to act upon, to obey. From Canonicus's perspective, the plural community depends upon both faithfulness, that is, one's willingness to act in a way consistent with one's words and, at the same time, one's readiness to act upon one's own beliefs. Taken together, the meaning of beliefs and knowledge is found in action, and actions are expected to correspond with beliefs.

The connection between action and belief also amounts to a pluralist ontological principle in Williams's discussion of Native religion. Shortly after the Pequot War in 1637, another English colonist, Thomas Morton, published a description of the Native people near the Massachusetts colonies. Morton was viewed as a renegade of sorts after setting up his own colony near Plymouth, called Merry Mount. Morton, like Williams, was sympathetic to Native calls for peaceful coexistence and welcomed Natives and Europeans to his town. Unlike Williams, however, Morton, in his 1637 volume *New English Canaan; or, New Canaan,* argued that the Native people of Massachusetts had no religion at all. "These people," Morton concludes, "are *sine fide, sine lege,* and *sine rege*" (Morton 1972, 27). Morton, perhaps in his interest to help justify his freewheeling life-style and community, found in Native people something like the quint-essential "noble savage." Williams, on the other hand, in an account of Native life which is arguably more consistent with later Native accounts of indigenous culture, begins his chapter on religion: "Manit, manit-tówock. *God, Gods*" (Williams 1973, 189). He continues, "He that questions whether God made the World, the Indians will teach him. I must acknowledge I have received in my converse with them many confirma-tions of those two great points . . . : 1. That God is. 2. That hee is a rewarder of all them that diligently seek him" (Williams 1973, 189). But despite promising similarities, Williams claims that Native beliefs go wrong when they "branch their God-head into many Gods" and "attrib-ute it to Creatures."

Although Williams dissents from Native beliefs, as he presents them, they nevertheless seem to be consistent with the principles of *Wunnaum-wáuonck* and *Coanáumatous,* faithfulness and belief. On the Native view, as represented by Williams, *Manit* is manifest in the actions of most things: death, certainly, but also in hunting, fishing, harvest, the winds, in femaleness, in maleness, in the sun, moon, fire, and so on. Just as *Wunnaumwáuonck* asserts a quality of character in action, *Manit* seems to be a quality of character as well. Presuming that those whose characters are manifested in action also act as they believe, then actions are manifest beliefs. Williams observes, "When I have argued with them about their Fire-God: can it, they say, be but this fire must be a God, or a Divine power, that out of a stone will arise a Sparke, and when a poore naked Indian is ready to starve with cold in the House, and especially in the Woods, often saves his life, doth dresse all our Food for us, and if it be angry will burne the House about us, yea if a spark fall into the drie wood, burnes up the Country?" (Williams 1973, 191). In this case, fire is "Manittóo," but this amounts to understanding fire as a distinct, active force in lived experience. What fire is, in other words, is significantly what it does.

The principles of *Wunnaumwáuonck* and *Coanáumatous* are supplemented by the acceptance of a complex form of epistemological pluralism that recognizes meaning can be made in a variety of ways. This principle, presented by Miantonomi in a dialogue related by Williams, recognizes that meaning is not always apparent and there are multiple ways of gaining access to meaning with differing results:

> After I had (as farre as my language would reach) discoursed (upon a time) before the chiefe Sachim or Prince of the Countrey, with his Archpriests, and many others in a full Assembly; and be night, wearied with travell and discourse, I lay downe to rest; and before I slept, I heard this passage:
>
> Qunníhticut Indian (who had heard our discourse) told the Sachim Miantunnómu, that soules went [not] up to Heaven, or downe to Hell; For saith he, Our fathers have told us, that our soules goe to the Southwest; did ever you see a soule goe thither?
>
> The Native replied; when did he (naming my selfe) see a soule goe to Heaven or Hell?
>
> The Sachim replied: He hath books and writings, and one of which God himselfe made, concerning mens soules, and therefore may well know more then wee that have none, but take all upon trust from our forefathers. (Williams 1973, 199)

Williams is subtle in his presentation. In the next paragraph he again explains how he thought it inappropriate to try to convert Miantonomi and his people before they had repented of "deade workes" and had "faith in God." While most of the Puritan leaders believed that evangelical efforts were necessary in order to help people achieve proper faith, Williams is careful to construct a case against evangelism and in favor of the practices of tolerance that he appears to adopt. The point of Miantonomi's brief dialogue seems more to assure the English Christian readers that Native American people are receptive to the claims of

Christianity while also presenting them as remaining committed to their own traditions. While Miantonomi seems to admit that the traditional beliefs could be wrong when challenged by knowledge acquired in other ways, he also seems to claim that becoming aware of other knowledge does not require the rejection of long-held belief. Anticipating later pragmatists, Miantonomi appears to suggest that meaning is more than truth.

The practices bound up with the process of *wunnégin* and the principle of interaction also serve to provide structure for relations within Narragansett communities. In his discussions of salutation, food, and sleep, Williams seems to rename *wunnégin* as the social principle of "civility" or "courtesie," where "courtesie" may be taken as a synonym for "nobleness, generosity, benevolence" as the *Oxford English Dictionary* suggests. Williams provides an instance. "Tawhítch mat petiteáyean? *Why come you not in?* . . . In this respect they are remarkably free and courteous, to invite Strangers in; and if any come to them upon any occasion, they request them to *come in,* if they come not in of themselves" (Williams 1973, 97). Implicit in the discussion is the idea that courtesy amounts to a kind of openness and willingness to share one's resources, ideas, time, and affection. Also implicit in the notion of courtesy instanced by Williams is the idea that courtesy is presumed mutual unless and until it is undermined by other factors. That Williams finds this principle a feature of Native culture not shared by European culture is reflected in his verse: "*The Courteous* Pagan *shall condemne* / Uncourteous Englishmen ,/ *Who live like Foxes, Beares and Wolves, / Or Lyon in his Den.* . . . *If Natures sons both* wild *and* tame, / *Humane and Courteous be: / How ill becomes it Sonnes of God / To want Humanity?*" (Williams 1973, 99). Williams himself, it seems, places *wunnégin* as the overarching context in terms of which he frames the *Key* and which, when established in practice, serves to frame the community he seeks.

The general context provided by the practices of welcoming strangers also seems to frame or perhaps rely on a central moral principle or rather a central set of expectations that help to frame interactions with the community. Williams finds these crucial expectations in the relationship between Canonicus, the senior sachem of the Narragansett, and Miantonomi, his nephew and secondary sachem. "Their agreement in the Government," Williams writes, "is remarkable: The old Sachim will not be offended at what the young Sachim doth; and the young Sachim will not doe what hee conceives will displease his Uncle" (Williams 1973, 201). The principle turns the Christian Golden Rule inside out. Where the Christian principle directs that people should do to others as they would have others do to them, the principle of the Narragansett locates the judgment of behavior in a context where individuals look to the interaction with others for standards; Miantonomi must try to know his uncle in order to behave well. At the same time, each person is also expected to trust other members of the community to do their share, to attend to each other, and behave in a way that recognizes the wishes and interests of others as well. In effect, the standard of behavior one looks toward is not within oneself but in interaction with others, and in accepting this standard one receives in exchange the trust of others to act in relation to the community. This is at once the sort of relationship generated through the practice of welcoming cannibals, and also the kind of relationship that serves to reinforce an ongoing respect for difference. This principle—call it the principle of *wunnégin*—is implicit in most of the other principles identified in Williams's *Key* and can be seen in the way Williams himself structures his responses to the doctrines and social policies of the surrounding European settlements.

The principle of *wunnégin* is also a central element in understanding the operation of the Narragansett attitude of meaning along the border between Native and European America. Although not an explicit part of the cannibal stories, it is clear, for example, that the interactive respect which characterizes the relationship between Miantonomi and his uncle also provides a pattern for the process of welcoming dangerous others into a community. Unlike patterns of assimilation or segregation, *wunnégin* establishes a pattern of mutual cooperation that at once preserves the distinctiveness of the participants and fosters their connectedness. The process does so not by trying to see others as if they were oneself, but by engaging in an active (and presumably experimental) process of attempting to see things as others do. Just as the principle appears to frame the response to outsiders in the cannibal stories, it also appears to ground the practices Williams advocates for preserving civil peace. What is often taken as a form of liberal tolerance in Williams's work is better understood as a combination of the principles he finds in Narragansett culture.

Finally, implicit in the Native notion of value as it emerges in the practices of *wunnégin* is the idea that what constitutes something good is not merely its conformity to a principle. Instead, it concretely contributes to the growth and well-being of those involved in the interaction. It is this aspect that is directly undermined by Josiah Cotton's notion of abstract good and what seems to be the basic reason for engaging in the practice of welcome in the first place. While Cotton's notion of *wunnégin* relies only on the relation of the "good" to God, *wunnégin* in its connection to the practice of welcoming strangers suggests that value emerges in a complex of relations. In the case of welcoming, of course, the process is itself framed as a process of establishing relations. This is implied as well by the use of the term "wunnêkesu," an adjectival form of the term "wunnégin," used for "proper" in the context of Williams's discussion of marriage and family in the *Key* (Williams 1973, 206). Presented in conjunction with the terms for loving, "Waumaûsu," and fruitful, "Muchickéhea," value seems to be found in developing relations that will sustain the family and the community. The locus of value, Williams suggests, is one's home place. "Nickquénum. *I am going home:* Which is a solemne word amongst them; and no man wil offer any hindrance to him, who after some absence is going to visit his Family, and useth the word *Nicquénum*" (Williams 1973, 117). The health or flourishing of the home place provides the central value frame. For Williams, this central value is called "sociablenesse". "The sociablenesse of the nature of man appears in the wildest of them, who love societie; Families, cohabitation, and consocation of houses and townes together" (Williams 1973, 128).

The commitment to establishing good relations in terms of *wunnégin* became formalized in the eighteenth century by members of the Massachusett Indian communities as an expectation about the proper relations between their people and the European colonials who came to surround them. This is well-illustrated in a series of documents written in Massachusett to record land transactions. Here, *wunnégin* in a variant form is taken to mean peace and friendship. In one case, for example, a sachem named Wompbamaog grants a piece of land to two women, Ales Setam and her sister, Kezia. He concludes his statement of their legal right to the land. "Wunnahtoae Ahtauhittich Micheme Yu Tahshin Ahsk," that is, "In peace may they own forever this amount of land" (Goddard and Bragdon 1988, 1: 125, 127). By connecting the practice of welcome and idea of good in the term for peace, "Wunnahtoae," and presenting it in the context of establishing land claims in both the Native and European worlds, Wompbamaog implies that an aspect of goodness will be not merely peace, but peaceful coexistence among recognizably different peoples.

The idea that *wunnégin* is bound up with a commitment to growth or the flourishing of particular communities is suggested by two entries in the *Key*. In one, the term for wealth is given as "wenawwêtu," combining the roots for "good" and "home." The term brings together two important aspects of Narragansett culture and does so in a way that suggests that success is not a matter of acquiring material goods or even acquiring eternal life, but rather is the concrete experience of a good home. To have a good home, on Williams's description, is to have a large, loving family and the resources necessary for it to flourish. This idea that what is good is a matter of growth is made clear in a letter of pro-

test sent by the Native people of Gay Head to the Indian commissioners of New England in 1749. They open their plea, "ne anue wannekik
[wunnégin] nukquennauwehukqunnan ongatog kottumm8ash nish
payom8ukkish," that is, "We need what (will) be better [or good] ("for
us") [in] other years that (will) come" (Goddard and Bragdon 1988, 1:
171, 173).[33] Here, what constitutes the "good" for other years is the possession of adequate lands and resources to sustain the Gay Head community. Here "goods" takes a most concrete form and amounts to a call
for survival. In short, Williams, in his familiarity with Narragansett culture, would have encountered not just a vision of a peaceful community,
but an alternative attitude, a way of understanding and acting in the
world. This alternative was one that viewed meaning as emerging from
interactions characterized by pluralism, framed by communities, and
evaluated in terms of growth.

33. Because of the lack of an accepted set of symbols to represent the Algonquian languages, Goddard and Bragdon (1988) used their own typography to represent the Massachusett documents. They used the character "8" to represent the "oo" sound as it would
be pronounced in the word "food."

CHAPTER SIX

Welcoming the Cannibals

HAD MIANTONOMI TOLD Williams a cannibal story as they sat across the fire on that cold January night, the contrast with Williams's own cultural notions of cannibalism may have helped explain to him the significance of the Narragansett's hospitality. After all, Williams was clearly an outsider and an outcast who came to Miantonomi in deepest winter from a people who had already proven to be disruptive and dangerous. From the Narragansett point of view, Williams was already a *Mohowaúgsuck,* that is, someone who can be welcomed and made part of the peace of the community despite differences in belief and interest. At the same time, from the perspective of the European colonials, Williams was also a cannibal of sorts—a dangerous and disruptive dissenter who must either completely transform his beliefs to accord with those of the group or be expelled. The different responses to his cannibal nature no doubt presented Williams with clear alternatives.

The Native response to strangers reflected in the *Mohowaúgsuck* stories stood in sharp contrast to comparable stories told among Europeans in America.[1] Cannibalism, of course, was a well-established feature of European traditions. In Greek mythology, Agamemnon's famous family, the House of Atreus, was cursed by cannibalism at its start. The Greek historian Herodotus describes a nation of cannibals to the north of the Black Sea. The early Christian church was accused of practicing ritual cannibalism by Roman authorities. Several of the early church fathers responded to the charge, including Tertullian, whose "Epistle to Scapula" Williams quotes in his own treatise on persecution (Williams 1848,

---

1. Alfred Cave provides a valuable summary of the English association of cannibalism and Native Americans (1996, 13–21).

14–15, 165–167). As Christianity became dominant in Europe, charges of cannibalism and practices of ritual murder came to be identified with Judaism instead. The connection became established, in part, as a consequence of the Christian belief in the magical power of blood as manifested in the transubstantiation of the elements in the Eucharist. Given the inherent power of the "blood of Christ," Christians themselves came to believe that their blood in particular must be a valuable commodity for consumption in certain Jewish rituals, including Passover, and in curing disease.[2]

The association of cannibalism with Judaism became public and formalized in a series of ritual murder trials during the twelfth through the sixteenth centuries. These trials, involving hearsay accusations against Jewish members of local communities and confessions obtained through torture, left the judges with little doubt about the guilt of the accused and the proper response. As R. Po-Chia Hsia summarizes in a discussion of a 1470 trial in the German town of Endingen, "The [confessions of the three accused] did not save them. Karl of Baden condemned all three to death. . . . [They] were stripped, wrapped in dry cowhide, tied to horsetails, dragged to their execution ground, and burnt. . . . Death by burning for a murder was exceptional. . . . Only heretics and black magicians were burnt. To Christians of the late fifteenth century, the Jews of Endingen embodied a despicable cross of both" (Hsia 1988: 26). The link between Judaism and cannibalism did not end in the years before Columbus's journeys to America, but it continued as a recognizable element of European culture. In 1600, for example, just three years before Williams was born, Shakespeare introduced his popular comedy *The Merchant of Venice.* Consistent with the expectations apparent in the German ritual murder trials, the protagonist is a Jewish moneylender who, in a bond for a substantial loan, asks that "the forfeit/ Be nominated for an equal pound/ Of your fair flesh, to be cut off and taken/ In what part of your body pleaseth me" (Shakespeare 1959, 43). Calling up the long-standing associations, when another character asks the moneylender, Shylock, what a pound of flesh is good for, he replies, "If it will feed nothing else, it will feed my revenge" (Shakespeare 1959, 71).

The association of Judaism with cannibalism, pervasive under Catholicism, persisted in the Protestant Reformation as well. Despite Martin Luther's initial stance of tolerance toward Judaism, his later writings reasserted the complex connections between Judaism, magic, and cannibalism, and joined them together with his condemnation of all "religions

---

2. See Hsia 1988, 8–12.

of the flesh." The Protestant Reformation was more than a reply to the hierarchies and ceremonies of the medieval church; it was also a reply to superstitious practices, witchcraft, and ritual murder. If true Christianity was a religion of faith and direct worship of God, then the embodied practices of Catholicism and Judaism must be the contrary, works of the devil to be found out and stopped. In his late works *On the Ineffable Name* and *On the Jews and Their Lies*, Luther reasserts a link between Judaism and practices of cannibalism and between Catholic ceremony and witchcraft.[3] It is not surprising that elements of the European conception of cannibalism and its connections with those who are outside the faith reemerge in immigrant America as witch hunts that recall in form and practice the ritual murder trials of the previous centuries in Europe.

Even as the European response to cannibals was imported to America, America was itself becoming identified with cannibalism. In Columbus's first account of the Americas cannibalism was an element of the description.[4] Vespucci's widely circulated letters further confirmed the idea that America was populated in part by cannibals, and later captivity narratives offered firsthand verification.[5] In 1557, for example, a German seaman named Hans Staden, with the help of a coauthor, recounted at length his captivity among the Tupi Indians of Brazil. In a process reminiscent of the one that came to associate Judaism with cannibalism, accounts of American cannibalism were rapidly offered and rapidly shared, often by tellings of apparently different incidents in nearly the same words.[6] Staden's account, for example, is nearly identical with a wide range of other accounts of American cannibalism which appear in the works of such diverse authors as Bartolomé de Las Casas and the geographer André Thevet. Whether any of the accounts are directly based on experience is unclear, but it is clear that cannibal stories were widely shared and very similar.

The two strands of European thinking about cannibalism, as Jewish and American, came together in the Northeast immigrant colonies. On one hand, it would have been "natural" for the American natives to be cannibals, not necessarily because of an expected primitivism, but because Native Americans were already associated with a lost tribe of Israel and therefore with Judaism. Daniel Gookin, writing in Massachusetts in the mid-seventeenth century, observes that "some conceive that [Native Americans] are of the race of the ten tribes of Israel, that Salmanasser

---

3. See Hsia 1988, 131–134.
4. See Columbus 1988, 14.
5. See Vespucci 1895, 11.
6. See Arens's discussion of Staden's narrative (1979, 22–40).

carried captive out of their own country . . . and that God hath, by some means or other, not yet discovered, brought them to America . . . and hath reduced them into such woeful blindness and barbarism."[7] He offers as evidence the conclusions of "historians" who write "that [the Natives of Peru and Mexico] used circumcision and sacrifices, though oftentimes of human flesh; so did the Israelites sacrifice their sons unto Moloch" (Gookin 1970, 2).

On the other hand, the prevalence of witchcraft "outbreaks" among the immigrants manifested, for example, in the Salem witch trials of 1692, seemed to confirm that Native people, like the Jews and Catholics, were in league with the devil.[8] Cotton Mather, in his description of one case of witchcraft, reports that the devil that appeared to the hapless victim had a "Figure of A Short and a Black Man. . . . [who] was not of a Negro, but of a Tawney, or Indian colour" (Burr 1914, 261). The victim, Mercy Short, further reported to Mather that "at their Cheef Witch-meetings, there had been present some French canadians, and some Indian Sagamores [leaders or sachems], to concert the methods of ruining New England" (Burr 1914, 281–282).[9] The association of Catholic Canadians and Native Americans in league to destroy the New England colonies brought together the worst fears of European Protestants: dangerous outsiders, known flesh-eaters, who sought to undermine the new Jerusalem. While Mercy Short was fortunate enough to be delivered from the devil by the efforts of Mather and his neighbors, others were less fortunate. Sharing the fate of the Jews convicted of ritual murder, twenty of these new cannibals were executed at Salem during 1692 and 1693.[10]

For Williams, the contrast between the cannibal stories of the Narragansett and the Europeans would have seemed ironic in the face of expectations that the "savages" of North America lacked civility and insight. Even though Williams himself sometimes exhibited a less-than-flattering view of the Narragansett lifestyle and ceremonial practices,[11] it was the New England colonies that proved to be uncivilized from his perspective. When found to be a dissenter in his own community, Wil-

---

7. Gookin cites II Kings 18:9–12 as his source (1970, 2).

8. Also see Cave 1996, 21–30.

9. Mercy Short, in addition to being one of the many women accused of witchcraft in Salem, was also the survivor of Indian captivity when she was a child (Burr 1914, 259).

10. Nearly two hundred people were accused of witchcraft during the "outbreak" of 1692–1693. Of those, twenty-seven people were convicted and nineteen executed by hanging. A twentieth person, after refusing to enter a plea, was also killed, in this case while being tortured (Karlsen 1987, 40–41). Significantly, the "witch hunt" raises important questions about colonial conceptions of gender. Nearly 75 percent of those accused and executed were women (see Karlsen 1987).

11. See Williams's *Key* (1973, 192), for example.

liams was first ordered to transform his behavior and his conscience according to the prescriptions of the magistrate, and when he refused he was banished. Such treatment, he argued later, is a breach of peace of the sort that emerges from the "wrong and preposterous way of suppressing, preventing, and extinguishing such doctrines and practices by weapons of wrath and blood, whips, stock, imprisonment, banishment, death, &c.; by which men commonly are persuaded to convert heretics, and to cast out unclean spirits" (Williams 1848, 53). It is his own community that rejects civility and a commitment to peace, and the so-called savages who remain committed in the face of disaster. Even as he was excluded from his colonial home, the Narragansett made room for him—not to convert him to their way of thinking, but to accommodate a stranger as part of the community, regardless of his history or beliefs. The cannibal stories and Narragansett practices of *wunnégin* may have made Williams recognize that he and his fellow immigrants were being recognized for what they were—dangerous outsiders—who were nevertheless granted an opportunity to become part of a broad American community. Williams concludes his discussion of government and justice in *A Key into the Language of America* with a verse from the indigenous American perspective ironically chastising the English: "*We weare no Cloaths, have many Gods, / And yet our sinnes are lesse; / You are the Barbarians, Pagans wild, / Your Land's the Wildernesse*" (Williams 1973, 204).

Miantonomi and his uncle responded to Williams's exile into their country by offering him a place to build a community for himself and those who were similarly rejected by the Massachusetts Bay Colony.[12] In a 1639 deed, Canonicus and Miantonomi confirmed their earlier grant and increased it. "We also, in consideration of the many kindnesses and services [Williams] hath continually done for us, . . . we do freely give unto him all that land from those rivers reaching to Pawtuxet river" (Knowles 1834, 107). As in the cases of hospitality toward cannibals, it would be difficult to imagine that either Miantonomi or Williams thought that the developing relationship between them was best understood as hospitality for its own sake. For Miantonomi, the coming of the English had at once helped to establish the Narragansett as a major power, but it had also been a disaster for Native people in general and for the flourishing international trade and culture along the Atlantic. Even if he did not outwardly identify the English in general and Williams in particular as *Mohowaúgsuck*, the general relationship between Native communities

---

12. In a letter written to Winthrop in 1638, Williams reports receiving Narragansett land as a gift (LaFantasie 1988, 165).

and the English would have suggested a similar pattern of response. In effect, it seems that Miantonomi may have been offering Williams a place to live not only for the sake of friendship or commonality of thought or interest, but because he had chosen to respond to the danger using the practices of *wunnégin.*

Williams perhaps understood something of this relationship because while it was clear to him that he need not adopt Native ways in order to coexist peacefully with the Narragansett and their allied nations, the relationship they established was one of reciprocal generosity:

> when the hearts of my countrymen and friends and brethren failed me, [God's] infinite wisdom and merits stirred up the barbarous heart of Canonicus to love me as his son and to his last gasp, by which means I had not only Miantonomi and all the lowest sachems my friends, but Ousamaquin also . . . ; and I never denied [Canonicus] or [Miantonomi] whatever they desired of me as to goods or gifts or use of my boats or pinnace, and the travels of my person, day and night, which, though men know not, nor care to know, yet the all-seeing Eye hath seen it. (Knowles 1834, 412)

In the contrasting responses to outsiders, the Narragansett and the English colonials provided competing conceptions of community and practices of interaction in the face of difference. While the colonial approach expected the elimination of that difference, the Narragansett conception included practices and a conceptual framework that could provide Williams with much more than a refuge—they provided him with a model for a pluralistic community.

Williams opens his argument for toleration in *The Bloudy Tenent of Persecution* by stating the twelve theses he will defend. While the general call is for doctrinal tolerance, the vision of a pluralist civil state becomes a necessary condition for achieving his goal. Recalling the diversity of the peoples on Massachusetts Bay and his own reception by the Narragansett, Williams says he will defend the claim that "*God* requireth not an *uniformity* of *Religion* to be *inacted* and *inforced* in any *civill state.*" Such uniformity, if enforced, "(sooner or later) is the greatest occasion of *civill Warre, ravishing* of *conscience, persecution* of *Christ Jesus* in his servants, and the *hypocrisie* and *destruction* of *millions of souls*" (Williams 1866, 3: 3–4). Much of the argument is focused on establishing a strict separation between spiritual and civil matters in order to make possible the wider field of a pluralist community. Once established, however, the Christian case for tolerance needs a still wider frame to accommodate the diverse community it demands. The problem is much like what Williams calls the "strange double picture" that arises when one asserts both the right of the church to assemble and practice as it sees fit and also asserts the power of government to govern matters of worship (Williams 1866, 3: 392–393). Here matters of "spirit" that determine the requirements of worship would be subject to the practical concerns of the "temporal community." To assert the control of one over the other leads to a confused conception of both spiritual and temporal matters. Neither the spiritual nor temporal point of view, Williams thinks, is an adequate perspective for governing a world in which both are important. A wider perspective is necessary and it is this that Williams develops by reconceptualizing the problem in terms of an analogy.

To argue that the civil magistrate should have authority for the conduct of worship or for religious leaders to have control over the governance of civil matters would be "as if the *Master* or *Governour* of a ship had power to judge who were true and fit officers, mariners, &c. for the managing of the Ship . . . and yet he should be an *usurper* if hee should abridge them of *meeting* and *managing* the *vessel* at their pleasure, when they please, and how they please, with and against his *consent*" (Williams 1866, 3: 394). By analogy, the two roles, ship owner and seaman, have different skills and interests. The ship owner is responsible for hiring the crew, securing a cargo, and so on, while the crew is responsible for sailing the ship. For the one to interfere with the other seems mistaken at best and disastrous at worst. A ship will operate best when those involved in its operation both attend to their interests and works while others do the same, each recognizing the other's concerns and trusting they will do their part. The analogy, Williams continues, will hold for Christians and non-Christians alike, and in this way the wider field of a pluralist community can be imagined. "All lawfull *Magistrates* in the World, both before the coming of *Christ Jesus,* and since, . . . are but *Derivatives* and *Agents* immediately derived and employed as *eyes* and *hands,* serving for the good of the whole: Hence they have and can have no more *Power,* than fundamentally lies in the *Bodies* or *Fountaines* themselves, which *Power, Might,* or *Authority,* is not *Religious, Christian,* &c. but natural, humane, and civill" (Williams 1866, 3: 398).[13] The magistrate, like the ship owner, is constrained and empowered by the interests served. With respect to the practices and interests of religion, a similar

---

13. Later, in *The Examiner Defended,* Williams identifies the common interests of human communities. "There are no generations of men, nor never were in the world, but by the dark light of nature, have condemned these four sins, *viz. Murther, Adultery, Theft, Lying,* as inconsistent to the converse of man with man: But all the Generation and Nations of men, have most constantly difference, and varied into many thousand differences about the true *God,* and his waies of worship, &c." (Williams 1963, 263).

relation holds. The civil or social context, in effect, coexists with and helps to sustain the practices of worship and belief. Such aspects, while demanded by God from a Christian perspective, can also be reformulated as part of an already complex human environment. Put succinctly, Williams concludes, "And hence it is true that a *Christian Captaine, Christian Merchant, Physitian, Lawyer, Pilot, Father, Master,* and (so consequently) *Magistrate,* &c., is no more *a Captaine, Merchant, Physitian, Lawyer, Pilot, Father, Master, Magistrate,* &c. than a Captaine, Marchant, &c. of any other Conscience or Religion" (Williams 1866, 3: 398–399). The resulting vision is of a plural community that at once affirms diversity of belief, occupation, and culture, including a diversity of overlapping limits that serve to constrain the actions and consequences of such a chaotic place. The "Christian Captaine" and the non-Christian or even anti-Christian captain nevertheless recognize a common ground of interest and function.[14] While Williams admits that a Christian captain may "act in [his] calling" to a "higher ultimate [end] from high principles," the non-Christian is not less a captain. The analogy that opens the community to pluralism also serves as the framing vision and the one that makes an explicit place for the otherwise excluded cannibals. "A *Pagan* or *Antichristian Pilot* may be as skilful to carry the Ship to its desired Port, as any *Christian Mariner* or *Pilot* in the World, and may performe that work with as much safety and speed" (Williams 1866, 3: 399).[15] In practice, the ship analogy provides Williams with an accessible European example of the principle of *wunnégin,* of establishing reciprocal and sustaining relations in a context of diverse and even conflicting interests, backgrounds, and beliefs.

The importance of the "ship of the commonwealth" analogy in framing Williams's conception of a community is made even clearer in his 1652 work *The Examiner Defended,* in which he summarizes much of the argument he proposes in *The Bloudy Tenent,* this time explicitly in terms of the analogy. "The *Ship* of the *Commonwealth,*" the book begins, "(like that gallant Ship now going forth, so called) must share her *weals* and *woes* in *common*" (Williams 1963, 203). If the Narragansett practices of *wunnégin* led to the peaceful coexistence of difference, the ship of the commonwealth reads like a description of the resulting community. "Now in a Ship there is the *whole,* and there is each *private Cabbin.* A

---

14. One might object that Williams is arguing for a kind of expert meritocracy with this emphasis on skill and function, but that is to read the issue of shared interests as a matter for the expert captain or lawyer alone. Just as the interests of the whole community govern the magistrate, so too the captain and lawyer must attend to the interests of those concerned with their work.

15. See Williams 1866, 3: 376–77 for several other examples of this analysis.

private good engageth our desires for the *publike,* and raiseth *cares* and *fears* for the due prevention of *common evils*" (Williams 1963, 203). The ship at once embodies commonality and difference while asserting their connection. The "private" world of the cabins engage desire for the public world, and the public world provides a frame and resources for addressing evil that affects the possibilities for flourishing "private" worlds. The problems faced by the community represent the potential for individual harm and also generate common concerns even as circumstances change. Shared circumstances require shared attention to the concerns, but not a uniformity of belief or practice. Williams continues, "[Not] to *study,* and not to *endeavour* the *common good,* and to exempt our selves from the sense of *common evil* is a *treacherous Baseness,* a *selfish Monopoly,* a kinde of *Tyranny,* and tendeth the destruction both of *Cabin* and *Ship,* that is, of *private* and *publike safety*" (Williams 1963, 203–204). The diversity does not, he thinks, stand in the way of particular beliefs and religious practices, including Christianity. In fact, while he is happy to "confess that all *Nations,* all *Peoples* . . . ought to *kiss the Son* [Jesus Christ]," he nevertheless believes in the value of a diverse world. "[W]hat a dreadful mistake is this," he asks, "that no people must live but *Christians?*" (Williams 1963, 204). Later, comparing civil leadership to the "Office of a Captain, or Master of a Ship at Sea," Williams says that such leadership ought to be "honoured and respected, paid and rewarded for [its] service" by the passengers regardless of their religious differences.

> But as to the *Consciences* of the Passengers, whether Jews, Turks, Persians, Pagans, Papists, Protestants, &c. whom he transports from Port to Port . . . I ask whether [the Captain goes] beyond the sphere of his *Activity,* if he act by any authoritative *restraining* them from their *own Worship,* or *constraining* them to *his?* And whether he have any more to do, but a shewing kindness and countenance, according to the quality and temper of his owne *Beliefe* and *Conscience?* (Williams 1963, 209)

In a world where "Jews, Turks, Persians, Pagans, [and] Papists" were most often viewed as evil and sometimes as cannibals, Williams asks that they be received with "kindness and countenance." And what goes for the metaphorical ship goes as well for communal life. Just as the Narragansett practices of *wunnégin* frame the idea of good as promoting flourishing communities, so too does Williams's notion of civility. Later, he is explicit. "But notwithstanding several *Religions* in one *Nation,* in one *Shire,* yea, in one *Family;* if men be either truly *Christian* . . . , or but truly *Civil,* and walk but by the rules of *Humanity* and *Civility;* Families, Townes, Cities, and Commonweals (in the midst of *Spiritual* Differences) may flourish" (Williams 1963, 263). Combining a Native vision of pluralism and European metaphors of the ship of the commonwealth, Williams joined Native and European practice and thought.

In the letter to the General Court of Massachusetts Bay written in October 1654 in an effort to avert war between the Massachusetts Bay Colony and the Narragansett, Williams explicitly identifies the Narragansett idea implicit in the "ship of the commonwealth" metaphor. "At my last departure for [England]," he writes, "I was importun'd by the Nariganset Sachims and especially by Nenekunat, to present their peticion to the high Sachims of England that they might not be forced from their Religion, and for not changing their Religion be invaded by War" (LaFantasie 1988, 2: 409). The Narragansett "peticion" is important in part because it confirms a Native starting place for the vision of a diverse community and in part because it represents an instance of the Narragansett people attempting to teach the Europeans an alternative way to understand themselves and their world. Williams continues, "With this their Peticion I acquainted (in private discourses) divers of the chiefe of our Nation, and especially his Highnes [Oliver Cromwell], who in many discourses I had with him, never exprest the least title [tittle] of displeasure." It is not clear that Cromwell's approval had any explicit policy implications, but it is clear that in their meeting Williams presented a Narragansett vision of a pluralist community and that the Narragansett leaders who asked for Williams to take the message to England can be seen as attempting to extend their well-established practices of *wunnégin* to an American environment that now included European outsiders, European cannibals.

Where the analogy of the ship provides a way to expand the pluralist community beyond Christianity, Williams also offers a range of crucial "internal" arguments in favor of toleration. These illustrate both the shape of his notion of tolerance as close to the Narragansett view and the ways in which Williams uses traditional Christian doctrine in its support. For example, despite the Puritan conviction that Christianity demanded assent to particular beliefs among all members of society, Williams argues that people need only behave with civility, that is, with a commitment to maintaining the peace of the community. Dissenters were neither to be banished nor forced to change their beliefs. Instead, the community would strive to maintain their membership in the community, asking only for their commitment to civil behavior. Using the New Testament parable of the wheat and tares, Williams argues that despite alternative interpretations, the parable reinforced his position.[16] He concludes:

16. See Matthew 13:24–30.

[In the parable] . . . the field is properly the world, the civil state, or commonwealth. . . . The tares here intended by the Lord Jesus, are anti-Christian idolaters. . . . The ministers or messengers of the Lord Jesus ought to
let them alone to live in the world, and neither to seek by prayer, or prophecy, to pluck them up before the harvest. . . . This permission or suffering
of them in the field of the world, is not for hurt, but for common good,
even for the good of the good wheat, the people of God. (Williams 1848,
89–90)

Just as the cannibals were to be welcomed among the Narragansett, Williams insists that the Narragansett, as "idolaters," be welcome among the
Christians.

Williams's interpretation of the parable of the wheat and tares marks
an important innovation from the established interpretations of the
time. These interpretations, authoritatively represented by John Calvin,
for example, hold that the field is to be understood as the church and
not the wider community. From this perspective, the tares or weeds il-
licitly planted by the "enemy" are to be left alone until the "harvest at
the end of the world." Calvin sees the central message not as a command
for tolerance, but as a reminder that there will always be weeds in the
wheat. He summarizes, "So long as the pilgrimage of the Church in this
world continues, bad men and hypocrites will mingle in it with those
who are good and upright" (Calvin 1981, 119).[17] Calvin discounts the
explanation of the parable that appears a few verses later in the Book of
Matthew.[18] He argues, for example, that Matthew's claim that "the field
is the world" does not refer to the world in general, but only to the
church and his claim that the tares are "created" by the "enemy" is properly understood as a reference to corruption and not to another creator.
Williams's interpretation emphasizes exactly what Calvin discounts. The
field is the world and good and bad seeds grow in accord with their
distinct origins.[19] If the parable is taken as a straightforward statement,
as Williams proposes, scripture directs believers to set aside evangelism
and its counterparts, excommunication and capital punishment, in recognition of the predetermination of salvation and, by extension, to focus
on worldly efforts to promote the growth of a diverse civil community.
In effect, the parable of the wheat and tares is transformed into grounds

17. John Cotton, whose critique of Williams is at the center of Williams's treatise *The Bloudy
Tenent of Persecution,* adopts Calvin's interpretation of this passage (see Williams 1848, 21).
18. See Matthew 13:35–43.
19. This point is strenuously opposed by the more recent commentator F. W. Beare,
who says that "this picture is pure myth—human beings are not seen as individuals with
personal character, capable of progress or degeneration, but as belonging to one of two
classes, according to their origin in the Son of man or in the devil" (Beare 1981, 312).

for a practice of cultural interaction that closely parallels the proper response to cannibals in the Narragansett tradition.

In order to reinforce the double claim that tolerance is possible for
non-Christians and that tolerance is more than a disinterested stance
toward difference, Williams develops the Old Testament example of
Artaxerxes. Artaxerxes was a king of Persia who, after the people of
Israel returned from their exile in Babylon, ordered that the Jews be
supported in the reestablishment of their religion and the rebuilding of
the Temple.[20] Even though Artaxerxes was not a Jew, he nevertheless
demanded that the Persians assist in the rebuilding and that the Jews
themselves take seriously their own religious traditions. As Artaxerxes
commands in his letter to Ezra, "according to the wisdom of your God
which is in your hand, appoint magistrates and judges who may judge all
the people in the province . . . all such as know the laws of your god; and
those who do not know them, you shall teach" (Ezra 7:25). For Williams,
Artaxerxes provides a model for a tolerant magistrate who will not only
tolerate different beliefs and practices, but will actively encourage them.
"What Law was the Law of *Artaxerxes* the *King*?" he asks. "[W]as it of
commanding the *Jewes* to his *Worship* and *Conscience,* in an *Uniformity* of
Worship to the *Nation* where they were captive?" It was, on the king's part,
"a Law of *Toleration* and *Freedome* to practice theire own *Religion, Conscience,* and *Worship,* and that with favourable *Incouragement* from himself"
(Williams 1963, 276). What is striking about Williams's use of Artaxerxes is that it is one of the few instances of overt toleration in the Old
Testament and it is tolerance practiced by someone not of the chosen
people. Against the varied examples of intolerance by the chosen people,
including the intolerance shown by Moses and Aaron, Williams selects a
Persian king as a proper model of tolerance. Further, while the tolerance
exhibited in the story is of the chosen people (which might seem appropriate from the perspective of those interested in the progress of human
salvation), Williams uses the relations to illustrate tolerance for outsiders. He claims a pagan king as a model for a Christian magistrate and
the chosen people for inclusion on his list of non-Christian others: "Jews,
Turks, Persians, Pagans, [and] Papists." Artaxerxes is, in fact, a fitting
type for Williams, a cannibal among cannibals on the borders of Christianity trying to shape a new and flourishing community.

In the end, Williams brings his conception of community back to
the problems of Christianity and those of nonbelievers. The relations in
such a community he likens to relationships between "a body or college

20. See Ezra 6 and 7.

of physicians in a city" or "a corporation, society, or company of East India or Turkey merchants . . . in London." The companies carry on their business, "hold their courts, keep their records, hold disputations, and in matters concerning their society may dissent, divide, break into schisms and factions, sue and implead each other at the law, yea, wholly break up and dissolve into pieces or nothing, and yet the peace of the city not be in the least measure impaired or disturbed" (Williams 1848, 46). The city continues to provide a sustaining frame that does not depend upon the particular spiritual or religious commitments of the groups or the individuals that make it up, and the city is sustained by a mutual interest in peace.

Williams cites the example of the city of Ephesus discussed by Paul in his letter to the Ephesian church. In this case, Christians were one group among many that made up the city. "Now suppose," Williams says, "that God remove the candlestick [of Christianity] from Ephesus, yea, though the whole worship of the city of Ephesus should be altered, yet, if men be true and honestly ingenuous to city covenants, combinations, and principles, all this might be without the least impeachment or infringement of the peace of the city" (Williams 1848, 47). In short, Williams adopts the language of Christianity and European politics to explain a conception of community remarkably like that of the Narragansett. In his response to the most difficult problem for such a community, that is, the presence of "Jews, Turks, Persians, Pagans [and] Papists," he rejects the European model of banishment and death in favor of something like the Narragansett model of *wunnégin*. The key to this alternative model is suggested in Williams's own *Key:* "[The Native people of the Northeast] have a modest Religious perswasion not to disturb any man, either themselves *English, Dutch,* or any in their Conscience, and worship, and therefore say: Aquiewopwaúwash, Aquiewopwaúwock. *Peace, hold your peace*" (Williams 1973, 193).[21]

Williams's adoption of the conception of a plural community based in part on a Narragansett model brought with it a range of commitments. At its core, the "ship of the commonwealth" described by Williams is framed by the principles that suggest the later development of pragmatism and begins to make clear an alternative attitude of meaning that seems grounded in Native thought and practice. The Narragansett atti-

---

21. Later, in *The Bloudy Tenent,* Williams makes an even more explicit connection. Describing the limits of civil authority, he writes "that no persons, papists, Jews, Turks, or Indians, be disturbed at their worship, a thing which the very Indians abhor to practice toward any" (Williams 1848, 217).

tude manifests a commitment both to the role of community as a context for meaning and to the value of pluralism. These framing commitments are supported by a commitment to the expectation that meaning is a matter of interaction and by an expectation that value is a matter of the way things and events contribute to the flourishing of the community in all its diversity. Unlike the colonial commitment to progress, the attitude displayed by the Narragansett and adopted by Williams favors a notion of flourishing that is relative to the community at hand, its opportunities and difficulties. There is, of course, much to be said about both the European influences that play a role in Williams's work and the ways in which the Narragansett people were themselves influenced by their contact with the European immigrants. Nevertheless, it remains that the vision of community and its underlying commitments in the Narragansett tradition and in Williams's work are strikingly different from the vision of community that came to dominate the Anglo-American philosophical tradition and the mainstream of American thought. This difference is well-demonstrated by considering the points of contrast between Williams's conception of a pluralist community and John Locke's conception of a tolerant community as presented in his *Letter Concerning Toleration*.

Published only forty-five years after Williams published his *Key into the Language of America* and *The Bloudy Tenent of Persecution*, Locke's *Letter Concerning Toleration* stands as a crucial argument for the toleration of difference in Western liberal society. Since both Williams and Locke make related arguments for tolerance, they are often associated. Perhaps because the bulk of Williams's argument appears grounded in theological doctrine, Locke's argument is generally accepted as the more enduring version. Despite their apparent similarities, however, the two arguments are substantially different, and their differences help display the alternative attitudes, the colonial and the indigenous.

Locke's argument is formed over a familiar pair of expectations, one regarding the nature of truth and the other regarding the nature of human beings. Following something like the colonial commitment to the reduction of meaning to a single timeline and a single hierarchy of value, Locke assumes with most of the English philosophical tradition that truth, despite difficulties accessing it, forms a single consistent system. Just as the history of God's wonders serves as the ground for Mather's *Magnalia* and the story of human progress forms the ground in Jefferson's *Notes* and Bancroft's *History*, the independent nature of truth serves as the ground for Locke's letter on toleration. This expectation that truth is a single consistent system provides both the crucial justification for toleration and its chief challenge. From the standpoint of truth, toleration is simply a moral requirement. Locke opens his argument by observing that Christianity itself, both in the way salvation occurs for individuals alone and in its moral prescriptions of charity and kindness, demand that Christians be tolerant. The conclusion, however, leads to a problem for the tolerance it demands. As in the "double picture" faced by those who claim civil authority over religious practices, the expectations about the nature of truth seem to undermine the diversity implied by tolerance. The challenge for Locke is to accommodate difference in the face of the expectation that in the end there is, as he puts it, "one truth [and] one way to heaven" (Locke 1955, 19).

The possibility for toleration emerges from the second expectation, that human nature must be understood in terms of a set of dualisms. From an ontological perspective, human beings are to be understood as composed of two substances: body and soul, or consciousness. In the temporal world of experience, body and soul work together and are experienced as a single being. But given the potential longevity of the soul and its separation from the troubles that plague the body, the soul has a special status, and its care stands as one's primary concern.[22] From the perspective of knowledge, the body-and-soul dualism leads to a parallel dualism in kinds of knowledge. Some things, things encountered through the senses, generate ideas that serve as sources for what the soul can know. Other ideas, however, those concerned with non-material things such as God, do not come through the senses but must be received directly by means of revelation. The result is two broad categories of knowledge: knowledge that is grounded in the senses and reflection on ideas of the senses, and knowledge that is acquired directly. This dual epistemology leads as well to a dual conception of realms of activity. Those that concern the body and the body and soul together relate to a public realm of knowledge and experience. Science occurs in this realm by means of systematic study, and its experimental method relies on its being a public process. Those activities related to the soul, however, are private. The result of these ontological and epistemological dualisms is a conception of human nature that emphasizes individual autonomy and universal rights. Under this model, individuals are capable of salvation and so have special standing, while their humanity provides a framework of rights and duties in terms of which individual salvation may be sought.

The possibility of tolerance emerges in recognition of the autonomy of individuals. Since the primary goal of human life is the care of a potentially everlasting soul, each particular soul is an independent respon-

---

22. See Locke 1959, Book II, Chapter XXVI, on "Identity and Diversity" for a discussion of personal identity and the role played by consciousness or the soul.

sibility and brings a vested self-interest that overrides any other concern. "[N]o man can so far abandon the case of his own salvation as blindly leave to the choice of another," he writes. "All life and power of true religion consist in the inward and full persuasion of the mind" (Locke 1955, 18). Given the autonomy of the search for salvation and the diversity of human experience, it follows that a diversity of churches would emerge to support the diversity of efforts to find salvation.[23] As a result, churches, in all this diversity, are to be understood as "voluntary societ[ies] of men, joining themselves together of their own accord in order to the public worshipping of God in such a manner as they judge acceptable to Him, and effectual to the salvation of their souls" (Locke 1955, 20). Attempts to control such societies or dictate truths that constitute salvation violate the logic of the separation of body and mind and its implications for salvation.

However, the crucial argument in favor of toleration relies on the implications of the epistemic dualism. For Locke, "There is only one of these [religious modes] which is the true way to eternal happiness: but in this great variety of ways that men follow, it is still doubted which is the right one" (Locke 1955, 31). Because the relevant knowledge is not the kind of knowledge one can acquire through the senses and reflection, such knowledge is ultimately to be gained by each person alone. Gaining such knowledge, however, is problematic. Certainty, for Locke, is a matter of the agreement or disagreement of ideas, and so certainty is dependent upon the ideas that come to the soul through experience or revelation. The origin of ideas and their outcomes are themselves inherently uncertain. Ideas gained through the senses are subject to the vicissitudes of finite material beings. Ideas gained through revelation are subject only to confirmation in comparison with other ideas. Ideas that come through the senses may be inaccurate pictures of the world, because the senses are limited and subject to deception. Ideas that apparently come through revelation may not be revelation at all. As a result, human knowledge is fallible. Given the importance of knowledge regarding the eternal status of the soul and the risk of error, it must fall to each individual to make his or her own choice about what to believe and how to worship. Suppose, Locke asks, that a prince knows better the way to salvation. In business, he observes, one might be willing to take the advice of a prince, since if he is wrong, he has the wherewithal to restore the lost wealth and allow one to begin again. With respect to salvation,

---

23. See Locke 1959, Book II, Chapter XXII, Of Mixed Modes, and Book III, Chapter V, Of the Names of Mixed Modes and Relations, for a discussion of the way diverse experience generates diverse ideas.

the outcome is final. "If there I take the wrong course," Locke observes, "if in that respect I am once undone, it is not in the magistrate's [or prince's] power to repair my loss, to ease my suffering, nor to restore me in any measure, much less entirely, to a good estate" (Locke 1955, 32). Given the human potential for error and what is at stake in the knowledge of God and salvation, the possibility for religious difference is crucial and grounds the case for a tolerant community.

The vision of tolerance is a powerful one in Locke, but it is a limited one. Although his argument is often viewed as general, Locke himself confines the scope of the argument from the beginning of his discussion. "Since you are pleased to inquire what are my thoughts about the mutual toleration of Christians in their different professions of religion," the letter begins, "I must needs answer you freely that I esteem that toleration to be the chief characteristic mark of the true church" (Locke 1955, 13). The focus on toleration within Christianity is confirmed by his discussion of those who are excluded from the tolerant community. Locke concludes the letter by describing four groups who are not to be tolerated by any state. The first excluded group includes those who have "opinions contrary to human society, or to those moral rules which are necessary to the preservation of civil society" (Locke 1955, 50). The second group Locke would exclude is made up of those who demand tolerance for themselves but deny it to others. The third group includes those who are members of a church "which is constituted upon such a bottom that all those who enter it do thereby *ipso facto* deliver themselves up to the protection and service of another prince" (Locke 1955, 51). The fourth category is more straightforward. Tolerance is not to be granted to those "who deny the being of a God" (Locke 1955, 52). While one may argue that Locke's tolerance ought to extend to at least some of these groups, Locke himself makes the case that given his starting principles, it is right to provide for this range of exclusions. For Locke, the first two groups most clearly represent the potential to undermine the ideal of a tolerant public, in effect, ruining salvation for everyone by potentially preventing the free search for one's own salvation. The third category carries with it a similar problem, because those who are loyal to some particular community have the potential to impose limits on their commitment to humanity in general (and so become intolerant) and to one's own salvation (because loyalty implies accepting someone else's beliefs as one's own). Atheists need not be tolerated either, because they represent a denial of a blatant truth. The consequence is, as Locke suggests, that such people cannot be trusted, and a failure of trust threatens the integrity of maintaining a tolerant public. "Promises, covenants, and oaths, which are the bonds of human society," he explains, "can have no hold upon an atheist. The taking away of God, though but even in thought, dissolves all" (Locke 1955, 52).

Williams's ideal of a plural community stands in strong contrast to Locke's notion of toleration on a number of points. Most important, while Locke begins with a supreme commitment to a singular framework for meaning and value, Williams begins with a supreme commitment to maintaining a peaceful and plural community. While Locke needs to find an argument to accommodate tolerance, Williams begins, in effect, on the other side. Tolerance is already expected as he begins *The Bloudy Tenent* and is made explicit at the beginning of *The Examiner Defended*, where the vision of community is presented as "the ship of the commonwealth." As a result, Williams's arguments are not arguments of the same sort as Locke's. In order to make tolerance plausible for those who share his starting expectations, Locke must argue for the necessity of toleration. Williams, in contrast, does not argue for the necessity of tolerance but focuses largely on showing that peaceful communities whose diversity includes more than varieties of Christianity are possible. The "ship of the commonwealth" metaphor is straightforward. In ordinary experience, one can see the possibility of a pluralist community. The metaphor does not carry with it some logical necessity, that if a ship can carry people with different beliefs so a community must be tolerant, but rather it is an appeal to recognize the possibility. In almost the same way that a cannibal story appeals to the possibility of responding to strangers with *wunnégin*, Williams offers a model of peace that makes a kind of experimental claim on his audience. His treatment of Native people in the *Key*, particularly the passages comparing Native people and Europeans, makes a similar argument. Tolerance is possible, he seems to say, and here is a model. Even as Locke argues for the necessity of a limited tolerance in service of the colonial attitude, Williams makes a very different sort of case for a peaceful community framed against the background of a radically different set of expectations. Finally, and perhaps most importantly, this sort of argument tries to reach beyond the "strange double picture" of offering a doctrinal argument in favor of doctrinal differences. By appealing to the experiences of human association and human possibilities, Williams can offer an open-ended case for trying pluralism and a model for maintaining it in changing circumstances. The cannibal stories as well as the arguments implicit in the practices of *wunnégin* propose a similar case.

At the same time, Locke and Williams are not completely at odds. It can be argued that Williams would accept Locke's first two categories of exclusion. In doing so, however, he would justify the exclusions in a different way. For example, it is not the case that Williams would exclude anyone who appeared to have "opinions contrary to human society or to those moral rules which are necessary for the preservation of society" (Locke 1955, 50). Anne Hutchinson, for example, clearly held such ideas as far as the Massachusetts Bay Colony and its leadership were concerned.[24] When Hutchinson and her followers were banished in 1638, they fled to the settlement of Aquidneck near Providence in the Rhode Island Colony. Despite letters from Winthrop condemning Hutchinson, Williams nevertheless talked with her at length and served as an intermediary between her and the Massachusetts Bay Colony.[25]

Not long after Hutchinson arrived at Aquidneck, Samuel Gorton, another exile from Boston, arrived at Providence and asked for shelter. Upon his arrival, however, he began to encourage other citizens of Providence to rise up against the overtly tolerant leadership of the colony and adopt his own version of evangelical Christianity. Williams and several other citizens of Providence worked to prevent Gorton from becoming enfranchised. The argument against Gorton was a difficult one for Williams, but he felt that Gorton had gone too far and threatened the survival of the wider community. In a letter to Winthrop, Williams reports that Gorton "is now bewitching and bemaddening poore Providence, both with his foule and uncleane censures of all the Ministers of this Country . . . and also denying all visible and externall Ordinances in depth of Familisme."[26] The problem, as Williams summarized it, was Gorton's "uncivill and inhumane practices" (LaFantasie 1988, 1: 21). Denied full citizenship at Providence, Gorton negotiated for a tract of land nearby from the Narragansett and established his own settlement. Significantly, the establishment of a separate community was the best solution. Gorton and Williams became friends over the years and aided each other in defending against the Massachusetts Bay Colony's efforts to bring Rhode Island under its control.[27] What marks the difference in approaches to the restrictions that Locke identifies is that while Locke establishes the exclusions in general, Williams adopts a case-by-case analysis where the standard of exclusion is not inconsistency with *a priori*

24. Given his argument for toleration, Locke might also have advocated for tolerance of Hutchinson's beliefs since she argued against the doctrinal requirements imposed by the Massachusetts Bay Colony on its residents. At the same time, from the perspective of Governor Winthrop there is little doubt that Hutchinson fit Locke's description of "such a degree of madness" (Locke 1955, 50) that she ought to be excluded from society.

25. See Williams's letter to Governor Winthrop, April 16, 1638 (LaFantasie 1988, 1: 149–150).

26. Familism is a version of Christianity that argued against predestination and original sin and in favor of direct communion with God. See Williams 1981, 32–33.

27. See LaFantasie's discussion of Gorton (LaFantasie 1988, 1: 208–215).

expectations about what will or will not undermine the community. Instead, Williams appears to have used a standard based on whether or not, in the present case, the general health and growth of the community would be promoted or undermined. Gorton was denied full citizenship because he did not respond to the welcome given by Providence. He was, as Williams put it, "uncivill." The response, however, was not unconditional exclusion, but a kind of negotiated settlement that held close to tolerance while it imposed some separation to preserve the peace of the community.

Although Williams would agree that some people ought to be excluded in various ways from a pluralist community, he would clearly have rejected Locke's third and fourth categories of exclusion. Locke's argument for the exclusion of atheists depends largely on the expectation that the truth of God's being is part of a single system of truths. To deny one truth and so to accept as true a single falsehood opens the door to every falsehood. While one's salvation is dependent upon one's particular knowledge of God, that God exists is a truth that is apparent to any reasonable person.[28] Should atheists work to undermine the possibility of belief in God for others, Williams would clearly object. But atheism on its own account, as a set of beliefs and practices, could be no *a priori* ground for exclusion.

When Locke excludes those who are loyal to a "foreign prince," he bases his exclusion on the idea that human beings can be understood in two ways only: as human beings and as individuals. The idea of loyalty to a group outside the tolerant public, Locke proposes, is impermissible on the grounds that it undermines individuality. For Williams, such an argument itself carries the danger of undermining the possibility of a plural community. This is perhaps best illustrated in Williams's last published work, *George Foxx Digged Out of His Burrows,* his critique of the doctrines of the Religious Society of Friends, the Quakers. The work was a summary by Williams of a public debate between him and representatives of the Quakers held at Newport in August 1671. For years, Williams's colony had gained a reputation as a haven for those who dissented from the rigid doctrines of the surrounding colonies. Along with people like Hutchinson and her followers, the Quakers also came to establish communities in Rhode Island. Ironically, the Quakers, who have come to have a well-deserved reputation themselves for tolerance and a strong commitment to social justice, came under attack by Williams. For Williams, the problem was that the Quakers, while they dissented from

28. See Locke 1959, Book I, Chapter III.

Puritan doctrines and advocated the equality of human beings, did so at the expense of the relations that join people into distinctive and sustaining communities. What is more, by militantly advocating Quaker doctrine and opposing all others, they undermined the possibility of maintaining a peaceful community because, again, they denied the value of human association grounded in distinctive belief.

Williams grounded his critique of Quaker doctrine in the work of one of their recognized leaders, George Fox, in particular in his book *The Great Mystery of the Great Whore Unfolded; and Anti-Christ's Kingdom Revealed into Destruction,* published in 1659. According to Williams, Quakers argued in favor of the equality of all human beings in their relationship with God. Each human being, in effect, was equally imbued with the spirit, no matter how profane or greedy or saintly the person appeared. Commitment to doctrines which admitted distinctions or suggested that some were better able to commune with God or which suggested the efficacy of ceremony were not only mistaken, but ought to be given up as false belief. Quaker advocacy of peace and justice was a direct consequence of the conclusion that every individual possesses the "light" or spirit of God. Williams's objection to this doctrine came from two directions. First, by focusing on the value of individuals, the doctrine had the effect of undermining the importance of connections with others. The importance of shared belief and of distinctive ceremonial worship was replaced by a formless interaction between individuals and God. Such advocacy of the individual, on Williams's view, was disastrous in that it set aside sustaining relations with others and the importance of others in interpreting religious and community experience, while making each person the sole judge and interpreter of humanity and God.

Williams makes this point clearly as he identified Quakers as sharing a view common with the "papists." "The Quakers are Papists," he says, "in that Spirit of Infallibility which they arrogate to themselves, pretending that the holy Spirit shall lead them into all Truth, speak Immediately in them, [for Quakers] all men have this spirit and need no Teacher, and yet what a horrible Contradictious noise is there of the Quakers, Apostles, Messengers, Ministers, Preacher" (Williams 1866, 5: 203–204). While Williams is quick to challenge the Quakers and the Catholics internally on matters of interpretation of their common Christianity, he challenges the Quakers more broadly on grounds that radical individualism leads at best to "horrible contradictious noise" and at worst to coercion and persecution. The "teacher," that is, the mediating role of others in forming beliefs and the consequent bonds of community are broken when teachers are replaced with the supreme confidence that individuals can know the truth "immediately." Of the demand to dissolve the communal aspect of belief he asks, "What is this but to cheat poor Birds with the chaff & fallacy of dividing the Body from the soul, the Letter from the Meaning, the Instrument or Tool from the Workman or Husbandman using it, the Gospel or glad news from believing of it" (Williams 1866, 5: 296).

At the same time, even as the doctrine directs people away from the importance of lived connections and shared belief, the practical consequence of valuing the individual alone is that it has concrete implications for how people live their lives. He concludes, "The spirit of Quakers tends mainly to the reducing of Persons from civility to Barbarism" (Williams 1866, 5: 307) where "barbarism" is not to be identified with Native ways of life, but rather with cannibalism and the dissolution of community, features already associated with the English colonies that banished Williams. Despite the implicit tolerance in the Quaker recognition of the presence of God in all people, the result, according to Williams, is potentially no different. Williams observes that, even as the Catholics and Quakers in America cry out against persecution, their own communities call for the persecution of those who do not share their beliefs. Just as persecution by the Puritans undermines the possibility of a peaceful community and flourishing life, so too do the commitments of the Quakers, he concludes, lead to the destruction of community. The "*Soul-Freedom*" advocated by Williams begins from an attitude focused on the life of a community which is overtly diverse and overtly committed to its diversity. Diversity in this case promotes the possibility that all persons can pursue their salvation in the company of others and in a non-coercive environment that will sustain them. Quaker doctrine fails both ways by severing relations and fostering coercion. Yet, while he criticizes the Quaker views, he does so in a way that does not demand their end, but rather reciprocal respect. It is only in this context, Williams believes, that people can flourish and find their salvation.

While it is clearly not the case that the ideas of tolerance advocated by Williams are the same as those offered later by Locke, it is clear that Williams's ideas are quite similar to the ideas of tolerance implicit in the Narragansett attitude. He recalls the Native attitude this way: "It is commonly known that as their garments hang loose about their Bodyes, so hangs their *Religion* about their Souls: so that (to my knowledge) they are so far from hindring any to come to God" (Williams 1866, 5: 258). While he believes that their religion is mistaken ("when they have seen the grave and solemn Worship of the English, they have often said of themselves and their own, that they are all one *Dogs* in comparison of the *English*" (Williams 1866, 5: 258)), their attitude of openness, of wearing "religion" loosely enough, is the key both to the maintenance of civil peace and the possibility of individual salvation. The Quakers, as well as the Puritan leadership, go wrong when they seek the latter without the former. The connection between the Narragansett attitude and the one evidenced by Williams emerges in the context of his experience in the border town of Providence and his commitment to the possibility of the coexistence of differences in a peaceful society. In sum, while Locke and Williams share an interest in toleration, their ways of understanding its meaning remain radically different. Locke's vision of toleration is comparable to the one that emerges in the Americas in the tradition grounded in the colonial attitude. Williams's vision seems framed by an alternative attitude much like the one already present in the philosophy of the Narragansett people.

Despite Williams's efforts, the European response to cannibalism and its attendant attitude became dominant. In 1642, John Winthrop, then the governor of the Massachusetts Bay Colony, received an unsigned letter describing a conspiracy to unite the Native peoples of the Northeast into a confederation that could destroy the rapidly growing English colonies. At the center of the conspiracy, according to the unnamed source, was an argument and plan credited to Miantonomi. In 1660, Lion Gardener, an engineer who helped design colonial fortifications, reported the speech Miantonomi gave to the Native people of Long Island:

> for so are we all Indians as the English [are English], and say brother to one another; so must we be one as they are, otherwise we shall all be gone shortly, for you know our fathers had plenty of deer and skins, our plains were full of deer, as also our woods, and of turkies, and our coves full of fish and fowl. But these the English having gotten our land, they with scythes cut down the grass, and with axes fell the trees; their cows and horses eat the grass, and their hogs spoil our clam banks, and we shall all be starved; therefore it is best for you to do as we, for we are all Sachems from east to west, both Moquakues and Mohauks joining with us, and we are all resolved to fall upon them all at one appointed day . . . and the next day fall on and kill men, women, and children, but no cows, for they will serve to eat till our deer be increased again. (Gardener 1833, 154–155)

Alarmed by the rumor of a conspiracy and its similarity to the beginnings of the Pequot War a few years before, Governor Winthrop asked Miantonomi to come before the leadership of the Massachusetts colony. As a long-time ally of the colony, Miantonomi responded to Winthrop's request and met with the commissioners in September 1642. After negotiating rules of the proceedings, Miantonomi gave "divers reasons, why we should hold him free of any such conspiracy, and why we should conceive it was a report raised by [Uncas, a rival of Miantonomi and a leader of the English-allied Mohegan Nation]. . . . in conclusion he did accommodate himself to our satisfaction" (Winthrop 1996, 410).

In the early summer of 1643, Williams departed for England to defend his title to Providence. In August, fighting broke out between Uncas and his allies and Miantonomi's people. In the ensuing battle, Uncas defeated Miantonomi and captured him. Consistent with his pledged relationship with the colonies, Uncas turned to the colonies for advice in settling the matter. Governor Winthrop, who only the year before had dismissed charges of conspiracy against Miantonomi as a rumor begun by Uncas, now reported that Miantonomi was to be executed. Among the reasons, Winthrop states that "it was now clearly discovered to us, that there was a general conspiracy among the Indians to cut off all the English, and that Miantunnomoh was the head and contriver of it. [Second,] he was of a turbulent and proud spirit, and would never be at rest" (Winthrop 1996, 472). The newly formed Commissioners of the United Colonies passed judgment that Uncas ought to "put such a false and blood-thirsty enemy to death, but in his own jurisdiction, not in the English plantations" (Pulsifer 1859, 11). They further recommended that "all mercy and moderation be shewed, contrary to the practice of the Indians who exercise tortures and cruelty" (Pulsifer 1859, 11–12). Even as Williams was writing his *Key into the Language of America* based on his conversations with Miantonomi and Canonicus, Uncas's brother "clave [Miantonomi's] head with a hatchet, some English being present. And that the Indians might know that the English did approve of it, they sent 12 or 14 musketeers home with Onkus [Uncas] to abide a time with him for his defense" (Winthrop 1996, 473).

Years later, in 1675, Metacom built an alliance among the Indian nations surrounding the Massachusetts colonies and attempted to regain autonomy for the Native nations nearby. William Apess, a Pequot orator writing in the 1820s, gives a version of a speech by Metacom from the beginning of the conflict:

> Brothers, you see this vast country before us. . . . Brothers, . . . you now see the foe before you, that they have grown insolent and bold; that all our ancient customs are disregarded; the treaties made by our fathers and us are broken, and all of us insulted; . . . our brothers murdered before our eyes, and their spirits cry to us for revenge. Brothers, these people from the unknown world will cut down our groves, spoil our hunting and plant-

ing grounds, and drive us and our children from the graves of our fathers, and our council fire, and enslave our women and children. (Apess 1992, 295)

Following the patterns established in the cannibal stories, the failure of *wunnégin* to establish a flourishing pluralist community gave way to another strategy. Within a year, however, Metacom and thousands of his people were dead and thousands of the survivors were refugees. As Metacom's (King Philip's) War began, Williams met with a delegation of the Native alliance outside Providence and tried to convince them to suspend the war. He argued, in part, for continued tolerance and support, but the young leaders of the alliance were determined to regain their lands and were confident they would succeed. A delegate replied, "You have driven us out of our own Countrie and then pursued us to our Great Miserie, and Your own, and we are Forced to live upon you." Williams replied, "I told them there were Wayes of peas [peace]" (LaFantasie 1988, 723). When the delegate asked what ways there were, Williams could only offer to go to Boston and negotiate. According to one narrative, the delegates concluded by telling Williams "that he was a good Man, and had been kinde to them formerly, and therefore would not hurt him" (Lincoln 1913, 87). The conference ended as the settlement of Providence was burned to the ground. Williams died in the winter of 1683, poor, forgotten by the European colonists except as an eccentric firebrand, and separated from the Native communities he had known.

While the Narragansett vision of a diverse and peaceful society ended in war, American experience at the border between European colonization and Native communities continued to be marked by reciprocal influence. Even as King Philip's War ended, new liaisons were being established between the Haudenosaunee people and second- and third-generation European immigrants that would lead to new possibilities as Native and European ways of thinking and cultural forms continued to interact and develop. The close examination of the case of Miantonomi and Roger Williams suggests four lessons that can help to frame further philosophical investigation.

First, the source of Williams's distinctive philosophical views may be less mysterious than commentators have found. While it is possible to see his conception of community as an original creation, it is also possible to see it as the product of philosophical reflection in the complex environment of the border between European and Native American cultures. Second, even as Williams presents his philosophical conception of a pluralistic community in terms drawn from the European Christian tradition, the means of presentation are only part of the history of the view. Williams's conception also emerges from and returns to the particularities of his own experience that is marked in part by sustained contact and friendship with Native people. If, as the evidence suggests, Williams did more than talk, that is, if he also listened to Miantonomi and others, he was clearly in a position to learn from the Narragansett tradition. Third, if the reconstruction that I propose is plausible, it opens the history of philosophy to the need to attend to the complex interactions and diverse cultural resources in the experience of those who produce the recognized American philosophical tradition. Finally, the reassessment of Williams provides evidence that the role of Native Americans was a potentially crucial element in the development of what is now viewed as American philosophy. On one hand, this means that it is no longer appropriate from a scholarly perspective to proceed as if Native culture were irrelevant to the development of philosophy. On the other hand, this means that pragmatism, for example, can be reexamined, not simply as an answer to the economic and social developments of the late nineteenth century, but as a way of thinking grounded in the struggle to maintain a pluralistic, open, and peaceful community in America.

By taking seriously the idea that American thought emerged from American experience, we have the potential to rethink the philosophical past. As in the case of Williams, such reconsideration can lead to new insights and new starting points for philosophical engagement with present problems. Philosophical investigations often start by recalling a philosophical past: Socrates' questions, Descartes's skepticism, Locke's empiricism. These past reflections help to frame new questions with which to consider present lives and problems. By reconstructing the history of American pragmatism, another set of past philosophical questions and answers becomes available to help frame new reflections, a philosophical past concerned especially with meaning and life in a united but irreducibly plural society.

CHAPTER SEVEN

The Logic of Place

WILLIAMS'S VISION OF A pluralist community was formed in a context where the problem of coexistence was shaped by the conflicts between radically different but also well-established communities. Although young, the New England colonies increased and grew stable with the help of their Native neighbors and a constant influx of immigrants. During Williams's time, although Native communities were devastated by disease and war, many nevertheless remained strong and together represented a majority of the population along the coast and its river valleys. The question for Williams was not primarily one of how to sustain the diverse communities, but how to provide for their peaceful coexistence.

When he began his pamphlet *The Examiner Defended* with the metaphor of a ship, Williams offered a logic of relations in terms of which some aspects of coexistence could be understood in light of present shared interests and others in light of fostering ongoing difference. The "*Ship* of the *Commonwealth,*" he says, "must share her *weals* and *woes* in *common.*" Those on board the ship "all agree (in their *commanding orders,* and *obeying stations*) to give and take the *Word,* to stand to the *Helm* and *Compass,* to the *Sails* and *Tacking,* to the *Guns* and *Artillery*" (Williams 1963, 203). And yet on this same ship, the "*Consciences* of the Passengers, whether Jews, Turks, Persians, Pagans, Papists, Protestants" are nevertheless to be treated with "kindness and countenance" (Williams 1963, 209). The shared interests and the diverse community were related in the same way that the ship as a whole relates to its private cabins. In this case, the cabins are not to be understood as "private" worlds in the sense that they are not or cannot be shared, but rather as marking the presence of distinctly different communities. Passengers can be expected to support the smooth operation of the ship as a present shared interest, while in their cabins they remain "Pagans" or "Turks" through their distinctive practices and beliefs. The sharp division between state and church that seems implied by the metaphor is not from this perspective either sharp or permanent, but rather marks a functional separation. The state is a changing collaboration that serves to preserve and promote the distinctive communities that make it up. As a result, the communities themselves, as lived interactions framed by history, shared attitudes, and future aspirations, form the ground both for the state and for the identity of individuals. The ship metaphor marks an adaptation of a European conception of social context to an alternative vision of coexistence. Just as the functional relations of *wunnégin* framed coexistence for the Narragansett, the functional relations aboard the ship of the commonwealth reconstructed coexistence for Williams.

By the end of King Philip's War in 1676, however, the context had changed. While many European and Native people still sought coexistence, others, particularly those who viewed themselves as part of the story of Christian progress, continued to press inland relying on the practices of slaughter, exclusion, and removal rather than either conversion or coexistence in their contact with Native peoples. During the last years of the seventeenth century, the English colonies of the Northeast consolidated politically and militarily even as they grew and became home to new German immigrants. Faced with new European influences and an apparent decline in the commitment to "original" Puritan Christianity, the shape of the westward colonial movement changed again in the 1730s. Now, the desire for land along parts of the western border of the European colonies combined with the evangelical efforts of a new movement: the Great Awakening.

For those Native and European people who still recognized the importance of coexistence, it was no longer to be understood as the problem of finding ways for flourishing communities to coexist peacefully. Instead, it was a problem of finding ways to resist the destruction of diverse communities in the face of territorial expansion and religious evangelism. Significantly, the Great Awakening did not begin in the urban areas like Boston, which were isolated from contact with Native people. It began on the borders of European settlement where the European American leadership faced nations from the Algonquian and Iroquoian traditions, the same traditions that, in league with Roger Williams, had challenged the authority and power of the Massachusetts Bay Colony. One branch of the new movement emerged along the Connecticut River, the old border of the Narragansett homeland. A second branch emerged along the Delaware River, the traditional home of a number of groups of Delaware people who shared both a common language family and narrative tradition with the Narragansett. Just as the first colonizers found themselves engaged with a Native tradition grounded in a commitment to pluralism and coexistence, so this later generation found itself engaged with the same tradition.

The message of the Great Awakening restated much of the Puritan theology that thirty years before had informed Cotton Mather's *Magnalia*. It differed primarily in its emphasis on the importance of the experience of conversion and its openness to people outside the educated elite. The general position reinforced the philosophical attitude evidenced by Mather and seemed to direct the same responses to the experience of difference. This response is well-illustrated in the work of Gilbert Tennent, who led the Great Awakening along the Delaware. A Presbyterian who had emigrated from Scotland with his family in 1715, Tennent was trained at the college his father founded in New Jersey. Tennent and a number of other graduates of the "Log College" became well-known for their preaching and ability to draw large crowds at revival meetings all along the border.[1] Tennent's passionate preaching demanded that people seek the experience of conversion and damned those who failed to achieve it.

In his 1740 sermon against other Presbyterians who had failed to show signs of the experienced conversion, Tennent used a crucial distinction between "natural" human beings, those who have not converted, and those who have been properly saved. "Now," he asks rhetorically, "are not all unconverted Men wicked Men?" (Heimert and Miller 1967, 76). Such "natural" people may use the rhetoric of "Fidelity, Peace, good Order, and Unity," but their works are necessarily for themselves and those with whom they associate. Without proper conversion, "natural men" are dangerous. "All doings of unconverted Men . . . are doubtless damnably Wicked in their Manner of Performance, and do deserve the Wrath and Curse of a Sin-avenging God" (Heimert and Miller 1967, 79). Tennent also makes it clear that such a policy stands as a guide for Christians' relationships with culturally different people. Quoting an unnamed source, he concludes, "*Be these Moral Negroes never so white in the mouth . . . yet will they hinder, instead of helping others in at the strait Gate* [of Heaven]" (Heimert and Miller 1967, 83; emphasis in the original). Recalling the dangers of the practices of welcome, Tennent hopes to guard his people against following those who will lead them into deadly alliances within the church and outside it. "Natural men . . . love those Unbelievers that are kind to them, better than many Christians, and chuse them for Companions. . . . Poor Christians are stunted and starv'd who are put to feed on such bare Pastures" (Heimert and Miller 1967, 79–80). Despite their

---

1. For an excellent discussion of Tennent's work and of the Great Awakening in general, see Lambert 1999.

danger and barrenness, "natural" people are nevertheless to be pitied and, for their own sake, are to be given the chance to convert by those already saved. "[W]e should pray to the LORD of the Harvest," he says, "to send forth faithful Labourers into his Harvest" (Heimert and Miller 1967, 84). The use of harvest as a metaphor for evangelism drew together both the demand for land and the expectation that what once grew in the field would be destroyed, marking the destruction of the indigenous attitude and the end of coexistence.

At Northampton on the Connecticut River, Jonathan Edwards led the Great Awakening. Edwards shared much of Tennent's theology, but added to his support for the movement by writing extensively on the psychology of conversion.[2] In contrast to Tennent, however, Edwards advocated a less aggressive stance toward "natural men." While Tennent demanded, for example, that unconverted ministers be driven from the church and scourged, Edwards argued that judgment and vengeance are not human matters (Heimert and Miller 1967, 285). Instead, at least for those already part of the church, vengeance amounts to "the devil obtain[ing] his end" (Heimert and Miller 1967, 286). The proper response to the unconverted is charity informed by a general commitment to the idea that all human beings are part of the same kind and as such are the same in all significant ways. The progress of humankind, from this perspective, is a story of unification, of recognizing sameness and manifesting it through conversion. As Edwards explains, "God has made of one

2. Edwards is a significant figure for a number of reasons, but I will not consider his work in great detail. At various points in the history of philosophy, Edwards was regarded as the preeminent American philosopher. See, for example, Schneider 1946, Blau 1952, and Flower and Murphey 1977. Most histories of American philosophy in the late nineteenth and twentieth centuries hold a prominent place for him. His biography also makes him a likely candidate for my study. He served as a minister to a congregation on the border between Native and European America. After leaving his call at Northampton, he served as a missionary to the Christian Indian community at Stockbridge. Edwards's work is often viewed as a highly original reconstruction of British Empiricism, under the influence of Locke and Berkeley. Among its innovations is a focus on experience that does not separate action and will. The emphasis on experience and in particular on things as they act in the world suggests connections with later American pragmatism and potential connections with the Native traditions we have considered. At the same time, Edwards remained a strong Calvinist committed overtly to the sort of view championed by Mather and supported at times in Edwards's work by the sort of attitude that, framed in terms of human nature, reemerges with Jefferson. He was known in the eighteenth century primarily in these terms and so is less directly relevant to the narrative at hand. In the end, Edwards clearly merits an extensive reexamination in terms of the problems and issues raised here. In a sense, his work embodies the same sort of tension we will find among the classical pragmatists as they are also torn between the demands of the colonial attitude and its expectation of progress and unification and the indigenous attitude that emphasizes growth and pluralism. In any case, I will not take up this further examination of Edwards here but will instead focus on the ways in which Edwards's promotion of the Great Awakening helped to generate the resistance movement among Native people.

blood all nations of men, to dwell on all the face of the earth; hereby teaching us this moral lesson, that it becomes mankind all to be united as one family" (Heimert and Miller 1967, 566). This view and its story of the monogenetic origin of humankind also gave Edwards a way to understand America and its people in the "history of redemption." "God," Edwards says, "made . . . two worlds here below, the old and the new" (Heimert and Miller 1967, 270–271). The arrival of Europeans marked the beginning of "the new and most glorious state of God's church on earth" (Heimert and Miller 1967, 271). "The old continent," he continues, "has been the source and original of mankind. . . . The first parents . . . dwelt there; and there dwelt Noah and his sons; and there the second Adam was born, and was crucified and rose again." In order to "balance things," he argues, it follows that the "glorious renovation of the world shall originate from the new continent" (Heimert and Miller 1967, 271). The beginning of the renovation, according to Edwards, was the Great Awakening. In agreement with both Tennent and Mather, the final triumph of God in the new world would be determined by war "wherein we must either conquer or be conquered, and the consequence of the victory, on one side, will be our eternal destruction, in both soul and body in hell, and on the other side, our obtaining the kingdom of heaven" (Heimert and Miller 1967, 274).

In the work of redemption, the place of Native Americans was either as allies of the enemy, Satan, or converts to Christianity. In his sermon series on the history of the work of redemption, he restates the story of the arrival of the first Americans. According to this version of the story the devil was "alarmed and surprised by the wonderful success of the gospel" and so "[by] the downfall of the heathen empire in Constantine's time . . . [the devil] led away a people from the other continent into America" (Edwards 1989, 434). The arrival of the Europeans marked the assertion of God's domain over the devil's kingdom and a prelude to "sending forth the gospel wherever any of the children of men dwell how far soever off" (Edwards 1989, 435). The evangelical movement was the Great Awakening, and its mission, in part, was to convert the allies of the devil.

When Edwards left his pulpit at Southampton, he was appointed as a missionary to the Christian Indian community at Stockbridge. Here Edwards worked out his own version of evangelism to Native people while he worked to establish an Indian boarding school. At the center of his plan was not simply the propagation of the gospel, but systematic cultural transformation. Anticipating the work of the Indian boarding schools established more than a century later, Edwards declared in a letter to the sponsor of the Stockbridge school: "'Tis . . . of great importance that [the children of Stockbridge] should be brought to the English language, as this would greatly tend to forward their instruction, their own barbarous languages being exceeding barren and very unfit to express moral and divine things." When the English language replaced the Native languages, it would "open their minds . . . and would tend above all things to bring that civility which is to be found among the English" (Edwards 1989, 389). As with Tennent, Edwards's "war" against Satan would be more than a process of acquiring land. It would be a process of destroying culture and acquiring souls.

For Native people, the Great Awakening combined with westward expansion of the English colonies marked an assault on both Native lands and culture. The result was a complex response. Some Native people, persuaded by the missionaries and pressured by European settlement, converted to Christianity. Along the border new towns like Stockbridge were established where Christian Indians and whites lived side by side. Other Native people abandoned traditional lands and moved further west, often into nations allied with the French, so that within a few years, with the outbreak of the French and Indian War, many Native people would find themselves at war with their traditional Native and European allies.[3] Still others responded by demanding the preservation of traditional Native lands and the autonomy of Native culture. The result of this last approach was a political, military, and philosophical movement that provided a new way of understanding cultural difference and coexistence in an environment where difference was constantly under assault. In response to attempts to eliminate Native difference, Native leaders emerged as prophets, leading a practical struggle against the acquisition of lands and efforts to destroy Native culture, while also establishing a logic of place, that is, an alternative philosophical framework that organized meaning in terms of place.[4]

The context for the emergence of the logic of place is well-illustrated by two encounters reported by David Brainerd in 1745. Brainerd, a Yale-

3. See White 1991 for a detailed discussion of the migrations and conflicts between Native people and the French and British during this period.

4. The discussion of the Native Prophetic movement is motivated by Gregory Evans Dowd's work *A Spirited Resistance*. Dowd argues, in part, that the emergence of Native prophets between 1745 and 1815 was a response to the Great Awakening in New England. Dowd focuses primarily on the political and military history of this movement, but he also argues that the rise and fall of the prophets should be understood as an attempt to utilize traditional Native powers to protect Native culture. Dowd concludes, "The nativists [the prophets] failed. Measured by their own goals, the failure was complete" (Dowd 1992, 191). I consider the Native Prophetic movement as a philosophical movement as well, and from this standpoint the nativists were not failures, but rather established the ground for a series of liberatory movements in North America including the Native rights movements of the twentieth century.

educated missionary and close friend of Jonathan Edwards, was one of a number of young ministers who became missionaries in the Great Awakening.[5] When Brainerd accepted the commission to bring the story of redemption to the Native people of what is now New Jersey and Pennsylvania, he brought a clear commitment to a vision of human nature understood in terms of the history of redemption. A key element in the process of conversion was acceptance of the transcendent timeline. To be saved, Native converts literally came to understand themselves in terms of the temporal progress of salvation. Resistance to conversion, on the other hand, meant resistance to attempts to reduce difference to sameness, and the resources for resistance were found in a conception of place.

The process of conversion is well-illustrated by Brainerd in his account of his work with an elder, who as a conjurer, or shaman, also called a "powwow," practiced traditional Native ceremonies despite an ongoing interest in Brainerd's preaching. Brainerd complained that when he preached about miracles performed by Christ, the people would downplay the miracles as the sort of thing the conjurer performed in their own experience. After the conjurer, while intoxicated, killed a young member of his tribe, he lost respect and became distraught. During the baptism of Brainerd's interpreter, the conjurer's "spirit of conjuration left him entirely" (Edwards 1985, 392) and his state of anguish deepened all through the winter. As he continued to attend Brainerd's sermons the agony became "utmost calmness and composure of mind [with] no hope of salvation" (Edwards 1985, 393). At this point Brainerd reports a dialogue in which the man retells his own history in terms of the history of redemption. When the man declared, in a kind of confessional catechism, that he must go to hell, Brainerd asked if he thought that it was right that he do so. "Oh'tis right," the man replied, "The devil has been in me ever since I was born" (Edwards 1985, 393). After much delay to ensure that the former conjurer was truly ready, Brainerd at last offered him baptism and he became a member of the visible church. "'Twas' . . . remarkable," Brainerd reports, "that in this season [the converted conjurer] was most diligent in the use of all means for his soul's salvation . . . So that he neither despaired of mercy, nor yet presumed to hope upon his own doings, . . . because he would wait upon God in his own way" (Edwards 1985, 394). Redemption, for the conjurer, became

---

5. Norman Pettit, who edited Edwards's *Life of Brainerd* for the recent Yale edition, argues that Brainerd, his work with Native Americans, and Edwards's reading of Brainerd's diaries were crucial for Edwards both in his assessment of the Great Awakening and in the development of his conception of experience (see Edwards 1985, 1–24).

a matter of setting aside the commitments of the indigenous attitude and reframing meaning in terms of the colonial attitude.

But even as Brainerd found success with the conjurer, there were other Native people who resisted missionary efforts. In the spring of 1745, while on a journey up the Susquehanna River, Brainerd encountered a person he describes as "a devout and zealous reformer, or rather restorer, of what he supposed was the ancient religion of the Indian" (Edwards 1985, 329). The reformer was strikingly dressed. "[H]e made his appearance in his pontifical garb, which was a coat of bear's skins, dressed with the hair on, and hanging down to his toes, a pair of bear-skin stockings, and a great wooden face, painted the one half black, the other tawny, about the color of an Indian's skin, with an extravagant mouth, cut very much awry" (Edwards 1985, 329). Although Brainerd was unsure about his purpose, the reformer challenged him ceremonially and "when he came near me," Brainerd says, "I could not but shrink away from him . . . his appearance and gestures were so prodigiously frightful!" (Edwards 1985, 329). After the ceremony Brainerd and the reformer retired to a lodge where they discussed religion. The reformer was an itinerant whose message was a complex argument to Native people to change their ways and recover certain lost traditions. When Brainerd talked about Christianity, there was much with which the reformer agreed. "He told me," Brainerd reports, "that God had taught him his religion, and that he never would turn from it, but wanted to find some that would join heartily with him in it; for the Indians, he said, were grown very degenerate and corrupt" (Edwards 1985, 329). The reformer, it appeared to Brainerd, had a developed theological perspective as well. "It was manifest that [the reformer] had a set of religious notions that he had looked into for himself, and not taken for granted upon bare tradition; and he relished or disrelished whatever was spoken of a religious nature, according as it either agreed or disagreed with his standard" (Edwards 1985, 330). Brainerd concluded that "he seemed to be sincere, honest and conscientious in his own way" and that "there was something in his temper and disposition that looked more like true religion than anything I ever observed amongst other heathens" (Edwards 1985, 330).

Regardless of his well-developed theology and good temper, however, the reformer remained in Brainerd's eyes an unfortunate pagan guilty of at least two important errors. First, the reformer refused to reconceive Native culture in terms of the history of redemption. "[H]e utterly denied the being of a devil," Brainerd reports, "and [he] declared there was no such creature known among the Indians of old times whose religions he supposed he was attempting to revive" (Edwards 1985,

330).[6] In addition to his failure to view his own tradition as the work of the devil, the reformer also failed to understand the process of redemption. "He likewise told me," Brainerd continues, "that departed souls all went southward, and that the difference between the good and the bad was this: that the former were admitted into a beautiful town with spiritual walls, or walls agreeable to the nature of souls; and that the latter would forever hover round those walls, and in vain attempt to get in" (Edwards 1985, 330). Brainerd says no more about the reformer and concludes the episode decrying the "deplorable state of the Indians upon this river!"

The reformer's view is a curious one. While he at once affirms certain European theological (and perhaps practical) principles, it is clear that he ultimately dissents from the general idea that Native people are part of Christian history. The views the reformer may have held are left obscure by Brainerd's account, but the reformer appears to be part of a Native parallel to the Great Awakening.[7] As the European American Great Awakening died down, Native prophets emerged across the Northeast and Old Northwest producing both Christian-derived theologies and moral principles and a general call for Native separation from European peoples. At some points the prophecies led to insurrection, including Pontiac's War of 1763–65 and Tecumseh's War of 1811–1813. Given the conflicts engendered in the adoption of Christian views and a call for a return to non-European ways, the movement is often viewed as a kind of confused conservatism. From this perspective, the reformer encountered by Brainerd is part of an early version of the later prophetic movement, before the politically efficacious prophecies that led to military resistance.[8] There is, however, another way to understand the encounter which views the reformer not as a conservative attempting to maintain static traditions in the face of dramatic change, but rather as an activist attempting to resist the colonization of Native people in part by reconstructing Native intellectual resources.

The encounter between the reformer and the missionary reveals at least four significant elements of Native resistance. First, the encounter is, in part, a ceremonial one, in particular, a version of a False Face ceremony. Although the reformer was probably a Delaware, the False Face

6. Despite the European colonial attempts to assign America to the devil, Northeast Native traditions do not appear to include an evil one of this sort. Good and evil are more often manifested in more ambiguous characters (see Haudenosaunee stories of the twins the Good Mind and the Evil Mind in Converse 1908).

7. See Dowd 1992, 29.

8. See Dowd 1992, Chapter 2.

ceremonies among the Haudenosaunee are generally used to "drive away sickness."[9] In the Haudenosaunee version of the ceremony, often called "the Travelling Rite," the wearers of the False Face masks travel from lodge to lodge "armed with turtle shell or bark rattles that they shake to scare away the spirit of sickness" (Fenton 1987, 267). Although Brainerd did not recognize it, the reformer, using the traditional resources of the False Face ceremony, may have been identifying him as a cause of illness and a danger to the people of the Susquehanna.

The attempt to drive sickness away using the powers connected with ceremony suggests a second aspect of resistance identified symbolically in the mask worn by the reformer: the importance of place. There are a wide variety of masks available to those performing the False Face ceremony. The one described by Brainerd is significant in that it makes manifest in the ceremony the importance of place. The mask, red on one side and black on the other, probably represented a person known in Onondaga as "Dehotgǫhsgá:yęh" or the "Split-Faced Man-Being." According to John Buck, a member of the Onondaga nation in conversation with the Tuscarora ethnologist J. N. B. Hewitt, "[t]he split-faced man-being dwells at the side of the midsky, the South, there along the margin of the earth. It is stated that the man-being, the east side of whose body is red, but the west side of whose body is dark, full black, dwells chiefly in darkness."[10] Properly understood, the mask of the reformer calls up the midsky, where the sunrise and sunset meet. It is the job of the one at that location to be available to "bear away or drive away whatever in the way of evil might menace or befall the inhabitants of the earth" (Fenton 1987, 104). Here, place emerges as a standpoint from which to challenge evil. A second version of the story connects the idea of a standpoint with a practice of tending to people in the places where they live. In this case, Dehotgǫhsgá:yęh is himself the product of the joining of a human being and a man-being.[11] After his beginning, Dehotgǫhsgá:yęh becomes a wanderer, "going from place to place considering the various peoples who dwell in diverse habitations" and providing support for their efforts to flourish in those places (Fenton 1987, 106). In Brainerd's encounter, the reformer ceremonially declares Brainerd a danger to the community and, in wearing the mask of Dehotgǫhsgá:yęh, proposes to sustain the people in their place.

9. See Fenton 1987, 267ff.

10. Buck describes Dehotgǫhsgá:yęh's attire in terms matching those given by Brainerd: "his robe is the flayed skin of a monster bear" (Fenton 1987, 104).

11. Hewitt identifies man-beings as mythical beings who occupy a cosmological place between human beings and gods. For present purposes it only needs to be noted that Dehotgǫhsgá:yęh is a union of different powers which are directional in nature.

A third element of Native resistance is suggested in Brainerd's conversation with the reformer. After the ceremony is performed, Brainerd challenges the reformer in conversation. "I discoursed with him about Christianity, and some of my discourse he seemed to like; but some of it he disliked entirely" (Edwards 1985, 329). The reformer seems to have surprised Brainerd in part because rather than simply railing against Christianity and the presence of Europeans along the Susquehanna, he presented a reasoned argument for his views and their implications. The views were, from Brainerd's perspective, well-thought-out but wrong. Native resistance is not only a political matter here, but also a philosophical and theological one. While it is surely valuable to track the course of movements of Native people, their economic relations with Europeans, and their military efforts to prevent the advance of European colonization, the encounter between the reformer and Brainerd makes it clear that it is also important to attend to the philosophical aspect of Native resistance.

A last element of Native resistance is suggested in the reformer's argument with Brainerd. As he reports it, the views advocated by the reformer are the product of visionary encounters with God. Combined with the use of ceremony and the particular traditions associated with the split-faced mask, the reformer illustrates a position of resistance grounded in Native traditions, but one which has also adapted key elements of European thought as resources. While some commentators emphasize the use of Christian notions such as monotheism to argue that Native thought was either hopelessly confused or hopelessly derivative, the encounter with Brainerd suggests that Native thought was rather innovative and constructive, maintaining key aspects of the Native tradition while acquiring new resources for its defense. Here even as Christianity found converts among Native people, many continued to resist the imposition of an all-encompassing history of redemption on lives framed in terms of places. In the Susquehanna Valley, that resistance emerged as an approach which would combine a traditional ceremonial dimension that ordered the response in terms of attention to particular places and was supported by overt philosophical reflection and the adaptation of available intellectual resources. Although the encounter leaves unclear how order and value conformed to place, it is clear that as the Great Awakening increased its efforts to impose history and unity on Native peoples who lived along the border, the border itself became a site of resistance to the practices and logic of the colonial attitude.

By 1761, resistance to European expansion along the border took clearer form. It is useful to consider in particular the work of Neolin, also known as the Delaware Prophet, whose visions and formulation of

Native resistance served as a framework for an armed insurrection led by Pontiac against the British in the Old Northwest. Neolin's development of a logic of place can be seen in two reports of his thinking. The first, given by Pontiac as an address to a council in preparation for an attack on British outposts, presents a paradox for those who accepted the colonial attitude and the logic of technometry. The second, reported by John Heckewelder and James Kenny, is found in Neolin's method of presenting his conception of Native resistance to European settlement and helps to identify the alternative logic of place.

There are several versions of Neolin's message. I will focus on the version included in Francis Parkman's history *The Conspiracy of Pontiac*.[12] In the account, Neolin had "an eager desire to learn wisdom from the Master of Life" (Parkman 1962, 167).[13] Since he did not know how to get to the Master's home, he used traditional means of "fasting, dreaming, and magical incantations" to divine the route. He found that he need only "move forward in a straight, undeviating course" (Parkman 1962, 167). Without telling anyone, he slipped out of his village and traveled for eight days. On the evening of the eighth day he set up his camp along a stream. As sunset arrived, he noticed three paths extending out from camp, which grew brighter and more distinct as the sun disappeared. He became impatient and in the darkness followed the first path. Eventually, however, the path was blocked by fire, as was the second path. Finally, after following the third path, he came upon a "vast mountain of dazzling whiteness" (Parkman 1962, 168). When he started to climb the mountain he was stopped by a beautiful woman who told him that he must purify himself before he started and that he must ascend the mountain using only one hand and one foot. So Neolin bathed and proceeded up the mountain unclothed. After a great struggle he reached the top, described as a "rich and beautiful plain" where he found three villages. He approached the largest and was invited to an audience with the Master of Life.

12. A second version of Neolin's story appears in Schoolcraft 1856. The versions differ in key terms, and it is useful to consider both versions.

13. The term "Master of Life" as well as "Great Spirit" came to be common in the speeches and writings of Native Americans in the late eighteenth century. There is some debate over the proper meaning of the term that seems at times to be a convenient English translation for a Native term that does not fully share the English meaning. For purposes of this discussion, the term is generally used (both in the texts I am considering and in other Native texts from the nineteenth century) as a kind of supreme power, consistent at once with the notion of power (often named *manitou* or *orenda*) which can have a variety of forms and with Christian monotheism. Given the pervasive use of the term, it seems that this is a notion that shows development in contact with European religion but should nevertheless not be read as identical with Christian conceptions of God.

In his speech to Neolin, the Master of Life makes four points. First, he asserts his standing as creator and because of this Neolin and his people have an obligation to act in accord with his direction. Second, the Master asserts that "the land on which you live I made for you, and not others" in such a way that Neolin's people were both fit to the land and others were not (Parkman 1962, 168–169). Third, the Master clarifies the fitness of Neolin's people and the land. The fitness, says the Master, is manifest in traditions and customs received from past generations and in the instruments of everyday life, e.g., clothes, tools, and food. The failure to attend to the ways that fit the people to the land had led to a destruction of game and a destruction of people. Finally, because fitness is undermined by the presence of whites, it is the responsibility of Neolin's people, in this case all Native people, to drive the whites away. The Master then prescribes several moral and religious principles for the people to follow. These include abstinence from alcohol, the practice of monogamy, maintenance of peace within Native communities, and the elimination of medical practices that call on evil spirits.[14] Neolin promised to relay the message and returned to his village to the surprise of the community, which had not known where he had gone.

To the general framework of resistance demonstrated by the Delaware reformer encountered by Brainerd, Neolin adds a crucial narrative. The report of the vision uses a variety of terms and figures that appear in stories throughout the Algonquian and Iroquoian traditions. What seems innovative about the presentation is that the Native sojourner encounters a single "Master of Life," who recounts a story of creation. Unlike the creation stories in the Judeo-Christian tradition, however, Neolin's account explicitly identifies at least two separate creations, one red and one white. The creations, however, are not simply creations of morphologically different people; they are complex acts in which the Master of Life literally places people in distinct locations and suits them physically and culturally to those locations. From this perspective the notion of place is no longer a simple idea of location, that is, a geographical location relative to others. Rather, place incorporates the land, its inhabitants, and activity of all sorts. In this sense, Neolin makes the land itself a contributor to the process by interacting with its residents to generate an integrated and distinctive whole. For the Master of Life, it is unacceptable for people so created as part of a place either to relocate themselves to a new land or to displace others from lands duly given. In

14. See Schoolcraft 1856, 201–202 for the moral and religious principles. Parkman only mentions that these were part of the message repeated by Pontiac (Parkman 1962, 169).

either case, the action violates the divinely intended life that flourishes when people (animals and plants as well) interact with their appropriate land. The result of these placed creations is a notion of fitness or suitability such that the place, as a complex interaction among properly suited people, practices, other living beings, and the land, is sustained. When taken up by Pontiac, the vision becomes a ground for a unified effort to restore places by restoring the sustaining interactions.

The logic of place, however, does not simply involve a process of affirming a complex notion of interaction in a geographical location, but rather extends to a redevelopment of a way of orienting one's understanding in the world. This is best seen by contrast. Salvation, from the viewpoint of Brainerd and the other Christian missionaries, is a matter of God's action on creation, whose reward is eternal life in a heaven either not of the earth or of a radically transformed earth. Neolin's notion of salvation involves individual and collective action and takes place in an earthly geography. When Neolin preached, according to several who knew his work, he often used a map as an element in making himself understood. The use is important. According to Heckewelder,

> [Neolin] had drawn . . . a kind of map on a piece of deer skin, somewhat dressed like parchment, which he called 'the great Book or Writing.' This, he said, he been ordered to shew to the Indians, that they might see the situation in which the Mannitto had originally placed them, the misery which they had brought upon themselves by neglecting their duty, and the only way that was now left them to regain what they had lost. This map he held before him while preaching, frequently pointing to particular marks and spots upon it, and giving explanation as he went along. (Heckewelder 1971, 291)

There are two detailed descriptions of the map. In each case, a central area is marked off as the proper place for Native people. In Heckewelder's description, the map includes two openings, one in the southeast and one in the northeast. The southeast passage had, according to Neolin, been closed off by white settlement, and the northeast passage, though open, was guarded by the "evil spirit." The map was marked at various points as well by lines which indicated, as James Kenny describes it, "all ye Sins & Vices which ye Indians have learned from ye White people" (Kenny 1913, 171). Parallel to the account of the speech of the Master, the map records "Sins & Vices" as concrete events ordered geographically relative to Native land. The actions, Kenny suggests, are marked as blocks to be overcome or gone around in order to travel the "Good Road" to a required Native place.

Following Heckewelder's account, Neolin described the central section of the map as "the heavenly regions," or as Heckewelder explains, "the place destined by the great Spirit for habitation of the Indians in future life" (Heckewelder 1971, 292). Later, quoting Neolin directly, the central section is described as "those beautiful regions that were destined for us" (Heckewelder 1971, 292). In this case, "heaven" becomes a beautiful region not necessarily transcendent or outside the present world but rather a place. Interpreted as well in light of the vision, the idea that the beautiful place is part of a destined "future life" should be understood as that region given to Native people in the first place by the Master of Life. The problem, as Neolin describes it, is that the access ways, the points of connection to the region, are blocked, in one case by the "evil spirit" and in the other by white settlement. The goal of restoration is to regain connections by overturning the "evil spirit" on one hand and moving the whites on the other. The place of the Delaware and other Native peoples has been, in a real sense, choked off by whites and by the adoption by Native people of evil practices brought by the whites. Restoration will involve reopening the passages and converting the destructive practices into constructive ones.

Significantly, the narrative Neolin told of Native history is now told as a particular geographic history, not a universal one. The coming of the Europeans does not require that European history conform to Native expectations, only that relative to the homeland of the Delaware, the Europeans arrived and literally transformed the landscape. Europeans, whose own origins do not appear in the story or on the map, appear relative to the lands of Native peoples and then serve as real, located obstacles to be overcome or driven off. Native resistance becomes one that requires the restoration of place by reestablishing a fit relationship to the land and the events that occur within its boundaries. Efforts to understand Native history, then, will more likely be discussions of lands, of movements of people, of concrete events occurring in particular locations and not a unifying story of all peoples and places. A narrative on such a model will be told as a process of circling away from and back to the home location, and the passage of time will be understood through a focus on the paths taken and landmarks along the way.[15]

The logic of the colonial attitude orders things and events according to their place in a larger unifying scheme. Mather's history, for example, makes the geography of New England meaningful in terms of a larger

---

15. Also see Pratt 2001.

plan, not in terms of the concrete places that serve as markers of human progress. Europeans move west, but their direction and the land over which they move do not provide their meaning. Neolin's vision suggests an alternative ordering where the meaning of the events is found in relation to the framing elements of the story and the interactions they involve. The logic of place can thus be understood as a way of understanding in terms of this process. From this perspective, experience gains meaning in ways that call on a variety of factors, including geography, operative traditions, and the fitness or suitability of the meaning to the context. The story, like Mather's, is directional, but the directions are relative ones, originating from Neolin's home village. The sequence of events is not presented in ways that overtly link to others' histories, but rather that link to Neolin and the troubles of his people. His journey is directed by his desire for wisdom, the needs of his people, and the instructions that emerge from the environment itself. His way is bounded by fire, for example, not clearly at the instruction of either the Master of Life or the woman who comes later to guide him. Instead, the fires provide direction in a way that suggests the cooperation of the land and its other inhabitants in the process. When the woman instructs Neolin to leave behind his "gun, . . . ammunition, . . . provisions, and . . . clothing," it reinforces the idea that Neolin needs to restore his relationship with the present place by setting aside the products of Europe fit not for the Delaware homeland but for another place. In effect, Neolin's experience is presented as a set of geographically related interactions whose purpose and meaning is found in the Master's message and Neolin's return home. In the Master's message, Neolin's journey is framed in terms of his homeland. "The land on which you live I made for you." And the consequences of this relation are clear: return to the homeland and reestablish your fitness for it. Neolin carries out the instruction and returns. In the end, it is Neolin's homeland, understood as its people, the land, and the land's other inhabitants, that give the journey its meaning.

The logic of Neolin's vision was a logic grounded in human experience. What made it compelling and what made the Master's message a truth to be heeded was that Neolin's "vision" was not an illusion or an allegory, but a "real" experience. The stages of the journey, the encounter with the Master of Life, the Master's account of human origin and purpose, all served to ground new knowledge and generate new meaning. In this sense, Neolin's vision was not unlike the conversion experiences of the Christian Great Awakening, which also served as sources of new knowledge and meaning. The logic of the colonial attitude that supported this conception of experience and knowledge owed much of its structure to the logic of Peter Ramus, a sixteenth-century French Protestant philosopher. According to Ramus and his successors, knowledge is the result of a process that begins in experience and is grounded in the confidence that what human beings experience is a reality determined by God.[16] Experience, in this sense, is a direct grasp of what is real and the experience of novelty and the unexpected is simply the experience of a part of creation not so far experienced or categorized. To know something is to experience the world directly and then to develop categories that can accurately represent the objects found in experience. Such a logic was important to the developing doctrine of Puritan Christianity as a way of understanding how individuals could come to know God without the mediating authority of the church. For the leaders of the New England colonies it was even more important as a means of shaping their response to the "American Strand."[17] Using this logic, the colonial experience of peoples, plants, animals, and topography that did not fit established categories could be accepted at face value as "real" differences that ultimately were part of a single system. As a result of this direct realism, those influenced by Ramist logic could engage the "New World" with the confidence that nothing significant would be missed, that the American experience was neither partial nor deceptive, but directly accessible for ordering and valuation.

Neolin's challenge, in simplest terms, begins by affirming what the evangelists of the Great Awakening had long argued: a single, all-powerful god created the world as it is experienced. This created world, Neolin says, includes a vast diversity of experiences including the experience of different deities, different relations with nature, different origins, and different ways of life. According to the logic of the colonial attitude, these experiences ought to be understood as the experience of real objects and so ought to constitute legitimate knowledge to be promoted and engaged, not reduced and destroyed. At the same time, however, the colonial expectation that all differences are part of a single system of order and value justified the attempt to eliminate differences through processes of conversion and assimilation, including the differences intrinsically involved in the fitness of a people to a land. The colonial attitude is at odds with itself, at once accepting the value of experience and denying its most pervasive feature, its diversity. The force of Neolin's message cut two ways. In one direction, it provided a framework for a Native logic of place. In the other, it challenged the very logic that

16. See Ramus 1969.
17. See Ames 1979 and Johnson 1929 for further development of Ramus's logic in the Puritan tradition.

was destroying Native places and making the coexistence of difference a fading possibility.

One might argue that Neolin's story was not aimed at challenging the logic of the colonial attitude and that it is better understood independently of European ways of thinking. Such an argument is clearly consistent with the standard view of Native people, especially by non-Native commentators, that suggests that Indians were intellectually isolated from European ideas, and so Native intellectual developments are largely internal. The evidence, however, challenges such a view. Brainerd, for example, did not encounter a narrow-minded Native radical unaware of European theology and philosophy. On the contrary, although Brainerd did not present the content of the reformer's words, he did credit the reformer with a well-considered view that was at least in part consistent with Brainerd's own views. From Brainerd's well-educated perspective, the reformer was no less thoughtful and well-spoken than Brainerd himself was, and that he could communicate such views in lively discussion suggests that the reformer was probably quite familiar with Brainerd's intellectual resources. Though Brainerd seems surprised about the reformer's views, he should not have been. Native people, as he well knew, had long been engaged in learning European ideas from missionaries and schools, even as they sought to preserve their traditions and return to their homelands. As part of that training, the Native students of European missionaries even had the opportunity to learn the formal logic of the colonial attitude. It is significant that John Eliot published a version in Natick of Ramus's *Dialectica* for distribution to the Massachusett people and other missionaries.[18] Although the scope of its circulation is unrecorded, its publication indicates the importance of the subject matter in the teaching conducted by the Puritan missionaries. Its publication also raises the possibility that reformers like Neolin and the one encountered by Brainerd could have more than an accidental knowledge of the logic that structured the European American ways of thinking. By the time Neolin presented his vision, the context of the telling would have been well-framed by the logic of the colonial attitude and its problems. Rather than seeing Neolin as a "religious" prophet or as a prophet whose message was aimed only at his own people, it is also possible to see him as a philosopher, proposing a critique of the colonial logic both to his own people who had given up on Native traditions and to the whites who sought to destroy them.

Neolin's vision was recognized as trouble for whites in his region.

18. See Miller 1939, 114, 120. Also see Eliot 1904.

Francis Parkman expresses a common view in his nineteenth-century re-telling of Pontiac's speech to a council of Native people at the Ecorces River. "Having roused in his warlike listeners their native thirst for blood and vengeance," says Parkman, "[Pontiac] next addressed himself to their superstition" and told the story of Neolin's vision as a justification for the impending attack on the fort at Detroit (Parkman 1962, 167).[19] Parkman was correct that the vision represented a powerful call for ac-tion, but not as a matter of vengeance or as a thirst for blood. In another part of the speech included as an appendix in Parkman's account, Pon-tiac is also reported to have said, "It is important, my brothers, that we should exterminate from our land this nation, whose only object is our death" (Parkman 1962, 494). Where Miantonomi initially chose *wun-négin* as a way to frame his response to Williams, Pontiac chose another mode of action: killing the cannibals. Despite the call for "extermina-tion," however, the purpose of the confederacy was not annihilation of all whites. Instead, Pontiac's War was an attempt to restore a place to Native people. Neolin's vision and the paradox at its center was a call for the restoration of place, in ways of understanding and acting. The demand was not the abstract assertion of a logic problem nor was it a simple demand for real estate. It was a call to change thinking bound up with concrete action. From the European American perspective, their communities along the border now faced a movement of Native prophets declaring in contexts accessible to all that the colonies embod-ied a deep contradiction. The colonial leadership, whose attitude was reinforced by economic advantage, the rewards of power, and long-standing hatred of the "servants of Satan," replied to the challenge with war. For others, Native and non-Native, the paradox demanded a differ-ent response that led to a reconstructed philosophical attitude.

Several important points emerge from this reading of Neolin's vi-sion. First, even as it proposes a paradox for the colonial attitude, it reaffirms features of the indigenous attitude apparent in the Narragan-sett people a century earlier, including the four principles that would later come to be a part of classical pragmatism. The process of under-standing people, land, practices, and beliefs ultimately relies on the prin-ciple of interaction. Rather than declaring the priority and indepen-dence of the land, Neolin's vision makes land an interactive part of the

19. Parkman uses several manuscript sources for his account of Pontiac's speech. See Parkman 1962, 493ff. While most of the sources may be non-Native, some are anonymous. The basic outline and figures in the texts agree across the different versions, including the one reported by Schoolcraft.

culture and practices of the Delaware. To talk about the land as though it was not the land of the Delaware or the Ottawa or the Shawnee given by the Master of Life is to fail to understand. The land, in this case, is part of a history of interactions among human beings and others. Its conception is not something that corresponds either to a point in a grand scheme or to a location in space and time, but is rather a record of what has happened combined with expectations about what might happen. Place, that is, the complex interactions involving land and its inhabitants, emerges from Neolin's vision not as a fixed element in the Delaware universe, but as an ongoing, open-ended process. Both Neolin's understanding of what has happened to his people and his responding call begin in the expectation that knowledge and being are to be understood in the interactions.

Even as Neolin declared the priority of place over the unifying demands of the colonial attitude, he also asserted the importance of the principle of pluralism. One might argue that pluralism is in fact contrary to Neolin's vision, especially as it was taken up by leaders such as Pontiac.[20] Yet while the message appears to assert a "pan-Indian" perspective, emphasizing the shared interests and histories of all Native people, the vision itself seems to assert something quite different. If Neolin is proposing or making clear a logic of place in order to preserve the differences between "red" and "white" people, the logic of the argument does not prohibit the recognition of other differences as well. Unless the logic of place is strangely constrained to Native–European relations alone, a similar distinction between peoples would also emerge, for example, when the Delaware and Haudenosaunee considered their relationship to each other and their own traditions. In fact, even as Neolin presented a logic of place, the Delaware also proclaimed the need for a relation of coexistence with the Haudenosaunee to the north involving distinct lands and the preservation of distinct cultural identities.[21] The Native–European differences did not exhaust the possibilities of cultural difference. Neolin's vision was a nativist vision, but in a significant way it was not pan-Indian. The logic of place establishes the expectation that there will be multiple geographical centers, multiple origins and histories relative to those centers, multiple "fit" relationships between the land and its inhabitants, and an ongoing need to determine relations between them. By calling for restoration of Native traditions, Neolin was not just

20. Dowd (1992), for example, focuses on the pan-Indian character of the prophetic movement and concludes in part that it aimed to reduce the importance of Native differences in favor of Native commonalities.

21. See Wallace 1990.

calling for the rejection of European alcohol and trade goods, he was arguing for a restoration of a logic that would provide a framework for maintaining differences "in place." Rather than challenging pluralism with pan-Indian unity, Neolin reaffirmed the principle that asserts the reality and value of differences.

The principle of community also plays a role in Neolin's vision. While the Master of Life dictated the need to return to traditions and restore the fit relations with the land, the directive was explicitly one that called Neolin back into his community and tradition. The vision needed to be heard by his people, and its result was to establish the expectation that the people would take their own community and traditions seriously and, in effect, listen to themselves. The expectation, on one hand, recalled the long-standing practices of interpreting visions through ceremony.[22] Ceremonies and the collective councils of which they are a part are the key for bringing the vision to action, and Neolin's vision was brought before Delaware councils and those of the other nations who joined Pontiac. Unlike Moses, however, Neolin did not bring tablets down from the mountain dictating new universal laws, but instead he came down with a message that demanded the reconstruction of community in a fit relationship with their land and traditions. Pontiac, as an Ottawa, took up Neolin's vision, because the call for the Delaware to reclaim their place could be applied as well to the Ottawa, Shawnee, Fox, Sauk, and other peoples who might join the insurrection. Its proclamation among the Ottawa and Shawnee was not a call to become Delaware, but rather a call to find the living traditions of their own communities. The call to arms was a call to fight for pluralism, not for union or even the elimination of the outsiders. In this sense, Neolin's vision drew together interaction, pluralism, and community.

The goal of the actions called for by Neolin recalls the principle of growth. Unlike the colonial vision of human action as a part of a history of redemption or the achievement of some ideal state, Neolin's vision was for the restoration of flourishing Native communities. According to Heckewelder, Neolin explained it this way: "[Y]ou are to return to that former happy state, in which we lived in peace and plenty, before these strangers came to disturb us" (Heckewelder 1971, 293). The notion of flourishing here is not merely a conservative isolation and recovery of a rigidly fixed past, but a reopening of connections as they were represented on Neolin's map. Just as growth is a matter of possibilities and connections, so Neolin's vision calls for the restoration of culture and,

22. See Pratt 1998.

at the same time, the reestablishment of the potential for connections by opening the interactive pathways. From this perspective, the logic of place becomes a logic of growth, recovering place and providing an alternative way of understanding and acting in a context of cultural pluralism. The coming war with the whites was not a war against growth, but a struggle to restore it.

Two decades before Neolin's vision became well-known, and nearly a century after Miantonomi was credited with a similar position, another Native reformer argued that the coming of the Europeans had not only been disruptive to human society, but it had contributed to the destruction of the other relations that flourished on the land. Describing his encounter with this earlier prophet, Conrad Weiser reports the speech of God heard by this prophet in a vision:

> You inquire after the cause why game has become scarce. I will tell you. You kill it for the sake of the skins, which you give for strong liquors and drown your senses, and kill one another, and carry on a dreadful debauchery. Therefore, I have driven the wild animals out of the country. . . . If you will do good, and cease from your sins, I will bring them back; if not, I will destroy you from off the earth. (Wallace 1945, 88)

The point was not that profits or productivity had been reduced by the presence of the Europeans, but rather that the ability of the place to sustain itself as a living complex had been compromised by the failure to sustain fit relations. Growth, in the sense of establishing connections and possibilities, had been undercut, and the call was for its restoration in the form of relations appropriate to the place. Neolin's vision and its logic reaffirmed the idea of coexistence that emerged in the contact between Miantonomi and Williams, but here it did not take the form of the practices of welcome. Instead, he offered a logic of place that demanded more than the coexistence of well-established communities; it demanded an active commitment to promoting and maintaining cultural difference through a reconstruction of the colonial logic and attempts to change the concrete relations of place by force.

Two important objections emerge to Neolin's vision and the consequent prosecution of Pontiac's War. The first regards the idea of racial difference, and the second regards the idea of land. One common response to claims of multiple creations or polygenesis is that it undermines attempts to see all human beings as part of one species. Put another way, polygenesis seems to be a preliminary case both for racial difference and for racial inferiority and superiority. The problem emerged at the same time in the eighteenth century in the work of Lord Kames, who argued along with Johann Gottfried von Herder that human difference is best understood in terms of different creations, each located in a specific region of the Earth.[23] While they argued that this did not require distinctions in value, others argued that it necessarily must since some peoples are more advanced than others. If it is true that peoples were not all created the same, then it must follow that those who lag in economics or education may lag for natural and therefore unchangeable reasons. Neolin's argument, one might conclude, surely supports such conclusions and as such ought to be set aside as mistaken. American philosopher Samuel Stanhope Smith, writing in 1788, expressed what was at stake in his *Essay on the Causes of Complexion and Figure in the Human Species* (1995). The risk of denying or ignoring the unity of humankind would be a disaster. "The science of morals would be absurd," Smith declares, "the law of nature and nations would be annihilated; no general principles of human conduct, of religion, or of policy could be framed." The problem, according to Smith, is that if nonunified human nature interacts with diverse environments, then human nature "could not be comprehended in any system" and a kind of radical relativism would necessarily follow. "The rules which would result from the study of our own nature, would not apply to the natives of other countries who would be of different species; perhaps, not to two families in our own country, who might be sprung from dissimilar constitution of species." The "doctrine of one race," combined with a recognition of the environmental causes of difference, "removes this uncertainty, renders human nature susceptible of system, illustrates the powers of physical causes, and opens a rich and extensive field for moral science" (Smith 1995, 164–165).

In reply, Neolin might have observed that polygenesis is not, properly speaking, the creation of different kinds of human beings, but rather different places in which people (as well as land and other animate creatures) are different from those in other places. Since life is tightly bound up with the context in which it goes on, it makes little sense to argue about universal standards of comparison at all. In order for the objection to get off the ground, it is necessary that one presume that there is some common standard in terms of which people in different places can be rightly compared. Since Neolin rejects this sort of unifying model as a required way of understanding all people, the objection to his view carries little weight, while the response implies a case for understanding

23. See, for example, Herder 1968, 7.

both the persistence of difference and the ways in which differences can be negotiated. Neolin suggests this reply in the speech reported by Heckewelder. "See what we have lost," he says, "by looking upon people of a different colour from our own, who had come across a great lake, as if they were a part of ourselves" (Heckewelder 1971, 292). Understood in terms of race, the idea of color difference represents different origins and fitness for different places. The resulting rejection of whites does not reflect some universal hierarchical ranking of human beings by race or culture, but rather a valuation relative to a particular place. European beliefs and practices were destructive, but it does not follow that European people are always evil. On the contrary, it appears that Europeans are as fit for their place, according to Neolin, as the Delaware are for theirs.

A second objection is more compelling. If Neolin is right, people and lands are rigidly and nearly inseparably connected. Relocations violate the creator's will and so, in a sense, the natural order of things. The resulting view appears to be a kind of land essentialism. If so, however, it would seem to condemn Native people and Europeans alike. It is well-known that just as Europeans migrated to the Americas, so many Native nations also migrated from their original homelands and came to occupy those of other nations.[24] In this case, if Pontiac's Ottawa people or Neolin's Delaware had come from other regions than those they claimed, a consistent application of Neolin's land essentialism should require that they also leave, returning the lands to their original people. In this case, an objector can conclude that Neolin's view is at best self-serving political rhetoric and at worst a tale of "erratic windings and puerile inconsistencies" as it is described by Parkman (1962, 167).

A response to the objection from Neolin's viewpoint, while implicit in his vision and map, is made more clear in the work of the Shawnee prophet Tenskwatawa, who, with his brother Tecumseh, led an attack on the United States in 1811–1813 by a confederation of Native nations. The visions of creation proposed by Tenskwatawa, unlike those of Neolin, include both the idea of polygenesis and a non-essentialist notion of land. In Tenskwatawa's story, human beings are created in the home of the creator and live there for some time.[25] The creator eventually decides that the people ought to relocate to an island and so prepares it to receive them by adding to it certain plants and animals. The island itself,

24. See White's (1991) extensive treatment of seventeenth- and eighteenth-century migrations, for example.

25. In this story, white people are created by "another spirit" who would use the white men to "thwart the [Indian Creator's] designs" (Trowbridge 1939, 3).

that is the land, was to become part of the new place as an active contributor. The creator says, "You are now about to go to the Island which
I have made for you, which rests upon the back of a great turtle that
carries it as a load. You must call the Turtle your grandfather. He will
hear all your complaints and will treat you as his Grand Children" (Trowbridge 1939, 2). The people travel until they reach the place where the
creator "had placed the heart of one of the old men [among them]"
(Trowbridge 1939, 4). Though created elsewhere, the people migrated
to a land where they could establish their place by making themselves
fit for the land and its other inhabitants even as the land and its other
habitants were made fit for the people.

   Tenskwatawa's account suggests that particular lands retain a crucial
connection to human beings, but not a connection so essential that a
change of practices or locations is impossible. Instead, the logic of place
directs that relocation and other changes be carried out in a way that
reestablishes suitability in response to the new land (or the new inhabitants of the lands). The link between land and people is close, but it is
also reciprocal and dynamic. This view is reinforced in a later episode
of Tenskwatawa's account in which an outsider arrives unexpectedly in
the newly founded village. The outsider, "a man unknown to them," appears in their council and was soon made a trusted part of the place. He
becomes a part, it seems, on the basis of his coming to fit the place and
its community.[26]

   What is important to note about Tenskwatawa's perspective is that
while it retains the features suggested by the Delaware reformer and by
Neolin, it modifies them somewhat to de-essentialize the notion of land.
On this view, relocation alone is not necessarily enough either to destroy
a people and their culture or to destroy the land. At the same time,
Tenskwatawa recognizes that not just any relocation is adequate. Within
his narrative is the idea that the development of a place requires a range
of practices that establish the necessary interactions with the land and
its other inhabitants so that a place comes to be. Land, it appears, is not
essential to a people or people to a land in the sense that their separation
necessarily destroys one or the other. Rather relocation and change
are possible, but only as collaborative efforts. Europeans, according
to Tenskwatawa, violated the logic of place by literally redrawing the
map. In the first encounter between Native people and the Europeans,
Tenskwatawa reports that "the whites brought from their vessel a chair

---

26. A similar illustration of fitness is found in Tenskwatawa's story of the Star Woman.
Here, an outsider comes to contribute to a new community by helping to establish a place
fit to flourish, in this case by repopulating the land with game (Shoerer 1962).

and after becoming a little familiar with the Indians they begged a piece
of land to place the chair upon" (Trowbridge 1939, 10). The request,
Tenskwatawa continues, was "so reasonable" that it was "readily granted."
Rather than seating themselves on the chair, however, the visitors dis-
assembled the cords in the seat of the chair and "surrounded the land
with it so as to make a quite large tract [and] telling the Indians that
such was the customary way among *them*" (Trowbridge 1939, 10).[27] Unlike the collaborative and interactive process of making a place, the
Europeans simply imposed their own standards and measures to make
the topography of the land conform to their interests without regard for
the land itself, its history, and its other inhabitants.

Tenskwatawa's version of place suggests a response to concerns
about essentializing land, but it recalls the first objection that polygenesis, now coupled with radically divergent ways of thinking, amounts to a
requirement that Native people and the descendants of Europeans remain strictly separate. Even in the cases of unknown people coming to
be part of Native places, the implication is that the strangers were at least
Native people and not European. Rather than bringing us to a view in
support of a pluralistic society of the sort advocated by Miantonomi and
Williams, the logic of place now seems to demand nothing less than multiple closed societies. The objector can conclude that differences may be
preserved but at the cost of establishing a kind of nationalism defined
by impassable boundaries. A response to this objection is implicit in both
Neolin's and Tenskwatawa's work, but it is made clearer in the work of
Sagoyewatha.

Sagoyewatha was born in the 1750s near the present city of Geneva,
New York, into the Haudenosaunee nation of the Seneca.[28] His original
name was Otetiani, or "Always Ready." Later, as he acquired a reputation as an orator, he came to be called Sagoyewatha, which translates as
"He-Keeps-Them-Awake." Most Europeans and European Americans
knew him as Red Jacket. Sagoyewatha rose to prominence in the years
after the American Revolution through his ability as an orator and
his ability to represent well the views of his community. The role of
orator is conferred upon individuals in the Haudenosaunee tradition by
the consensus of those men and women recognized by the wider community as leaders. Sagoyewatha's frequent presence as a speaker for the

---

27. Trowbridge suggests that this story is of European origin (Trowbridge 1939, 10).
Whether it is or not, however, is beside the point in that Tenskwatawa used it to explain
the relationship of Europeans to Native people and to American lands.
28. See Densmore 1999 for a recent biography of Red Jacket.

Haudenosaunee suggests that he was widely respected by his people and, despite his alliance with the British in the American Revolution, became the primary point of contact between the new United States government and the western Haudenosaunee.

Sagoyewatha's response to the nationalist objection to the logic of place is suggested in a series of speeches given in response to requests from various missionaries to conduct their work among the Haudenosaunee. In one of the speeches, given in 1805 in response to a missionary, Rev. Jacob Cram of the Evangelical Missionary Society of Massachusetts, Sagoyewatha recalls much of the position taken by Neolin and Tenskwatawa.[29] Cram's purpose was to ask for the support of the Haudenosaunee Council for his missionary work among them. His speech as it is recorded argues that his work ought to be supported by the Haudenosaunee leadership in light of certain facts consistent with the logic of the colonial attitude. "There is but one religion," he declares, "and but one way to serve God, and if you do not embrace the right way you cannot be happy hereafter" (Densmore 1999, 136). The way proposed, however, is not that of the Haudenosaunee. "You have never worshipped the Great Spirit in a manner acceptable to him: but you have all your lives been in great errors and darkness. To endeavor to remove these errors, and open your eyes, so that you might see clearly is my business with you." After a period of deliberation, Sagoyewatha responded on behalf of the Haudenosaunee leadership. He began by recalling stories of origin taught by his ancestors. In the beginning, indigenous Americans had sole possession of the land. "There was a time when our forefathers owned this great island," he said.

> Their seats extended from the rising to the setting sun. The Great Spirit had made it for the use of Indians. He had created the buffalo, the deer, and other animals for food. He had made the bear and the beaver. Their skins served us for clothing. He had scattered them over the country, and taught us how to take them. He had caused the earth to produce corn for bread. All this he had done for his red children, because he loved them. If we had some disputes about our hunting ground, they were generally settled without the shedding of much blood. (Densmore 1999, 137–138)

The arrival of Europeans, however, was an "evil day." They were welcomed at first and given sustenance, but eventually they returned poison.

---

29. See Densmore's discussion of Sagoyewatha's meeting with Cram (Densmore 1999, 63–70) and a reprint of the speeches of both (Densmore 1999, 135–40).

In time, Europeans came in great numbers, and, even as the indigenous population became smaller, the European population grew and demanded Native lands.

Like Neolin, Sagoyewatha uses the logic of the colonial attitude to lay the ground for his reply to the missionary. By framing the account in terms of the work of a single creator whose intentions actively structure the shared world of Europeans and Americans, he establishes a common ground of "invention," of "facts" drawn from Native experience, with which to assess Cram's requests. The picture of America before the Europeans arrived seems romantic in its natural ease and beauty, but this seems consistent with alternative stories of origin, including the Judeo-Christian story of Eden. In this case, the "fall" that follows the early state of the Native American people comes with the arrival of the Europeans. The fall is not brought on by the actions of a naïve woman deceived by a snake, but rather by the aggressive invasion of downcast Europeans who begin to destroy the first people of the Americas by starvation, sickness, and alcohol. The logic of the story is apparently not lost on the missionary. As Sagoyewatha finishes laying responsibility on the Europeans for the destruction of "thousands" of Native people, the missionary appears to be in a hurry to leave. "Brother," Sagoyewatha calls. "Continue to listen." Cram apparently keeps his seat.

Sagoyewatha then identifies several ways in which the claim that there is one religion is undermined. Observing that the source of the religion Cram offers is exclusively European, he asks, "You say that you are right and we are lost. How do we know this to be true?. . . . If [your religion] was intended for us as well as you, why has not the Great Spirit given to us, and not only to us, but why did he not give to our forefathers, the knowledge of that book, with the means of understanding it rightly?" (Densmore 1999, 138). In effect, experience suggests that there is indeed more than one religion in the world. If Cram is right about a single creator, then it seems that the work of the single creator was to generate immediately a diversity of people and religions. Sagoyewatha observes, "The Great Spirit has made us all, but he has made a great difference between his white and red children" (Densmore 1999, 139). The reason that the missionary will not be supported in his efforts is that it seems clear that the Great Spirit intended for there to be a difference between people and that giving up one's tradition is itself a violation of the will of God. Implicit in polygenesis is cultural pluralism. "We do not wish to destroy your religion, or take it from you," he concludes, "We only want to enjoy our own."

Significantly, however, Sagoyewatha's version of the logic of place recognizes the possibility of change and a standard according to which change can occur. "We are all told," he says, "that you have been preaching to the white people in this place. These people are our neighbors. We are acquainted with them. We will wait a little while, and see what effect your preaching has upon them. If we find it does them good, makes them honest and less disposed to cheat Indians, we will then consider again of what you have said" (Densmore 1999, 139). As he concludes elsewhere, "Let us know the tree by the blossoms, and the blossoms by the fruit" (Stone 1866, 291). While it is clear that Sagoyewatha and the council do not wish to support Cram's missionary work, they will not decline the opportunity to learn something of it and its benefits. In effect, though they do not adopt Christianity, they are nevertheless willing to adapt it to their own needs. Adaptation, however, depends largely upon how the set of beliefs and practices work out in action in the context of a logic of place. In the end, if there is something that can be suited to the needs of the Haudenosaunee, they will consider adopting it. The notion is important because it both upholds the conclusion of his argument against Cram, that it is necessary to preserve difference, and at the same time supports the idea of dynamic change based on things learned in experience. In short, Sagoyewatha emphasizes the transformative possibilities of place where place is a process of ongoing interaction. It is destructive, on this view, to lose the past in a forced or *ad hoc* way, but it is also contrary to the logic of place to ignore new ways to contribute to the flourishing of a place. It is expected that new ways, when they help to maintain the land, its history, and its inhabitants, should also be considered and in some cases made part of the place.

In another speech given in this period by Sagoyewatha, he offers to provide Seneca missionaries to provide training to European Americans to "teach them our religion, habits, and customs." In particular, Sagoyewatha believed that Haudenosaunee ideas would provide ways for whites to avoid the conflicts generated by their own beliefs, in effect by providing a ground for a tolerant and diverse community. He continues, "We would be willing they should be as happy as we are, and assure them that if they should follow our example, they would be more, far more happy than they are now. We cannot embrace your religion. It renders us divided and unhappy—but by your embracing ours, we believe that you would be more happy and more acceptable to the Great Spirit" (Stone 1866, 288–291). Although the interpreter translates Sagoyewatha's interest as religious, it is clear from the way he frames his proposal as an offer to give whites an opportunity to "follow an example" that the interest is in practices and attitudes. If whites would only follow the Native example, he claims, then European Americans could both sustain their identity and community while at the same time maintaining fruitful interactions with the other inhabitants of the land. In this way, recalling Neolin and the Delaware reformer, the whites will act in a way consistent with the creator's will and in so doing act in accord with the general framework of Christianity and in accord with a logic of place. Sagoyewatha's conclusion is significant when "religion" is taken to mean a way of acting in the world. "But as you have our good will, we would gladly know that you have relinquished your religion, productive of so much disagreement and inquietude among yourselves, and instead thereof that you should follow ours" (Stone 1866, 288–291).

The demand for separation that seems embedded in the logic of place, when understood in concert with the other commitments of the indigenous attitude, leads not to absolute separation but rather to the possibility of interaction and even cultural exchange. From this perspective, cultural contact, no different from any other form of action, is properly an interaction. Interaction implies pluralism and demands the presence of a wider context in the form of a community. Even so, interactions can lead to a destructive unrestrained sharing that amounts to an attack on difference. The principle of growth provides a frame to moderate the exchange and direct it in ways that sustain diverse communities. Applied to Neolin's context, the Native Prophetic movement saw the problem as one embedded in the colonial logic and its solution in the possibility of an alternative logic of place. In the alternative, the boundaries asserted by the demands of unity and reduction are set aside in favor of attention to the boundaries asserted by place: the interaction of land, people, practices, and beliefs. The logic of place, in a way, adopts the language of experience found in the colonial logic but takes it up into a context that interprets action as interaction and in a context framed by pluralism, community, and growth.

CHAPTER EIGHT

"This Very Ground"

IN THE SPRING OF 1757, a Delaware leader, Teedyuscung, whose name means "one who makes the Earth tremble," was in Philadelphia to demand that the citizens of Pennsylvania respect the boundaries of Native lands along the north fork of the Susquehanna River. One evening during his stay, Teedyuscung visited the home of a Quaker acquaintance. As they sat at the fireside, according to the Quaker, both he and Teedyuscung "were silently looking at the fire, indulging in their own reflections and desiring each other's improvement" (Harvey 1909, 309). Earlier, Teedyuscung had said that, in his meeting with the governor of Pennsylvania, the governor's words "came only from outside of his teeth," and asserted, "I will talk so too." After thinking about Teedyuscung's response, the Friend replied, "I will tell thee what I have been thinking of. I have been thinking of a rule delivered by the founder of the Christian religion, which, from its excellence, we call 'The Golden Rule.'" Teedyuscung interrupted. "Stop! . . . Don't praise it to me, but rather tell me what it is and let me think for myself. I do not wish you to tell me of its excellence; tell me what it is." "It is," said the Quaker, "for one man to do to another as he would the other should do to him." The Delaware responded, "That is impossible—it cannot be done" and then fell silent, smoking his pipe and pacing. After fifteen minutes of silence, he addressed the Quaker again. "Brother, I have been thoughtful of what you told me. If the Great Spirit that made man would give him a new heart, he could do as you say; but not else." He continued, "Now, Brother, it is no harm to tell you what I was thinking before you spoke. I thought that the Great Spirit who made the land never intended one man should have so much of it as never to see it all, and another not to have so much as to plant corn for his children. I think the Great Spirit never meant it should be so" (Harvey 1909, 309).

The scene reflects the character of the border between Native and European America at the end of the Great Awakening. The conversation, apparently between two friends, emerges from the wider context of cultural conflict along the border and is framed in terms of Christianity and land. The Quaker, in the context of a peaceful rest, responds to the Delaware leader's comment on the governor and the conduct of negotiations with an admonition to adopt a Christian principle. Teedyuscung responds in a tone that seems half-weary and half-angry, perhaps tired of the press of missionaries on one hand and land-greedy settlers on the other, caught in the middle between the Haudenosaunee to the north, the French to the west and the British to the east and south. Here, over a pipe, Teedyuscung made an intellectual declaration of independence to accompany the military and political declarations he had already made in conferences with the Pennsylvania leadership. He would decide for himself, or rather for himself as a Delaware and as spokesperson for a confederacy of Native peoples, whether the Golden Rule ought to be followed. Probably to the great surprise of the Friend, Teedyuscung immediately responded that the rule is impossible. Yet how could anyone reject a rule that stood as the cornerstone of the Quaker commitment to peace? Teedyuscung's deliberate explanation of his conclusion, that its practice would require that God change the human heart, seems to have lessened the surprise and satisfied the Quaker's concern. For the Friend, Teedyuscung seemed to be saying that to obey the Golden Rule one must be able to see oneself in others. To say that human beings needed a "new heart" might simply mean that the disposition to consider only oneself must be replaced with a disposition to consider others as oneself. In effect, Teedyuscung might have seemed to say that the Golden Rule is impossible in a selfish world. While this might be a plausible reading of Teedyuscung's reply, it is also an interpretation in overtly colonial terms. The barrier to obeying the Golden Rule is the failure to see everyone "as oneself." The standard of comparison in the rule is one's own interests and needs as a human being and the crucial perspective is the ability to see others in those terms. Others, in this case, are extensions of oneself, or rather one's own conception of what humanity requires. Following the logic of the colonial attitude, if something is necessary for me as a human being, it is also necessary for others as human beings. If I wish to treat others properly, I will treat them in the same way I wish to be treated, that is, as a human being. Under this approach, I become the model and standard for the others I encounter.

Another reading of Teedyuscung's response seems more likely. For many Native people along the border, the Great Awakening seemed to be a demand that they submit to a doctrine that predicated action on the assumption of human sameness. The expectations set by different origin stories, the recognition of distinctive cultural practices, and the importance of place all stood in sharp tension with the unifying message of the Great Awakening preachers. A reading of Teedyuscung's response to the Golden Rule that simply affirms pessimism while presuming a logic grounded in the colonial attitude misses the potential message. From the perspective of resistance as manifested in the Prophetic movement, Teedyuscung's rejection of the Golden Rule is not because he thinks that God must "give [humankind] a new heart" so that people can see others as themselves, but because God has already made people different and provided an appropriate moral standard for such a creation. Given "human nature" from the Native prophets' viewpoint, the proper rule is not seeing others as oneself but seeing oneself from the perspective of others as a member of a particular nation, as part of a particular place. Recalling the principle of government adopted by Miantonomi and Canonicus, the proper principle is to act in a way that does not displease others, confident that others will "not be offended" by the efforts one makes. Teedyuscung's rejection of the Golden Rule from this perspective is not on the ground of human inability to see others in terms of one's own conception of humanity, but on the ground that the rule is inadequate for a richly diverse humanity. In effect, Teedyuscung's rejection marks an alternative logic. Rather than seeing particular cases in terms of some universal standard, Teedyuscung expects standards to emerge from interactions involving shared interests and using established resources as a means to settle present concerns. It is a local logic, not a universal one, and its implications are significant for Teedyuscung and his negotiations, and for the European Americans who sought to maintain a peaceful and diverse American society.

Teedyuscung reinforces this alternate interpretation when he reveals what he has been thinking about: land. As part of the Prophetic movement developing along the border and anticipating Neolin's conclusions, Teedyuscung is thinking about Native lands and, from the standpoint of the logic of place, lands as integral components of human and other life. Recalling the Great Spirit (or "Master of Life" in Neolin's terms), Teedyuscung implies the Delaware expectation of polygenesis and its logic. Whites are violating the proper relations established by polygenesis by isolating Native people and reducing their lands in a way that will necessarily destroy them. The issue does not admit of easy interpretation under the Golden Rule. From this perspective, Native people must be understood in terms of human nature and progress. Places are not as important as the need to adopt the ways and interests of civilization. Such ways do not cling to places and the lands involved, but view the land as a resource to be subdued and made to support human progress. To treat the Delaware properly, that is, as "he would the other should do to him," is to foster ways of life that commodify the land and contribute to human progress. If it is human nature to move toward civilization through progress and progress involves leaving traditional homelands or selling parts of it, then the Golden Rule amounts to a justification for the Native dispossession. By making land a commodity to be acquired, the whites and the Delaware can participate in all of the economic and social processes that ensure progress. As made clear in Edwards's educational plans (and those of missionaries before and after him) the process of reducing Native lands and demanding other modes of living was precisely to see Native people as fundamentally the same as the Europeans, as part of one humanity and one process of development. Teedyuscung rejects the Golden Rule because it seems to lead to the policies of dispossession he was in Philadelphia to oppose.

Teedyuscung had long experience with the preachers and the doctrines of the Great Awakening just as he had a long family history of removal and dispossession.[1] Born near the village of Trenton in New Jersey, Teedyuscung grew up in close proximity to the rapidly growing European American people. While living in a Delaware village, he nevertheless learned English and the crafts of basketry and broom making.[2] By 1730, increasingly pressed by the expanding white settlement, Teedyuscung and his family moved across the Delaware River to another established Delaware village near the Lehigh River in the region called the Forks of the Delaware. When English settlers began to arrive in the vicinity of the Delaware villages in 1734, the leadership was called to the village of Durham by the Pennsylvania government. Here, James Logan, chief justice of the Pennsylvania Supreme Court, informed the Delaware that the lands in question, including the Forks, had been sold to Penn-

---

1. The biographical information included here is from Wallace 1990. Wallace presents a detailed account both of Teedyuscung's life and of the social and political circumstances that surrounded his controversial career. Wallace's account is invaluable in studying Teedyuscung and in establishing resources for understanding the Native background to the peace conferences attended by Franklin in the 1750s. At the same time, Wallace tends to present Teedyuscung as an unstable figure struggling to maintain his Native identity while wanting to be viewed as European. At minimum, however, Teedyuscung's public speeches need to be understood as not merely his own views, but as views representing the viewpoint of his people and himself as Delaware. The identity question that interests Wallace, at least in these cases, is not the question. As Teedyuscung is willing to accept aspects of European culture, even asking for a secretary to keep minutes of the proceedings for him, he never seems troubled by a confused identity. Teedyuscung is Delaware and is advocating for peaceful coexistence, not assimilation.

2. See Wallace 1990, Chapter I.

sylvania in 1686. The Delaware leadership was shocked. Nutimus, the acknowledged speaker of the Native villages at the Forks, explained that there was no record at all of the Forks' inclusion in the earlier purchase. Logan, whose ironworks at Durham was running out of wood fuel, needed the lands north of the Delaware River to provide a fresh supply. The old land deal provided the justification for expansion into the Forks, and after convincing the Haudenosaunee allies of the Delaware to stay out of the negotiations, Logan recalled Nutimus and his people to the table in 1737. At this meeting, Logan showed Nutimus a map supposedly showing the extent of the 1686 sale and convinced Nutimus to reaffirm the deal by signing a new deed. The deed specified the western boundary of the purchase and the extent of the sale to the north as the distance that could be measured by "a day and a half's walk along the Delaware" from the Durham ironworks. This settlement, in honor of its method of measurement, became known as the "Walking Purchase." In September of 1737, "three young woodsmen" began the walk to determine the boundaries of the purchase along a trail that had been cleared for the purpose earlier by Logan's people. The pace was so fast that one of the woodsmen and the Native observers had to drop out. By midday of the second day, the walk ended fifty-five miles up the Delaware in a territory that now included twelve hundred square miles of land (Wallace 1990, 26).

With the forced conclusion of the Walking Purchase by Logan and the Pennsylvania government, European settlers began to arrive at the Forks. In 1740, a renowned preacher of the Great Awakening, George Whitefield, purchased a tract of land from Pennsylvania to establish a college for freed blacks. The college was abandoned the next year and the land sold to a group of German Christians led by Nikolaus Ludwig Count Von Zinzendorf. The Moravian sect, as the group was known, was a Protestant group that favored a communal lifestyle and a Reformation theology that included harsh discipline and dissent from earthly governmental authority. The group had not been well-received in North Carolina and the move to Pennsylvania, whose Quaker leadership was more tolerant of such dissent, was to be a new start. On December 24, 1741, Count Von Zinzendorf officially established the Moravian village of Bethlehem on the banks of the Lehigh River. Consistent with the atmosphere of evangelism that pervaded the Delaware River valley, the Moravians began a concerted effort to convert their neighbors. Within a few years, the Moravians had expanded their evangelical efforts to the Native people further up the Lehigh and established a mission named Gnadenhütten, "The Huts of Grace."

According to Anthony F. C. Wallace, Gnadenhütten was a "little syl-

van utopia. At the foot of the hill, on the west bank of the creek, stood
the chapel and the barns and farmhouses of the white Brethren; on the
east side were the log huts of the Indians spread in a half-moon, part
way up the hillside" (Wallace 1990, 41). The village served as a refugee
center for displaced Native people throughout the region. While not all
Native residents were Moravian converts, many were, and the result of
the joined cultures was a distinctive "Praying Indian" culture that maintained Native cultural forms and practices while incorporating Christian
practices and European economic forms.[3] By 1750, Teedyuscung and his
family had moved from the Native village of Meniolagomeka to Gnadenhütten and in March of that year he and his wife were baptized by the
Moravian bishop there (Wallace 1990, 40).[4] While there is necessarily
some debate about the meaning of Teedyuscung's baptism and move to
the Moravian mission and whether it constitutes a challenge to his identity as Delaware, it is important to recognize the force of dislocation in
the Forks and the need for the Native people there to find ways of maintaining their own identities while also maintaining peaceful relations
with the surrounding peoples. From this perspective, it is not surprising that when the Haudenosaunee asked the Delaware to settle in the
next valley to the west along the north fork of the Susquehanna River,
Teedyuscung's people were eager to accept.

For some time, relations between the French and the British had
deteriorated. When hostilities broke out along the border between the
territories of the Native allies of the French and the Native allies of the
British, the Delaware and other Native people in the vast Ohio River
drainage northwest of Philadelphia found themselves in the middle of a
European war. In order to prevent the French Indian allies from occupying the territory between Philadelphia and the British allies to the
north, the Haudenosaunee Confederacy (who also claimed the Delaware people as dependents) asked the Delaware to take up residence in
the abandoned Haudenosaunee village of Wyoming on the upper Susquehanna River.[5] The offer not only represented a chance for the Forks
peoples to establish a new place for themselves away from the evangelism
of the Moravians, it also amounted to an offer to improve the standing
of the Delaware from subservient status to semi-independence. They

---

3. See Wallace's description of Gnadenhütten (1990, 41–42).
4. The Moravian bishop noted the baptism in his journal. "Today I baptized *Tatiuskundt,*
the chief among sinners" (quoted in Wallace 1990, 40). The reference to the "chief among
sinners" suggests that those like the earlier "chief sinner" Roger Williams, who advocated
for coexistence, continued to be viewed as a threat.
5. See Wallace 1990, Chapter IV.

were to occupy Wyoming as their permanent home and would, of course, maintain a firm alliance with both the Haudenosaunee and the British.

In 1754, Teedyuscung and his people arrived at Wyoming to start their lives again in a place independent of the Europeans. Within months, however, as the French and British began to fight to the west, Teedyuscung learned that a group of settlers from Connecticut had "purchased" the land of Wyoming and were about to establish a settlement there. Setting aside the details of the negotiations and agreements that gave the Connecticut settlers a "right" to the Wyoming valley, Teedyuscung and the other leaders of Wyoming sent appeals north to the Haudenosaunee and south to the British asking for assistance in maintaining their place as an independent community on the Susquehanna. The call for help, however, went unheard or unheeded and the lack of response quickly placed the Wyoming people in a difficult situation. Without support from the British and Haudenosaunee, they were left alone to deal with the French and their Native allies to the west and the invasion of the Connecticut settlers from the east. When the French made offers of support in exchange for military assistance against the British, the Wyoming people reluctantly agreed. After long supporting the peace party, Teedyuscung led a group of thirty warriors in January 1756 and attacked several white plantations to the east along the Delaware. After killing several and capturing prisoners, the party returned home only to find that his people had moved in fear of British attack. He rejoined his people at a village further up the Susquehanna until spring when the group returned to Wyoming. The attack on the British plantations earned Teedyuscung respect as a war leader, and when negotiations opened later in July 1756, Teedyuscung was chosen as the speaker for the Native people living in the area of Wyoming.[6]

6. Despite his repeated selection as speaker for the Native people of the area around Wyoming, Teedyuscung was not widely respected by the European Americans who knew him. He drank heavily on occasion and periodically turned up at important meetings drunk. He also appeared to be remarkably vain, demanding that he be called "king" and often declaring himself to be a chief of the Six Nations (the Haudenosaunee). Wallace ascribes Teedyuscung's drinking and vanity to his location on a border between dramatically different cultures. As a result of his double identification, Native and British, and the conflict generated between them, drinking and extreme behaviors are to be expected. While this might be a correct assessment, it is also possible that the criticisms of Teedyuscung are influenced by his challenging both British and Six Nations authority in his attempt to negotiate a place for his people in the midst of warring factions. The demand to be called "king" could easily be viewed as a demand that the selected speaker of the Native people in the north Susquehanna valley deserved respect. His drinking, while no doubt a problem, could also be read as a problem not of "coping" with a split identity but of alcoholism. His speeches at least leave little doubt that if Teedyuscung faced warring identities in his personal life, as the Delaware speaker the war was only in the background.

Eventually, when he sat at the fireside of the Friend in Philadelphia, the discussion of the Golden Rule can be seen as a focal point, not just for Teedyuscung's assessment of European military and political policies, but also for the Delaware resistance to the European ways of thinking and acting in the world that had brought so much hardship to his people. While he could have used the Golden Rule as a means to condemn European policies and practices, he instead challenged it. From Teedyuscung's perspective, the European practices that ignored the importance to Native people of land and boundaries clearly violated the expectation that actions ought to take into account how they will be viewed and how they will be understood by others. By destroying Native places, that is, the complex interaction between people, land, and the land's other inhabitants, the Europeans failed to see things through others' eyes. The imposition of the European ways of thinking meant starving children and a dying culture, failed lands, and an inability to participate as people in community. The story of Teedyuscung's response to the Golden Rule, in a sense, identifies both the key issues along the border and the key confusions facing any attempt to foster coexistence instead of assimilation or annihilation.

The Native resistance to the presence of whites in the Forks of the Delaware River became clearer to the Proprietors of Pennsylvania at the peace conferences held at the village of Easton at the confluence of the Lehigh and Delaware Rivers first in July and then in November of 1756. Teedyuscung opened the conference between the Delaware people from the area of Wyoming and representatives of the Pennsylvania colony under the leadership of the new governor, William Denny. After reminding his listeners that this conference continued the work of one held in the same place during the summer, Teedyuscung began, "In Conformity to an antient and good Custom established among our Ancestors, I now proceed to open your Eyes and Ears, and remove all Obstructions out of your Throats, that nothing may impede the Attention necessary to be used in a Matter of such Importance as is now going on" (Van Doren and Boyd 1938, 151). Observing that "bad reports" had recently circulated about Delaware attacks on white settlements along the border with Pennsylvania, Teedyuscung said that they should be "no more minded than the Whistling of Birds" and, by giving a belt of wampum he would "take away the bad Impressions."[7] The governor rose

---

7. "Wampum" refers to strings or belts made of light and dark colored shells or beads used for a variety of purposes by Native people and European Americans. Sometimes wampum was used as a form of currency, especially along the border between Native and Euro-

and, following the instructions of his advisers, thanked Teedyuscung for his speech, agreed that the "idle Reports" should be "no more regarded than the chirping of Birds" and gave a string of wampum to reinforce his agreement. The conference adjourned until the following day.

Among the representatives of Pennsylvania that day was Benjamin Franklin. Already well-known in the British colonies and in Europe, fifty years old, a writer, printer, scientist, and promoter of the public good, he attended the conference as a commissioner of the colony and was one of the four signatories on the official report of the conference. Franklin, like Roger Williams, is a key figure in tracing the influence of Native thought and, beyond Williams, a key figure in the development of pragmatism.[8] In this chapter and the next I will examine Franklin's connections with Native thought, particularly with the logic of place as it developed in the Native Prophetic movement, and its implications for Franklin's own views. In this chapter, I will consider Franklin's connections with Native people in the context of diplomacy and in light of his commitments to the importance of community and the standard of growth. In the next chapter, I will examine the influence of Native thought on the development of Franklin's experimental science as it was framed by a commitment to the principle of interaction, and the development of his commitment to pluralism that finally framed his vision of American democracy.

Franklin's attendance at the Easton conference was important because it was here, as the author of several crucial speeches to the Delaware, that he gained experience with the logic of place. Franklin already had some experience in such negotiations. Beginning in 1736, he began to print accounts of Native and British treaty negotiations for sale to the general public. They proved to be popular reading and served both as a kind of original American literary form and as a means by which Europeans and European Americans removed from the border could learn about the formal practices and concerns of Native people. Franklin himself became part of a negotiation in 1753 when he attended a conference at Carlisle between the Pennsylvania government and representatives of the Delaware, Haudenosaunee, Shawnee, Twightwee (or Miami), and

pean American nations. In cases of the sort described here, from the perspective of the European Americans, wampum served as a formal gift used to show "good faith" in the process of negotiations. From a Native perspective in this case, the belt may also have been seen as part of the process of communication between different nations. For discussions of wampum see Jennings et al. 1985, "A Glossary of Figures of Speech in Iroquois Political Rhetoric," and Foster 1985, "Another Look at the Function of Wampum in Iroquois-White Councils."

8. See Campbell 1999, for a valuable examination of Franklin's pragmatism.

Wyandot. The issues of the conference were left unclear until the commissioners arrived, but when they sat down for informal talks before the official conference, the chief spokesperson for the Natives, Scaroyady, made it clear that the proximate need for the conference was the incursion of the French and their Native allies into the Ohio River valley.[9] Although some see the purpose of the conference as a request for presents to keep the Ohio Indians friendly to the British,[10] it is more likely that the conference was called to convince the British to help the Ohio Indians maintain their territories and autonomy as the French prepared for war.

The Carlisle conference, unlike the one held in 1756 at Easton, began with a ceremony of condolence. Traditionally condolence ceremonies served to provide an opportunity for neighbor groups to set aside their differences and help condole a group that had lost a leader. The ceremony combined features of a funeral in the Christian sense as a framework for grieving, but it also served the function of dissipating anger and reaffirming the connections between groups in a peaceful setting.[11] The condolence ceremonies traditionally began with a ceremony called the "woods edge" in which those visiting approached but did not enter the village of a people who had lost a leader. The grieving people would then send emissaries to welcome the arriving group and to invite them into the village. The welcoming ceremony included an exchange of words to "clear the dust" of the road from the eyes, ears, and throat of those participating in the ceremony to make it possible for the parties to engage each other fully. At the Carlisle conference, after condolences and gifts were given for the losses suffered by the attending Native peoples, the commissioners, aided by an interpreter, began the business of the conference by offering to reaffirm the standing friendship between the nations and Pennsylvania. The speech by the commissioners, perhaps read to the assembled conference by Franklin, concludes, "Let no Differences nor Jealousies subsist a Moment between Nation and Nation; but join all together as one Man, sincerely and heartily" (Van Doren and Boyd 1938, 129).

Following the ceremonial form of peace conferences, after those who spoke first introduced issues for discussion and confirmed them by giving a string or a belt of wampum, it was proper that the receiving

9. Scaroyady was an Oneida who had been chosen as speaker by the nations attending the conference.

10. See Van Doren 1938, 207.

11. See Fenton 1985 for a discussion of the connections between the traditional condolence ceremony and the ceremonial form of peace conferences.

side consider the points raised and then respond to them in order. To the matter of joining "all together as one Man," the Indians, in the voice of Scaroyady, declined to accept the proposal but deferred an answer by agreeing to take the belt that was given back to the Ohio valley for consideration by a larger council of the associated nations. The deferral was at once consistent with a general Native commitment to involving the people represented in negotiations in the process of making agreements and with a rebuke of the Pennsylvania commissioners' request that the Ohio valley people ally as "one Man" with Great Britain in their war against France. By delaying a response, the Ohio Indians also remained neutral in the conflict as they tried to make the best arrangements for their own continued national and cultural autonomy. After setting aside the issue of alliance, Scaroyady seemed to raise the real issue on which the question of alliance turned. "We desire a Commission may be given to the Person intrusted by the Government of *Pennsylvania;* and that he may be directed to warn People from settling the Indians Lands and impowered to remove them" (Van Doren and Boyd 1938, 130).

The commissioners' response to Scaroyady's speech refused to take up the matter of land directly but rather focused on a range of issues relating to trade. The issue of lands and the logic of place that provides a framework for their importance is set aside by the collective action of the commissioners and governor, but it appears that the issue made a deeper impression on Franklin. In 1755, when a delegation of people including Scaroyady visited Philadelphia, the issue of stolen lands was raised again. The complaint, however, was not detailed in the official records of the Carlisle conference and the only existing notes about the issue of Native land rights were Franklin's.[12] Although Franklin was not willing to conclude that the complaint was well-founded,[13] his interest in issues of national autonomy, national union, and aspects of place were clearly present in his thinking about Native people and the British colonies. Although not specifically in the context of land, the report on the Carlisle conference coauthored by Franklin, Richard Peters, and Isaac Norris ends with a demand for justice for the Native people of the Ohio valley.

> [In] Justice to these *Indians,* and the Promises we made them, we cannot close our Report, without taking Notice, That the Quantities of strong Liquors sold to these *Indians* in the Place of their Residence, and during their Hunting Seasons, from all Parts of the Counties over *Sasquehannah,* have

12. See Franklin 1959, 6: 254, 287–288, 288n.
13. See Franklin 1959, 6: 287–288.

encreased of late to an inconceivable Degree, so as to keep these poor *Indians* continually under the Force of Liquor, that they are hereby become dissolute, enfeebled, and indolent when sober, and untractable and mischievous in their Liquor, always quarrelling, and often murdering one another. (Van Doren and Boyd 1938, 134)

It is both the unregulated sale of liquor and the violation of Native lands, "the Place of their Residence," that is behind the injustice to Native people. It is not merely selling liquor (elsewhere Franklin argues that traders may sell liquor in their own stores outside Native lands), it is the violation of the relations of place that led to the undermining of Native culture and autonomy. Franklin appears to have made strong connections between lands, people, and culture that would serve to frame his developing notions of a pluralist American society, although these connections were indirect at the time of the Carlisle conference.

The following year, 1754, Franklin's view of Native people and the potential he saw in Native ways of understanding and acting in the world emerged even more clearly at a conference at Albany in the province of New York. Called primarily in order to reinforce the alliance between the British colonies and the Six Nations and their allies, the colonial representatives arrived before the Six Nations representatives did and took advantage of the time to discuss how best to respond to their mutual interests. Franklin and others used the opportunity to propose the "Albany Plan of Union." In partial response to the need to do justice to Native people and in part to form a united military alliance among the British colonies against the French, Franklin proposed that the colonies unite in a confederation.[14] The model for the confederation maintained at once clear boundaries between colonies, autonomous state governments, and a single federal council to conduct a limited range of business on behalf of the union. The confederation structure was similar to the form of confederation embodied in the Haudenosaunee Confederacy, which was itself the union of five (and later six) distinct nations. Each nation, in joining the confederacy, preserved its own boundaries, governance structures, and traditions, but also agreed to participate in a central council that made decisions about issues that affected the common interests of all the nations.[15] In 1744, the Onondaga speaker Canassatego, in the conference report published by Franklin, is reported to have closed his discussion with the Pennsylvania governor with a rec-

14. See Franklin 1959, 5: 357–417 for documents related to the Albany Plan of Union.
15. See Parker 1968 for two versions of the constitution of the Haudenosaunee that describe both its origin and governing structure.

ommendation that proposed the union of the colonies in just these terms. "We heartily recommend," Canassatego says, "Union and a good Agreement between you and our Brethren. Never disagree, but preserve a strict Friendship for one another, and thereby you, as well as we, will become the stronger" (Van Doren and Boyd 1938, 78). The recommendation was given with crucial evidence. "Our wise Forefathers established Union and Amity between the Five Nations," Canassatego reminds the conference, "this has made us formidable; this has given us great Weight and Authority with our neighbouring Nations. We are a powerful Confederacy; and, by observing the same Methods our wise Forefathers have taken, you will acquire fresh Strength and Power." Franklin recalls Canassatego's remarks in a letter to James Parker in 1751. "It would be a very strange Thing," Franklin says, "if six Nations of ignorant Savages should be capable of forming a scheme for such an Union, and be able to execute it in such a Manner, as that it has subsisted for Ages, and appears indissoluble; and yet a like Union should be impracticable for ten or a Dozen English Colonies, to whom it is more necessary, and must be more advantageous and who cannot be supposed to want an equal Understanding of their Interests" (Franklin 1959, 4: 118–119).

The Albany Conference provided Franklin with an opportunity to propose "a scheme for such an Union."[16] In the end, the individual colonial governments did not accept the plan, but it did provide a precedent and background for the later unions of the European American colonies during and after the Revolution. As significant as the details of the plan are (the structure of the "Grand Council," the particular powers assigned the confederate government, and so on), the general framework is especially important for understanding the ways in which Franklin began to understand communities and the possibilities of pluralism. The plan was based on a twofold need to respond to common concerns (Native trade and the French) and to minimize "disputes and quarrels" in the process of responding to such needs. The union, then, was pre-

16. The Albany Plan and its connection with Native American practices through the Albany Conferences and references to Native governance by Franklin are often cited as evidence that the United States Articles of Confederation and Constitution are based on Native forms of government. See Grinde 1977, Johansen 1982, Grinde and Johansen 1991, and Johansen 1998 for discussions of the case for the influence of the Haudenosaunee on North American political institutions and ideas of freedom. See Tooker 1988 for a counterargument. This debate provides another useful perspective on the issues of Native American influence on European and European thought and ideas closely connected with the pragmatic commitments to community and pluralism.

sumed to involve the maintenance of colonial differences while providing a common framework for interaction.

The plan itself was not presumed to descend from laws about human
nature or the directives of God, at least according to Franklin's notes.
Rather, the commissioners "proceeded to sketch out a *plan of union,*
which they did in a plain and concise manner, just sufficient to shew their
sentiments of the kind of union that would best suit the circumstances
of the colonies, be most agreeable to the people, and most effectually
promote his Majesty's service and the general interest of the British Empire" (Franklin 1959, 5: 400). Curiously, in a context dominated by the
colonial attitude, Franklin was here proposing a government and laws
that were judged in relation to the details of fostering a place. It was the
interaction of the colonies' concrete geographical, cultural, economic,
and historical locations that provided the standard with which to determine a good union. That the union was the best "to suit the circumstances" reinforces the idea that the frame for Franklin's thinking about
the problems of governance and coexistence was grounded in concrete
circumstances and, in the language of the Native Prophetic movement,
sought to establish a place, a complex of interactions. The idea that such
a union was "agreeable to the people" is not merely a democratic sentiment, but, in context, an affirmation of the relational and located nature
of his case and the proposed union itself. Even the reference to the Empire fits the logic of place in that it includes the interests of the Empire
as one of the relations involved in the place but not as the unquestioned
authority in terms of which proposals would be judged.

As violence spread along the border in 1755, Franklin became an
advocate for establishing a militia in the province of Pennsylvania despite
the province's long commitment to the Quaker ideal of pacifism. The
proposal recognized the pacifist tradition of Pennsylvania but also argued that, in light of the Quaker commitment to freedom of conscience,
non-Quakers who wished to defend Pennsylvania should be free to do
so. Given the large number of non-Quakers now in the province, volun-
teers were not in short supply. The Militia Act authored by Franklin
passed in November 1755, just days before a group of French-allied Indians attacked the Moravian mission at Gnadenhütten. Since the Christian Indians who lived at the mission were told of the coming attack,
they escaped, but ten whites were killed and the buildings of the town
burned.[17] With the attack, Franklin himself led a detachment of soldiers
and supplies to aid in the defense of the Moravian villages in the Forks.

17. See Wallace 1990, 76ff.

In January 1756 he arrived in the destroyed village of Gnadenhütten, even as Teedyuscung and his group attacked the plantations north of Easton on the Delaware.

By November 1756 when the peace conference convened at Easton, Franklin's experience with Indian affairs and reputation as a leader, military and otherwise, led to his appointment as one of the commissioners to the conference and apparently the author of many of the speeches delivered by Governor Denny. The experienced interpreters, including Conrad Weiser, a German Moravian who spoke several Native languages and had been adopted by the Mohawk, expected a traditional peace conference beginning with a condolence ceremony and an exchange of gifts. When Denny actually opened the discussion, he set aside the established protocol to ask an open question:

> You was pleased [*sic*] to tell me, the other Day [at the opening meeting], that the League of Friendship made by your Fore-fathers was as yet fresh in your Memory; you said that it was made so strong that a small Thing would not easily break it. As we are now met together, at a Council-Fire, kindled by us both, and have promised on both Sides to be free and open to one another, I must ask you, how that League of Friendship came to be broken? Have we, the Governor or People of *Pennsylvania* done you any kind of Injury? If you think we have, you should be honest, and tell us your Hearts. (Van Doren and Boyd 1938, 154)

Denny concludes by giving a wampum belt that he "may obtain a full Answer to this Point" (Van Doren and Boyd 1938, 154). Weiser described Denny's question as "a very absurd one in the Indian Light," claiming that the Delaware at the conference "wanted nothing but forgiveness" for the attacks on the white plantations, and "old Friendship restored" (Wallace 1945, 461).[18] Whether Weiser's assessment was correct or not, it is clear from what followed that the question marked both a turning point in Franklin's conception of Native perspectives of themselves and the whites and a turning point in Teedyuscung's ability to speak to the issue of Native place.

The speech read by Denny that day had been drafted the previous day by Franklin.[19] Denny, a novice in Native affairs, probably had little idea about the importance of asking for a Native perspective on the borderlands that made up much of Pennsylvania's territory. Franklin,

---

18. Regardless of how the Delaware viewed it, Weiser also noted in his journal, "I was not pleased with the Question, but protested against it." The Six Nations representatives present were also angry about the question. See Wallace 1945, 461–462.

19. See the draft of Denny's speech by Franklin (Franklin 1959, 7: 15–17).

however, given his experience and attention to issues of justice for the Native people, surely knew both the risks of the question and the possible results. Even as he had tried to offer a plan of Union to the colonies two years earlier that would ensure the integrity of distinctive provinces in alliance with Native nations, so here was a chance to find out how best to settle the conflicts along the Delaware in a similar way. Familiar as he was with the ceremonial demands of a peace conference, he knew that because he framed the question as he did, Teedyuscung would be obliged to answer on behalf of his people as best he could. In such a forum Franklin probably expected that he might find keys to defusing the war that had killed so many whites and Indians over the previous three years. At the same time, if Teedyuscung sought to speak freely to the whites who had dispossessed his family, isolated his people between competing powers, and placed his own village at constant risk of destruction, Franklin had given him the chance that he otherwise would not have had in the context of a formal conference.

Some have argued that Teedyuscung in this context was little more than a pawn in the ongoing struggle between the Proprietors of Pennsylvania and a group of Quaker business people. The Proprietors, as the heirs of William Penn, had absolute power over the province but blamed the Quakers and their pacifism for the war. At the same time, the Quakers wanted the Proprietors to pay a share of the costs of maintaining the province and its defenses and blamed the war on the Proprietors' Indian policies. Paul Wallace puts this interpretation succinctly. "Weiser recognized [Denny's question] for what it was: a maneuver by Israel Pemberton's Quakers to escape the political consequences of Pennsylvania's military unpreparedness (for which they were responsible) by blaming the war itself on the Proprietors" (Wallace 1945, 461).[20] While the evidence from journals of the time suggest that Teedyuscung received support from the Quakers (including gifts and money) and that they met with Teedyuscung periodically throughout the conference, it is not clear that Teedyuscung was just a pawn in another conflict. In light of the interests and approach of the Native Prophetic movement already flourishing along the border, it is more likely that the Quaker interests and Teedyuscung's nationalist interests intersected. That Franklin appears to have penned Denny's speech and was himself a moderate who had a

20. Anthony F. C. Wallace shares Paul Wallace's conclusions about the motivations behind Denny's speech and Teedyuscung's reply (Wallace 1990, Chapter XI). This interpretation may be best with respect to understanding the development of Pennsylvania politics of the time, but it overlooks both the intellectual tradition brought to the conference by Teedyuscung and the perspective and interests brought by Franklin.

well-informed interest in Native issues suggests that the speech and its response marked a crucial moment when Native and European American concerns were brought together for open consideration.

After retiring to reflect on the questions posed by Denny, Teedyuscung returned the next day with an answer prepared. Although presented in a translation using the first person singular pronoun, the content of Teedyuscung's address suggests that the translation should have used the plural. "According to your . . . Question . . . last Night, to know of me why I struck you, without first giving you a Reason for it; I will tell you the Truth" (Van Doren and Boyd 1938, 156). "The King of England, and of France," he says, "have settled, or wrought, this Land, so as to coop us up, as if in a Pen." The attacks by the Susquehanna Indians focused on the English and not the French because "Our foolish and ignorant young Men, . . . were persuaded by this false-hearted [French] King to strike our Brethren the English." The attack on the English was made swifter and heavier by the "lies" of the French, but the encouragement of the French was not the "principal Cause."

The "principal Cause" Teedyuscung at first leaves aside, content to talk about the progress of his diplomatic mission during the late summer as he tried to reestablish alliances with other Ohio River valley peoples. The governor, perhaps at the prodding of Franklin and his colleagues, presses the issue and asks Teedyuscung to explain his grievances. In response, he says that he did not need to go far for an example of the primary cause of the Native attacks. "This very Ground, that is under me (striking it with his Foot) was my Land and Inheritance, and is taken from me by Fraud" (Van Doren and Boyd 1938, 157). The point, Teedyuscung says, is not that no land may be sold: "A Bargain is a Bargain." It is rather that the whites have failed to establish the relations expected of them when they entered into agreements to occupy parts of Native lands. He gives an analogy. Suppose, he says to the governor, that "you had a Pipe in your Mouth, smoking, of little value; [and] I come and take it from you." After a time, "you remember it and take Revenge: I had forgot and wonder at the Cause and ask you Brother, Why you have done so?" The key problem is not that the pipe was taken or even that the pipe's original owner remembers the incident and seeks revenge. The problem is that the pipe's origin has been forgotten. The network of relations in which the pipe lived was broken, not by the stealing or the seeking of revenge, but by forgetting and so ending the relation. Teedyuscung returns the analogy to the land. "Now, although you have purchased our Lands from our Fore-fathers on so reasonable Terms, yet now at length, you will not allow us to cut a little Wood to make a Fire; nay, hinder us from Hunting, the only Means left us of getting our Livelihood." The problem is not the exchange, but the failure to maintain proper relations afterwards. For Teedyuscung, "selling" the land does not mean turning over the land exclusively to someone else, but rather means something like entering into an ongoing relation where there was none before. When the whites "bought" the land, they took exclusive hold of it and began to destroy the crucial relations long established between the land and its inhabitants. Perhaps following cues from Israel Pemberton and his Quaker allies, Teedyuscung uses the language of land fraud.[21] His illustration, however, is not of land fraud of the legal sort, but rather is framed as a process of blocking interactions and so undermining the life of the people and the land.

The governor, however, hears only of fraud and asks Teedyuscung to be specific. Teedyuscung, in turn, describes two kinds of fraud (Van Doren and Boyd 1938, 157). The first, the Walking Purchase, is a "fraud" in which an established relationship was broken when the heirs of Penn redescribed the geography of the agreement through a forged map. While Penn had been given the opportunity to live with the Native people in the region, his children now claimed exclusive right to land outside the first agreement, including Teedyuscung's home in Wyoming and his family's home in the Forks. The second form of fraud occurs when one party sells land that they do not have a right to in the first place to someone else, as when Pennsylvania sold the Wyoming valley to investors from Connecticut. In this case too, the issue is not strictly an issue of purchase but an issue of violating established relations. It is not that Connecticut settlers could never be welcome at Wyoming, but rather that the process of "buying" Wyoming from someone who is not related fails to establish the proper relations. Teedyuscung concludes his speech with a perplexing challenge: "not that I desire that you should now purchase these Lands, but that you should look into your own Hearts, and consider what is right and that do" (Van Doren and Boyd 1938, 158).[22]

The commissioners considered Teedyuscung's reply and two days

21. Weiser affirms this problem of communicating Teedyuscung's own concerns in terms suggested by his Quaker allies. Weiser explains, "Many Expressions Teedjouskon made use of, were no Indian Phrases, and he could not afterwards answer to them, before he spoke with Israel, or some others; This very Thing cost Pennsylvania much Blood and Treasure" (Wallace 1945, 462). This does not, however, mean that Teedyuscung and his councilors had no voice in the proceedings. Rather, it is better understood as a case where Teedyuscung was attempting to take advantage of the support and arguments of the Quakers to reinforce his own people's position.

22. Teedyuscung here follows the sort of principle that stands as an alternative to the Golden Rule. By leaving the proper response open, he expects that the whites will try to see things from the Delaware perspective and behave accordingly. By leaving the answer open, Teedyuscung also offers to trust the whites to accept their role in the interaction.

later Denny read a speech drafted by Franklin and his colleagues.[23] While the governor said that it would be difficult to prove the accusations of land fraud, he nevertheless sought a way to respond to the Delaware's accusation. "[T]o show our sincere Desire to heal the present Differences, and live in eternal Peace with you our Brethren tell me, what will satisfy you, for the Injustice you suppose has been done you in the Purchase of Lands in this Province; and if it be in my Power, you shall have immediate Satisfaction, whether it be justly due to you or not" (Van Doren and Boyd 1938, 160). In particular, the commissioners wanted to offer money and goods to settle the matter. When they asked Teedyuscung to set a price, he refused and instead tried to illustrate the reason with a comparison.

> When you chuse a Spot of Ground for Planting, you first prepare the Ground, then you put the Seed into the Earth; but if you don't take Pains afterwards, you will not obtain Fruit—To Instance, in the *Indian Corn,* which is mine (meaning a native Plant of this Country) I, as is customary, put seven Grains in one Hill, yet, without further Care, it will come to nothing, tho' the Ground be good; tho' at the Beginning I take prudent Steps, yet if I neglect it afterwards tho' it may grow up to Stalks and Leaves, and there may be the appearance of Ears, there will only be leaves and cobs—In like Manner, in the present Business, tho' we have begun well. Yet if we hereafter use not prudent Means, we shall not have Success, answerable to our expectations. . . . Therefore, let all of us, Men, Women, and Children, assist in pulling up the Weeds, that nothing may hinder the Corn from growing to Perfection. When this is done, tho' we may not live to enjoy the Fruit ourselves, yet we should remember, our Children may live and enjoy the Blessings of this good Fruit, and it is our Duty to act for their Good. (Van Doren and Boyd 1938, 162)

Consistent with the logic of place made manifest in the Prophetic movement, Teedyuscung denies that the issue of land dispossession will best be understood or responded to in terms of a single settlement. As with the growth of corn, the process is one that is a matter of developing sustaining relationships in a cooperative environment over an extended period. It is little wonder in light of a view that sees land as a part of place that Teedyuscung would decline to put a value on the damages done by the whites in the Delaware valley. The idea of replacing lands with money or goods could make little sense. Besides, he concludes,

23. See the draft of the speech given by Denny offering "immediate satisfaction" written by Franklin (1959, 7: 18–21).

"there are many more concerned in this Matter, not present; and tho' many, who have suffered are now in the Grave, yet their Descendents feel the Weight and the more now for the Time they have waited" (Van Doren and Boyd 1938, 163).

The conference ended with only a resolution to meet again. For Franklin, however, the conference marked a significant turn of events. While he had entered the diplomatic process in part to find out the cause of the troubles, when he did, it provided a new insight and a new purpose. Within four months, Franklin was appointed as an emissary to the king, and his job as such was in part to present Teedyuscung's complaint. He left for England at the beginning of April with the conflict along the border far from settled. For Franklin, the issue of British treatment of Native people and the resulting conflicts amounted to further evidence for the establishment of a union of British American colonies. The absolute power of the Proprietors combined with their own narrow interests and the lack of shared interests with England meant that the Pennsylvanians were blocked from establishing fit relations with their Native neighbors and lands. In a draft of his petition to the king, prepared in September 1758, Franklin is specific. "It has allways been thought advisable," he says, "to make purchases there or from the Native Indian Possessors." When purchases have been made the Native people and new white settlements develop a relationship of coexistence and mutual support. The Native people "there forming a kind of frontier, where they are Capable whilst Maintaining in Friendship of doing Great Service to the English and of Contributing to the Prosperity of Their Settlements" (Franklin 1959, 8: 266). When these relations are violated as when "[the Indians] are Deprived of these Lands without their consent," the result is war. The petition was forwarded to the Board of Trade for more study in April 1759 and ultimately referred back to the British Commissioner of Indian Affairs, William Johnson. In a letter to Pemberton in 1759, Franklin observes that "It is everywhere represented here by the Proprietor's Friends, that this Charge of the Indians against him, is mere Calumny, stirr'd up by the Malice of the Quakers, who cannot forgive his deserting their Sect" (Franklin 1959, 8: 299). For Franklin, the denials and counterattacks by the Proprietors amounted only to an attempt to deny Pennsylvania the possibility of establishing a peaceful coexistence with Native peoples and as a result a flourishing Pennsylvania province. "I believe," he concludes, "that it will in time be clearly seen by all thinking People, that the Government and Property of a Province should not be in the same Family" (Franklin 1959, 8: 299). Teedyuscung's plea for justice became a part of a plea for resistance against the colonial government of an increasingly pluralistic North American society. But the political message is only part of Franklin's development.

Even as he was learning alternative ways of conceiving social and cultural relations, he was also developing deeper transformation of attitude.

Franklin was born in 1706 in Boston, just two years after Cotton Mather published his *Magnalia Christi Americana*. The environment of his youth was already affected by the indigenous attitude, especially as it became manifest in the work of Williams and in the practices of his settlement at Providence, which supported both a flourishing colony of dissenters and served as a way station for newcomers who rejected the dominant Puritan viewpoint. At the same time, the colonial attitude continued to frame daily life in Boston and the philosophical outlook of its inhabitants. Cotton Mather was the dominant theological voice during this time, and Franklin often heard him preach. In this case the colonial attitude was manifested in the context of Mather's *Essays to Do Good*, reinforcing a standpoint that combined unquestioned acceptance of doctrine with a tireless commitment to doing good works in and for one's own community. Franklin's own philosophical development stood at the intersection of these conflicting attitudes, demanding a critical stance toward the dominant view while affirming the importance of public service.

Franklin's father, Josiah, was a candle maker who was a member of Boston's Old South congregation and a respected community leader. In his *Autobiography*, Franklin declared that his father's "great Excellence lay in a sound Understanding, and solid Judgment in prudential Matters, both in private and publick Affairs" (Franklin 1987, 1315). This prudential character reinforced his father's commitments to both hard work and the value of learning that extended even to promoting lively table conversations. Although Benjamin was enrolled for a time at Boston's Latin school because his father intended to "devote" him "to the Service of the Church," the high cost of tuition changed his father's plans, leading first to Benjamin's leaving the Latin school for a less expensive option, and shortly after making him a printer's apprentice. To his father's stalwart character was added the influence of his uncle, Benjamin, who was an advocate of the liberal philosophy that began to flourish in England after the Glorious Revolution in 1689. The elder Benjamin collected political tracts and sent them to his nephew and for several years lived with his brother's family in Boston. For young Benjamin, his environment brought together commitments to practicality and dissent, the rejection of elitism, and a commitment to work for one's own sake and for the sake of one's community.

The role of dissent for Franklin became more prominent after he was apprenticed at twelve years old to his older brother James, who was a printer. As part of his printing business, James began to produce a weekly paper, *The New England Courant,* that, in addition to carrying small news articles, became a forum for political ideas often at odds with the Boston leadership. The first issue of the *Courant* was produced in the summer of 1721 in the midst of a smallpox outbreak in Boston. In an effort to end the epidemic, Cotton Mather and, at Mather's encouragement, a leading doctor named Zabdiel Boylston advocated the practice of inoculation against the disease. Unlike the later smallpox vaccine, this early method involved infecting a healthy person with smallpox collected from the sores of someone already ill from the disease. Although the inoculated person would still be ill (and potentially could die), those who survived would not become infected again. By infecting healthy people, as opposed to people already weak from other conditions, the danger of the infection could be controlled. The *Courant* stood firmly against the practice, and its inaugural issue was committed to public opposition.[24] The attacks on Mather, who served as the primary advocate for inoculation, were sharp, and in response Mather declared the writers at the *Courant* the "Hell-Fire Club." In terms reminiscent of his attacks on Williams and other dissenters in the *Magnalia,* Mather wrote, "the practice of supporting and publishing every week a libel on purpose to lessen and blacken and burlesque the virtuous and principal ministers of religion in a country, and render the services of their ministry despicable . . . is a wickedness that was never known before in any country, Christian, Turkish, or Pagan" (in Van Doren 1938, 20).

In the spring of the following year, Benjamin himself joined the ranks of the Hell-Fire Club as the anonymous author of a series of letters from Mrs. Silence Dogood. In an obvious play on Mather's *Essays to Do Good,* the Dogood papers began as an autobiographical account of a New England widow who, contrary to the usual expectation, became well-educated by her own efforts and was prepared to offer Boston her views on important matters. Mrs. Dogood's letters became a popular feature of the *Courant.* Among her early efforts was an elaborate parody of Bunyan's *Pilgrim's Progress.* The satire criticized the elitism of Harvard College and the materialism of its students, but it also stood against the emptiness of the curriculum. Mrs. Dogood described the "Temple of Learning" she saw in a dream of Harvard, as a place where students "for want of suitable Genius, . . . learn little more than how to carry themselves handsomely, and enter a Room genteelly. . . . And from whence they return, after Abundance of Trouble and Charge, as great Blockheads as ever, only more proud and self-conceited" (Franklin 1907, 2: 13).

24. Franklin himself became an advocate of the practice. See Franklin 1959, 8: 281 ff.

In June of 1722 the conflict between Mather and the *Courant* worsened. When James Franklin published a fictionalized account of the inaction of the Boston government in the face of pirates, the city council took action and arrested James. In his absence, Benjamin, now sixteen, took charge of the paper and continued its publication, including a new letter from Mrs. Dogood reprinting an article from the *London Journal* by the libertarians John Trenchard and Thomas Gordon in support of freedom of speech. After James's release, he resumed his role as publisher and continued to attack the Boston leadership. In January 1723, the Boston city council prohibited James from publishing a newspaper without prior censorship. Benjamin was made publisher again, but in September, angered by his brother's poor treatment of him, he sailed to New York and then to Philadelphia.

Franklin's dissent from Puritan belief came to its fullest expression a few years later when, after joining a printing office in England, he wrote and published a short pamphlet called *A Dissertation on Liberty and Necessity, Pleasure and Pain.* In the pamphlet, in part a response to William Wollaston's volume *The Religion of Nature Delineated,* Franklin argues that in light of a deterministic understanding of the world of the sort conceived by Newton, there is properly no such thing as human free will and no real evil. He frames such determinism, while it might lead to concerns in particular about freedom of action or moral responsibility, as an attack on how things are valued. If all things are determined in the way they must be in a Newtonian universe, then despite human experience, nothing in the universe is more esteemed than any other thing. In light of this determinism there can be no truly free will, and so everything may be as it is intended to be by the creator. From this perspective *"there can be neither Merit nor Demerit in Creatures"* and *"every Creature must be equally esteem'd by the Creator"* (Franklin 1987, 62). Experienced good and evil, pleasure and pain, and even virtue and vice must be viewed through the same transcendent lens and the same conclusion, that each is equally valued, must follow.

While Franklin uses the equality of esteem to argue against the possibility of an afterlife, the argument itself completes another trajectory begun while Franklin was still in Boston. In an unsigned letter in the *Courant,* written at the time his brother was banned from printing, Franklin proposes the problem that human beings are so fallible that they can never be certain of the truth. As he observes, "There is nothing in which Mankind reproach themselves more than in their Diversity of Opinions" (Franklin 1987, 49). Diversity here is not a thing valued but a reproach, a verification of human weakness. Those who demand priority for their own views or special honor for themselves overstep human possibility. It is a criticism of the censors and those who demand authority and respect on the basis of inheritance or position, because these people, despite their confidence, have no solid ground upon which to stand even as they persecute the publisher of the *Courant*. The *Dissertation* provides a ground for the view by arguing for the radical equality of things and ideas in Newton's deterministic world, making the world safe for freedom of speech while simultaneously undermining the grounds on which one can make judgments. At the same time, dissent and its consequent skepticism threaten to make doing good indistinguishable from simply doing. As he explains in his *Autobiography*, showing that "Vice & Virtue were empty Distinctions, no such Things existing: appear'd now not so clever a Performance as I once thought it" (Franklin 1987, 1359). Instead of the transcendent perspective and deterministic universe of "metaphysical Reasoning," he shifted his focus to lived human relationships. "I grew convinc'd that *Truth, Sincerity & Integrity* in Dealings between Man & Man, were of the utmost importance to the Felicity of Life." Doing good, in short, became the focus, but the metaphysical speculations were not without their impact, because now Franklin needed to find new ways to understand the good to be done. When framed by Mather, there was little doubt about what was to be done. With the transcendent viewpoint undone, Franklin needed to establish a new standard.

By the time Franklin returned to Philadelphia in 1726, the importance of community was a given. Having separated the idea of public good from the doctrines of the reformed tradition, he set about promoting both his own welfare and the welfare of the public as an increasingly successful publisher. The point of view he had adopted was perhaps best manifested in his *Poor Richard's Almanack*, issued for the first time in 1733. Franklin's "author," Poor Richard Saunders, was portrayed as a hard-working family man whose almanac was intended to serve both the public good by providing useful information (and entertainment) even as it served himself, lessening the strain of poverty and allowing him to better support his family. Implicit throughout Poor Richard's work is the idea that the public good involves at least two elements, the possibility of individual success and the simultaneous need for an individual's wider community to flourish as well. From this perspective, it was clear that some actions and principles were better than others in terms of making a contribution, and so the new challenge for Franklin was trying to establish a way to define good with respect to one's community.

The shape of Franklin's response to the need to weld together his commitment to the public good and the possibility of judgment emerged in two papers written in 1735. The first, a Socratic dialogue between Socrates and Crito, considered the character of a "man of sense." Such a person, Franklin seems to conclude in the voice of Socrates, will be a person who has "Knowledge of our true Interest; that is, of what is best to be done in all the Circumstances of Human Life, in order to arrive at our main End in View, HAPPINESS" (Franklin 1959, 2: 245). Knowledge, however, is not enough. Just as "Knowledge of all the Terms and expressions proper to be used in Discoursing well upon making a good Shoe" does not make one a shoemaker, one must also "know how" to use the knowledge in making shoes (Franklin 1959, 2: 17). Similarly, a "man of sense" is one who both knows what is good and how to use the knowledge to affect the conduct of life.

At the same time, it remains unclear how one best determines what constitutes knowledge of what is good. In the second paper, a "Letter" to the *Pennsylvania Gazette* by "Veridicus," Franklin argues that "the love of truth is not more essential to an honest Man than a Readiness to change his Mind and Practice upon the Conviction that he is in the wrong" (Franklin 1987, 254). Truth and openness are, he says, "inseparably connected in our present fallible Condition." The paper concludes in a way closely related to Locke's argument for tolerance on the grounds of fallibilism that one must sacrifice "*darling Prejudice*" in order to attain truth. One condition of judgment, on Franklin's account, is that inquiry be pursued with an attitude of openness and involve not only statements of one's positive conclusion, but also of one's errors. The difficulty here as in his critique of values in the *Dissertation* is that what constitutes the standard according to which something will be taken as true remains obscure, although there are hints about what the standard will involve. In the Socratic dialogue, for example, Franklin concludes in a critical vein, challenging those who "are ignorant" of the "science of virtue." Such a person, he says, "since he is ignorant of what principally concerns him, tho' it has been told him a thousand Times from Parents, Press, and Pulpit, the Vicious Man however learned, cannot be a Man of Sense, but is a Fool, a Dunce, and a Blockhead" (Franklin 1959, 2: 248). The standard, "what principally concerns him" is not something found by consulting religious texts or transcendent principles, but by listening to members of one's own network of relations. Whatever constitutes good will be found, in a sense, in the context of one's life as lived.

In 1747 Franklin published a satirical speech in the voice of a woman named Polly Baker that helps clarify how one seeks a standard in the life of one's community. Polly Baker's speech is framed as an address to the magistrates of a New England town who had charged Baker with the crime of giving birth to a child out of wedlock. It was her fifth offense. Against the fines and imprisonment that the magistrates were likely to levy, Baker argues that she ought not be punished on account of her behavior. "I cannot conceive (may it please your Honours) what the Nature of my Offence is," she says, "I have brought Five fine Children into the World, at Risque of my Life: I have maintained them well by my own Industry" (Franklin 1987, 306). In effect, Baker argues, she has contributed to the community by increasing it in terms of population but also in terms of its possibilities. "Five fine children" in a community struggling to maintain itself is not an inconsiderable contribution. When such living contributions are compared with the apparent violation of religious doctrine, there is no comparison. In fact, she argues, to enforce laws without regard to the community can only have disastrous effects:

> do not turn natural and useful Actions into Crimes. . . . Reflect a little on the horrid consequences of this Law in particular: What Numbers of procur'd Abortions! And how many distress'd Mothers have been driven, by the Terror of Punishment and public Shame, to imbrue, contrary to Nature, their own trembling Hands in the Blood of their Helpless Offspring! (Franklin 1987, 307)

For Baker and her author, the standard of what constitutes a good is found in the complex interactions of one's life in community. The things and actions to be favored are those that contribute to the growth of the community and its people. "[To] increase and multiply," Baker says, is the "Duty" according to which she acts. Beneath the satire of the speech remains a figure for how people ought to act in general. Baker's duty (and the duty of the magistrates) is to promote the growth of the community.

Taken together, Franklin's views developed a commitment to the importance of community both as a formative context for individuals and as a source of the standards according to which one ought to act. Developed in the context of a tension between the colonial attitude of Mather and an attitude of dissent that undermined the universal standards Mather sought to apply, Franklin turned to lived experience as a ground and source of judgment. As displayed in his paper on prejudice, however, there remained at least two problems. How can one organize one's thinking in a way that attends to present circumstances in a way that can lead to good judgment, and how can one adapt one's views in the face of disagreement? Both of these issues were to be addressed over the next decade of Franklin's life in the face of two new developments: his practice of experimental science and his experience along the border with Native American thought.

CHAPTER NINE

Science and Sovereignty

ALTHOUGH FRANKLIN WAS largely self-educated, he nevertheless became quite familiar with a version of the new science developing in Europe as a result of the work of Isaac Newton. I. Bernard Cohen has argued that this new science should be seen not as a single monolithic approach to experimental science but one conditioned by two different works by Newton (Cohen 1990, 14). The first, the work best-known to later philosophers and scientists, is Newton's *Principia Mathematica,* a treatise written in Latin that set out to provide a mathematical description of the laws of motion following a geometrical model. Despite his interest in Newton's *Principia,* however, it is unlikely that Franklin had an adequate background in math to use the text (Cohen 1990, 15). At the same time, the other work by Newton, *The Opticks,* published in English with a minimum of math, would have both been accessible to Franklin and would have presented a strategy of conducting science that could serve as a model of the experimental approach Franklin adopted. While the *Principia* presented a picture of science struggling toward a single unified picture of the world, the *Opticks,* while it shared the goal of the *Principia,* proceeded by experiment. "My design in this book," Newton says, "is not to explain the Properties of Light by Hypothesis, but to propose and prove them by Reason and Experiments" (Newton 1931, 1). The volume presents a series of propositions, each followed by a detailed description of an experiment that confirms the proposition. The volume ends with thirty-one "queries," or speculative propositions, that had yet to be confirmed by experiment or mathematical proof. While the method of the work did not claim the certainty of the *Principia,* it provided a model for scientific investigation that could contribute to the larger project of a unified theory of the universe that was accessible to people with limited formal training and resources. "As in Mathematicks, so in Natural Philosophy," Newton says in the concluding section of the *Opticks,* "the Investigation of difficult Things by the Method of Analysis [making Experiments and Observations] ought ever to precede the Method of Composition [the process of combining hypotheses into a general theory]" (Newton 1931, 404). As a result, Franklin could feel justified in pursuing science piecemeal as a process of responding to particular questions and phenomena, particularly those present in ordinary experience.

In 1747 Franklin began a series of experiments on electricity the results of which he presented to his friend Peter Collinson, who in turn presented them to the Royal Society and then published them in a pamphlet in 1751.[1] Franklin's 1750 letter, published later as "Considerations and Conjectures," reveals a crucial innovation in Franklin's approach to experimental science. He begins, following Newton, by presenting electricity as "subtile" particles that behave like a fluid (Franklin 1959, 4: 10–11). After introducing his findings on the way pointed objects conduct electrical fluid, he admits that he has "some Doubts about them," but "even a bad Solution read, and its faults discovered, has often given Rise to a good idea in the Mind of an ingenious Reader" (Franklin 1959, 4: 17). "Nor is it of much Importance," he continues, "to know the Manner in which Nature executes her Laws; 'tis enough, if we know the Laws themselves. 'Tis of real Use to know, that China left in the Air unsupported, will fall and break; but how it comes to fall, and why it breaks, are Matters of Speculation. 'Tis a pleasure indeed to know them, but we can preserve our China without it." The conclusion is a key to understanding the way in which Franklin differed from Newton in his understanding of the meaning of experiments. For Newton, experiments are preliminary to the development of a deductive mathematical system that will explain "why" things work the way that they do. Particles and their motions were not merely ways of explaining experiments or of providing resources for solving other problems, but are the real things of the universe.[2] Franklin affirms the importance of theories framed in terms of particles and fluids, but is primarily interested in the actions and interactions they describe. What is important is what happens and what can be learned to guide future actions and expectations.

The principle at work in Franklin's experimental science appears to be closely related to the work of another European American, Cadwallader Colden, twenty years Franklin's senior and a well-respected scien-

1. See Franklin 1959, 4: 125–128.
2. See Newton 1931, 401–402.

tist and philosopher. Born in Ireland of Scottish parents in 1688, Colden graduated from the University of Edinburgh in 1705 and emigrated to America in 1710. He tried to establish a practice as a physician in Boston until 1718 when he moved to New York and became a surveyor. In this capacity, Colden spent several years along the border between lands claimed by New York and the homeland of the Haudenosaunee. During this time, he was adopted by the Mohawk and given a Mohawk name, Cayenderonque (Beauchamp 1907, 405). In 1727 he published the first English language history of the Haudenosaunee, *The History of the Five Indian Nations*. The work was widely circulated and beginning in the 1750s served as a resource for Franklin in working out his views on Native concerns.[3] In light of his education, experience with Native people, and scientific interests, Colden was a natural choice for lieutenant governor of the growing province of New York. From this position, to which he was appointed in 1761, Colden helped manage the relations between New York and the Haudenosaunee and often served as a mediator in conflicts between Native people and whites. In 1743, Colden and Franklin met for the first time by chance along a trail in New York.[4] Soon after their meeting, they began to exchange work. Colden sent Franklin, among other things, a copy of his critique of Newtonian physics, *An Explication of the First Causes of Action in Matter* (published in 1746), treatises on the "vital motions" of animals, mathematics, the "First Principles of Morality," and the revision of his work on Newton published as *The Principles of Action in Matter.* Until his death in 1776, Colden was well-respected as one of America's most prominent intellectuals. After the Revolution his work was largely forgotten, in part because he remained a British loyalist throughout his career. His influence, nevertheless, seems to persist in the work of the younger generations of American scientists and philosophers, in part because Franklin and others appear to have adopted something very much like Colden's basic methodological framework.

At the beginning of *The Principles of Action in Matter,* Colden gives what amounts to the central epistemological principle of his work. "We have no knowledge of substances, or of any being, or of any thing, abstracted from, the action of that thing or being. All our knowledge of things consists in the perception of the power, or force, or property, or

---

3. For example, Franklin used Colden's book extensively in his response to a report on the Ohio valley by the Commissioners of Trade and Plantations in 1772 (Franklin 1907, 5: 480 ff.). Franklin purchased a copy of Colden's *History* in March 1751 (Franklin 1959, 4: 76n).

4. See Colden's letter to Franklin (Franklin 1959, 2: 385–386).

manner of acting of that thing." The epistemological principle leads to an ontological one. "Every thing, that we know, is an agent, or has a power of acting" (in Anderson and Fisch 1939, 102). Like the pragmatist principle of interaction, Colden's principle is both epistemological and ontological and has the effect of making the meaning of things and events a matter of what happens. In a paper written in 1760, Colden asks, "what idea or conception can I have of a thing which does nothing? . . . A being absolutely inactive can produce no phenomenon; it is absolutely useless" (Colden 1946, 298). What a thing does is what matters and the rules or laws that describe such actions emerge in the process of knowing. In his manuscript, "The First Principles of Morality," Colden describes the process this way: "In making of these observations of the difference in actions, the mind proposed some view or purpose to itself; and according to this view or purpose judges of the actions from whence its ideas arise: what effects can be produced by them, or how fit or unfit they are for the purposes or views the mind has set to itself" (Fay 1950, 62–63). Franklin's concern about the use of "laws" makes the same point. It is enough to know the rules based on experiment and present interests because these rules make further plans and actions possible.

The principle of interaction as developed by Colden is important for at least two reasons. On one hand, it probably helped Franklin to frame his own experimental science as it began to take shape in the years after the two met. While Newton framed experiment as a process in service of acquiring resources for more comprehensive theory, Colden's version of the principle of interaction asserted a ground for scientific theory in service of its implications for use, for future action. Second, the principle of interaction seems to mark a distinctive American methodological innovation. Colden's own work has little precedent in European thought. It is not the empiricism of Locke or the pan-psychism of Leibniz, and even among American historians of philosophy it has been hard to classify.[5] In fact, the principle of interaction as it is developed by Colden is more like a view held by Haudenosaunee peoples and often identified as the concept of *orenda* or power. Following the analysis by the Tuscarora philosopher and ethnographer J. N. B. Hewitt, *orenda* is the idea that things both are and are known by what they do. The term Hewitt uses, *orenda*, suggests a way of understanding the idea. The word root of *orenda* is "(C)ɛn(ɔ>)-," the same root used for the word for song and voice as well as for ceremony and wishing.[6] From this perspective, *orenda* can be

5. See Pratt 1996 for a detailed discussion of Colden's relation to Native traditions. Also see Riley 1907 and Blau 1952 for contrasting discussions of Colden's work. Also see Pratt and Ryder (forthcoming).

6. See Pratt 1998; Hale 1883; Chafe 1967, 50.

understood as song or voice or, more generally, the way things express themselves. In the introduction to his collection of Iroquoian origin stories, Hewitt argues that for the Haudenosaunee and other Native people, "[t]hings animate and things inanimate were comprised in one heterogeneous class, sharing a common nature" (Hewitt 1903, 134). What is "common" in this case is not a substance but rather the potential for agency. "All things," Hewitt continues, "were thought to have life and to exercise will, whose behests were accomplished through *orenda*—that is, through magic power, reputed to be inherent in all things." Despite Hewitt's critical view of the idea of a "magic power," perhaps realizing that anything less in the world of turn-of-the-century anthropology would be unacceptable, the idea captures the notion of both an epistemological and ontological claim. "Thus," he concludes on behalf of those who framed experience in terms of *orenda*, "all phenomena, all states, all changes, and all activity were interpreted as the results of the exercise of [*orenda*] directed by some controlling mind" (Hewitt 1903, 134). In effect, what things are and what things are known as emerges from their ways of expression, their actions.

Hewitt illustrates the concept by connecting it with the idea of music. If *orenda* is understood as the song or voice of individuals, then the practices of music take on special meaning. As Hewitt puts it, from an Iroquoian perspective, "singing or to sing had a significance and a purpose which greatly differ from the meaning and the motive associated with it today" (Hewitt 1902, 35). In the Iroquoian tradition, "the phenomena of environing nature" is nothing other than "the operations of the bodies and beings thereof," that is, the songs of "independent and self-sufficient personages."

> The speech and utterance of birds and beasts, the soughing of the wind, the voices of the night, the moaning of the tempest, the rumble and crash of the thunder, the startling roar of the tornado, the wild creaking and cracking of wind-rocked and frost-riven trees, lakes, and rivers, and the multiple other sounds and noises in nature, were conceived to be the chanting—the dirges and the songs of the various bodies thus giving forth voice and words of beastlike or birdlike speech in the use and exercise of their [*orenda*]. (Hewitt 1902, 35–36)

Although Hewitt's account emphasizes the importance of the agent or will of each singer, *orenda* also disposes one against the idea that such singers or agents have an existence apart from their interactions with their environment. *Orenda* understood as a song or voice carries with it the implication of a context in which at least sometimes the speaker will be heard.

Hewitt illustrates this idea of song as communication when he identifies an Iroquoian term for the cicada, "kaněⁿ'haíq-thǎ," literally "it habitually ripens the corn" or "corn ripener." As Hewitt tells it, "this insect acquired this name because when it sang in the early morning the day became very hot . . . its singing was held to signify that it was exerting its *orenda* to bring on the heat necessary to ripen the corn" (Hewitt 1902, 40). While the song of the cicada might only be a sign that power is being used, it can also be understood as a kind of power. The song of the cicadas can be understood rather as a call to others in the environment to do the things that they do. The sun and clouds answer the call of the cicadas and "sing" to the corn, experienced as hazy skies and hot, humid air. The corn responds as its ears dry and harden, taking on the experienced qualities that mark it as ready to act as nourishment for still others in the environment. The "corn ripeners" do not "make" the corn ripen, but rather through their song gain the responsive cooperation of others to carry on the processes of life. Here song is a causal power in the same way that asking for a drink of water or singing a lullaby are understood as causes. As in these cases, *orenda* as voice or song marks not just an utterance but an interaction. From this perspective, the notion of *orenda* stands at the center of a complex of expectations about the world. If things are their "songs," then they can only be understood in the process of singing, interacting, with an environment disposed to understand and respond. *Orenda,* therefore, implies as well a community and the complex interrelations that promote singing and listening.

Just as *orenda* provides a means of distinguishing individuals through their particular voices or songs, the idea of *orenda* also provides grounds for understanding classes of things. As implied by the cicada example, *orenda* marks both the songs of individuals and songs that are shared among many individuals. While one may, after listening closely, distinguish the song of one cicada from another, there is also a way in which one's first experience is of a choral or collective voice. While Hewitt doesn't discuss the implications of this aspect of *orenda,* it is an important one because it also suggests the ways in which things can become divided into particular groups. What makes an individual is clearly one's own particular expression, but that expression, while unique, is also not unrecognizable. A particular cicada's song, while unique, that is, emanating from a particular place, starting at a particular moment, is also recognizably cicadian. The key to hearing it as unique is to hear it also as part of a larger class of singers. To be utterly unique, a song without precedent would, in a sense, be a song beyond comprehension and response. From this perspective, *orenda* marks both one's particularity and one's connections. To be part of a group is to share a style of song, but to be part of one's group is to also have a distinct voice, a distinct *orenda*. When a cicada sings, and by analogy, when things take action, they gain both their individuality and their character as a kind.[7]

Orenda connects as well with the ideas of the Native Prophetic movement and the idea of place. For national or cultural difference understood in terms of *orenda*, the voices of different peoples, while they sustain individual differences, also sustain culturally shared commonalities. These commonalities, however, are not understood in terms of some inherited substratum, blood, or genes, but rather in terms of a distinctive song or style of song. To learn such a song, however, is not merely a matter of making certain sounds. Since physical presence, practices, language, and expectations are, on this view, matters of *orenda*, it is clear that the distinctive Delaware voice will not simply be a way of speaking or a way of dress or a way of looking, but rather all of these and ways of answering calls, of listening and responding. As a result, to be Delaware as distinct from being English or Pennsylvanian will be a matter of the entire context in which one lives and learns. Practices, physical appearance, beliefs, sensitivities, and ways of response will all be a product of and part of the complex interactions of place.

The Native literature accessible to non-Native people in the eighteenth century and after does not provide a complete picture of Native ideas such as *orenda*. At the same time, what was accessible, through everyday contact, intermarriage, formal ceremonies, and more formal study (especially in the mid and late eighteenth century) seems to have included many illustrations of the concept of *orenda* both as a subject matter and as a principle guiding interactions. While Colden may not have been aware of the concept in just the terms presented by Hewitt, it seems clear that Colden was familiar both with a wide range of traditional stories and with the formal ceremonial practices of the Haudenosaunee and their Native allies. While he does not discuss Native metaphysics in his work, it seems likely that someone living with Native people for more than five decades, studying their history, politics, and ceremonies, may have incorporated key aspects of their philosophical attitude and its ideas into his own way of understanding and acting in the world. When in the 1740s Colden began an early retirement from his post as surveyor general of New York to conduct philosophical research, he had already spent nearly thirty years on the border at the edge of the province of New York and well inside the homeland of the Mohawk. When he became

---

7. See the description of the Thanksgiving ceremony in Gibson's version of the Haudenosaunee origin story for an example of the way *orenda* marks both difference and sameness (Hewitt 1928, 563 ff.).

dissatisfied with Newton's treatment of matter as passive, the Native ideas of *orenda* may have already asserted an alternative.

For Newton the idea of inertia is essential to a theory of motion, but on his account, inertia is something passive. If it is passive, Colden argues, then it cannot be known at all and so violates Newton's own commitment to not using what he called "occult qualities" to explain physical phenomena.[8] While Newton took gravity, fermentation, and cohesion to be "general Laws of Nature," he accepted the idea of passive particles. In this case, matter itself, since it could be known, became a quality "supposed to lie hid in Bodies, and to be the unknown Causes of manifest Effects" (Newton 1931, 401). In order to solve the problem, Colden proposes to understand phenomena in other terms, that is, in terms of their actions. "The differences of things (so far at least as we can know)," he says, "consists in their different actions, or manner of acting. And the actions of several things be such, as that we evidently perceive, that they cannot proceed from the same power of force, or kind of power of force, such things are said to be in their nature different" (Anderson and Fisch 1939, 103). In short, Colden proposes to understand physical phenomena in terms of their *orenda*.

Colden proposes four sorts of principles of action: inertia, motion, elastic or communicating power, and intelligence. The first principle, inertia, is the power of resisting, and the second, the power of motion, provides the framework for understanding extended things. The power of communication, or "aether," provides a way to understand the spaces between objects. Elasticity or aether, although invisible, nevertheless can be known by its varying ability to communicate action. Air and water have different communicating powers, as do human flesh, pieces of metal, and sticks of wood. Intelligence, unlike either the rationalist idea of a thinking substance separate from matter or the materialist view of thinking as matter in a particular arrangement, is understood as a way of behaving or acting in the world. To be intelligent is to act in a particular way. To know that a thing is intelligent is to find it disposed to act in particular ways in ongoing interactions. Taken together, the powers provide a framework for classifying the things in the world and also a way to devise rules about their various operations. Inertia, motion, and aether provide the conceptual starting point for discussion of what is thought of as the "material" world, and intelligence provides the starting point for understanding the processes of reasoning, creativity, and morality. Like *orenda,* the principles of action provide an account for both

8. See Newton 1931, 397ff..

what is common among things, their potential for action, and what is distinctive, their potential for particular and distinctive action.

While Franklin does not adopt Colden's framework explicitly, when he takes up his experiments in electricity, he nevertheless proceeds with the expectation that the actions of electricity as they are demonstrated experimentally ground the rules according to which electricity can be understood and used. By starting with something like Colden's principle of interaction or the Iroquoian notion of *orenda*, Franklin is able to approach science free of the usual expectations about the importance of finding truths. The principle of interaction in its various forms focuses instead on the concrete results of experiments and the potential for the results to lead to new action. Cohen, in his discussion of the practicality of Franklin's science, is right to downplay the role of use as the purpose of Franklin's science, because the principle of interaction does not demand that use justify or even frame science, but rather it demands that science focus on what happens.[9] The development of the lightning rod, as Cohen observes, is based on the results of Franklin's electricity experiments, but the experiments are not justified or made true by the success of the lightning rod. They are not even begun in search of finding a way to protect buildings from lightning strikes. Instead, Franklin's science, after dismissing an interest in the reasons behind the rules, turns instead to a readiness to see the possibilities that experimental results can bring. There is, in a sense, no truth to be procured, only new possibilities: batteries, light, and means of protecting buildings. They are successful conclusions because they lead to new possibilities.

By 1749, Franklin displayed a deep commitment to both the importance of community, through his work in the public service, and to a version of the principle of interaction, through his developing experimental science. But Franklin remained uncommitted to the sort of pluralism characteristic of both the later pragmatists and the Prophetic movement. In 1751, as if to confirm his opposition to pluralism, Franklin prepared a brief paper inquiring into the process of population increase. He argues, among other things, that the populations of a region will involve the complex interaction of human beings, their cultural practices and expectations, and the environments in which they live. His view anticipates the later conclusions of Thomas Malthus, Buffon, and Herder, among others. At the end of the discussion, he reveals a strong commitment to a view much like that found in Mather. "[T]he number of white

9. See Cohen 1990, Chapter 3.

people in the World is proportionately very small," he says. "I could wish their Numbers were increased. And while we are, as I may call it, *Scouring* our Planet, by clearing *America* of Woods, and so making this Side of our Globe reflect a brighter Light into the Eyes of Inhabitants in *Mars* or *Venus,* why should we in the Sight of Superior beings, darken its People?" (Franklin 1959, 4: 234).[10] While Franklin's racial hierarchy is presented as a preference and not a necessity as it is in Mather's work, Franklin nevertheless affirms a hierarchy in which the diversity of human culture will eventually succumb to the superior Anglo-Saxons.

The obvious racism of Franklin's 1751 paper becomes increasingly less apparent in his later work. His 1753 letter to Peter Collinson, for example, reworks much of the earlier essay on human population by explicitly adding an account of human nature. On this view, Native cultures mark a different set of relations with their environment. Their "laziness" is not an inferior disposition, but a particular mode of interaction with an already productive environment. Just as the principle of interaction frames the electricity experiments, it now reemerges as a background for recognizing differences without imposing a necessary hierarchical relation. The explanation is reinforced by the insights of a "Transylvanian Tartar," a Greek Orthodox priest named Samuel Domein, who visited Philadelphia. "He asked one day," says Franklin, "what I thought might be the Reason that so many and such numerous nations, as the Tartars in Europe and Asia, the Indians in America, and the Negroes in Africa, continues a wandring careless Life" (Franklin 1959, 4: 481). Before Franklin could answer, Father Domein continued in broken English. "I'll tell you . . . God make him for to live lazy; man make God angry, God turn him out of Paradise, and bid him work; man no love work; he want to go to Paradise again, he want to live lazy." From this Franklin concludes that the "hope of becoming at some time of Life free from the necessity of care and Labour, together with fear of penury, are the mainsprings of most peoples industry." The ways of living practiced by diverse peoples do not amount to degrees of progress toward some fixed end, but different responses to the environments in which people live. Human diversity on this view is not a matter of skin color, but a matter of environment and goals. The apparent "laziness" of Native people and their disinterest in "civilization" is not "bad" or less valued, but rather a legitimate response to a flourishing environment motivated, as Father Domein suggests, by the desire to "live lazy." The shift is significant because, for Franklin, it provides a way to understand goods not in univer-

---

10. Franklin rejected this view within a few years and when the paper was republished in 1760 and 1761, this paragraph and the one preceding it were omitted (Franklin 1959, 4: 234n).

sal terms but in terms relevant to the situation in question. The desire to "live lazy" and the desire for "growth" are both relative standards that can be responsive to different cultures and lands.

When Franklin participated in the conferences with Teedyuscung in 1756 and prepared Governor Denny to raise the issue of British responsibility for the outbreak of war in the Delaware valley, he was already listening to the Native perspective. By the end of the November conference, he appeared to take the Native perspective seriously. The report on the Easton conference prepared by Franklin concludes, "as we apprehend it of Importance to the Province, that the complaints made by the Indians whether justly founded or not, should be fully represented and the Sense of them and Earnestness with which they insisted on the Wrongs that had been done them in the Purchases of Land, are much too faintly expressed in this Account of the Conference" (Van Doren and Boyd 1938, 166). The commissioners go on to assert that the Walking Purchase was "universally given up as unfair, and not to be defended" and that no one objected when "Teedyuscung claimed the Lands even those on which the Conferences were held." Further, while some saw Teedyuscung's refusal to settle for "immediate satisfaction" an invalidation of his claim, the commissioners saw it as a responsible action by a chosen representative of the people. In short, Franklin already had well-developed ideas about the principle of interaction, the role of community, and the value of growth, and his negotiations with the Delaware mark an increasing appreciation for pluralism.

Franklin returned to America in 1762 and remained active in the government of Pennsylvania. His son was appointed governor of New Jersey, and Franklin traveled much, inspecting fortifications and carrying on a lively scientific correspondence. In the summer of 1763, inspired by the prophecy of Neolin, Pontiac laid siege to Detroit. In the aftermath of his defeat, a group of whites near the village of Lancaster decided to continue the war, this time as an effort to exterminate Native people from the province.[11] On December 14, the vigilante group called the Paxton Boys armed itself and traveled to the Christian Indian community at nearby Conestoga and murdered six of the twenty Native people who lived there. The remaining residents, who had been away at the time of the murders, were invited into nearby Lancaster to take shel-

11. See Parkman's account of the Lancaster massacres as well (Parkman 1962, 348–375). Parkman's assessment is dramatically different from Franklin's. According to Parkman, the massacre "had no other definite result than that of exposing the weakness and distraction of the provincial government, and demonstrating the folly and absurdity of all principles of non-resistance" (Parkman 1962, 374).

ter. When the vigilantes learned that the survivors of the Conestoga attack were being protected in Lancaster, they went there, stormed the
building in which they were staying, and killed all fourteen people.
Franklin was outraged. In January, he and two others introduced a bill
in the Pennsylvania Assembly requiring that those accused in cases of
capital offenses between whites and Natives be brought to Philadelphia
for trial. The bill was tabled.[12] In February, the Paxton Boys armed themselves again and set out for Philadelphia, intent on killing the Native
people who had taken refuge among the Quakers there. Franklin responded by mobilizing the militia to meet the group and turn them away.
The Paxton group dispersed, but the damage was done both to the Native people of Pennsylvania and to Franklin's political career. His political
enemies used his defense of the Indians against him as evidence that he
no longer represented the interests of the province, and later that year
Franklin was defeated in an election for Speaker of the Pennsylvania
Assembly. In November 1764, Franklin left America for England.

Franklin's pamphlet on the massacre provides a good example both
of his emergent pragmatism and the ways in which that pragmatism is
connected with the Native philosophical perspective which he had come
to know over ten years of border diplomacy. The *Narrative of the Late
Massacres in Lancaster County, of a Number of Indians, Friends of this Province,
by Persons Unknown* was composed quickly in January 1764 and published
as the Paxton Boys prepared to march on Philadelphia. According to
Franklin's letter to Lord Kames, written in 1765, the pamphlet was written "to strengthen the hands of our weak Government, by rendering the
proceedings of the rioters unpopular and odious" (Franklin 1907, 4:
374). The pamphlet, he says, "had good effect" when news of the insurgents' march on Philadelphia came. Franklin reports that he was able
to mobilize "near 1000 citizens" who were able to convince the rioters
to disperse. At the same time, with "the fighting face we put on, and the
reasonings we used with the insurgents . . . I became less man than ever;
for I had, by these transactions, made myself many enemies among the
populace" (Franklin 1907, 4: 375). At issue were not merely the condemnation of the Paxton Boys and the "face" of military action, but "reasonings," ways of thinking about Native and white relations. After more than
a decade of war in Pennsylvania, Franklin seemed to propose an alternative that aimed to satisfy the demands of Native people as he had come
to understand them and provide a means for the whites to live at peace.

---

12. See Franklin 1959, 11: 27–28. While the bill violated expectations that trials would
be conducted locally, the virulent anti-Indian sentiment along the border in the Ohio valley
made Franklin and others demand that the only way for justice to be done in such cases
was with a change of venue to Philadelphia.

Those in power rejected the stance. "The Governor," Franklin concludes to Lord Kames, "thinking it was a favorable opportunity, joined the whole weight of the Proprietary interest to get me out of the Assembly." Despite the unpopularity of the views when applied to Native and white relations, the views developed and expressed in this context became for Franklin the guiding views that he and others used to make a case for the separation of the colonies from England and to produce a framework for a social structure that could at least sustain a union among the independent colonies. It also reveals the increasing importance in Franklin's thought of the idea of pluralism in relationship to community and growth. In particular, the *Narrative* illustrates Franklin's adoption of a logic of place comparable to the one developed within the Native Prophetic movement as a way of assessing and responding to issues of cultural difference.

The *Narrative* can be divided into four parts.[13] The first part establishes a view of the existence of difference in Pennsylvania prior to the Lancaster massacres. The second part describes the destruction of a Native place, the third proposes an alternative way to foster coexistence modeled on the logic of place and the practices of *wunnégin,* and the fourth demands that European Americans reconstruct themselves along these lines. Franklin opens the *Narrative* by invoking place and the possibilities of coexistence and death. The *Narrative* begins, "These Indians were the Remains of a Tribe of the Six Nations settled at Conestogoe, and thence called the Conestogoe Indians" (Franklin 1959, 11: 47). Not only does Franklin begin by concretely locating the Native people, the first two paragraphs mark a kind of geographical summary of the situation. The Conestoga Indians, according to Franklin, were one of the tribes associated with the Haudenosaunee and were present when William Penn arrived in America to establish a colony. Unlike discussions by Mather, for example, the account begins not with an assertion of the geographical connections between Native people and Europeans, but rather an assertion of the geographical separation of the peoples. The Europeans are presented by Franklin as newcomers and visitors. "On the first Arrival of the English in Pennsylvania, Messengers from [the Conestoga] Tribe came to welcome them, with Presents of Venison, Corn and Skins" (Franklin 1959, 11: 47–48). The formal process involved in the arrival is crucial, because it marks both the overt use by the Conestoga people of the practices of *wunnégin* and the idea that proper relations among distinct people is, or at least can be framed as, a formal

---

13. In contrast, see Lemay 1993. Lemay argues that the *Narrative* should be seen as a classical oration of eight parts.

practice that preserves the character of both. The product of this "first" meeting is a "Treaty of Friendship . . . that was to last 'as long as the Sun would shine, or the Waters run in the Rivers'" (Franklin 1959, 11: 48). Implicit in this initial paragraph is the sort of position taken by Teedyuscung when, at the 1756 Easton conference, he followed the approach of the Native Prophetic movement and declared, "this land, was made, by that Almighty Power, that has made all Things, and has given this Land to us. I [the Delaware] was the first, to whom he gave it; and as it pleased him to convey you to us, and unite us in Friendship . . . it is now in your Power, and depends, entirely, on your Care and faithful Diligence, that it may not be broken . . . and if broken, it will be owing to you" (Van Doren and Boyd 1938, 197). As Neolin had done in his challenge to the colonial attitude, Franklin begins by granting the reality and standing of cultural difference in experience, and he frames it geographically.

The geographical history continues in the second paragraph where Franklin recapitulates the geographic relations of the "first" contact, now in changed circumstances. Over time, Native people sold their lands and whites flourished even as the Native population declined. "As [Native] Lands by Degrees were mostly purchased, and the Settlements of the White People began to surround them, the Proprietor [of Pennsylvania Province] assigned them Lands on the Manor of Conestoga, which they might not part with" (Franklin 1959, 11: 48). Although the problematic central action of "assigning" lands reminds the reader of the colonial relationship between the Proprietor and the Conestoga people, it also reasserts the original relationship between distinct peoples each tied to their place. Despite changes of circumstance, the Native people are still viewed as connected with a geographical location and in being so located retain the character of a culturally and geographically distinct group. Taken together, the beginning paragraphs of the *Narrative* start with a recognition that the lands of the people are both "owned" by and constitutive of peoples.

The *Narrative* then turns to a strategy that serves to establish a complex notion of Conestoga and its people.[14] Franklin brings the reader closer to the experience of the destruction of a village and a way of life by relating brief descriptions of some of the individuals killed in the attack by the Paxton Boys. The individuals here are described largely in terms of their connections with others, a process that traces the relations

14. The strategy recalls the strategy of preaching in the Great Awakening that focused on the importance of accounts of the personal experience of conversion both as a guide to others as they prepared themselves for conversion and as a means of verifying that a conversion had occurred. See, for example, *Faithful Narrative of the Surprising Work of God* (Edwards 1972, 191 ff.).

of each, both inside the community and outside. The first introduction is of an elder named Shehaes[15] who serves as the center of the village. Shehaes, a "very Old Man" assisted with the treaty signed with William Penn in 1701 and "ever since continued as a faithful and affectionate Friend to the English" (Franklin 1959, 11: 49). The next introduction, of Shehaes's daughter Shee-na-wan (or Peggy) and her husband Saquies-hat-tah (or John Smith), helps to construct a vision of the community radiating out from Shehaes, who serves both as the center of the Native relations and as the point of contact with the English. The remaining descriptions set out a chain of personal connections among the people of Conestoga and conclude by recalling their ties with the English. "The Reader will observe," he says, "that many of their names are English." The practice of taking the names of "English persons they particularly esteem" is, he explains, a common practice (Franklin 1959, 11: 49). Such renaming, however, does not diminish the character of Conestoga as a distinctive community, a "little Society." Even as names are adopted, the community continues its traditions, in particular, the custom of welcoming each new Pennsylvania governor and "assuring him of their Fidelity" (Franklin 1959, 11: 50). The custom returns the description of the state of affairs to its beginning, reasserting the national relations established between Native people and the whites who surround them.[16]

The second section begins, "On *Wednesday,* the 14th of *December,* 1763, Fifty-seven Men, from some of our Frontier Townships, who had projected the Destruction of this little Common-wealth, came all well-mounted, and armed with Firelocks, Hangers and Hatchets, having travelled through the Country in the Night, to *Conestogoe* Manor" (Franklin 1959, 11: 50). The opening sentence serves to reframe the event for his

15. Shehaes was a close friend of Franklin's friend James Wright (Franklin 1959, 11: 48n).

16. It is important to note that while Franklin implies the passivity of Native people in his description of Conestoga, such passivity must not be taken at face value. Franklin's argument in the third part of the *Narrative* emphasizes the power and value of Native cultures. Carla Mulford, in her paper "*Caritas* and Capital," argues on the contrary that Franklin's treatment of Native people as passive should be viewed as a rhetoric that "at once seems to locate Native Americans in a moral sphere equal to whites while ultimately placing them in a social position subordinate to the white colonists" (Mulford 1993, 355). Mulford's examination focuses largely on the first and fourth parts of the *Narrative* and overlooks the role of the third section in particular. Mulford also dismisses the point of the context of the *Narrative*'s writing and audience. The *Narrative* can be seen as an argument offered within the context of a Quaker Christian society in favor of a non-colonial perspective on cultural conflict and racism. By presenting the Conestoga Indians in ways that make them appear passive in the face of persecution, Franklin associates them for the reader with their own conception of early Christianity. The point is not to see all Native people as passive (he argues explicitly against taking such universal claims), but rather to see the Conestoga people, like the persecuted Christians, as people wrongly judged. Rather than a rhetorical strategy designed to subordinate Native people, the strategy is to call Christians to do justice and in so doing to affirm the autonomy of Native communities.

Philadelphia audience. It begins by reminding the reader of the particular day and date of the first of the two massacres, placing the massacres in a direct relationship to the people of Philadelphia, as if to say "about a month ago, as you went about your business, a great injustice occurred." The day and date make a strong connection with the reader even as the action itself begins ambiguously, corrosively, along the "frontier." As the sentence unfolds, however, the action gains form and detail, and finally it asserts the particularity of location: the Conestoga Manor. Having arrived at the village, the details of the place make the massacre vivid. The Paxton Boys surround the "small village of *Indian* Huts." "[J]ust at the break of day" (the reader can see a red sun just breaking through the trees and reflecting off the frosty ground), the vigilantes "broke" into the houses "all at once" (Franklin 1959, 11: 50). "The good Shehaes," he says, "among the rest, cut to Pieces in his Bed." If the first part of the *Narrative* established Conestoga as a place, the second draws the reader from their own point of view into the place and then graphically displays its violation, the destruction of the relations that made it what it was. Of the six people in the village at the time of the attack, "all of them were scalped and otherwise horribly mangled." However, the destruction did not stop with the murder of the people, but rather it widened to include their homes, "their Huts were set on fire and most of them burnt down." The attackers, "pleased with their own Conduct and Bravery, but enraged that any of the poor Indians had escaped the massacre, rode off and in small parties, by different Roads, went Home." The attackers vanish into the geographically ambiguous frontier from which they came.

Thirteen days later, the survivors of the first massacre, who had been away from the village at the time of the attack, were followed by the Paxton Boys to their refuge in the workhouse of the nearby white village of Lancaster. Apparently with little resistance from the white villagers who had decided to shelter the refugees, the vigilantes broke into the workhouse and killed the remaining fourteen Conestoga Indians. As Franklin describes it, "When the poor Wretches saw they had no Protection nigh, nor could possibly escape, and being without the least Weapon for Defence, they divided into their little Families, the Children clinging to the Parents; they fell on their Knees, protested their Innocence, . . . and in this Posture they all received the Hatchet! —Men, Women, and little Children—were every one inhumanly murdered! —in cold Blood!" (Franklin 1959, 11: 52). Although Franklin probably created the details of the scene, the fact of the murders was unquestionable and his depiction of the slaughter completes the process begun in the first massacre. The destruction of Conestoga as a place was completed when the Paxton

Boys killed the remaining people and did so in a way that destroyed not only the present community but its future as well.

The account of the massacre ends with an argument that recalls the situated logic of place used by the Native Prophetic movement to argue against the imposition of a single timeline and a single hierarchy and in favor of establishing a coexistence of different cultures. Franklin notes that some commentators had justified the "enormous Wickedness of these Actions" in light of the ongoing war with the Ohio River valley peoples and the recent attacks by Pontiac and his confederacy by claiming that "The Inhabitants of the Frontiers are exasperated with the Murder of their Relations, by the Enemy Indians" (Franklin 1959, 11: 55). Franklin replies that such an argument "can never justify their turning in to the Heart of the Country, to murder their friends." He illustrates the absurdity of the defense of the Paxton Boys by observing that just as Native people are of different nations and traditions, "In *Europe,* if the French who are White People, should injure the Dutch, are they to revenge it on the English, because they too are White People?" To carry out racially based revenge is nothing less than agreeing that a person's real crime is to have particular physical features, of having "reddish brown Skin and black Hair." "If it be right to kill Men for such a reason," Franklin concludes, "should any Man with a freckled Face and red Hair, kill a Wife or Child of mine, it would be right for me to revenge it, by killing all the freckled red-haired Men, Women and Children, I could afterwards any where meet with" (Franklin 1959, 11:55).

Franklin's analogies are curious in that they do not rely on the expected argument that it is not right to kill the Conestoga Indians because all people are fundamentally the same. In light of the Golden Rule, the argument might go, we are obliged not to kill others because we ourselves do not wish to be killed. Franklin argues instead that since people are different it does not make sense to judge them as though they are the same, if they share a particular feature. Neither all Native people nor all white people are the same, and their differences, their actions, their interests, are significant. The killing of the Conestoga people is recognizably wrong, not because it violates a universal law, but because it does not take differences seriously enough. Further, by arguing against the authority of skin color as a marker of relevant differences, Franklin throws the reader back on the original picture of Conestoga defined by its place, that is, its geography, history, and relations. The Conestoga Indians were a community with a particular history and location as well as "color." To suppose that their racial classification marked universal traits that could justify the massacre was a logical mistake, in effect, of seeing universals where there are none. Just as the case for Native autonomy demands attention to differences of place, so Franklin demands attention to differences of place as a condition of justice. The problem with the demand is that whites do not know how to negotiate such differences. What is needed is a model of interaction that can sustain places. This model, recalling the work of Roger Williams and the Narragansett practices of *wunnégin,* is found in the practices of what Franklin calls "hospitality."

The third section sets out to show that there is a well-established "practice of what is right" and that most other peoples carry it out. "We pretend to be Christians" Franklin says, "and from the superior Light we enjoy, ought to exceed Heathens, Turks, Saracens, Moors, Negroes, and Indians" (Franklin 1959, 11: 56). White Americans are nearly alone, he thinks, in failing to adopt what he calls *"the Rites of Hospitality."* Franklin proceeds to introduce eight illustrations of the point. Like the first sections, the examples are not abstract but have a strong place component, each related to a particular geographical region: Greece, Persia, North Africa, Spain, Cuba, Guinea, and Carolina. Unlike the progressive geography of Mather, Franklin's geography of hospitality is localized; connections are not a matter of progress but points of comparison. Even as Mather brings the English to the American Strand as a matter of progress toward salvation, Franklin undermines the progressive movement by making particular locations valuable as they are. The first example, from Homer, argues that the ancient Greeks had well-established practices of hospitality. Rather than presenting a past people superseded by the new stage of Christianity, the Greek practices are left sufficient in themselves (Franklin 1959, 11: 56–58). The Turks as well, barbarians from the perspective of most of his readers, also have well-established practices of taking care of visitors. These again are viewed not as part of a progressive history, but rather as part of a place in terms of which the reader can understand the process (Franklin 1959, 11: 58–59). The seventh example, although probably fictitious, takes place in Guinea where a white man, Captain Seagrave, takes refuge with an African man, Cudjoe, who protects him from a mob. "The White Men, said [the mob], have carried away our Brothers and Sons and we will kill all White Men, give us the White Man that you keep in your House" (Franklin 1959, 11: 62). Cudjoe responds that *"the white Men that carried away your Brothers are bad Men, kill them when you can catch them; but this White Man is a good Man, and you must not kill him."* The mob "seeing his Resolution, and being convinced by his Discourse that they were wrong, went away ashamed." The example restates the circumstances of Lancaster and of the refugees in Philadelphia, but here non-whites admit their mistake and adopt the practices of hospitality.

What is remarkable in each of these cases is first the use of non-Christian and non-English instances as exemplars for appropriate behavior. Despite a Quaker tradition of using Christian scripture to justify their efforts to maintain peace (as did the Quaker friend of Teedyuscung), Franklin steps outside and uses different cultural perspectives. Instead of using the Golden Rule, Franklin relies on the principle of interaction as a means of advocating for hospitality. The illustrations exhibit the practices of hospitality and do so despite different justifications for the practices. In the case of Cudjoe, for example, when asked why he saved the white man, he answered that had they killed him *"their God would have been angry, and would have spoiled their Fishing"* (Franklin 1959, 11: 62). In an earlier example, the Spanish governor of Cuba during the English war with Spain exhibits the same practices when an English ship damaged by a storm seeks refuge in the harbor at Havana. Despite the war, the governor releases the ship and its cargo of gold and justifies his actions saying that he is bound by the "Law of Humanity to afford Relief to distressed Men, who ask for it" (Franklin 1959, 11: 61). It is, in short, not the justification, the "why," that is important, it is the interaction, the practice and its consequences. The argument recalls Franklin's electricity experiments begun fifteen years before. It is "not of much importance to know the Manner in which Nature executes her Laws," it is enough to know how to "preserve our China." Put another way, the action of hospitality is not "explained" or justified by its conformity to rules, but in its results. The rules serve only as guides to be used to reinforce and promote the practice.

Second, the examples of hospitality are geographically and culturally located, and the practices, like those of the *wunnégin* in the Narragansett tradition, are explicitly cross-cultural practices. The Saracens practice hospitality toward Christians, the Moors toward the Spanish, the Spanish toward the English, Africans toward the Americans, and Native peoples toward each other. If attention to difference provides the starting point for justice, then the practice of hospitality provides the framework for such recognition. The result, again paralleling the basic position of the Prophetic movement, is the recognition that there are distinct cultures with particular locations that have value and that relations between such different peoples will be structured as a practice of hospitality.

Franklin concludes that the Conestoga Indians would have been safer anywhere "except in the Neighbourhood of the CHRISTIAN WHITE SAVAGES of Peckstang and Donegall!" (Franklin 1959, 11: 66). The last section of the *Narrative* is an appeal on behalf of the 140 Indians who had taken refuge in Philadelphia, not simply to protect them against the killers, but to do so by adopting a principle of hospitality. Unlike the Golden Rule and its implicit principle of charity that helps others in terms of the giver or the giver's notion of humanity, the principle of hospitality recognizes difference and maintains it while maintaining a critical attitude. Franklin does not advocate uncritical acceptance, but rather a careful hospitality of the sort captured by Poor Richard in 1754: "Love your neighbour; yet don't pull down your hedge" (Franklin 1959, 5: 184). In the end, Franklin's demand for sustained Native communities can be seen as a reflection of the case he had taken to England in 1757 on behalf of the Delaware people of Wyoming. Teedyuscung anticipates Franklin's conclusion when he says, "we intend to settle at Wyoming, and we want to have certain Boundaries fixed between you and us; and a certain Tract of Land fixed, which it shall not be lawful, for us, or our Children, ever to sell, not for you, or any of your Children, ever to buy. We would have the Boundaries fixed all round, agreeable to the Draught we give you, that we may not be pressed on any Side, but have a certain Country, fixed, for our own Use, and the Use of our Children, for ever" (Van Doren and Boyd 1938, 197–198). Hospitality is a matter of coexistence and new possibilities, and for Franklin it seems to require two things: the practice of hospitality and a transformed logic that takes place as a starting point. Significantly, the same sort of argument and outcome helped Franklin to frame his defense of American independence a few years later.

At the center of the English colonies' demand for independence was the claim implicit in the opening lines of the Declaration of Independence, co-authored by Franklin, that "peoples" could be distinct and valuable. While the declaration is often cited as establishing individual "rights," its central claim is for the standing of sovereign communities. Not long after his return to England after the Lancaster massacres, Franklin became a vocal advocate for the autonomy of the American colonies. His argument, repeated in various forms around various particular issues, is reminiscent of the very points he used against the Paxton Boys and their advocates. In a letter to the *Pennsylvania Chronicle* in December 1768 Franklin responded to critics who argued that a candidate for Parliament, one Barlow Trecothick, should not be elected because he had, for a time, lived in America. The issue gives Franklin an opportunity to say why English domination of the American colonies ought to end. The letter begins, in the manner of the *Narrative,* by specifying a placed relation. "I am, sir," he says to the printer, "a native of *Boston,* in *New England,* but I do not concern myself in your *London* election, nor do I believe that any of my countrymen think it of importance. . . . And yet I hear a great Clamour, as if [Trecothick's] nomination were to promote a Boston interest" (Franklin 1959, 15: 63). The controversy turns on the failure to recognize the importance of place in judgments that affect the governance of a people. Geography, in this case, is exactly the issue.

Trecothick is to be rejected by the Londoners because he may represent the interests of the Americans even as these same Americans "have an evil disposition to Old England" with "hostile intentions," and making "barbarous resolutions against it" (Franklin 1959, 15: 64). By failing to pay the taxes levied by the Stamp Act, the Americans are "inhuman," that is, Franklin explains, "the horrible inhumanity of resolving to live within compass, and manufacture what they [the Americans] can for themselves!" (Franklin 1959, 15: 65). The conflict, Franklin says clearly, is a matter of "living within compass," of operating as a community bound together not by language and genealogy alone, or even by a tenuous connection of human sameness, but by the interactions of a place. Setting aside his sarcastic criticism of English policies that denied food and support to their own poor, he declares, "I that am a stranger among ye, cannot be qualified to judge. I can only say, that, as you live together, you have better opportunities of knowing one another than you have knowing us at 3000 miles distance and that therefore what you say of one another is rather more to be depended on" (Franklin 1959, 15: 66).

The consequent logic of place reconstructs communities in local terms and provides a reason for declaring independence from England. It also provides a model for constructing a set of relations that can maintain difference while promoting union through a kind of sovereignty based on the relations of place. When Franklin is called on to propose an alternative model for the new union of American colonies in 1775, his proposed Articles of Confederation make the connection with the logic of place overt. In Article II, for example, recalling the very terms which established the relationship between Shehaes and William Penn, Franklin states that the English colonies in American will "enter into a firm League of Friendship with each other, binding on themselves and their Posterity" (Franklin 1959, 22: 122). As a league of friendship the relationship among the colonies will be one that recognizes the colonies as different places. This is not a process of becoming "as one Man," as Franklin had proposed to the Ohio Indians at Carlisle, but a union of different peoples, as Canassatego had proposed to the Pennsylvania commissioners at Lancaster. The third article is explicit: the colonies will agree "that each Colony shall enjoy and retain as much as it may think fit of its own present Laws, Customs, Rights, Privileges, and peculiar Jurisdictions within its own Limits." Here again, Franklin proposes a geographically bounded cultural sovereignty in conjunction with the proposed union of interests.

Finally, Franklin's proposal expands the model of English colonial union to Native peoples as well. In the eleventh article, Franklin proposes "A perpetual Alliance offensive and defensive, it to be entered into as soon as may be with the Six Nations" (Franklin 1959, 22: 124). The agreement with the Six Nations is not just a military alliance but one that includes recognition of the same sovereign standing as that held by the colonies of the union. The geographical "Limits" of the Six Nations will be "ascertain'd and secur'd to them; their Land not to be encroach'd on." Such recognition does not however stop with the Six Nations but extends implicitly to a continental cultural pluralism. "The Boundaries and Lands of all the other Indians shall also be ascertain'd and secur'd to them in the same manner." Much like Teedyuscung's proposal for the peaceful coexistence of the Delaware and English in geographically and culturally defined places, Franklin carries the model further as a way of establishing a standard for coexistence of distinct places on a continental scale. While Franklin's proposal was not accepted in full and his model was overturned by degrees in favor of the federalist constitution, it is clear that for Franklin the logic of place was both crucial to understanding the developing American society and to establishing the possibility of the coexistence of different cultures in America.

In the end, Franklin's conception of scientific inquiry, structured by the principles of interaction, is joined with his commitment to the political and cultural sovereignty of place through the practices of "civility." Just as hospitality or *wunnégin* serves as the ground for the coexistence of places, civility serves as the attitude crucial to producing knowledge in such an environment. Franklin makes this point in a late paper, "Remarks Concerning the Savages of North America," written in 1783 while he lived in France. The paper begins, "Savages we call them, because their manners differ from ours, which we think the Perfection of Civility; they think the same of theirs" (Franklin 1987, 469). The claim of cultural parity is not surprising given the development of Franklin's thought, and his reassertion of it as a way of introducing his remarks suggests that, unlike popular accounts that presented Natives as savages, Franklin will offer a view of Native civility. The paper presents four brief stories, each an element of what Franklin takes to be a Native version of civility. The third story in particular outlines the role of civility in the context of belief. It begins in a way that almost undermines the point. "The Politeness of these Savages in Conversation," Franklin begins, "is indeed carried to excess, since it does not permit them to contradict or deny the Truth of what is asserted in their Presence" (Franklin 1987, 971). He concludes that given the responses of Native people to the "Truths of the Gospel," one "would think they are convinc'd." However, it is "[no] such matter. It is mere Civility." He illustrates his conclusion with the story of a Swedish minister, perhaps during the Great Awakening, who gathered a group of Susquehanna Indians to give a sermon and acquaint "them with the principal historical Facts on which our Religion is founded, such as the Fall of our first Parents by Eating an Apple, the Coming of Christ, . . . &c." When he was done, a speaker of the group stood and thanked the preacher for telling them "those things which you have heard from your Mothers. In return," he said, "I will tell you some of those we have heard from ours" (Franklin 1987, 971). The speaker then told the preacher the story of the origin of corn, beans, and tobacco. When the speaker was finished "[t]he good Missionary, disgusted with this idle Tale, said, what I delivered to you were sacred Truths; but what you tell me is mere Fable, Fiction & Falsehood." The speaker, offended by the missionary's outburst, replied, "my brother, it seems your Friends have not well instructed you in the Rules of common Civility. You saw that we who understand and practice those Rules, believed all your Stories; why do you refuse to believe ours?" (Franklin 1987, 972).[17]

"Mere Civility" in this case must be understood not as a phrase dismissing the practice of civility, but rather as an affirmation that it at once promotes exchange and new alternatives without undermining the expectation that people nevertheless hold particular convictions and seek truths. Civility, in this case, recalls the virtue of humility Franklin proposes in his *Autobiography* and describes as "a Rule to forbear all direct Contradiction to the Sentiments of others, and all positive Assertion of my own" (Franklin 1987: 1393). As he explains, "When another asserted something that I thought an Error, I deny'd my self the Pleasure of contradicting him abruptly, and of showing immediately some Absurdity in his Proposition; and in answering I began by observing that in certain Cases or Circumstances his Opinion would be right, but in the present case there appear'd or seem'd to me some Difference, &c." (Franklin 1987, 1393). Civility in this sense provides an effective way to defuse

---

17. This story is repeated by Charles Eastman, a Sioux author, in *The Soul of An Indian* (1911, 119–120), and by Vine Deloria Jr. in *God Is Red* (1994, 85–87). Deloria uses the story to illustrate the Indian point of view of the historicity of "creation legends."

conflict and promote conversation, and combined with virtues like silence, it is a way to learn about alternative ways of thinking. He concludes in the *Autobiography*, "The modest way in which I propos'd my
Opinions, procur'd them a readier Reception and less Contradiction; I
had less Mortification when I was found to be in the wrong, and I more
easily prevail'd with others to give up their mistakes when I happen'd to
be in the right."[18] This sort of civility is "excess" only when read against
an expectation that alternatives ought not receive serious consideration. The story is compelling at least in part because the missionary
rejects without consideration the story of the origin of corn in the
Susquehanna tradition. Civility of the sort practiced by the Susquehanna
serves to grant the missionary's story some standing, not as knowledge
perhaps, but as something preliminary to knowledge, as something to be
believed.

At the same time, the civility is "mere" in that it does not deny the
importance of pursuing inquiry in search of answers. Civility does not
demand that one simply give up believing something, but rather that
one adopt an attitude that will entertain the possibility of believing something else, an attitude that can promote belief—the attitude of humility.
In his study of electricity, this sort of attitude is present in the double
commitment to scientific explanations that work, that "preserve our
China," and to the possibility of new scientific explanations that may be
better. As he explains, "These Explanations of [electricity], when they
first occurred to me . . . appeared perfectly satisfactory: But now that I
have wrote them, . . . I must own, I have some Doubts about them. Yet
as I have at present Nothing better to offer in their Stead, I do not cross
them out: for even a bad Solution read, and its Faults discovered, has
often given Rise to a good one, in the Mind of an ingenious Reader"
(Franklin 1959, 4: 17). The practices of experimental science, understood broadly as the practices of civility, provide the intellectual resources for sustaining differences in a culturally plural context. In short,
politically and culturally sovereign places are sustained by an attitude

18. It is significant that Franklin's last speech at the constitutional convention is an
admonition to the participants to adopt humility as a guide in their deliberations. Long
experience, he says, has taught him that he can be wrong and that others can be right.
Collective deliberations will not produce perfect results, but after as careful deliberation
as possible, they nevertheless have produced a result that, given the deliberation, is worth
a try. Humility, in the end, sets aside the rigid concerns of truth and consistency in favor
of a respect for the process and a willingness to acknowledge one's own limitations. "Thus
I consent," he says, "to this Constitution because I expect no better, and because I am not
sure that it is not the best" (Franklin 1987, 1140).

that at once acknowledges and engages the beliefs of others while still recognizing the need for knowledge that works in particular places.[19]

In his volume *Recovering Benjamin Franklin,* James Campbell argues that the philosophical vision of pragmatism can be understood in light of four of its themes that are closely related to the commitments that emerged along the border between Native and European America that I have identified as central to pragmatism. For Campbell, the key pragmatic themes are natural place, experience, possibility, and community (Campbell 1999, 270). In the idea of natural place, Campbell identifies the pragmatic interest in understanding the world in a situated and experimental way, manifested in Franklin's commitment to science. Like the commitment to the principle of interaction, natural place focuses pragmatic attention on what happens. The theme of experience, almost as a corollary to natural place, identifies both the importance of experience as a test for ideas and as an antidote to dogmatic beliefs. In Franklin, the appeal to experience is an appeal to the common ground of experiment in science and social practice in the context of human communities. Again, like the principle of interaction, experience is a kind of interaction that serves as the context in which things both are and are known. The third theme, possibility, recalls the pragmatic commitment to the principle of growth. Franklin, Campbell observes, "focuses on how the individual can make more of his or her life in a directly Pragmatic fashion" (Campbell 1999, 271). At the same time, the possibilities for individuals can only be understood in a larger context, and this larger context, community, frames the other themes.

The four themes of pragmatism found in Franklin's work also form a crucial step in the development of pragmatism. "Franklin," Campbell concludes, "was thus a presenter of a vision of life that grew in the hands of others into a self-conscious, articulated philosophy. Emerson and James and Dewey performed this task without being themselves particularly cognizant of his contribution" (Campbell 1999, 271). Although Campbell does not trace the history, Franklin helped to lay the groundwork for the development of "formal" pragmatism in a number of ways. As a pioneering scientist he helped to establish a context for scientific re-

19. The importance of this sort of knowledge is illustrated in the first of Franklin's stories in his "Remarks" where he recalls an offer by officials from the Virginia colony to provide a college education to the sons of several Native leaders. The Native leaders rejected the offer on the grounds that such education actually made Native people unsuited to their homelands. See Franklin 1997, 970.

search in North America that was driven by the principle of interaction and its focus on science as a means of improving the life of the community. His close friend Benjamin Rush, for example, helped to establish both public health research and a form of empirical psychology, in large measure as a way to seek "rules" to solve the ongoing crises of public health in the increasingly crowded urban areas of the new United States. The same sorts of commitment to science for the sake of improvement became part of educational theory with the work of Horace Mann and Bronson Alcott. Franklin's attention to the development of cultural difference became an important framework for the development of an "American" identity in the work of Emerson. His experimentalism and his treatment of a logic of place became the aspects of early American political and scientific theory that Dewey identified as a key development in the history of pragmatism.[20]

Emerson himself was aware of Franklin's potential for influence on future generations of American philosophers. In a letter written to his aunt in 1824, Emerson writes, "Don't you admire (I am not sure you do) [Franklin's] serene and powerful understanding which was so eminently practical and useful . . . ; which seemed to be a transmigration of the Genius of Socrates—yet more useful, more moral, and more pure, and a living contradiction of the buffoonery that mocked a philosophy in the clouds?" According to Emerson, Franklin was a "sage who used his pen with a dignity and effect which was new, and had been supposed to belong only to the sword." From this perspective, Franklin appears as the ideal philosopher for Emerson, a public intellectual, concerned with the results of his words, committed to bettering himself and others, and whose reason is united with character.[21] Emerson concludes, "One enjoys a higher conception of human worth in measuring the vast influence exercised on men's minds by Franklin's character than even by reading books of past ages. . . . .many millions have already lived and millions are now alive who have felt through their whole lives the powerful good effect both of Franklin's actions and his writings" (Emerson 1909, 375–377). To the extent, then, that Franklin's commitments are an extension of the pragmatic commitments of the Delaware and the Haudenosaunee,

---

20. Dewey identifies the experimentalism of eighteenth-century American science with Jefferson and there is little doubt that Jefferson conducted such a science. It is also clear, however, that the pioneer and person who set the stage for the experimentalism of Jefferson was Franklin. See Dewey 1940, 201–223.

21. See Bier 1970 and Hedges 1976 for discussions of the connections between Franklin and Emerson.

Emerson can be seen as a transitional figure, continuing the line of development connecting the indigenous attitude with the Native Prophetic movement on one side and the classical pragmatists on the other.[22] In the end, as Campbell puts it, "Franklin's vision is . . . continuous with those of Emerson, James, and Dewey" (Campbell 1999, 270).

22. At the same time, however, Emerson may have been more directly influenced by Native thought through the work of his brother Charles, an activist against the removal policy, and by his close friend Margaret Fuller. As early as 1819, while a student at Harvard, Emerson debated on the questions "Whether the conduct of the U.S. towards the Indians can be reconciled to the principles of justice and humanity?" and "In which state of society, the civilized or the savage, is the greatest degree of happiness to be found?" Later on, at the encouragement of his brother, Emerson attended speeches by Native orators who frequented Boston in the 1830s to protest governmental policies toward Native Americans. In 1832, for example, Emerson wrote his brother, "Your friends the Cherokees are in town[.] Mr. Walker-on-the-Mountains addressed a great meeting the other [evening] at Federal St. Ch. and put to shame our orators A. H. Everett and Mr. Hoar and Dr. Beecher who spoke on the same occasion" (Emerson 1939, 1: 346). Emerson's public commitment to Native Americans was most fully expressed in a published open letter to President James Buchanan protesting the removal of the Cherokees to Oklahoma. "You, sir," he says, addressing Buchanan, "will bring down that renowned chair in which you sit into infamy if your seal is set to this instrument of perfidy [the order to remove the Cherokees]; and the name of this nation, hitherto the sweet omen of religion and liberty, will stink to the world" (Emerson 1929, 1197). See Pratt 1997a.

CHAPTER TEN

The Logic of Home

IN THE SUMMER OF 1827, fifty-two years after Franklin proposed the Articles of Confederation recognizing the political and cultural sovereignty of Native people, the prophet Wabokieshiek led warriors of several nations from the region between the Wisconsin and Rock Rivers in what is now Wisconsin in an attack on a flatboat transporting people and equipment to the lead mines in the heart of Indian country.[1] The attack reaffirmed the failure of Franklin's vision of North American pluralism in the face of United States Indian policy in the aftermath of the Revolutionary War and the soaring demand for new land in the wake of the War of 1812. A few days later Wabokieshiek's confederacy attacked again, this time killing all members of three families living near the mines.[2] United States soldiers were rushed by flatboat up the Mississippi River from St. Louis and quickly brought the Native allies to a conference at Green Bay to end the fighting. The U.S. soldiers demanded that hostilities cease and that the leaders be turned over to the troops for judgment and punishment. The Winnebago prophet Wabokieshiek, also known as White Cloud, and a war chief, Red Bird, surrendered on their own in order to protect their people from retribution by the U.S. Army. Red

---

1. Wabokieshiek was of mixed national heritage, part Winnebago and part Sauk. It is likely that he was among the Winnebago and Sauk who met with Tenskwatawa in the early days of the War of 1812. See Black Hawk 1990, 58 and Radin 1990, 21–25. According to one of Paul Radin's Winnebago informants, Tenskwatawa's message to the Winnebago began, "Younger brothers, we are not doing the right thing and that is why we are not getting along very well in life" (Radin 1990, 22). Wabokieshiek appears to have taken a similar stand. According to Black Hawk, Wabokieshiek recommended peaceful relations with the neighboring whites, but that Native people should continue in their traditional ways (Black Hawk 1990, 119).

2. For accounts of the Winnebago War see Stevens 1903, 71–76; Sultzman (http://www.dickshovel.com/win.html); and *The American Quarterly Review*, September 1828.

Bird died in prison the following February. Wabokieshiek was pardoned as a last act by the outgoing President of the United States, John Quincy Adams, and then retired to a village along the Rock River some forty miles from its confluence with the Mississippi River. The allied Indian nations that met with the United States at Green Bay signed a new treaty that sold off much of their remaining land to satisfy U.S. demands for access to lead and copper mines. New borders were established, but even these would fall within a few years.

In 1832, Wabokieshiek became an adviser to the Sauk leader Black Hawk. After Black Hawk's home village, Saukenuk, was occupied by settlers, Wabokieshiek encouraged him to take up arms against the United States in order to reassert Native borders and to ensure a place where Native culture could continue to flourish.[3] After an initial victory against the militia deployed to drive Black Hawk and his people out of their traditional lands, regular army troops arrived from St. Louis and pursued Black Hawk into Wisconsin. When his people decided to recross the Mississippi and leave their traditional lands to avoid a one-sided fight with the army, they were met at the crossing and nearly 150 men, women, and children were killed by U.S. troops, who held a position on the bluffs overlooking the river. Members of the Winnebago nation turned over Black Hawk and Wabokieshiek to the United States.

The conflict that began the forced removal of the nations of Wisconsin and northern Illinois, the Winnebago War, combined with events in the Southeast to generate a renewed attempt by some white Americans to advocate in favor of recognizing Native American land rights in some form. In December 1828, the ongoing conflict between the state of Georgia and the Native people of the Southeast worsened when the state approved legislation that "all Indian residents would come under its jurisdiction after six months" (Satz 1975, 3). The crisis precipitated by Georgia led to debate about the future of Native and white coexistence, a debate settled in part by the passage in May 1830 of the Indian Removal Act. Against those who favored taking Native lands without apology or compensation, there were a number of Native and white activists who advocated Native land rights in one form or another and opposed the policies that worked for the immediate elimination of Native people east of the Mississippi. This advocacy divided into three sorts.

One sort of advocacy, connected with the policy of Andrew Jackson and supported by the philosophical perspectives of Jefferson and Bancroft, argued in favor of removing Native peoples from lands in the East

---

3. See Black Hawk 1990, 121–122.

and relocating them to "equivalent" lands in the West. From this perspective, human progress depended upon the availability of land. Native people, to the extent they maintained their ways, could only be viewed as outside progress or as obstacles to it, destined to vanish in the face of "civilization's" inevitable triumph. Removal to alternative lands out of the path of civilized progress, these advocates argued, was the only humane course of action. The state of Georgia, in its drive to make progress, needed Indian lands, and if Native people remained, they would be placed at risk as the irrepressible planters of Georgia expanded their holdings. Removal alone could save Native people from these unfortunate circumstances. Thomas McKenney, a commissioner to the Fond du Lac conference of 1826, put it this way: "[A]fter all, they are just like ourselves, and had it pleased God that you and I should have been born and brought up as these poor ignorant savages have been, we should have been in all respects such as they are, even to the dirt . . . which in any quantity attaches to them" (McKenney 1827, 340). The fortunate circumstances of the whites, in fact, brought with them certain obligations as well. "These [obligations]," McKenney concludes, "are deep and lasting as their own native hills" amounting to the need to "preserve" the "remnants" of Native life. Such a task, McKenney argues, could be completed in "one spirited and just act, followed up by vigorous measures . . . [in order] to place [Native people] in a condition which they may be prosperous and happy" (McKenney 1827, 341).

Governor Cass of Michigan was more straightforward in his case for removal. "A barbarous people," he says, "depending for subsistence upon the scanty and precarious supplies furnished by the chase, cannot live in close contact with a civilized community" (Cass 1828, 4).[4] Given the impossibility of coexistence, Cass continues, "the only means of preserving the Indians from that utter extinction which threatens them, is to remove them from this sphere of influence" (Cass 1828, 6). Relocation, far from depriving Native people of their rights, was a process of recognizing land rights. Traditional lands, legitimately held by Native people but now needed for purposes of progress, were to be quantified and exchanged for "equal" lands farther west. The process both recognized the

---

4. Despite Cass's renown as an Indian "expert," his most famous work, *Considerations on the Present State of the Indians and Their Removal,* is often simply mistaken. While most knew, for example, that many Native peoples had long been agriculturists, Cass repeatedly adopts the view held by European anthropologists including Rousseau and Buffon that "primitive" people lived by hunting and gathering alone. His conclusion that Native people could not live near whites makes the problem a Native one even though it was well-known that Natives often advocated coexistence. It appears that whites, not Native people, were in fact incapable of coexistence.

importance of land and held the potential for a "humane" settlement of the issue. Cass concludes, "Now, when the time of severance has approached, we owe it to them, to ourselves, to the opinion of the world that the process should be conducted with kindness, with liberality, and above all, with patience" (Cass 1828, 60). Like Mather and Jefferson, Cass and the removal advocates saw Native people from a perspective framed by the colonial attitude. Every kindness, from this perspective, would at best make the inevitable less painful.

The second form of advocacy was also informed by the colonial attitude exhibited in the first approach, but disagreed with what constituted a "humane" approach.[5] The work of the American Board of Commissioners for Foreign Missions adopted this approach. Their chief spokesperson during the removal debates was Jeremiah Evarts, who is often viewed as a powerful advocate of this view. From this perspective, Native people ought not be removed from traditional territories but given the opportunity to learn "civilized" ways and become a part of the movement of human progress where they lived. Unlike the Jacksonian advocates of removal, these assimilationists argued that as human beings, Native people were no less qualified than European descendants to learn the ways of advancing civilization and no more subject to involuntary removal. A humane approach to the "Indian problem" according to this view was to preserve small Indian reservations in traditional homelands and then provide Native people with the resources necessary to "become civilized." While these activists disagreed with the removal advocates on the potential for Native people to learn new ways, they agreed with virtually everything else claimed by Jackson and his allies. Native culture was clearly inferior to European civilization, whose progress was inevitable. In the long run, Native people as such must disappear from the world.[6] Some Native leaders adopted this view as well, particularly after the Civil War and the passage in 1887 of the Dawes Act. The best way to survive, some believed, was to set aside Native traditions and connections and adopt as fully as possible the ways and ideas of the whites. Boarding schools like the one at Carlisle, Pennsylvania, under the leadership of Richard Pratt (and founded in 1879), were important in convincing many Native people of this view. This conclusion is confirmed by the story of human history and the picture of human nature affirmed on one hand by the Puritans and on the other by the new science of anthropology anticipated by Jefferson and advocated by Ban-

5. See Francis Paul Prucha's introduction to Evarts's work (Evarts 1981).
6. Native authors like Charles Eastman and Arthur Parker are often viewed as later advocates of this position.

croft. Despite its "humane" face, however, such an approach still understood Native culture from an attitude that saw all history as a unified story and all its characters related hierarchically. Native people as human beings could change roles, but to the extent they remained Indian, they also remained a less valuable and disappearing people.

The third form of advocacy appears to share aspects of the positions taken by both the removal advocates and the assimilationists. On one hand, like those in favor of removal, these advocates believed that Native culture was distinctive and ought to be "preserved" in a place, that is, in relatively autonomous communities. Native survival, in this case, depended on the ability of Native culture to flourish, and such flourishing could only occur when Native people maintained both traditional practices and traditional lands. On the other hand, these advocates argued that Native people nevertheless should have access to the "benefits" of civilization, including education and agriculture. Like the assimilationists, these advocates believed that Native people were human beings and perfectly able to learn the ways of European American society. At the same time, they rejected the idea that all Native people ought to give up traditional ways and argued that Native people should have the option to be "traditional," choose to adopt Euro-American ways, or to do some of each. This position appears contradictory on its surface. To advocate for assimilation must naturally demand that Native people give up traditional views and lands in order to become civilized. To advocate for preservation of the tradition necessarily involves the rejection of civilization and its trappings and the acceptance of safe removal to the west. On the contrary, the view represents a fundamental shift and not a compromise between the positions informed by the colonial attitude. These advocates, taking their lead from Native people themselves, adopted an alternative attitude from which to view the problem in the first place. From this perspective, grounded in a logic of place, advocacy will be a matter of responding to the circumstances of Native people as they are, not as an attempt to generate answers based on some already-determined principles from another place and relevant to another people. The third form of advocacy approached the question of Indian removal by proposing an awareness of places and a commitment to maintain their integrity in a context of coexistence.

Further, while the advocates of removal and assimilation tended to overlook Native perspectives on the process, advocates of the third stance both attended to Native voices and actively attempted to make the Native perspective part of their advocacy. Since many of these advocates came to the debate already explicitly influenced by Franklin and Roger Williams and familiar with the positions of leaders such as Sagoyewatha,

Tenskwatawa, Wabokieshiek, William Apess, and John Ross, they came to the debate already influenced by Native ways of thinking.[7] Taken from a starting point that already recognized the importance of pluralism, community, and growth, the Native-influenced activism can be seen instead as an effort to carry out these commitments and make it possible for culturally distinct peoples to coexist peacefully. At the same time, the changing character of European American communities and the fragmentation of borders between Native and European America also led to new developments in how the indigenous attitude was applied. It is in this context that the logic of place transformed again into a new logic of resistance—what might be called a "logic of home"—that came to inform other resistance movements in nineteenth-century America.

The logic of home emerged at a crucial time. In the 1820s Europeans began to face the problem of how to understand and respond to human difference. The problem came in a three-sided crisis: Indian removal, slavery, and women's suffrage. At the center of one range of responses to this crisis were the philosophical traditions of Native people, some already a part of European American internal strategies of critique and resistance, some becoming a part of new forms of European American activism. As the practices of *wunnégin* helped Roger Williams to envision a pluralist community and as the Native Prophetic movement and the emergent logic of place helped Franklin to frame both a vision of sovereign communities and a practice of science grounded in the needs of the community, so the efforts of Native leaders and speakers in the era of removal helped to provide resources for the feminist and anti-racist movements begun in the 1820s. Here the pragmatic commitments are inherited from both the earlier tradition of influence and the Native cultures of the time as they were manifested in the logic of home. Taken together, all three of these moments of influence became the context out of which classical pragmatism emerged at the end of the nineteenth century.

The transformation of the logic of place into a logic of home is best illustrated in the work of a range of women writers who developed a narrative method focused on what will be called "domestic details." This approach, though perhaps influenced by developments in English fiction

---

7. William Apess was a Pequot Indian who became an ordained minister and published author. In 1833–34, he helped to prevent the removal of the Mashpee Indians from Massachusetts and then spoke against the general policy of removal. He often spoke against removal in Boston at lectures attended by white activists. In 1838, Apess vanished without a trace. See Apess 1992, Barry O'Connell's introduction.

of the time, emerged most clearly in the work of women authors who lived at the border between Native and European America. At the same time, a comparable logic emerged within Native communities as they developed strategies for cultural survival against the genocidal policies of Indian removal. In this context, the logic of home helped to organize both internal and external resistance to the colonial attitude.

One of the earliest examples of the narrative form of the logic of home is found in the widely circulated story "The Forsaken Brother," by Bamewawagezhikaquay, a Chippewa woman also called Jane Johnston Schoolcraft. Johnston Schoolcraft was the granddaughter of Waub Ojeeg, one of the principal chiefs of the Chippewa living near Sault Ste. Marie, where Lake Superior joins the lower Great Lakes.[8] Her mother, Oshauguscodaywaygua, was also a well-known and well-respected Chippewa leader, and her father was a trader of Irish descent.[9] In 1823, Jane Johnston married Henry Rowe Schoolcraft, the Indian agent who had been assigned to Sault Ste. Marie the year before. Before her marriage, Johnston Schoolcraft traveled widely with her father and studied for a time in Ireland.[10] After her marriage to Henry, she joined him as a co-author of a "manuscript magazine," *The Literary Voyager,* that circulated widely in the Northeast in 1826 and 1827. With the help of Johnston Schoolcraft's family, especially her mother, the magazine included versions of traditional stories, descriptions of Chippewa customs, as well as poetry and brief news articles. Although edited by Henry, *The Literary Voyager* also includes some of the earliest and most influential publications of Native women.[11]

Johnston Schoolcraft's story "The Forsaken Brother" begins, "It was a fine summer evening; the sun was scarcely an hour high,—its departing rays beamed through the foliage of the tall, stately elms, that skirted the little green knoll, on which a solitary Indian lodge stood" (Schoolcraft 1962, 93). In the lodge, an elderly man prepared to die. In his final wish,

---

8. The Chippewa are also called Ojibwe or Anishnaabeg. Waub Ojeeg's biography is presented in several entries in *The Literary Voyager.* See Schoolcraft 1962, 23–26, 39–42, 50–56, and a poem by his granddaughter, "Invocation To My Maternal Grandfather on Hearing His Descent from Chippewa Ancestors Misrepresented," in Schoolcraft 1962, 142–143.

9. Oshauguscodaywaygue is discussed at length by Thomas McKenney in his journal *Tour to the Lakes* (1827, 182–184). Also see Phillip Mason's introduction to *The Literary Voyager* (Schoolcraft 1962).

10. See McKenney's brief biography of Johnston Schoolcraft (1827, 184–185).

11. The persistent issue of the "authenticity" of Native voices emerges here as it has whenever Native texts have been considered in this discussion. Here there is little question of Johnston Schoolcraft's self-identification as a Chippewa, but it is also clear that in addition to her education in the Native community, she was also well-schooled in European and European American settings.

he asked his three children, in the face of the "unkindness, and ingratitude, and every wickedness" they will encounter, "to cherish each other, and on no account to forsake [the] youngest brother" (Schoolcraft 1962, 94). The old man died, confident that his children would stay together. The mother of the children, despondent over the death of her husband, died as well within six months, asking her children to renew their promise to cherish one another. The children were left alone. After a time, the oldest brother became restless. "My sister," he says, "are we always to live as if there were no other human beings in the world? . . . I shall seek the villages of men." His sister, the oldest of the three, admits that she cannot deny her brother's desire to seek society, but she cautioned him, "we were told to cherish each other. . . . If we follow our separate gratifications, it will surely make us forget [our brother] whom we are alike bound to support" (Schoolcraft 1962, 95). The elder brother left and in time married and "settled on the shores of the same lake, which contained the bones of his parents and the abode of his forsaken brother."

After a time, the elder sister also grew restless. So, "[o]ne day, after she had collected all the provisions she had set apart for emergencies, and brought a quantity of wood to the door, she said to her [younger brother]. 'My brother, you must not stray far from the lodge. I am going to seek our brother: I shall soon be back'" (Schoolcraft 1962, 95). Instead of returning, however, she became "so much taken up with the pleasures and amusements of society, that all affection for her brother was obliterated." She married and "never more thought of the helpless relative she had abandoned." The boy who was left behind eventually used all of the stored food and supplies his sister had left for him and, as winter came on, began to forage for food, sleeping in trees and eating the "refuge meats of the wolves." After a time the wolves took pity on the boy and began to leave him extra food. By spring, the boy traveled in the company of his new friends, the wolves, and on a particular day they came to the lakeshore. At the same time, the boy's brother happened to be fishing nearby from his canoe when he thought he heard a child cry. He came near the shore and recognized his brother who sobbed, "*Neesya, neesya, shyegwuh gushuh! / Ween ne myeengunish! / ne myeengunish!*" "My brother, my brother / I am now turning into a Wolf! / I am turning into a Wolf!" (Schoolcraft 1962, 96). The elder brother quickly came to shore and tried to catch his brother, but as he approached, the boy fled and as he fled he began to physically transform into a wolf. After a long pursuit, the younger brother became a "perfect wolf." His sibling gone, the older brother "felt the bitterness of remorse all his days, and the sister, when she heard of the fate of the little boy whom she had so cruelly left, and whom both she and her brother had solemnly promised to foster and protect, wept bitterly; and never ceased to mourn until she died" (Schoolcraft 1962, 96).

The story is a simple one in which the bonds of family relations are broken by the selfishness of the older siblings. In the end, despite promises to their parents, both older siblings leave home and abandon their brother to the wolves. At the same time, the story is also one of a home place. The opening lines, like the speeches of the Native prophets, make a particular geographical location the center of both the action and the meaning of the story. Parallel with the abandonment of the boy is an abandonment of the traditional home of the children's family. The underlying geographical story pictures the older siblings not simply leaving their young brother behind, but leaving their home as well, marked significantly by the "bones" of their parents. When the older brother leaves, it is to seek society. When he finds it, he establishes an intimate connection through marriage, and though he has not left the lake of his family, he has turned away from his brother with no thought of return. The sister, despite her promise to return, becomes enamoured with the "pleasures and amusements of society" and literally marries these amusements with no thought of her origins or obligations. Her abandonment, like her brother's, is in part selfishness, but it is also a matter of greater displacement, of physically separating herself from her home. The younger brother also leaves home in search of food. In his wandering, he is taken in by still another people, the wolves. Even as his siblings establish intimate, embodied relations which separate them from their homes, so the younger brother embodies a new people that will serve to permanently separate him from his family and, by degrees, from his home. The destruction of the home is complete.

"The Forsaken Brother" exhibits a logic of place as it recounts the breakdown of geographically framed relations. The Indian children abandon their traditional place to join with other Native people in one case, with the whites in another, and with the wolves in the third. The relations that were the place dissolve. The cause of the dissolution adds a further dimension to the tale. At its root, the problem is a breakdown in the relations of the human community that was part of the place. While the deaths of the children's parents opened the situation to change, the children themselves gave up traditional connections and adopted others that finally led to the breakdown of the original place. A logic of home, as I use the term, marks attention paid to the sustaining relations within the community and the way interactions transform them, both within and between communities. Not only does the Native family stand in the midst of other peoples, its relations with the world are viewed as particular interactions of the people who are part of the place. As the members of the family fall out, establishing different relations with others, the character of the children's home place changes, leading to its destruction.

Why this is a story of something understood as undesirable rather than as something good is relative to the home place itself. Forsaking the younger brother is not presented as an example of something that is bad because it violates some general principle such as the rule that one must keep promises, but because it destroys particular relations and possibilities. When the sister is described as mourning the treatment of her brother until her death, she is clearly not mourning that her brother had died, since he continued to live as a wolf. Rather, what is mourned is the process of disconnection that resulted from her leaving the boy behind. Here, the relations of place, in this case the relations of the Native community to the surrounding peoples, and the relations of home, in this case the familial bonds of the children, break down, and the home place disappears. The outcome is disconnection, the elimination of possibilities, and, consequently, the undermining of growth. As it is told, the story makes no larger claims but stands as a kind of situational analysis of a particular place and so seems to offer no general advice, no conclusion about the particular case that illustrates some truth or moral prescription. Just as Teedyuscung left open what the Pennsylvania government ought to do in the face of the violation of Delaware lands, so Johnston Schoolcraft leaves open the message of "The Forsaken Brother." What the listener consequently learns is not a rule of behavior, but a logic, a way of ordering and valuing experience so that things can be seen from different angles. The features of the "home" then serve as variables with which to take up other situations. There is no moral, only method.

At the same time Johnston Schoolcraft was publishing versions of Native stories, new strategies of resistance were developing among Native peoples in response to increasing demands by the United States that Native people leave their traditional homes. In the Southeast, this pressure led to a meeting of the Cherokee nations in the summer of 1827 at which the nation wrote and adopted a formal constitution. While the Cherokee and most other eastern peoples had long lived under well-known governmental structures, the Cherokee decision to adopt a formalized and written constitution marked an important adjustment in Native attempts in the Southeast to maintain a place. While the earlier generation of Native prophets had conceptualized relations within Native nations in terms of long-standing tradition, the Cherokee explicitly began to change the sustaining relations of home and place, that is the relations both within Cherokee society and between the Cherokee and others. This strategy is well-represented in the work of John Ross, born in 1790 of mixed Cherokee and Irish descent. Ross was educated both in white schools and within the Cherokee nation and served as a clerk to the principal chiefs of the Cherokee in their dealings with the United States in the aftermath of the War of 1812 and Tecumseh's War in the north.[12] When the Cherokee approved the new constitution, Ross became the first principal chief elected under the new system. Ross led the Cherokee nation during attacks by Georgia and the United States, political and otherwise, risked assassination, and finally helped to lead the Cherokee out of Georgia when the United States military came to drive them out by force. He continued as an elected leader of the nation after it reached Indian Territory, now Oklahoma, until the Civil War. Although a slave owner himself, Ross opposed Cherokee involvement in the war on the side of the Confederacy, and when the Confederates convinced surrounding Indian nations to join the South, Ross left and went to Washington, where he spent the remainder of the war trying to convince the North that the Cherokee support of the South had been coerced.

Ross's response to removal, representing the collective views of the Cherokee leadership, began where the arguments of the earlier generation of Native prophets had begun: asserting an original right to traditional lands granted by the creator. As pressure increased for removal, however, Ross and the Cherokee leadership argued against forsaking the Cherokee place and advocated instead for transforming it and establishing new sustaining relationships. In his first annual message to the nation in 1828, he explicitly responds to the claims made by Georgia against Cherokee lands. According to Ross, Georgia claimed Cherokee lands by the rights of discovery, conquest, and compact (Ross 1985, 1: 142). None of the three were legitimate claims, Ross argues. The claim of discovery he dismissed in language that recalls the earlier prophets: "[T]he claim advanced under the plea of discovery," he says, "is preposterous. Our ancestors from time immemorial possessed this country, not by a 'Charter' from the hand of a mortal king, . . . but by the Will of the King of Kings, who created all things" (Ross 1985, 1: 143). The arguments of conquest and of compact do not apply either, he concludes. The Cherokee were not conquered in any previous war with the United States or Georgia and had never sold the lands in question. Rather than ceding their home place, the Cherokee would work to sustain it. Recalling the

12. See Ross 1985, Gary E. Moulton's introduction.

logic of place, Ross concludes, "In all our intercourse with our neighboring white brethren, we should endeavor to cultivate the utmost harmony and good understanding, by strictly observing the relations which we sustain to the United States" (Ross 1985, 1: 144).

In order to sustain such ongoing relations, however, Ross argued for the need to transform Cherokee society internally, even as he argued for its integrity as a distinct culture and nation. Ross's letter to the Seneca, written in 1834 and signed by four other Cherokee leaders, provides both a modification of the logic of place and a strategy with which to answer the problems posed in cases of the sort described by Johnston Schoolcraft in "The Forsaken Brother." In April 1834, the Cherokee delegation in Washington met a delegation from the Seneca nation who delivered an address. A few days later, the Cherokee responded, thanking the Seneca and advancing their own view on the proper response to the common threat posed by the United States. After the formalities of thanks, Ross presented a brief description of the problem faced by Native nations in the face of the European invasion. The description, following the patterns set by the prophets and speakers like Teedyuscung, explains the destruction of the relations that sustained Native home places. The problem, Ross claims, is not a matter of natural inferiority, military weakness, or a matter of the inexorable progress of the whites, but rather a problem of wisdom. The great "leading cause" of the destruction of places is the "superiority of the white people . . . in their cultivation and acquirements of the arts and sciences" (Ross 1985, 1: 85). "[In] wisdom," he says, "and Superior Knowledge, the force of power exists." The result for whites is the possibility of growth. At present, he continues, "the existence of Indian Nations as distinct Independent communities within the limits of the United States seems to be drawing to a close." In order not to forsake Native homes, Native people needed to take two steps: to pursue education and to build alliances with other Native peoples.

In effect, Ross argues that rather than forsaking homes, Native people must attend to the sustaining relations both within and between Native communities, at once fostering their place, its history, land, and people even as they adopt resources to maintain their homes in the face of circumstances changed by the presence of the whites and their arts and sciences. The problem, in short, is that the Cherokee were failing to take advantage of the resources available to sustain flourishing communities even as the whites established their own. The struggle within Native communities had undermined Native homes as much as the assault on Native places undermined the sustaining relations to land and history. In order to restore Native homes, Native people needed to learn the resources of the whites even as they maintained their place as distinct from whites. Within the community, education, the development of a written language and publications, and governmental reform provided the proper response. Outside the community, the proper response involved promoting sustaining relations with the other Native peoples. In the end, Ross concludes:

> From the uncertainties of bettering our condition by removal, we have determined to cling to our original rights in the country where we first drew the breath of life—for there our rights have been recognized and secured by treaties under the solemn pledge of the U. States to protect them unto us. And as Cherokees we cannot but feel a deep interest in the welfare of all red people—and for this reason we would most earnestly recommend unto them unity of sentiment and action among themselves, as the only security for their own welfare and happiness. (Ross 1985, 1: 286–287)

For Ross, the Native home place ought not be abandoned. It ought to be held and sustained by understanding and acting in terms of the logics of place and home.

The logic of place as it emerged from the Native Prophetic movement made a case for cultural pluralism in places by adopting a way of understanding the relationship between people, culture, and land. The invasion by European Americans undermined the places of Native people, not because whites sought a place to live in America, but because they did so in a way that undermined the sustaining relations of place. The prophetic logic of place, at least as it emerged in the interaction between Native people and whites, focused largely on the interactions of cultures and communities. Johnston Schoolcraft's story follows a similar logic but takes up the consequences of cultural interaction within communities. The presence of other peoples shifts the attention of the children away from their home place, forsaking their brother and "the country where [they] first drew the breath of life." When the relationships of place are undermined, they are undermined in part by the intracommunity relations of particular people. The sister and older brother leave home and their brother by becoming part of other communities and in so doing forget their origins and the obligations their home place demands. This understanding modifies the expression of the indigenous attitude again. The Narragansett practices of welcome provide, in a sense, a context for the interaction of radically different peoples. The logic of place makes explicit the elements that sustain different cultures and interactions among them: history, people, practices, and land. The logic of home focuses on the complex relations that constitute the interaction of difference within culturally distinct communities.

At the center of the development of the logic of home in European American thought is the work of Lydia Maria Child. Other writers, including Catharine Maria Sedgwick, Lydia Sigourney, Anna Brownell Jameson, and Margaret Fuller also played important roles in its development and had connections with Native people and issues. Child stands out from these other contributors both because of her close relationships with Native people in the Northeast and because her work was published before the relevant works of the others.[13] Child was born in Medford, Massachusetts, in 1802, the youngest of five children.[14] Her brother, Convers Francis, attended Harvard and became the pastor of the Unitarian church in Watertown, Massachusetts. After Child's mother died of tuberculosis in 1814, Child was sent to live with her sister, Mary Francis Preston, and her husband in Norridgewock, Maine (then a territory of Massachusetts). In 1814, Norridgewock was a border town along the Kennebec River, sustaining a growing European American population surrounded by small settlements of Eastern Abenaki people.[15] Although Child had attended grammar school in Watertown, her formal education ended with her move to Norridgewock. Instead, she read widely, especially the works of Sir Walter Scott, Shakespeare, and Samuel Johnson. She also spent time in conversation with the people of the village and the Native people in the surrounding lands. Her contact with Native people was transformative. "Actually," writes Child's biographer Carolyn Karcher, "as Child seems to have realized by the time she wrote her first novel, *Hobomok,* the move from Medford [Massachusetts] to Norridgewock turned out to be as liberating as [her heroine's] sojourn in the wilderness" (Karcher 1994, 9). Not only does Child's first major work call upon her experience in Norridgewock, she continued to write about Native subjects throughout her career and to work as an advocate of Native rights.[16]

13. See Zwarg 1995, Chapter 3 for a discussion of Fuller's connections with Native people.
14. The biographical details are from Carolyn Karcher's invaluable biography of Child (1994).
15. Among the Eastern Abenaki are the Kennebec peoples, including the Norridgewock Indians (dispersed after the 1724 massacre at Norridgewock), the Wawenock, and the Penobscot. See Snow 1978. The Malecite and Passamaquoddy peoples live to the west and north and the Western Abenaki lived to the west. Their territories included the headwaters of the Connecticut River and the St. Francis River. See Erickson 1978 and Day 1978.
16. See Child 1986 and Child 1997, collections of Child's work collected by Karcher.

Among the prominent Native people Child came to know while living in Maine was John Neptune, then the governor of the Penobscot
nation, whose central village at the time was Old Town along the Penobscot River.[17] In 1816, John Neptune became a prominent voice for Native
people in the region when he testified on behalf of a Penobscot man,
Peol Susep, who was charged with murdering a white man.[18] Apparently
trying to set Susep's actions in context, Neptune argued that Native
people had been the subject of a great many wrongs by the European
Americans who had come to the Penobscot valley. "You know," Neptune
said, speaking to the court, "your people do my Indians a great deal of
wrong. They abuse them very much: yes, they murder them; then they
walk right off, . . . nobody touches them . . . and this makes my heart
burn" (Vetromile 1866, 162). Four years later when Maine became a
state, Neptune visited the new governor to complain about white viola-
tions of Native hunting and fishing rights (Eckstorm 1945, 11). In 1825,
Neptune reached an even wider audience when he dictated a letter published both in Maine and in Boston protesting the destruction of Native
forests in the Penobscot valley (Eckstorm 1945, 12). Child's impressions
of Neptune were strong enough that on meeting several Native people
from Maine in 1841, she recalled having dinner with him at his camp
"on the shores of the Kennebec [River]" more than twenty years earlier.
She recalled as well Neptune's nephew, Etalexis, whom she described as
"a tall, athletic youth, of most graceful proportions" (Child 1998, 19).[19]

When Child began to write stories for her popular children's magazine *The Juvenile Miscellany,* she included a number of stories based on
her experiences with Native people in Maine. In one, "The Indian Boy,"
published in 1827, Child recalls a young Penobscot named Alexis, perhaps the nephew of John Neptune, with whom she spent much time. In
the story, Child provides a meal and some supplies for Alexis and his
grandmother when the grandmother has fallen ill. Alexis invites Child
to visit his grandmother, which she does the following day, bringing a
beaded string for Alexis and more supplies for his grandmother. Alexis
gives Child a basket he had woven. She concludes about Alexis that he

17. Henry David Thoreau also met John Neptune and briefly describes him in *The Maine Woods* (1966).
18. The date and name of the man on trial are taken from Eckstorm's account (1970, 11). Eugene Vetromile published a slightly different account, dating the trial in 1817 and the name of the man on trial as Piol Zusep (Vetromile 1866, 162). Vetromile's account contains a brief quotation from Neptune's speech. Child herself wrote an apparently fictional ac-count of a Penobscot artist named Pol Sosef, published in the *Juvenile Miscellany* in 1831.
19. Karcher speculates that Etalexis may have served as the model for Hobomok in her novel written only a few years after their meeting (Karcher 1994, 12).

"could tell little white boys a great many things they never heard of; and he was as kind to the old and sick as ever any child was in the world" (Child 1827, 31). The conclusion suggests that Child may have herself learned much from young Alexis, his family, and perhaps the other Penobscot who lived in the area. Of her time in Maine, she wrote, "I used to go to the woods and visit the dozen wigwams that stood there very often."[20]

Norridgewock itself became the scene for two of Child's important early stories. Both are based on the 1724 attack on the Catholic mission to the Norridgewock Indians. A company of English soldiers attacked the mission, located just north of the town where Child lived, and most of the Native people and the mission priest, Father Sébastien Râle, were killed and the mission burned to the ground. In 1815, shortly after Child arrived at her sister's house in Norridgewock, a strong summer storm blew down a tree north of town. Entangled in its roots was the bell from the old Norridgewock mission. The discovery generated much discussion in town, enough discussion that the thirteen-year-old Child would recall the incident and make it the centerpiece of her 1827 story "Adventures of a Bell." Told from the perspective of the bell, the story presents a kind of eyewitness account of the massacre. In this version of the story, the English settlers who lived near the mouth of the Kennebec, described by the bell as "malicious, blood-thirsty dogs," were planning to attack the Norridgewock Indians to the north who were allied with the French. As the Norridgewock Indians prepared to strike first, they were called by the bell to the mission for prayer. Once the Norridgewock people, including the warriors, were in the church and unarmed, the English attacked. This element of the story is important to note. According to Fannie Eckstorm in her critique of the literature on the Norridgewock massacre, the story that the Native people were called into the mission just prior to the attack was part of the Native oral tradition about the massacre but never part of the written histories. Both she and ethnologist Frank Speck were surprised to learn this aspect of the story during their investigations in the region at the end of the nineteenth century. Eck-

---

20. Child wrote several other autobiographical stories about her experiences along the border, including "Buffalo Creek." This story describes a lengthy visit to the land of the Seneca in New York where she met the daughter of Joseph Brandt, the Mohawk leader who led many Haudenosaunee people into Canada at the end of the Revolutionary War. She also met Red Jacket, Sagoyewatha, whom I discussed in an earlier chapter. In addition to those prominent Native Americans she met as a youth, Child probably met many of the Native activists who visited the Boston and New York areas in the 1820s and 1830s. She also knew the Cherokee leader John Ross through her husband, who was also an activist against removal and a well-known abolitionist.

storm used the story as a reason to reevaluate all the published accounts of the attack, concluding, in part, that many of the French documents appear to have been written in order to obscure the events of the massacre and the actions of Father Râle. That Child was familiar with this oral tradition and used it in her stories suggests that she had the opportunity to hear at least some of the stories of the Penobscot during her years in Norridgewock.[21]

Child's earliest stories, including her novel *Hobomok*, are striking, in part because they mark a dramatic shift in how stories were told in the developing European American tradition and in part because this shift came to focus on what Child called "domestic detail." While there were already a number of novelists writing stories that included the details of relations (loves, murders, misunderstandings, and so on), these novels were more often structured as didactic exercises to illustrate important moral principles through concrete example.[22] Child's novel, as I will suggest, reverses the relations and develops the details and logic of situations as the sources of judgment. *Hobomok* does not provide moral principles that can serve to guide the reader through the troubles of their own lives. Rather it provides a concrete examination of a particular situation where the method of examination is the lesson to be learned. Rather than repeating accepted moral truisms, Child challenges them, strains them, and sometimes overturns or transforms them. While the moralizing short story and novel would flourish in America and elsewhere, this alternative model, initiated in large part by Child, became the form for stories that set out to transform American attitudes to support a pluralistic society in which different people of all sorts could coexist.[23]

In order to see the ways in which Child applied the lessons of the logic of home as it emerged in her experience with Native people at Norridgewock, it is useful to consider *Hobomok* in contrast with another popular novel published a year earlier. In 1823, James Fenimore Cooper published a milestone in the history of American literature, the first of his "Leatherstocking Tales," *The Pioneers*. As if to assert a new version of

21. Convers Francis, Child's brother, lends support to the idea that the story of the massacre was not one found in the literature with which he was familiar. Francis says, "A tradition is sometimes mentioned in that neighborhood that when the English troops reaches Rale's village, the Indians and their priest were all in their church, . . . I know not the slightest historical evidence for such a story" (quoted in Eckstorm 1934, 545). Eckstorm herself does not mention Child's use of the story and perhaps was not aware of it. Child's second version of the story, in the following year, retains the tradition that the Norridgewock people had been called to the mission just before the attack, but tells the story from a perspective focused on Father Râle. See Child 1997.

22. See Brown 1940 for a discussion of the development of novels of this sort.

23. See Tompkin 1985; Solomon 1994; and Mills 1994.

the logic of place as the framework for the narrative, he begins, "Near the center of the state of New York lives an extensive district of country, whose surface is a succession of hills and dales, or, to speak with greater deference to geographical definitions, of mountains and valleys" (Cooper 1954, 618). While it is clear that location matters to his narrative, as Cooper widens the scene it also becomes clear that the location in question is not the source and frame of the meaning of the tale. Instead, the location itself gains meaning from a larger story that literally transcends any particular places along the way, the story of American progress. Cooper leaves little doubt about how the topography becomes important. After observing the "picturesque" quality of the valley, he continues, "Beautiful and thriving villages are found interspersed along the margins of the small lakes or situated at those parts of streams which are favorable to manufacturing; neat and comfortable farms with every indication of wealth about them, are scattered profusely through the dales to the mountaintops." While the valley is a scene of interaction for Cooper, it is the interaction of an acquisitive and aggressive people on what is presented as a passive environment. "Only forty years have passed," he concludes, "since this territory was a wilderness" (Cooper 1954, 619). Following his predecessors, Mather and Jefferson, Cooper begins his narrative in the colonial attitude, literally capturing the valley from which the Delaware River emerges as a moment in the relentless progress of humanity.

Even as Cooper's narrative makes the Delaware valley a passive resource for the movement of progress, his second chapter establishes a similar relationship between Native people and Europeans and, by implication, between women and men. The wilderness, of course, is not for Cooper an empty land, but rather a land filled with resources and thrills that feed the needs of an expanding nation. As he reminds his readers, "Before the Europeans, or, to use a more significant term, the Christians, dispossessed the original owners of the soil, all that section of country which contains the New England States, and those of the Middle, which lie east of the mountains, was occupied by two great nations of Indians from whom had descended numberless tribes" (Cooper 1954, 631). These nations, the Haudenosaunee or Six Nations, and the Delaware, illustrate the role of Native people as instrumental to the advancement of European settlement. In Cooper's novels, the Six Nations, a powerful military alliance, served to toughen the Europeans for their work in North America. Through them and their allies, the Europeans learned skills of survival and war. The Delaware, on the other hand, marked the necessarily submissive quality of Native peoples to stronger rivals. When the Delaware had been worn down by war and disease, they were "induced to suffer themselves to be called *women*" and in doing so agreed to "cultivate the arts of peace, and to entrust their defence entirely to the *men,* or warlike tribes of the Six Nations" (Cooper 1954, 632). When the Delaware reasserted their "manliness," they were nearly destroyed, and now the "sole survivor" of the Mohegan tribe of the Delaware people, a Christian convert named Chingachgook, comes to the house of a powerful white man as a servant. On his arrival, Chingachgook enters the house from the cold, bares himself to the waist, and assists in treating a wound accidentally inflicted by the master of the house on a young hunter. In effect, as *The Pioneers* begins, the land and those who populate it are to be understood relative to the advancement of European civilization as surely as Mather's "American Strand" became meaningful when the chosen people came to "irradiate" it. As the land itself is a resource, so Native people are to be understood as resources as well, teaching the skills of survival and testing the mettle of the "men" who would survive, while themselves taking up the role of subservient women or passing from the stage.

The next year, 1824, Child published her novel *Hobomok* about Native and white relations. Child's novel, though it shares many of the stereotyped images of Native people used by Cooper, nevertheless takes a different narrative approach. *Hobomok* is set nearly 150 years earlier than *The Pioneers* and is set in Massachusetts rather than in New York. It opens with three distinct beginnings. The first, a preface by a fictional friend of the author, establishes the work as a contrast to the fiction of Cooper. When the "author" of the book, presented by Child as a man, declares that "he" has decided to write a novel, his friend replies that there seems little reason to do so in light of the numerous and popular works by Sir Walter Scott and James Fenimore Cooper. "'The Spy'," he says, "is lurking in every closet,—the mind is every where supplied with 'Pioneers' on the land, and is soon likely to be with 'Pilots' on the deep" (Child 1986, 3). The author replies that the history of New England as "barren and uninteresting as it is" when compared with Cooper's New York, is still "enough to rouse the dormant energies of my soul." Significantly, rather than viewing the works of Cooper as stories of humanity's progress, the author of *Hobomok* takes them as local tales, histories of a place, and in so doing can justify her own narrative as the story of a different place.

The second introduction to the novel illustrates the strategy of place as opposed to a tale of progress. The author begins "his" promised story with "I never view the thriving villages of New England, which speak so forcibly to the heart, of happiness and prosperity, without feeling a glow of national pride, as I say, 'this is my own, my native land'" (Child 1986, 5). In contrast to Cooper's opening line, the author places herself, or rather the author of *Hobomok,* in the scene. The villages thrive, as they do in *The Pioneers,* but what makes them meaningful is not their role in a larger scheme. It is rather that they are connected with the author and provide, in a sense, the complex context of the author's own identity. The identification by the author of "his" "native land" marks a crucial shift. Rather than seeing "himself" as part of a larger story of progress, Child's narrator presents himself as bound to the land. While such identification implies the dispossession of indigenous people from a particular place, it also asserts a first step toward peaceful coexistence of different places. By seeing himself as a part of a place, the narrator announces the possibility of a pluralist American society framed by growth, not a progressive one bent on using the resources of the land and moving on.

As the Delaware valley is picturesque for Cooper, so is New England for Child. But the aesthetic quality is not a matter of its potential as a resource, but because it calls up a frame for understanding of the past. "The remembrance of what we have been, comes rushing on the heart in powerful and happy contrast" (Child 1986, 5). While in most nations, history is "shrouded in darkness," in this place, "[e]ach succeeding year has left its footsteps distinct upon the soil." Two hundred years of settlement, she says, have made the past accessible for better and worse. Even as she recalls Mather's image of "irradiation" in the coming of Christianity to America, it is not as part of the story of redemption but as the story of the place itself. The villages are held under the light of a steady sun "which for ages beyond the memory of man had gazed on the strange, fearful worship of the Great Spirit of the wilderness" and then "upon the altars of the living God" (Child 1986, 5–6). Here, the "steady sun" marks the spot, not progress from an oriental dawn. The place is not by this process made part of Europe, but rather a place now influenced by the presence of Europeans. "The bold outlines of [the] character [of the first European immigrants] alone remain to us. The varying tints of domestic detail are already concealed by the ivy which clusters around the tablets of our recent history" (Child 1986, 6). These details from which the "bold outlines of character" emerge will be revealed in the story she will tell. For Child, the history of the place is not a matter of the relations of the events to a transcendent story. It is found in the "domestic detail," the particulars of the lives and relations that occurred in a particular location. More than a story of place, then, meaning becomes a story of the domestic context where "domestic" is taken in its oldest sense of having to do with where one lives, one's home and relations. When the narrative itself begins, it is now a first-person voice presented as emerging literally from the place in an "old, worn-out manuscript." *Hobomok* begins from a logic of home.

The novel begins in 1629 and is the story of a young woman, Mary Conant, who had come to New England among the earliest settlers. At the center of the story is Mary's love, on one hand, for Charles Brown, a young Englishman who, despite the separatist inclinations of the colony, retains his commitment to the Anglican Church, its doctrine, and its ceremony. On the other hand, it is a story of Mary's other love for a Wampanoag man named Hobomok. Early in the story, her two loves are confirmed when Mary goes into the woods and performs a "ceremony" of sorts to determine whom she will marry. According to the narrator who observes the ceremony, Mary draws a large circle on the ground and, after appropriate incantations, declares that the man she will marry will step in the circle. At once, Hobomok, who is passing through the clearing, steps in, and moments later Charles, who has come in search of Mary, also walks through it. Although Mary wants Charles as her husband, the ceremonial connection with Hobomok remains. Later, when Charles is reported dead at sea, Mary proposes marriage to Hobomok and flees the English village to take refuge at the Wampanoag village. Mary and Hobomok eventually have a son and live happily for some time when Charles, who had survived the sinking of his ship, reappears in search of Mary. On Charles's arrival, Hobomok decides to leave his wife to her former lover and vanishes from the scene. Their son is adopted by Charles when he and Mary wed and return to the English village of her father.

Child's selection of "Hobomok" as the name of her central Native character is important. Historically, there was a Wampanoag of that name who assisted the Puritans in their efforts to build a colony at Plymouth. The name is also shared with a powerful "spirit" being, also called "Cheepi," whom the English identified with the devil. Edward Winslow's report on Cheepi in his history of New England includes the observation that he is not "wholly bad," and other reports suggest instead that he is rather a trickster who does things that both help the community and challenge it.[24] The name "Cheepi" is itself a form of the word for "to separate," "chippe," which serves as the root in the terms for soul, ghost, and death as things that involve separation from the body or life (Trumbull 1903, 27). While such separation is not necessarily viewed as evil, when applied to a person's relations with others it marks problems

---

24. See Simmons 1986, 41–44.

of divisiveness and the breakdown of community. Ironically, Trumbull, in his Natick dictionary, notes that "chippinnin" is also the term for "free man," literally "a man apart, not subject to any sachem or master" (Trumbull 1903, 24). In this case, the recommended and literal translations lead in different directions. While the missionaries no doubt felt confident in their use of "chippinnin" for freedom as a good, those who spoke Natick and related languages may have been less enthusiastic. To be separated also could mean the destruction of one's connections and community. To be free in this sense is to be more like the cannibals who live separate from others and whose presence is a danger to others. When missionaries incorporated the term into their description of Christian doctrine, their use of the term "chippinnin" to translate, for example, Revelation 6:15, "He is a free man," might mean "he is without community or family."[25] From this perspective, the efforts of the missionaries to make Native people "free" might have been viewed as an effort to separate Native people from their communities and traditions. "Hobomok," in addition to its historical reference, also suggests the notion of English freedom and a parallel potential to destroy Native places even as it marks the problems of cross-cultural communication.

Hobomok's name also calls up associations with visions reported in the early histories of New England written by Wood, Winthrop, and Josselyn. In these visions, Hobomok or Cheepi appeared to the Native people "to warn them against departing from their ancestral ways [and] urging them to uphold custom and guard socially correct values and behavior" (Simmons 1986, 118). One vision, reported by Josselyn, saw Cheepi appearing in two different forms. "[A]n Indian," he reported, "sitting in the Corn field belonging to the house where I resided, ran out of his Wigwam frighted with the apparition of two infernal spirits in the shape of Mohawkes. Another time two Indians and an Indess, came running into our house crying out they should all dye, Cheepie was gone over the field gliding in the Air with a long rope hanging from one of his legs." When Josselyn asked what Cheepie looked like, they said he was an Englishman. The connections are instructive. The first vision appears to warn the Indians about the "Mohawkes," a name with triple meaning: the Mohawk people of the Six Nations, cannibals, and dangerous outsiders. The second vision dresses the warning in English "hat and coat, shooes and stockings" (Simmons 1986, 119). By choosing Hobomok, Child brings together all the conflicts and demands of

---

25. Trumbull apparently did not notice the potential for irony in this translation. See Trumbull 1903, 24.

cross-cultural relations, both the potential for disaster and for the practices of welcome that emerge in encounters with dangerous outsiders. That Child herself was aware of the complex meaning of Hobomok's name is suggested in a footnote to Hobomok's prayer to "Abbamocho" early in the novel. "Abbamocho," in fact, is another version of the name "Hobomok" and, Child notes, "Abbamocho" means "'very good devil,' a term they generally applied to those prophets or priests who had effected any great cures" (Child 1986, 14n).

The story of Mary Conant and Hobomok is important for several reasons. First, while still representing a dichotomy between people who are classed as civilized and people who are classed as savage, the story sets aside the sharp hierarchical relation between them. While some Native people are viewed as dangerous and unpredictable, others, including Hobomok and his people, are viewed as lovers, neighbors, and allies.[26] By setting aside the rigid hierarchy, the possibilities of cultural exchange and coexistence emerge and are illustrated in the interactions of Child's characters. Coexistence becomes a set of attitudes and established relations in terms of which the radically different cultures can interact. Child could have chosen from a vast array of historical instances in which Puritan relations with Native Americans were violent. Instead, and in contrast to the narratives of Cooper, she chooses a context in which Puritan and Native communities flourished side by side.

Second, Child does not simplify the relations involved in such a coexistence. Not all the English view Indians as people with whom they can coexist. The governor, Endicott, renowned for his brutality in the colony's wars with the Indians, is portrayed as unwilling to accept the intermixing of the communities. Mary's own father refuses at first to accept her marriage to Hobomok. In the end, some of the white attitudes about the Wampanoag and about Mary change from anger to acceptance, but at no point does Child transform the tensions of multiculturalism into anything like "perfect harmony."

Third, even as the English resist coexistence, Native people are portrayed as modeling the practices of coexistence, the practices of *wunnégin*. Hobomok himself serves as an intermediary between the English and the surrounding Native communities and with the help of other Native people, routinely assists the English in their struggle to survive, to the point of leading several of the English, including Mary, on a nocturnal deer hunt (Child 1986, 87–90). Just as Miantonomi and Canoni-

26. See the discussion between John Collier and James Hopkins about the potential danger of a Native leader named Corbitant (Child 1986, 51–52) in contrast with the dialogues involving Hobomok (Child 1986, 36–37 and 84–87).

cus welcomed Williams in his flight from the Puritan leadership, so Hobomok and his people welcomed the first generation of English immigrants. It is ultimately their practices of welcome that serve to support the interaction of the two communities, and it is the practices of *wunnégin* that ultimately transform the attitudes of many of the colonists to accept Mary's and her son's return.

Fourth, the central figure in the story is Mary Conant, a woman who uses the logic of home to rebel against the cultural constraints of her community. Mary is portrayed throughout as thoughtful and independent, but she is also portrayed as one who accepts "traditional" responsibilities of women as the framework for her understanding and action. Even as she is clearly not motivated by the demands of Puritan doctrine, she is portrayed as bound by relations to her father and mother, to her friends, and to her lovers. Given her apparent commitment to her place as a woman in Puritan society, the people of her village find her decision to marry Hobomok inexplicable. How can a woman who recognizes the importance of family and home nevertheless abandon it in favor of "the company of savages" (Child 1986, 122)? The only response, as Goodman Collier put it, was that "she was bereaved of reason when she did this deed" (Child 1986, 133). And yet from the perspective of the logic of home, Mary is better seen as acting in accord with an alternate rationality.

After receiving the news of Charles's death, Mary visits her mother's grave where Hobomok finds her. Although Child describes Mary's "mind" as "chaotic," she is also portrayed as reflecting on her circumstances. "What now," Mary asks herself, has "life to offer? If she went to England, those for whom she most wished to return, were dead. If she remained in America, what communion could she have with those around her?" (Child 1986, 121). Hobomok's presence seems to stand as an alternative. "Even Hobomok, whose language was brief, figurative, and poetic, and whose nature was unwarped by the artifices of civilized life, was far preferable to them." The alternative is reinforced as well by the power of the ceremony with which she and Hobomok came to be linked at the beginning of the story. Taken together, the relations that were Mary's home and her understanding of them lead directly to her decision to marry Hobomok. The decision, however, is not irrational. It is instead the product of an examination of the interactions that constitute her home and her decision that, with Charles's death, the interactions no longer could contribute to growth. Symbolically, Charles represented the dissenting voice in the community without which the ways of the Puritan leaders would stand unchallenged. His death, in a sense, undoes the possibilities of growth for her community as well. "It was strange," the narrator remarks, "that trouble had power to excite her quiet spirit to so much irascibility" (Child 1986, 122). Though the decision was not without pain, it was nevertheless a decision made not of desperation but in light of the developing relations of home and the need for growth. The logic of home here becomes a resource for assessing and responding to trouble, both as Mary leaves her home village for another and as she returns. Whether her decision is correct is a matter left open by the narrator, whose emphasis, in the end, is on the importance of understanding and acting in light of a logic of home, in light of emotion, established commitments, the demands of place, and the possibilities of growth. Such an approach does not provide the certainty of established laws, but it does provide a way for people to sustain themselves in "a world of hazards."[27]

A second example of the kind of narrative strategy used by Child is found in Catharine Maria Sedgwick's novel *Hope Leslie*, written the year after Child published *Hobomok*.[28] Like Child's novel, Sedgwick's also involves an interracial marriage, but in this case, the white woman, Faith Leslie, decides to stay with her Native husband, a Mohawk named Mononotto. The story also includes a strong Native woman character, Magawisca, who serves as a bridge between Native and European worlds. Even with their differences, the two novels involve stories that undermine directly and indirectly the dominant view of both Native people and women. Each novel is also overtly the story of a place rather than an illustration of the progress of humanity. In *Hope Leslie*, the Puritans are viewed as a people removed from their places and seeking to make a new place in America. Sedgwick's narrator expresses doubt that a people whose roots are firmly in Europe can do so. "Home," she writes, "can never be transferred; never repeated in the experience of an individual." Home, in this case, is to be understood as the complex interaction of relations among people, but also the interactions that involve material circumstances and the land as well. "The place consecrated by parental love," Sedgwick says, "by the innocence and sports of childhood, by the first acquaintance with nature; by linking of the heart to visible creation, is the only home. There is a living and breathing spirit

27. See Dewey 1929, Chapter 1.
28. See Philip Gould's discussion of both books in *Covenant and Republic: Historical Romance and the Politics of Puritanism* (1996). Gould sees the two works as a continuation of the work of the American Revolution in establishing republican virtues. He sees the historical fiction of the period as an effort to reinterpret the experience of the Puritans in ways that will support the new United States. This reinterpretation involves in part the feminization of republican virtue. Read in the context of Native pragmatism, the novels need to be reexamined as well in terms of the logic of home and the role of pluralism.

infused into nature: every familiar object has a history—the trees have tongues, and the very air is vocal" (Sedgwick 1987, 18). In addition to recalling the Native idea of *orenda,* Sedgwick's conception of home is one that focuses on its particularity and the need, as time and circumstances change, to continually renew the meaning of the place.

Like Child, Sedgwick grew up and lived most of her life on the border between Native and European America. She was born in 1785 in Stockbridge, Massachusetts, the place where Jonathan Edwards came as a missionary to the Indians in 1751 and where Lyman Beecher still preached to the Native congregation forty years later (Harding 1991). Sedgwick's family, long residents of the border area of Massachusetts, had a history of interactions with Native people. In 1821, Sedgwick visited Oneida, New York, and met a distant cousin, the descendant of Eunice Williams. Williams had been abducted by the Haudenosaunee in 1704 and, although she had visited her family in later years, never left the people who had adopted her. The story of Eunice parallels the story of Faith Leslie in Sedgwick's novel.[29] In addition to her personal experience with the people of Stockbridge, her own family history, and her visits to the Haudenosaunee, Sedgwick also read the available histories regarding the Narragansett and Pequot, as well as Roger Williams's *Key into the Language of America,* which she quotes in the novel. The work of Child and Sedgwick represented a new direction in American fiction, but just as importantly, it displayed and promoted a changing philosophical attitude, ways of understanding and acting in the world. Their stories constructed meaning around a central place, acknowledged differences, presented meaning embedded in context and community, and used the process of narration to frame new possibilities. What Child and Sedgwick shared was a background framed by both the work of people such as Franklin and Williams and a close connection with Native people and Native traditions.

In the end, *Hobomok* suggests that Child approaches the processes of meaning in a framework intended to challenge the one displayed by Cooper. In so doing, she sets her story in terms that conform broadly to a logic of place, and more closely to a logic of home. As a result, her approach overtly takes up the issue of cultural pluralism in a way that does not rest on a set of rules that will determine all cultural interaction. Instead, she offers a model for understanding coexistence, identifying relevant relations, and seeking a settlement that will, in the present circumstances, promote further possibilities. At the same time, the story

---

29. See Foster 1974, 73–80 for a discussion of Sedgwick's connections with Native people.

also turns on being able to understand intracultural differences in a way that does not lead to fixed roles and hierarchies. Mary is portrayed as a woman who accepts traditional roles as guides, but such roles do not lead to submissiveness or exhaust her potential. The roles become instead a valid frame for her interactions within her community and outside it. In a sense, Child begins to transform the idea of womanhood from a fixed and subservient caregiver to an independent person informed by women's roles but still free to interpret those roles in ways that fit the circumstances.

One might argue that the dichotomies Child uses to organize the women and men, Natives and Europeans in her story undermine claims that *Hobomok* is a novel resisting the hierarchies that are part of Cooper's tales. It is clearly the case that the character of Hobomok, for example, is as much a picture of the "noble savage" as he is of the complex Native man who assisted the Plymouth colonies in their first years. The description of Mary as well seems as much a part of the "cult of domesticity" as it is a picture of an emergent feminism. Her concern about leaving her father in his old age and her pining about Charles when he first leaves her to return to England might be seen as verifying her inability to control her own life. Mary and the narrator show little sadness as Hobomok vanishes from the story, leaving behind his son, his mother, and his village. And when Hobomok's son leaves America to complete his studies at Cambridge, it is not clear that he or anyone else thinks of him as part Wampanoag. This, one might conclude, is a story of the final triumph of European society over the primitive peoples of America.

While the concerns suggest that Child presents a less-than-revolutionary rethinking of race and gender, such a reading sets aside the construction of the narrative itself and its potential as a way to make things and events meaningful. If Child is recommending a logic of home, then she is clearly modeling a method as much as offering a content. From this perspective, the proper response to those aspects of the narrative that one will criticize 180 years after the story was published is to take seriously the problematic points and use them to identify other details, other aspects of the story, and its context that will respond to new concerns. As Sedgwick puts it in the preface to her novel *Redwood*, published in 1824, "As times and manners change, it must be evident that attempts to describe them must be as constantly renewed and diversified" (Sedgwick 1969, vi). For Child, the story is an interactive process connecting the writer and the reader to a place in order to be both critical and constructive of new experiences. Just as Johnston Schoolcraft's story in part presents an opportunity to see the consequences of undermining the relations of a place, Child's narrative provides an opportunity to see what works and what does not in establishing the relations for the coexistence of different cultures and genders. It is significant that at the end of *Hobomok* both the English and Wampanoag villages continue to exist side by side. In fact, the only character who explicitly vanishes is Hobomok himself, but this, in a sense, was to be expected. Hobomok, or Cheepi, is a figure in Native traditions who negotiates borders by marking the separation of people and places. He represents interaction *and* the maintenance of difference. His disappearance, like the vanishing visions of Cheepi, keeps alive the possibility of diverse and flourishing places in America.

Cooper's text, in contrast, does not itself direct alternative readings and reconsiderations. We may choose to read Chingachgook, the last Mohegan, as an example of successful coexistence between Native and European American worlds, but to do so would be to set aside the logic Cooper recommends. Chingachgook is the *last* of the Mohegan. He is not a figure that represents coexistence, but a figure that represents the end of coexistence. He is, in short, a representative moment in a great story of progress. Although he can be read against this story, to do so reframes the story in terms that take seriously the "domestic details" that Child recommends even as Cooper rejects their relevance. For Child, such details always transform the meaning, making the logic of home a means of understanding a pluralistic world even as it changes.

CHAPTER ELEVEN

Feminism and Pragmatism

THE NARRATIVE STRATEGIES that made the work of Child and Sedgwick distinctive were already a part of the Algonquian narrative traditions. Traditional Algonquian stories embody a logic of home of the sort illustrated by Child. In doing so, they also show that with the logic of home comes an understanding of women's roles and status within a community that could serve as a starting point for a women's movement in European America. The logic of home, in recognizing and valuing difference within a community, made women crucial members of the community as women, not as subservient or ornamental members whose value came from the men they served. As the logic of place affirmed the value and even the necessity of culturally different places, so the logic of home affirmed the value and necessity of differences within a place. Stories that follow the logic exhibited by "The Forsaken Brother" are common in Algonquian traditions. Although few were recorded before Johnston Schoolcraft began to publish, such stories were nevertheless part of the longstanding oral traditions of Northeastern Native peoples. Perhaps among the most striking Native stories to European and European American ears were those that not only illustrated the logic of home but that also illustrated varying Native conceptions of women. It was well-known that many Native traditions were matrilineal, where membership in nation and clan was based on the mother's descent, and not, as in most European traditions, on the father's. In the Haudenosaunee Confederacy, women were responsible for appointing and dismissing male leaders of the confederacy council. And, much to the chagrin of white male diplomats, women often attended and participated in treaty conferences. Such a view of women was deeply opposed to the received European view in which women were understood to be subservient to men and dependent upon them, limited in ability and so in opportunities, and most importantly, limited in their ability to think rationally.[1] As a result, European women often had no property rights, no access to education, no right to their children in the event of divorce, and no voice in government. At best, European women would carry out their natural biological functions as mothers and serve as helpers to their husbands, who would sustain the family.

By the end of the eighteenth century, women were arguing against the legal, economic, social, and educational limitations placed on them. The leading voice in the English resistance to the established status of women at this time was Mary Wollstonecraft.[2] Wollstonecraft adopted Locke's empiricism and transformed it into a resource for arguing against the idea that women were naturally less able than men with respect to intellectual and creative work. Since the ideas and relations of human thought are all, according to Locke, the product of experience, Wollstonecraft argued that the incapacities of women can be explained as the product of limited experience. The narrowness of women's experience ensured that they would not develop the complex ideas necessary for rational thought, but instead would only develop ideas applicable to their lives as mothers and domestic servants. On the other hand, if women were provided with the same kinds of opportunities that were provided to men, they would be able to develop the ideas and skills necessary for rational thought and so could participate in government, attend universities, and participate in other forms of intellectual work in society. Further, there would be no reason for women to be limited in their property holdings or other contexts of life where they had been all but excluded. Wollstonecraft's ideas crossed the Atlantic with Frances Wright, an activist for women's suffrage and a famous cofounder of the utopian community of New Harmony. Wright was also a well-known speaker who presented a case for the need to provide education to women and workers as a necessary condition of their freedom.[3] The difficulty with this view, according to some, is that it seemed to adopt the all-or-nothing attitude of European thought. Either women were utterly equal to men or they were not equal and so related hierarchically to men as the lesser sex. Even as Frances Wright's movement gained momentum in America, another way of understanding women emerged from the intersection of Native and European American thinkers as they worked against the policy of Indian removal.

Much has been written about the probable influence of Native

1. See Tuana 1993.
2. See Wollstonecraft 1975.
3. See Wright 1829.

women on the founding of the women's suffrage movement in the 1840s.[4] Well before that movement gained a clear public identity, Native conceptions of women were already becoming a part of European American thought through Native stories commonly told and practices that illustrated both women's roles and women's power within Native culture. For many who lived along the border, such stories were a common part of life, and the opportunity to see Native women exercising their power was common as well. When Johnston Schoolcraft published her stories in 1826, she was among the very first Native women to publish in English, but she also was simply placing in print what had been part of the experience of the border for hundreds of years. In a sense, the publication of Native women's stories in *The Literary Voyager* simply confirmed what many may have already suspected, that Native women had distinctive and important roles in many Native cultures and also had a way of understanding that was both different from the "rationality" of European thought and compatible with the need to sustain a richly plural society.

The logic of home illustrated in Johnston Schoolcraft's work is illustrated as well in the Abenaki traditions with which Child was familiar. This logic and its difference from the dominant European approach are well-illustrated in Charles Leland's 1884 collection of Algonquian stories. Although published after Child's work, Leland's collection nevertheless records versions of stories that, according to his informants, had long been told in Native communities of the Northeast. One story, from the Passamaquoddy tradition, recounts part of the history of Mt. Katahdin.[5] The mountain is the highest peak in Maine and is understood to be the "spiritual center" of the world by the Eastern Abenaki nations.[6] The mountain is a sacred place whose character is that of a powerful and handsome man. Roaming in the region of Katahdin is the spirit Pemúle, described as a homeless wanderer, who "has a head, legs, and arms or wings but no body, and can alter his size at will" (Speck 1935, 15). Like Hobomok, Katahdin and Pemúle are neither absolutely good nor absolutely evil, but rather act in ways that are sometimes good and sometimes bad. Pemúle in particular is represented both as friendly and as the "evil spirit of night" (Speck 1935, 15 and Leland, 1884, 257). There is a wide

4. See especially Wagner 1992 and Landsman 1992.
5. Mt. Katahdin is the scene for the first third of Thoreau's book *The Maine Woods.* Fannie Eckstorm's *The Penobscot Man* provides an interesting alternative perspective on Thoreau's excursion in her biography of Thoreau's Penobscot guide Joseph Attien (1970, 65–102). Also see Robert Sayre 1977.
6. Calloway 1990, 12. Also see Speck 1940, 7–26.

range of stories told about Mt. Katahdin. In one such story, reported by Tomah Joseph, a Passamaquoddy hunter traveled to Mt. Katahdin in search of game. As he approached the mountain, he met a young and beautiful woman who invited him to follow her into the mountain. The hunter passed through the rock and into a cavern where he met the woman's father, a giant with stone eyebrows and cheeks (the person, Mt. Katahdin). After a time, Katahdin's sons, Thunder and Lightning, visited their father and then left to go "over the world" to defend their friends and attack their enemies.

What is significant about the story for this discussion is that it illustrates a crucial narrative strategy. Here the center of the story is the place and literally the person of Mt. Katahdin. The editor, Leland, unintentionally reinforces the importance of the geographical grounding when he explains in a footnote, "This minuteness of detail is very characteristic of Indian Tales. I do not think that it is introduced for the sake of local color, or to give an air of truthful seeming, because the Indian simply believes the whole, as it is. I think the reason may be that, owing to their love of adventures, they enjoy the mere recitation of topographical details" (Leland 1884, 259n). From the perspective of a logic of place or a logic of home, the "topographical details" and "local color" are not merely enjoyed, but make the meaning of the story. Leland may be correct in saying that such stories are "believed" as a "whole," because it is the interaction, the storytelling, listening, details of the land, history, interests, and expectations that together are the meaning of the story. For those who expect stories to serve as illustrations of universal principles or fixed moral laws, such details are unnecessary. In a sense, where Leland expects the logic of the colonial attitude, a logic of laws revealed in particulars, the Native storytellers appear to give him a logic of place. This is confirmed in the last line of the story. Joseph concludes, "Now when the day was done the hunter returned to his home, and when there found that he had been gone seven years" (Leland 1884, 261). Chronology and its power to synchronize meaning across space is explicitly violated by the place, Mt. Katahdin. The focus on events in place radically shifts the narrative focus from the rigid frame of time and space that hold disparate worlds together to a particular place whose relations and events provide the context of meaning.

In two of her early stories, Child takes an approach similar to the one used by Tomah Joseph in his story of Mt. Katahdin, but enriches it with attention to relations within a place of the sort illustrated by Johnston Schoolcraft. The first story, "The Lone Indian," published in 1828, begins with an invocation from the poetry of William Cullen Bryant. "A white man, gazing on the scene / Would say a lovely spot was here, / And praise the lawns so fresh and green, / Between the hills so sheer. / I like it not—I would the plain / Lay in its tall old groves again" (Child 1986, 154). Child uses Bryant's verse to announce that the story will be both a story of a place and its transformations. The invocation gives way immediately to the story of a Mohawk sachem named Powontonamo. Recalling Cooper's approach to lauding the prowess of Native leaders, Child does so as well, tracing Powontonamo's career and his marriage to an Oneida named Soonseetah. The Cooperesque beginning is interrupted literally in mid-celebration by an observation. "The Prophets of Powontonamo's people like it not that the strangers [the English] grew so numerous in the land" (Child 1986, 155). The coming of the whites, they foresaw, will destroy the interactions that are their place. Powontonamo replied, "[T]he land is very big. The mountain eagle could not fly over it in many days. Surely the wigwams of the English will never cover it" (Child 1986, 156). But Powontonamo was wrong; as game animals fled and he was unable to hunt successfully, his family was left hungry. Faced with starvation, he took stock. "Wherever he looked abroad, the ravages of the civilized destroyer met his eye. Where were the trees, under which he had frolicked in infancy, sported in boyhood, and rested after the fatigues of battle? Where were the holy sacrifice-heaps of his people? The stones were taken to fence in the land, which the intruder dared to call his own. Where was his father's grave?" (Child 1986, 156–157). Here the details serve to present the destruction of the things and activities that sustained Powontonamo's home place. With its destruction came the death by disease of Powontonamo's son and wife. He buried his son beneath an oak seedling and his wife beneath a vine that he entwined with the young tree. When he stood at the graves of his family, a white man passed by on the road and asked, "Will you go home?" (Child 1986, 159). "Home!" he answered with bitterness. "I will go home" and he then began to wander to the west only to return each autumn to stand at the graves of his wife and son. The destruction of place became the destruction of home. For thirty years, Powontonamo continued to return until, the tree cut down and the vine withered, he "disappeared forever."

While "The Lone Indian" presents a more or less standard view of the disappearance from the east of Native people, it does so not in terms of a story of inevitable progress, but rather as a story of a place. Powontonamo must leave in the end, but not because he is "primitive" or unable to "civilize." He leaves because his home place has been destroyed by the systematic undermining of all of the interactions that made it his home. The conclusion cuts two ways. So long as Europeans continued their unfit practices, the places of America would be destroyed. At the same time, should the Europeans stop their unfit practices, places, perhaps even including the Europeans', could flourish. Just as the Prophetic movement argued for the need for newcomers to conform to the place with fit practices, so Child indirectly argues that such adaptation by whites is necessary. The Bryant verse makes it clear that the destruction of such places through the interaction of cultural difference is not acceptable. Like the story of Mt. Katahdin, Child develops her story on the details of the place and even makes the strategy explicit by citing "the prophets," the Native Prophetic movement itself. Such details combine with a conception of home that identifies both the problems of European settlement and possible strategies for resolving the problem through the adoption of fit relations.

It is tempting to see Child's appeal in "The Lone Indian" as a one-sided affair, arguing that whites have a moral responsibility to preserve Native homes, but whether they do so or not, the cost is to be borne by Native people. It is, in a word, sad that Powontonamo's home is destroyed, but it appears to have cost the invading farmers little but guilt. A second story, "Chocorua's Curse" published in 1830, makes it clear that the price of failing to sustain homes will be paid by whites as well. Here, the story is of a place called Chocorua's Cliff in New Hampshire, told from the perspective of the Europeans who settled there. The founder of the village near the cliff was Cornelius Campbell, a righteous dissenter from the Puritan fold whom Child describes as "too liberal and philosophical for the state of the people" (Child 1986, 163). To avoid persecution, he, his wife, and their son established a small village where he and the others who joined him lived in peace with each other and the nearby Native people. "From the Indians," Child writes, "they received neither injury nor insult" (Child 1986, 164). Among the Native people lived a prophet named Chocorua who had a young son. Over time, Chocorua's son became a friend of the Campbell family and spent much time with them. One day, Campbell's wife prepared a poison intended to kill a "mischievous fox." Chocorua's son found the poison first, ate it, and became ill. He ran home and died in his father's arms. Chocorua was enraged and took revenge on the Campbells, killing both the mother and son. Cornelius, discovering his family dead, leads a posse in pursuit of Chocorua and after cornering him on the precipice that would carry his name, mortally wounds Chocorua. As he died he proclaimed, "A curse upon ye, white men! May the Great Spirit curse ye when he speaks in the clouds, and his works are fire! Chocurua had a son—and ye killed him while his eye still loved to look on the bright sun, and the green earth! The Evil Spirit breathe death upon your cattle! Your graves lie on the war path of the Indian! Panthers howl and wolves fatten over your bones!" (Child 1986, 166). Within two years the village was abandoned and Cornelius Campbell was dead. Child concludes, "To this day the town of Burton, in New Hampshire, is remarkable for a pestilence which infects its cattle; and the superstitious think that Chocorua's spirit still sits enthroned upon his precipice, breathing a curse upon them" (Child 1986, 167).

Unlike the story of Powontonamo, "Chocorua's Curse" involves the destruction of two home places. At first, peaceful coexistence seems possible, but in time, the whites act in a way that is unfit for the interactions that can sustain the homes. The attempt to poison the fox goes awry and kills Chocorua's son, destroying the relations that sustained the Native home. As the Native home is destroyed, the European American home is destroyed as well. By cursing the whites and their efforts to make a home, Chocorua simply makes explicit the consequences of failing to establish fit relations. These consequences are not limited to original inhabitants but extend to the newcomers. The other side of the destruction of Native culture is the inability to achieve a home place at all. By destroying the differences and relations that made a home, the whites put their own survival, their own home, at risk.

These two stories suggest that Child adopted the logic of home as it emerged in Native traditions, while crediting the traditions indirectly with embedded references to prophets like John Neptune and Sagoyewatha. In a sense, the logic of home provides a diagnosis of the problems faced in the United States in the 1820s with the rise of Jacksonian democracy, the policy of Indian removal, and the battles over the extension of slavery into new states. The logic of place is enriched by tightening the focus on the effects of differences within communities as well as between them. Like Johnston Schoolcraft's story of "The Forsaken Boy," these stories frame the destruction of homes in part as a matter of the ways human and non-human interactions have failed to establish the means to sustain a home place. Child found in the logic of home a critical logic based on "domestic details" that provided the framing logic for both her Native American stories and her stories about slavery published in the 1830s and 1840s. In stories such as "The Quadroons," the details of home provide a means to identify the relations that are destroyed in places given to slavery (Child 1841). In her *Appeal in Favor of That Class of Americans Called Africans* (1833), she focuses almost entirely on the details of the slave trade and the condition of places where slavery is the rule. This leads her not only to display the evils of slavery but their concrete effects on the slaveholders themselves.[7] Slavery, she implies, de-

---

7. See her chapters I, IV, and VIII (Child 1833).

stroys the possibility of flourishing places. It is not merely a question of moral right and wrong but the actual quality of lived experience. So long as slavery dominates, places will, like the New Hampshire town in "Chocorua's Curse," be unable to sustain a flourishing community.

Significantly, much of the abolitionist literature that emerged in the 1830s and 1840s adopts a strategy like the one used by Child in the 1820s. Works such as Frederick Douglass's *Narrative* and even Harriet Beecher Stowe's *Uncle Tom's Cabin* implicitly frame their challenge to slavery in terms of the logic of home. Douglass's *Narrative of the Life of Frederick Douglass An American Slave* is particularly illustrative. He begins his story focusing on the place of his birth, its "domestic details," and the relations that he found formative. "I was born in Tuckahoe," he says, "near Hillsborough, about twelve miles from Easton, in Talbot County, Maryland. I have no accurate knowledge of my age, never having seen any authentic record containing it" (Douglass 1984, 18). Place as a source of meaning in contrast to chronology marks the difference between slaves and masters, blacks and whites. "I do not remember to have ever met a slave who could tell of his birthday," Douglass says. Instead, lives are defined by place-framed times: "planting-time, harvest-time, cherry-time, spring-time, or fall-time." This separation of his own history from the chronological and unified history of the slave owners provides a means of organizing his narrative. Douglass presents a placed story that follows his geographical movements as the framework for the story of his own growth and widening range of possibilities.

Douglass's approach stands in sharp contrast with another famous autobiography of the time, this one by P. T. Barnum, published less than a decade after the *Narrative*. Barnum's narrative begins in a way that makes the differences in autobiographical approach striking. "My first appearance upon this stage," he says, "was on the 5th day of July, Anno Domini 1810. Independence Day had gone by, the cannons had ceased to thunder forth their remembrances of our National Anniversary . . . and when peace and quiet were restored, I made my *début*" (Barnum 1854, 12). For Barnum, the date of his birth was propitious, linking his "*début*" to the greater history of the United States, setting aside location and detail in favor of seeing himself as a piece of a bigger story. For Douglass and Child, the story is not and perhaps cannot be seen from such a transcendent perspective.[8] Instead, the domestic details are re-

---

8. See *Incidents in the Life of a Slave Girl*, by Harriet Jacobs under the pseudonym of Linda Brent and edited by Child (1987). This autobiography also seems to reflect a logic of home, framed initially with the domestic details of Brent's early childhood in which she "never knew" she was a slave. The story is a narrative of the destruction of the sustaining relations of home.

quired both to establish the character of the circumstances that stand
in the way of sustaining a home place and in order to use those circumstances as resources for change. From this perspective, Douglass is able
to generate a striking critique of American slave-holding and slave-
sanctioning societies. When Douglass and Child turn to offer the post–
Civil War world a way to preserve differences peacefully, neither offers
a final prescription. Instead, the analysis itself, the narrative attention to
place and home combine with an interest in the possibilities of growth
to provide an alternative means for promoting a pluralist American society. Child develops this strategy in detail in her 1829 work against
Indian removal, *The First Settlers of New England; or, The Conquest of the
Pequods, Narragansetts, and Pokanokets.*

Although framed as a history, the last section of *The First Settlers* uses
the lessons of the history of the earliest English in America to focus on
the issues emerging in the late 1820s, when Andrew Jackson assumed
the White House and worked to make Indian removal a reality. Child
begins the last section of the book by citing a commentary on the Winnebago War published in the *American Quarterly Review*. The author of
the commentary proposes that the war was largely the consequence of
the unthinking policies of European American settlers who negotiated
the dispossession of some of the lands of the Winnebago and then violated the terms of the agreement when it became clear that the remaining Native lands were a rich source of copper and lead. "The writer,"
Child says, "is of the opinion that our treaties with the Indians are not
only useless, because no equivalent can be given them for their lands,
but that the most deplorable results are often produced" (Child 1829,
226). In this case, the writer continues, the Winnebago might have actually supposed "the most solemn assurances that the boundaries then
established or recognized would on the part of the United States, at least,
be carefully respected" (Child 1829, 228). From this perspective, the
Winnebago might have believed that they had achieved an arrangement
where they could peacefully coexist with the whites who came to settle
on their borders. Unfortunately, they did not understand the character
of those with whom they dealt. "Is it surprising," the writer asks, that
when settlers in search of lead and copper violated the treaty only
months after its approval, "so prompt and palpable a violation of the
treaty should have produced some act of retaliation?" (Child 1829, 229).
Child agrees with the writer's assessment of the cause of the war. By
failing to uphold the treaty protecting Native lands, the United States
should have expected war and could continue to expect war until it began to respect its ratified treaties.

The *American Quarterly Review* writer goes on, however, to give an assessment of the results of the war. In the end, the Winnebago's "valuable land and rich lead mines will invite the enterprise of our restless western population, and the miserable remnant of the Winnebagoes, retaining their ancient habits and feelings, will be compelled to seek westward of the Mississippi, amid hostile lands, and in a desolate region, a precarious existence" (Child 1829, 230). Such a result, the writer confesses, "is not, perhaps, to be greatly regretted." For the writer, it is an outcome that "must speedily have arrived, whatever probable course events might have taken." And its inevitability is to be understood as a consequence of Native cultural inferiority. "A people so rude, so obstinately averse to settled industry, so incapable of patient, connected, and useful thought, must soon have yielded their place to a more enterprising, and, we hesitate not to say, a better race of men" (Child 1829, 231). Child rejects the writer's conclusion. "It is, in my opinion, decidedly wrong to speak of removal or extinction as inevitable" (Child 1829, 281). Her grounds for rejection, however, are neither a common humanity nor universal law, but on the grounds that the writer fails to understand the issue. First, what the writer takes to be "rudeness" amounts to cultural practices that are at least honest and "vastly preferable to the underhand dishonest conduct . . . so commonly practiced by white men" (Child 1829, 231). Second, what the writer takes to be an aversion to "industry" is, in practice, a way of life suited to the circumstances. "[T]he industry of the Indians," she says, "is fully adequate to the supply of all their wants, when they are allowed to reap the fruits of their toil." "Proof" of her conclusion is found in the support Native people had given whites in need and "that no beggars or destitute persons were found" in Native communities (Child 1829, 232). Further proof, she suggests, can be found in the dispatches of the military "where thousands of acres of corn are boastingly stated to have been destroyed in their hostile expeditions against the Indians." Third, rather than being "incapable" of reason, she cites Charlevoix and concludes that Native people are not only capable of reason, but are an instance of a people whose behavior is entirely governed by a form of reason that does not require coercive authority.[9] In short, what the writer takes to be an unsuccessful mode of life is, on closer examination, a matter of fit relationships between Native people,

9. Charlevoix probably meant that Native people behave well because they behave in accord with natural reason alone, untroubled by civilization. This is closely related to Rousseau's view of the state of nature. Child seems to advocate a related view that holds that human beings have a moral sense but that such a moral sense is not contrary to either "civilization" or traditional ways.

their traditions, land, and circumstances. Dispossession and disappearance are not a natural necessity but the result of destructive ways of
thinking and acting embedded in European American culture. From a
Native perspective, an alternative society that recognizes differences and
changing circumstances but does not lead to the end of differences is
possible.

In order to achieve such a society, Child argues that European
Americans, not Native people, must be transformed. The proper solution is suggested by an unnamed Seneca orator. "[T]he great injuries we
received from white men, and the wickedness we constantly saw practiced among them, greatly strengthened our minds against their ways
and their religion; thinking it impossible that any good could come out
of a people, where so much wickedness dwelt" (Child 1829, 236). Coexistence, from this Seneca perspective, would be possible when whites
transformed their own behavior in a way that made it possible. Child
agrees. Like other advocates of Native rights, she thinks that the key to
establishing an environment in which Native people and whites could
flourish side by side will ultimately depend upon a form of evangelism.
"Missionaries and teachers," she proposes, "might be sent to instruct the
barbarous inhabitants on our borders to practice the virtues of justice
and humanity, as essential to the Christian character; and to assure them
that massacre and plunder are wholly opposed to its essence and spirit"
(Child 1829, 278). The "barbarous inhabitants," in this case, are not
the Native people, but rather "our own people," the whites who have
come to live along the border. Unlike the program advocated by missionaries for Native conversion and assimilation into Christian society,
Child reverses the formula and argues that the way to sustain peaceful
coexistence is to make it possible for European American society to accept as their own those principles already practiced by the Native people.

The First Settlers was published at Child's expense in 1829, and though
its impact was probably limited because it was not widely distributed, it
nevertheless marks a crucial moment in her philosophical development
and a moment in which the influence of the Native logic of home entered both the American feminist and anti-racist movements.[10] Four
years later, Child published her *Appeal in Favor of That Class of Americans
Called Africans*. Following the arguments of *The First Settlers* and not the
arguments popular in much of the abolitionist material published by
white authors, Child argued against the removal of freed slaves to Africa

---

10. See Karcher's assessment of the receptions of *The First Settlers* (1994, 96–100).

and in favor of transforming the anti-black convictions of white society into attitudes that respected and supported interaction with non-white peoples. Her publication of the *Appeal* placed her at odds with many of the eastern intellectuals who had come to accept her as a woman writer.[11] Despite the rejection, however, the work provided key resources both for the abolitionists and others who fought racism in the years after the Civil War.

The key to Child's argument in *The First Settlers* is a critique of an attitude that had both prevented the development of a multicultural American society and provided a way of thinking that would destroy the possibility of such a place. The argument develops two lines of thought. First, European settlers imported a way of thinking that undermined peaceful coexistence between European and Native peoples. In terms of the logic of place, this attitude worked against establishing fit relations between people, practices, and lands and instead overrode differences to establish the conditions of progress. At the same time, the very attitude that prevented peaceful coexistence also worked to undermine the relations that would sustain the Europeans in America by blocking opportunities for women and imposing fixed hierarchies. For Child, the cause of Indian removal and the cause of the oppression of European American women were inextricably connected. The answer to both problems was to set aside the attitude inherited from Europe and to adopt one that emerged in the Native responses to differences in culture and gender.

Native conceptions of gender differences were probably apparent to Child in her life at Norridgewock. If she was able to hear Native stories framed by the logic of home, it is also likely that she heard stories about women of the Northeast nations that would have both reinforced the logic of home and introduced an alternative conception of women. In Frank Speck's collection of traditional Penobscot stories, many take women as their central characters, and most develop aspects of womanhood that would stand in tension with the ideas of women in European American society.[12] Several of the stories are presented as the stories of a particular place, an island that is probably the place now known as

---

11. See Karcher's review of the reception received by Child's *Appeal* (1994, 191–192).

12. It is difficult, of course, to know the contributions of Speck to the stories he presents. However, since there is a commonality of themes and action among the stories (and stories from other sources), it seems likely that the general outlines of the stories are similar to the ones long established in the Penobscot narrative tradition. Despite what might be lost in translation of the stories, the examples given by Speck can be seen as representative of the stories Child might have heard.

Indian Island in the Penobscot River near Old Town, Maine. In one version of the story, it is said that a man became angry with his wife and "to get rid of her, he took her away, and deserted her on an island . . . thinking that before long she would die of hunger and cold" (Speck 1935, 86). The woman, however, was "wise and knew what to do" and over time used the resources of the island to make herself a flourishing home place by establishing sustaining relations with the island and its inhabitants. After a time, "her brothers found her and took her back home" where her husband "was found and killed." In another version of the story, the woman abandoned on the island is "a woman so old and covered with vermin that she could not help herself in any way" (Speck 1935, 88). Her relatives left her on the island to die, but she found a way to snare rabbits and after a time built a place to live. Her relatives, who had continued on their journey after abandoning her, were not successful in their attempts to find food and eventually they passed the island again. Since a great deal of time had passed, the relatives thought that they should stop and bury the bones of their grandmother. When they landed, however, they discovered that their grandmother was not only alive but had become a successful hunter. She shared her food and shelter with her relatives, saving them from starvation and cold. The narrator concludes, "The old woman, who had saved them, they kept with them, and there is the end" (Speck 1935, 89).

In each story, the woman, who is expected to perish when left behind, survives instead by establishing a place for herself using the resources at hand. At issue in these stories is not the relationship between a people and dangerous outsiders like cannibals, but rather the relationships within a community. In the second version of the story in particular, the community, apparently uninterested and disgusted with the old woman, abandons her to starve. Rather than perishing, the old woman flourishes even as her relatives nearly starve. At Indian Island, it is the women in particular who are able to survive by establishing fit relations with their situation, and it is when, in the second story, the old woman's community reestablishes fit relations with the woman that it is restored to health. Perhaps as important from a European American perspective is that the women, in both cases, take up roles that are outside those recognized as women's roles. While such openness in role is common in Eastern Algonquian stories, for a European American woman like Child the overt and successful adoption of men's roles by women may have suggested a striking alternative to the expectations of her own community. That women could adopt such roles as a response to violence may have added still another important aspect to the stories. Other common Penobscot stories reinforce this view that at once recognizes a distinct role for women but also the possibility of going beyond the established role in order to foster growth and new possibilities.[13] When Child took up the project of advocating for Native rights in *The First Settlers,* the link between a logic of place, that is, understanding meaning in terms of a people, land, history, and shared interests, and a logic of home, that is, an examination of the sustaining relations inside Child's own community, asserted the importance of women in establishing relations that would lead to growth.

Significantly, *The First Settlers* is set as a dialogue between a mother and her two daughters, Elizabeth and Caroline. By offering her criticism of Indian policy in this form, Child seems to assert a starting point within the logic of home. It is not that men are to be excluded from the discussion, but rather that the perspective that can challenge the dominant attitude will not start from a male perspective. It will instead be the voices and viewpoints of others within European American society that will make the problems apparent and begin to identify resources for a response. Much as the grandmother of Indian Island was able to foster the fit relations of place that could save her starving family, so the mother and her daughters in *The First Settlers* can, as women, help to establish the fit relations necessary to avert the disaster of removal.

The dialogue format, while it locates the process as one framed by gender, also offers a methodology with which to use the logic of home as a process of social inquiry. The historical content of the work goes beyond a simple history and uses the story of the earlier interactions between Native people and Europeans as resources for reexamining the crisis that developed as Jackson pressed for Indian removal. Unlike Mather and Bancroft, whose purpose in writing history is to make the truth explicit from a single point of view, Child is interested in complicating history and re-presenting it from alternative viewpoints where the focus shifts to points of view outside the dominant perspective and reconstructs the events with a new meaning. Anticipating Du Bois's efforts in *The Souls of Black Folk,* Child declares it to be her purpose to present an "unvarnished tale" that will serve an educative purpose. "I ardently hope that this unvarnished tale, which I have offered to view, will impress our youth with the conviction of their obligation to alleviate, as

13. Several of Speck's stories are stories of incest. See "Magic Flight from the Amorous Cousin" (1935, 87–88), "The Legend of Profile Rock (1935, 90), and "A Man Marries his Cousin and Becomes a Loon" (1935, 90, 91). In each case, the woman victim is able to take action against the incestor, sometimes alone and sometimes with the help of others. Significantly, the women are not portrayed as passive victims or as willing ones, but rather as potentially powerful people able to restore the relations necessary to fostering their own growth in the context of a community that took their perspective seriously.

much as is in their power, the sufferings of the generous and interesting race of men whom we have so unjustly supplanted" (Child 1829, iv).

Child's "tale" of the Pequot and Narragansett will provide a way to address the present problem of the state of Georgia's attempt to drive the Creek, Cherokee, and Seminole nations across the Mississippi. The dialogue will do so, Child suggests, in terms that were initiated by the Native prophets who stood as the most vocal defenders of Native rights along the border. Child concludes the introduction, "'What are states' rights,' exclaims an indignant Cherokee Chief [probably John Ross], 'in comparison to original possession, and inheritance from the King of Kings'" (Child 1829, vi). *The First Settlers,* like the "tales" of the Native prophets and the "unvarnished tale" sought by Du Bois, are reconstructive accounts of the history of Native and European relations that begin with an affirmation of difference, an "inheritance of the King of Kings," develop a critique of European ways of thinking and acting, and then point toward a way of thinking that will help to sustain a world in which diversity is conserved and respected.

The dialogue between the mother and her daughters begins in the middle. Mother says, "Having concluded what I have to relate of our Southern Indians, I will now give you some account of those who inhabited this part of the country when it was first visited by our ancestors" (Child 1829, 8). The opening both insists that her listeners are already in the midst of an ongoing story, and by citing the "Southern Indians" at the beginning, Child hints that what will follow in her discussion of the history of Native and European relations will have bearing on the circumstances in the 1820s in the South. As if to reinforce the genealogy I have presented, Child, who the previous year had published a short biography of Benjamin Franklin and who would soon publish a Franklin-inspired book of practical advice called *The Frugal Housewife,* begins her discussion of the dispossession of Northeastern peoples by discussing the Narragansett sachem Miantonomi and his friend Roger Williams.[14] Miantonomi models a way of structuring the coexistence of English and Native people. Using the logic of home, Child argues in favor of Miantonomi's approach by developing a critique from within European American society of the attitudes inherited from the Puritans.

14. Child's work helps to remind later readers that Williams and Franklin were influential and controversial figures in the first half of the nineteenth century. While they came to be viewed as less than significant thinkers from a twentieth-century viewpoint, both were renowned as activists opposed to dogma and hierarchy and in favor of ways of thinking that were both distinctively practical and committed to pluralism.

The strategy of an internal critique, that is, attention to the ways in which the relations within the European American community sustain or undermine growth, is developed early in the dialogue when Caroline observes that "whenever I speak of the Indians, and compassionate their condition, I am asked how I can feel so much for these miserable hordes?" The voice of the mother offers a striking diagnosis. "[T]he Indians have been strangely misrepresented, either through ignorance or design or both; and men have given themselves little trouble to investigate the subject. People seldom forgive those whom they have wronged, and the first settlers appear to have fostered a moral aversion to the Indians, whom they barbarously destroyed" (Child 1829, 13). The problem is not one of inconsistency or a failure of conviction, but a "moral aversion," a prejudice in terms of which colonial thinking went on. In effect, the problem was an attitude that took up questions already disposed to be answered in a way that could not include the possibility of peaceful coexistence. "This disposition," she says, "has been transmitted to their descendants, who appear to think themselves justified in following the example of men who have been so much extolled and venerated" (Child 1829, 23). When Elizabeth asks how such a disposition and consequent actions could be justified by people who proclaimed Christianity, Mother explains that far from serving to block the systematic extermination of Native people and its attendant cruelty, Puritan religious doctrine actually justified it. "Yet we may in truth imagine," Mother says,

> that a sect,—who ascribe to God passions highly vindictive and unjust,— who represent this universal Parent as having formed rational creatures for the express purpose of inflicting on them torments the most excruciating and endless, without allowing them any chance or power to escape,—and who also believe that the small number, whom he has ordained to be happy, have been redeemed . . . ,—may have believed themselves authorized to inflict all the evil in their power on wretches who are born to suffer. (Child 1829, 31)

For Child, in the voice of "Mother," the Puritan attitude was grounded in a set of commitments that took things and events in terms of a single timeline where the central actors are God's chosen people. By framing the story in this way, the attitude also imported a value structure that placed all peoples in a hierarchical relation. Those most valued in the scheme, the English immigrants, by virtue of their place in God's determinate universe, had both the right to conquer the Native peoples of

America and the obligation to do so as part of the progress of God's people. In other words, Child sees the treatment of Native people by whites as a consequence of what I have called the colonial attitude.

Parallel with her discussion of the colonial attitude and its implications for cultural and racial difference, there is a second tale of the role of women. Women are introduced as an issue in the discussion when Caroline asks why the Puritan women did not express sympathy for Native people as she had expected (Child 1829, 35). Her mother gives a twofold answer. On one hand, Puritan women, like Puritan men, were subject to the colonial attitude. Rather than taking an active interest in the consequences of English actions on Native people, "at this period the women were, like the other sex, much addicted to questions engendering strife and division, and were, without doubt, also engaged with those weighty matters . . . respecting the manner in which women should be allowed to adorn themselves" (Child 1829, 36). This attitude overrides what Child takes to be the woman's role of enhancing growth in new American places. "It would indeed have been highly honorable, and congenial with those impressions which are supposed in a peculiar manner to influence the actions of women, and will, I trust, ever distinguish them; had they acted in conformity with the spirit of peace, Christian charity and forgiveness." Just as the practices of *wunnégin* are undermined by colonization, so too are the practices associated with womanhood. The result is that both women and Native people are made subjects to an oppressive structure that blocks what Child will later call the "true culture" of women and Native people. At the same time, just as Williams and Franklin found a crucial alternative structure in Native ways of interaction, so Child finds value in Native societies and in the potential contributions of women in all societies. The key to unlocking the potential is resistance to the colonial attitude and the cultivation of an alternative in dialogue with others.

The importance of valuing both gender and cultural difference as a means of resisting oppression and fostering the coexistence is carried further in Child's discussion, largely quoted from Washington Irving, about the "conquest" of the West Indies. The central illustrations Child cites are of two women, Queen Isabella of Spain and Anacaona, a Native leader on Hispaniola. In contrast to Columbus and Ovando, his successor, Isabella and Anacaona exemplify the practices of welcome as a means of structuring interaction across differences. In Isabella's case, in addition to her opposition to the persecution of the Moors and the exile of the Jews, she also rejected the idea of enslaving Native people. When presented with several Native people who had been abducted from Hispaniola and brought to her in Spain, she ordered them returned to

America. Even as Columbus and the other colonial leaders adopted policies of enslaving the Americans, Isabella continued to oppose them from Europe. Anacaona, when faced with the Spanish army, welcomed them into her city and treated the Spanish well. Although the approach worked at first in maintaining peaceful relations, when Ovando arrived he distrusted Anacaona's generosity and decided that it was part of a plot to kill the Spaniards. Anticipating the worst, he captured the leadership of the city, including Anacaona, and killed them. When Isabella learned of the massacre on her own deathbed, she extracted a promise from her husband, King Ferdinand, to recall Ovando.

Isabella and Anacaona are an important illustration of how the European conception of women is mistaken and how the colonial attitude oppresses both women and Native Americans. By linking the two, Child both provides a way of reconceptualizing the value of women and Native culture and, at the same time, provides a frame in terms of which the oppressive and male-dominated colonial attitude can be resisted. Just as the argument that Native people cannot be civilized falls quickly in the light of Native accomplishments such as those of the Cherokee, so too the argument for women's inferiority falls in light of women such as Isabella and Anacaona. "The common notion, that women are incapable of occupying high and responsible stations in society is not sustained by history or experience" (Child 1829, 241). But further, just as Cherokee "civilization" is not the same as European "civilization," so women's leadership is different from men's. "The few females," Child observes, "who have attained sovereign power, have, in most instances, discharged the important duties which devolved on them, with dignity, and an attention to humanity and the rights of their subjects, which is commonly not found in kings" (Child 1829, 241). The historical reconstruction of women's roles leads to the conclusion that "[a]though the duties, which are by nature assigned to females, are of a different character from those which men are called to perform, they are assuredly not less important." At the center of these distinctive duties are those surrounding the "proper management of the family" and the education of children. The significance of women's roles and evidence of women's abilities then serve to justify the conclusion that "it is certainly essential that women should not only receive an enlightened education, but that they should possess a degree of independence, which will secure to them respect and attention" (Child 1829, 242). The claim for women's rights here takes a distinctive turn. Rather than viewing rights as an implication of one's humanity, Child views rights, or rather independence, as a necessary aspect of the distinctive duties of women.

The result of Child's argument is the general expectation that the logic of home, which has the potential to resist the colonial attitude and its assaults on Native people, can also provide a justification for women's rights and a way to resist sexism even as gender difference is valued. The recognition of women *as* women necessarily leads to a transformation of women's roles and status in society from that of household servants denied freedom and influence to an active role marked by a distinctive viewpoint and approach. The association of Isabella and Anacaona serves to link the oppression of women and Native people. By this link, Child implies that the indigenous attitude can also support the idea that "women were created to be the companions and equals of man, and, although different stations have been allotted them, the duties which devolve on women are assuredly not the least important" (Child 1829, 246). The key to challenging both racism and sexism is the adoption of a critical and constructive method that is grounded in the logic of home as it emerged from Native American thought.[15] Child summarizes her response to the colonial attitude in the advice that the mother in the dialogue offers to her daughters. "I ardently desire, my dear children, to impress on your minds the important part you are designed to act in life; and with the full conviction that you are endowed with the powers adequate to the performance of the high duties, which devolve on your sex in all relations of life. Home should be the centre of attraction, where all the virtues and graces should be exhibited in their most perfect form" (Child 1829, 252). Respond, she might have said, from the logic of home.

The emphasis on home, despite Child's own illustration of its liberatory potential, may nevertheless sound more like a recommendation that women accept "the cult of True Womanhood" as a model for their lives. In her classic paper on the subject, Barbara Welter defines the "cult" as affirming that women ideally ought to possess four "cardinal virtues," "piety, purity, submissiveness, and domesticity" (Welter 1966, 152). In light of the context in which the advice is offered, however, it appears that Child has something else in mind. For her, the centrality of the home must be understood with the coequal demand for independence. In a sense, for Child, the relevant virtues of piety, purity, and submissiveness are to be understood only in light of understanding framed around a flourishing home place. What piety might mean in one place will not necessarily mean the same thing in another. In her 1855 work *The Progress of Religious Ideas*, she offers a comprehensive survey of world religions.[16]

---

15. Ward Churchill makes a similar point in his book *Struggle for the Land* (1993). He argues that the problems of poverty, racism, and sexism that pervade European American society would be addressed by first restoring Native lands and traditions.

16. The work begins with advice to the reader. "I would candidly advise persons who are conscious of bigoted attachment to any creed, or theory, not to purchase this book.

She argues that humanity shares a common "religious sentiment," a disposition to wonder and seek wider interactions, and that the sentiment is grounded in experience located in concrete places. "In all ages and countries, the great souls of humanity have stood on the mountain peaks, alternately watching the clouds below, and the moonlight above, anxiously calling to each other: 'Brethren, what of the night?' And to each and all an answer has returned, varying in distinctness: 'Lo, the morning cometh'" (Child 1855, 2: 418). The common sentiment owes to the kind of creatures human beings are, living in the places they live. The manifestation of such sentiment, however, is not uniform but is as diverse as the places in which people live. What comes to be venerated in each place depends upon that place. "Whatever condition of things grows out of a certain state of society, must necessarily be in some degree best adapted to that state" (Child 1855, 2: 456).

The virtue of purity, as illustrated in many of her stories, is also a matter of particular circumstances transforming the idea from an abstract and absolute virtue into sexuality appropriate to a place. Child's advocacy for the elimination of miscegenation laws, for example, was aimed at reconstructing a notion of purity relative to the reality of a racially diverse world.[17] Interracial marriage in this case does not mark a policy of assimilation by breeding, but rather an aspect of community life in which relations across cultural and racial boundaries are opened and made intimate and influential.[18] In her story "Hilda Silfverling," Child challenges accepted views of "fallen women." Here, she uses a science fiction plot to transform Hilda's circumstances so that her sexuality made unfit by a sexist society becomes fit in a new and open place.[19] Here the "fitness" of behaviors in a place marks their relative "purity" just as the fitness of religious practices marks their "piety."

Submissiveness may also be understood as a "virtue" responsive to context. As a virtue, traditional submissiveness marked a woman's rec-

---

Whether they are bigoted Christians, or bigoted infidels, its tone will be likely to displease them" (Child 1855, 1: vii). The work itself is a singular achievement as one of the first works in comparative religion that takes an explicitly multicultural approach to the investigation. See Karcher 1994, 374–381.

17. See especially Child 1833, Chapter 8.

18. "The Quadroons," for example, examined this issue, showing in part that social prescriptions against interracial marriage can destroy the sustaining relations of a home place. See Child 1841.

19. See Karcher's discussion of "Hilda Silfverling" (1994, 240–341) and the story itself (Child 1997). After having been wrongly accused of the murder of her illegitimate daughter, Hilda is sentenced to participate in an experiment in cryogenics. She is made to sleep 100 years. When she awakens, she flees from her native Norway to Sweden, where she falls in love with a man who is actually her own great-grandson, identified by Karcher with the folk-hero Alerik.

ognition, on one hand, of her dependence on men and, on the other, of her purpose in service of the good of others.[20] While Child affirms that in order to foster growth women and men must respond to the needs and interests of others, she also holds that success in fostering growth is not a product of submission or blind obedience. Instead, "submission" to others involves the cultivation of sufficient independence and resources to sustain oneself and others even in the face of difficult situations. In *The First Settlers*, Child makes this explicit by arguing for property rights for women. For those who have property, they should not be obliged to "resign all their right to disposal of it" when they marry or at any other time. For those who marry with no property, they ought to "have a certain portion of the property, or income of their husband's secured to them for their use exclusively." The consequence, she argues, "would be no abject submission on one side, or arbitrary interference on the other" (Child 1829, 243). Instead, women would gain the power to leave "cruel and humiliating" circumstances, have both the right and resources to support their children and the freedom to change their circumstances to ones that would restore growth (Child 1829, 245–246).

When Child published *The Frugal Housewife* in 1829 and *The Mother's Book* in 1831, it was not to support the virtue of domesticity as it came to be understood, that is, as a complete withdrawal from affairs outside the home. Rather, she sought to provide resources for women to gain the independence and knowledge necessary to foster a flourishing home as part of a wider community. Unlike other works published in the next decade that promoted the four virtues as abstract standards for women to attain, *The Frugal Housewife* aimed to provide accessible tools of survival for women who did not have the advantages of wealth. "[T]he information conveyed is of a common kind; but it is such as the majority of young housekeepers do not possess, and such as they cannot obtain from cookery books. Books of this kind have usually been written for the wealthy: I have written for the poor" (Child 1972, 6). Her recipes and home remedies emphasize the results of proven practices shared among New England families, including Native American recipes and remedies, coupled with the sort of advice found in Franklin's *Poor Richard's Almanac*.[21] Almost explicitly combining the perspectives of Franklin and the Native prophets, she offers a central principle for the development of the alternative attitude that she seeks to promote. "In early childhood,

20. See Welter 1966, 158–159.
21. See for example Child 1972, "General Maxims for Health." Child mentions Franklin directly as well (1972, 5).

you lay the foundation of poverty or riches, in the habits you give your children. Teach them to save everything,—not for their *own* use, for that would make them selfish—but for *some* use. Teach them to share everything with their playmates; but never allow them to *destroy* anything" (Child 1972, 6–7). The admonition to share and not to destroy operates at many levels, within and between communities with respect to environmental resources and cultural ones as well.[22] Rejecting the traditional cult of domesticity, Child argues for a kind of activism that fosters connections with one's home as a starting point.

The Mother's Book, like most works on education in the nineteenth century, begins with an empiricist psychology, emphasizing the role of experience in forming ideas and in forming character.[23] Mothers, as those particularly responsible for childhood education, are presented as responsible for organizing a child's environment in ways that promote learning and, especially, character development. Child provides much advice on games, food, hygiene, and even topics for conversation. At the center of her discussion is the claim that both girls and boys ought to learn a wide variety of skills and develop characters that, while adaptable to changing circumstances, do so in a way that promotes further possibilities.[24] Welter, in her discussion of "True Womanhood," cites Child's *Mother's Book* in particular as a work designed to emphasize the virtues of womanhood. While this is true in a sense, it is also true that when read from the standpoint of the logic of home, both *The Mother's Book* and *The Frugal Housewife* are better understood as resources with which to undermine the idea of a fixed ideal of womanhood. Taken this way, the "cult" whose primary works were not published until the 1840s may be seen as an effort to block the spread of the attitude promoted by Child and others on behalf of women and non-white peoples in America.

In the end, the logic of home, like the logic of place, embodies the four pragmatic commitments. The notion of a home, from the perspective taken by Child, is not a thing or an abstract ideal, but rather begins with the principle of interaction by taking a home as an ongoing complex of interactions. It is the "domestic details" that make the home place what it is, and it is these same details, moments of interaction, that serve

22. Sedgwick uses the logic of home to challenge one aspect of the "frugality" advocated by devotees of Franklin's "Way to Wealth," including Child. Taken up by the colonial attitude, the commitment to wealth itself destroys home places. Sedgwick's story "Daniel Prime" (1850), for example, portrays the destruction of relations within a community when frugality is made an absolute principle.

23. See Child 1831, 1–6.

24. See especially Child's chapter on "Management During the Teens" (1831, Chapter 10).

as its meaning. Child illustrates the principle in her *Letters from New York* in a story about a fire that destroyed part of her neighborhood. "It began," she says, "at the corner of Chyrstie-street, not far from our dwelling; and the blazing shingles that came flying through the air like a storm in the infernal regions, soon kindled our roof" (Child 1998, 70). While Child's building survived the blaze, most of the surrounding tenements were destroyed. Reflecting on the fire, she reports that her greatest sympathy was with a black neighbor, Jane Plato, who lost, in addition to her other possessions, the small garden that she had long cultivated. While Child was criticized for her focus on a garden, the point of the focus is not to argue for the particular value of a garden over a kitchen or bedroom, but rather to illustrate how she understands what was lost.[25] "Jane Plato's garden," she says, "might not be worth much in dollars and cents; but it was to her the endeared companion of many a pleasant hour" (Child 1998, 71). By turning the garden into a person, a companion, Child illustrates a way of understanding things in their interactions. The garden is a living, responsive being whose character and value emerge in its interactions with Jane Plato. This does not deny the importance of other things that are necessary to one's survival; it is rather to focus on what makes things meaningful. This approach contrasts ways of assigning meaning and value independent of particular interactions in terms of money or independent hierarchies. "Cash value" is here not a matter of money, but a matter of how things interact. Child knows, she says, "by experience how very dear inanimate objects become under such circumstances" and explains that she has "dearly loved the house in which [she] *lived,* but could not love the one [she] merely *owned*" (Child 1998, 71). The point is not that gardens or houses have some given value, but that what they are is bound up with how they interact and the connections they involve. From this perspective, even if things have a kind of vague existence in anticipation of interaction, it is in their interactions that they gain their being, as Jane Plato's garden or Child's own home.

The principle of interaction leads as well to a basic commitment to pluralism. In the second series of *Letters from New York,* Child asserts both the unified and pluralistic character of a world in which interaction defines being. She proposes an analogy to understand the relation. "Light is one and unchangeable, but the objects on which it shines absorb

---

25. Child refers to the criticism of the original publication of the letter in the National Anti-Slavery Standard. In her own defense, she remarks in the revised letter published in *Letters from New York,* "Will your kind heart be shocked that I seem to sympathize more with Jane Plato for the destruction of her little garden-patch . . . ? Do not misunderstand me. It is simply my way of saying that money is not wealth. . . . Our real losses are those in which the *heart* is concerned" (Child 1998, 71).

and reflect its rays so variously, that modifications of colour therefrom are infinite" (Child 1845, 120). Despite the apparent unity of things, the processes of interaction replace unity with an irreducible pluralism. What unity there is will only be a starting point for diversity. Just as a single creator gave rise to valuable differences in the origin stories of the Native Prophetic movement, so the unity of the world for Child serves as a starting point for ineliminable differences. The same conjunction of interaction and pluralism applies to questions of knowledge as well. After recounting the story of the fire, Child uses the principle of interaction she established in understanding what was destroyed in the fire to propose a way to understand human knowledge. "[A]ll the highest *truths*, as well as the genuine *good*, are universal" (Child 1998, 72). Here, "universal" does not signify a fixed set of truths, but rather that truths and goods are, as she puts it, "open to all who wish to receive." When recognized as the product of particular interactions, truths and goods are emergent from the situations in which they are sought. Every place, in effect, has truths and goods. What they are known to be in one situation or another is a matter of the logics of place and home. In the second series of *Letters from New York*, she makes this idea explicit. "Truth," she says, "is one and unchangeable, but no two minds receive it alike; hence the innumerable colourings and shadings of human opinion" (Child 1845, 120). Human knowledge, like being, is a matter of particulars. While it is useful to recognize the connections among things, what they are and how they are known will always be plural and a matter of interaction.

Even as her friends in the 1840s adopted an increasingly transcendental version of the commitment to unity, Child, like her pragmatist successors, retained her commitment to the principle of interaction and its pluralist implications. Responding to the assertion that she was a Transcendentalist, Child says that she might be understood as one by the language that she used to express her position, but that she nevertheless should be seen as standing on the side of the practical world of interaction and pluralism. Writing about her Transcendentalist friends, she concludes that "there are people, very intellectual ones too, who mystify me in the strangest fashion. After talking with them, my spirit always has to bite its finger, to know whether it exists or not; and even then, the questions arise whether a sensation *is* a sensation" (Child 1845, 129–130).[26] For Child, even if a transcendental perspective is possible, interactions provide ground of what is and what is known.

---

26. Child's letter on Transcendentalism provides a useful perspective on the relationship between her work and the other philosophers of the time. In the end she concludes that while she is sympathetic to Transcendentalism, she adopts a perspective that not only

All four pragmatic principles are part of the framework for Child's conceptions of gender and race as developed in *Letters from New York*. For Child, true womanhood, like true manhood, is a process of growth, beginning from the place where one is as a woman or a man. "True culture," she says, "in [women], as in men, consists in the full and free development of individual character, regulated by their *own* perceptions of what is true, and their *own* love of what is good" (Child 1998, 154).[27] She notes that her friend Ralph Waldo Emerson had argued a similar point in his lecture, on Being and Seeming, when he "urged women to *be,* rather than *seem.*" The advice, she says, "was excellent, but the motive by which it was urged, brought a flush of indignation over my face. *Men* were exhorted to *be,* rather than to *seem,* that they might fulfil the sacred mission for which their souls were embodied; . . . but *women* were urged to simplicity and truthfulness, that they might become more pleasing" (Child 1998, 155). Emerson's motive, she believes, is not uncommon and it indicates that "society is on a false foundation." Despite this, she continues, "I must acknowledge that much of the talk about women's rights offends both my reason and my taste." Her justification for the offense, however, is important. "I am not of those who maintain that there is no sex in souls; nor do I like the results deducible from that doctrine." Women and men, on this view, are distinctive ways of interacting framed by history, physical bodies, institutions, interests, and expectations. "True cultures" are distinctive in that who one is and how one is known begins from one's place, but, like the women of Indian Island, such a place serves only as a starting point. The principle of community is embodied in the place as part of what sets the conditions for gender interactions. The principle of growth provides a means to look beyond "given" aspects of gender and toward new possibilities. From this perspective there is "sex in souls."

Gender differences are not simply relevant to the lives of individuals, however. As part of the diversity of a place, they also contribute to the growth of a community. "The nearer society approaches to divine order,

---

grows out of experience but also returns to it. There are striking similarities between her views and those of James and Dewey. See Child 1845, 125–130.

27. While the view Child here proposes is implied in her earlier work, especially *The First Settlers*, its presentation here takes advantage of the language of William Ellery Channing's idea of "self-culture," made famous in an address given by Channing in Boston in September 1838. The lecture brought together many of the ideas that would help Emerson and the Transcendentalists develop a way to talk about the growth of individuals and the idea of self-reliance. Channing introduces the idea this way using the metaphor embedded in the saying, "To cultivate anything, be it a plant, an animal, a mind, is to make [it] grow. Growth, expansion, is the end" (Channing 1877, 15).

the less separation will there be in the characters, duties, and pursuits of men and women," but the diminishing separation will be a product of learning from the differences. "Women will not become less gentle and graceful, but men will become more so. Women will not neglect the care and education of their children, but men will find themselves ennobled and refined by sharing those duties with them; and will receive, in return co-operation and sympathy in the discharge of various duties, now deemed inappropriate to women." Although framed in the language of progress toward a "divine order," here heaven is better understood as a concrete place. "The more women become rational companions, partners in business and in thought, as well as in affection and amusement, the more highly will men appreciate home—that blessed word, which opens to the human heart the most perfect glimpse of heaven" (Child 1998, 155–156). Here, even "rational" must be understood in the context Child proposes. As women and men attend to the "domestic details" of place and the goals of growth, then they will also come to understand and act in terms of home places. Rationality here is to understand and act in context, in accord with a logic of home.

Even as souls are marked by sexual difference, they are also marked by racial difference. In one of her *Letters from New York,* Child tells the story of her visit to P. T. Barnum's American Museum in New York in March 1843 where she witnessed the "visit" of fifteen Native people, several of whom were veterans of the Winnebago and Black Hawk Wars. The fifteen were all members of the Fox, Sauk, and Iowa nations and included an Iowa prophet named Wacontokitcher and Nonosee, a niece of Black Hawk. Child appears horrified by Barnum's display of Native people alongside "monkeys, flamingoes, dancers, and buffoons" (Child 1998, 164). Turning away from the spectacle in the text, she discusses how Native ways of understanding and acting seem radically different from her own and concludes that such differences are both fundamental and inaccessible, at least on their own terms. In desiring to see the world through the eyes of the Native women at the museum, she was, she concludes, making a "foolish wish." "The soul *is* ME, and *is* Thee," she writes, "I can only look *at* people" (Child 1998, 164–165). It is only in the interaction between people that they can be known at all. Who they "really" are, in a sense, is not relevant, at least to embodied life. What serves as the common ground among people, as implied by the principle of interaction, is rather what people do, the ways they act in the context of a community.

Child illustrates the point in her letter by comparing Wacontokitcher with Johann Gottfried von Herder. Despite the "distance" between them, "they are both prophets; and though one looks through nature with the

pitch-pine torch of the wilderness, and the other is lighted by a whole
constellation of suns, yet have both learned, in their degree, that matter
is only the time-garment of the spirit" (Child 1998, 165). Here, Herder,
whose work takes advantage of a culturally diverse literature, and the
Iowa prophet, who, Child presumes, calls only on central Algonquian
traditions, nevertheless share a common function and, from this perspective, a common conception that human life exceeds material particularity. At the same time, even such commonality, that is, the soul that
extends beyond material locations, is necessarily subject to the material
particularity it seems to transcend. It would be "worth a kingdom to
hear" Wacontokitcher's vision, she says, but to do so would require that
she could "borrow the souls of his tribe." Understanding the prophet is
a matter of being part of the prophet's community in its place. She
writes, "That the races of mankind are different, spiritually as well as
physically, there is, of course, no doubt; but it is as the difference between
trees of the same forest, not as between trees and minerals." The differences, like that of trees, are a matter of location, perspective, and the
soul, while physical similarities and common needs and interests provide
an embodied ground of interaction. Differences can, she argues, be affected by experience, but even so, they will retain a character that reflects their origin and history. "Similar influences brought to bear on the
Indians or the Africans, as a race," would "enlarge their perceptions of
moral and intellectual truth." But, she cautions, "[t]he *same* influences
cannot be brought to bear upon [these truths]; for *their* Past is not *our*
Past; and of course never can be. But let ours mingle with theirs, and
you will find the result variety, without inferiority" (Child 1998, 163).
Interaction and pluralism support a conception of human differences
that exists in the context of distinct communities understood in terms
of place. From this perspective, growth is not a matter of unification or a
matter of progress toward some single end, but a matter of the coexistence of diverse groups, ideas, and interests.

In Child's work, the pragmatic commitments of the indigenous attitude became bound to the logic of home as a way of responding from
inside European American society to the colonial attitude as it was manifested in Jacksonian democracy. Here the legacy of Native thought becomes both a way of fostering the growth of diverse American places
and a way of fostering differences within those places. In the logic of
home as Child developed it, the principle of interaction served as the
starting place, ontologically and epistemologically. In a context of domestic detail, things gained their meaning and character. By attending
to the context, Child could take seriously the role of differences and
their value. Understanding and action also required recognition of one's

own home and the existence of other homes that served as alternative centers of meaning. Such homes were not simply other isolated individuals, but complex relations among people, land, histories, and interests. The views of individuals from this perspective do not stand alone but are bound up with the interests and expectations of others within communities and as they emerged in interactions between communities. In the end, Child affirmed the principle of growth as the standard according to which judgments can be made despite the radical located pluralism of the world. Child's admonition in *The Frugal Housewife* to share and not destroy recalls not only the Native practices of *wunnégin* and Franklin's and Dewey's ideas of hospitality, but also Jane Addams's notion of "lateral progress." Child, standing at the border between Native and European America, also stands as a pragmatist whose work served as the starting point for the line of pragmatist thought that developed in the work of nineteenth-century feminists and helped form the context from which classical pragmatism emerged.

CONCLUSION

The Legacy of Native American Thought

I HAVE ARGUED THAT Native American thought contributed to European American philosophy at key moments in its development. At each of these moments, the principles that came to characterize classical pragmatism emerged in Native American responses to European-descended ways of understanding and acting. In time, these Native responses were taken up by European Americans as well and became part of a new American philosophical tradition. In the earliest moment of connection, Native thought expressed in the practices of *wunnégin* proposed a model for a pluralist American society. The model was grounded in an indigenous attitude that was committed to the principles of interaction, pluralism, community, and growth. The model, however, was not enough to check the dominance of what I have called the colonial attitude. This way of understanding and acting in the world, empowered by its logic of technometry, saw America as part of a story of human progress defined by a single conception of human nature and purpose. Guided by the colonial attitude, European Americans pushed inland from their first settlements and over time applied the assimilating power of the colonial logic to the people and lands that had originally offered them welcome.

In the eighteenth century, Native resistance to the colonial attitude generated another important period of contribution. Against the background of the Great Awakening and the imperial battles of England and France, the Native Prophetic movement spoke out and in so doing presented another version of the indigenous attitude. This attitude, now expressed as a logic of place, proposed to organize meaning in terms of the relations between people, lands, histories, and interests. *Wunnégin* still characterized potential interaction between places, but the logic of place also argued for adopting ways of thinking and acting that recognized the integrity of diverse places and valued their differences. The logic of place became a key component in the development of European American thought by providing both an orientation toward science and philosophy and by providing a vision of political and cultural sovereignty. Here Native thought entered the European American tradition as a distinctive conception of science and sovereignty that affirmed the principles of interaction and pluralism and framed the work of science and government in terms of a commitment to community and the growth of new possibilities.

The vision of a pluralist society supported by the logic of place was challenged in the aftermath of the American Revolution by a series of policies and practices that promoted the colonial attitude as the dominant way of understanding American society. Practically, this new dominance was expressed in the policies of Jacksonian democracy, including the policy of Indian removal. As if to declare an end to the vision of the Narragansett, who first proposed a pluralist American community in the seventeenth century, and the vision of the Native prophets who envisioned a similar community in the eighteenth century, Indian removal sought to settle the matter by eliminating the presence of Native people and influence. In the 1820s Native resistance to Indian removal, following the lead proposed by the Native prophets, took up a new logic that tried to offer again the idea of a pluralist American society now supported by the process of social inquiry and adjustment that I have called the logic of home. Here the indigenous attitude and its new logic entered the European American tradition through the work of women writers who both opposed Indian removal and sought a way to respond to the oppression of women within European American society.

The legacy of Native American philosophy did not end with Indian removal and the work of the early American feminists. In a way, it became even more pervasive. Even as one line of Native influence persisted in the development of American conceptions of science and community, the other, emerging from anti-removal activism, helped set the stage for other activist movements in the nineteenth century. Two of these, the black anti-racist movement that began in the 1810s and the feminist pragmatism that emerged in the 1880s, have yet to be traced in detail. In this conclusion, I will briefly summarize the genealogy of these other crucial movements. In the end, it is the combination of all these lines of Native influence that formed the rich intellectual environment from which classical pragmatism emerged. And it is in seeing pragmatism as continuous with Native American thought that its commitments to the principles of interaction, pluralism, community, and growth can be taken up again as potential resources for responding to a new vision of a pluralist American society.

The development of a logic of home in the work of nineteenth-century feminists was paralleled by the development of related ways of thinking in the work of black anti-racist activists. African American thinkers, beginning in the 1810s, had already begun to adopt the commitments and strategies developed in the resistance movements. Consider the address by William Hamilton, a leader of the black community in New York, delivered in 1815 on the seventh anniversary of the end of African slave trade with the United States. Hamilton presents an account of the history of African Americans that parallels the place accounts then emerging from the Native tradition. Just as the Native Prophetic movement proposed a conception of human origins that affirmed a single creator and multiple creations, so Hamilton proposes a similar view. In this case, he argued that while Africa served as the "original" of humankind, the world was nevertheless populated with diverse peoples, each bound to a place and manifesting a distinctive character. Using a logic like the one used by Sagoyewatha in his story of Native history, Hamilton says that the ancestors of blacks in America were, in ancient times, driven from their original homelands in Egypt by "a wicked nation" that "entered and laid waste their country, making slaves of some of the inhabitants, and [putting] to death others" (Foner and Branham 1998, 93).

The people driven from Egypt took up the land from the Tropic of Cancer to the Cape of Good Hope, where they established a place of their own. They were, says Hamilton "an industrious, honest, peaceable people," establishing fit relations with their new land, which was "very fertile, producing its fruits with very little labour of the husbandman." Eventually Europeans arrived and established the slave trade. "They set to work," Hamilton says, "that low, sly, wicked cunning peculiar to the Europeans, to the creating of jealousies and animosity, one horde or nation with another" (Foner and Branham 1998, 94). Even plying the people of Africa with "spirituous liquor," the Europeans "laboured until Africa became one continuous scene of suspicion, mad jealousy, confusion, war, rapine, blood and murder." In effect, the European invasion had, as in the Americas, destroyed the interactions that provided for the flourishing of African peoples. Finally, through the slave trade, the fates of Africa, Europe, and America became joined. "Would to God," Hamilton exclaims, "that Columbus with his exploring schemes had perished in Europe ere he touched the American Isles, or that Americus had perished in the ocean ere he explored the southern parts of the Continent; or rather that the hateful Cortes, with his murderous band had been swallowed by an earthquake" (Foner and Branham 1998, 95). The destruction of Africa as a place, like the destruction of America, was the consequence of European colonialism.

Hamilton's narrative against the European invasion, like Sagoyewatha's, became the starting point for the demand for establishing new home places where African people in America could flourish. The year after Hamilton's address and in the wake of a growing population of free blacks in European American communities, a group of leading white activists founded the American Colonization Society.[1] It was the policy of the colonization society to return all free blacks to Africa, in effect removing them from white communities in America. The parallel with the Indian removal policy of the same period is striking, and its connection was made apparent when Andrew Jackson became a member. The response by black activists, like that of Native activists, was to argue against removal and in favor of establishing distinct black communities. Speaking on Independence Day 1830, Peter Williams Jr., a black minister and activist, argued against the policy of removal and in favor of founding a black community on purchased lands in Canada. "We are NATIVES of this country, we ask only to be treated as FOREIGNERS" (Foner and Branham 1998, 117).[2] Rather than being sent to Africa, Williams asserted a black connection with America and argued that "we need not go to Africa nor anywhere else to be improved and happy." Rather than leaving America, blacks who had become a part of it were to join together in communities that could flourish side by side with communities of Europeans who had also become part of America. Just as the strategies of the Native prophets would preserve the places of Native people, so Williams advocated a plan that would establish African American home places. The program proposed by Williams and others before the Civil War was carried forward again after the war. Sojourner Truth, for example, in a speech in 1871 also advocated establishing black lands within America. Unlike a program primarily interested in establishing individual property as the Dawes Act would do in the next decade, Truth was interested in a grant of lands as a way both to foster the growth of African American communities and a wider multicultural American society. "[T]he United States," she says, "ought to give [freed

---

1. See Foner and Branham 1998, 114.
2. See Marilyn Baily's discussion of the Canadian colony (1973).

blacks] land and move them on it" (Foner and Branham 1998, 505).
"We've ain't land enough for a home," she says, "and it would be a benefit
for you all and God would bless the whole of you for doing it."

While the failure of Reconstruction rekindled race hatred against
blacks in both the North and South, those who opposed race prejudice
often advocated a policy of submission designed to minimize conflict
with whites. The policy, generally associated with the work of Booker T.
Washington, amounted to a program of "industrial education, concilia-
tion of the South, and submission and silence as to civil and political
rights," as Du Bois described it (Du Bois 1989, 30).[3] Blacks who opposed
this approach began to advocate for sharper separation between blacks
and whites in America. In doing so, they turned even more directly to a
conception of difference and a logic of place of the sort used by the
Native prophets against the Great Awakening and its demands for conversion. In 1895, at the Cotton States and International Exposition in
Atlanta, Washington asked those blacks who would abandon the South
to stay and cultivate "friendly relations with the Southern white man,
who is their next door neighbor" in hopes that conditions would eventually improve (Foner and Branham 1998, 803).[4] John H. Smyth, the black
editor of the *Richmond Reformer* who had also served as a missionary in
Liberia, replied to Washington in an argument against submission and
in favor of establishing black autonomy.

Smyth's position in favor of black nationalism begins with an argument nearly identical to the one used by the Native Prophetic movement
to undermine the logic of technometry and establish a logic of place.
"We are taught by holy writ," he says, "that God set bounds to the habitations of men. One race he established upon the continent of Africa,
another upon the continent of Asia, another upon the continent of
Europe, and a heterogeneity of races upon the continent of America"
(Foner and Branham 1998, 820–821). Such diversity of origin leads to
the diversity of peoples, and that diversity is good. "In this various ap-
portionment of races, wisdom and beneficence are shown. If we fail to
see the former, we cannot doubt the latter, since 'He does all things well'"
(Foner and Branham 1998, 821). From this perspective, Smyth argues,

3. Du Bois notes that Washington's policies were not new, but had been advocated before the Civil War by the American Missionary Association, whose work also involved "civi-
lizing" the Indians. Washington himself was educated at Hampton Institute, whose program served as a model for the Carlisle Indian School in Pennsylvania. The superintendent
of Carlisle, Richard Pratt, first served as the head of the Indian division at Hampton before
opening Carlisle. See Hertzberg 1971 for a brief discussion of Carlisle, and see Lindsey
1995 for a detailed discussion of Native Americans at the Hampton Institute.

4. See the discussion of Washington's speech, Foner and Branham 1998, 800–802.

Americans need to adopt a perspective that will recognize both shared interests and the irreducibility of difference. "Though we are part of this great national whole," he says, "we are a distinct and separate part" (Foner and Branham 1998, 823). Unlike Washington's position and its supporters, Smyth's position represented an alternative that both demanded the recognition of racial difference and the elimination of race prejudice. Anna Julia Cooper, whose book *A Voice from the South* was published in 1892, anticipated his position, and Du Bois echoed it in his 1897 address "The Conservation of Races."

When Du Bois published *The Souls of Black Folk* in 1903, he brought together the arguments for racial and cultural difference affirmed by the logic of place and at the same time took up the methodology of social inquiry implicit in the logic of home. In the first chapter, he asserts that as a black in America he "feels his twoness—an American, a Negro; two souls, two thoughts, two unreconciled strivings; two warring ideals in one dark body, whose dogged strength alone keeps it from being torn asunder" (Du Bois 1989, 3). The geography of his body and soul are grounded in the geography of America and Africa. Differences here are to be understood as a complex interaction of history, body, ideas, and aspirations together with concrete locations. In the end, he wants to preserve the geography of twoness, but in a way that will sustain both.[5] Such a logic of place gives the parameters for his social inquiry, but the work itself uses the logic of home to critically analyze the interaction of different cultures within places. Du Bois's work, like Child's *First Settlers*, combines social history and stories framed by domestic details in a unified social inquiry. Writing at the beginning of the twentieth century, Du Bois reasserts the perspective developed by Native activists at the beginning of the nineteenth century and carries it forward as a resource for twentieth-century responses to the problems of the coexistence of different peoples.[6]

As the black anti-racist movement took up versions of the logic of place and home, so too did the developing American feminist movement. By the 1840s even as Child's claims about women and non-white

5. "He would not," Du Bois says, "Africanize America, for America has too much to teach the world and Africa. He would not bleach his Negro soul in a flood of white Americanism, for he knows that Negro Blood has a message for the world. He simply wishes to make it possible for a man to be both a Negro and an American, without being cursed and spit upon by his fellows, without having the doors of Opportunity closed roughly in his face" (Du Bois 1989, 3).

6. Much more needs to be said about the development of African American thought in the nineteenth century and its relation both to Native American thought and feminist

people were resisted by the Northern intellectual elite, her approach to understanding home as a liberatory framework took hold even among conservatives. In 1843, Catharine Beecher published her *Treatise on Domestic Economy*. On one hand, the *Treatise* transformed Child's *Frugal Housewife* into a domestic science.[7] By emphasizing the value of both scientific results and the method of experimental science in the home, Beecher argued that the home could become a better place. Where Child presented simple recipes lacking in detail, Beecher advocated for precise instructions in order to use resources efficiently and to promote the health and well-being of the family. Where Child offered home remedies, Beecher advocated familiarity with medical science. In 1869, Beecher and her sister, Harriet Beecher Stowe, prepared an expanded version of the *Treatise*. The purpose of the work, entitled *The American Woman's Home*, is "to elevate both the honor and the remuneration of all employments that sustain the many difficult and varied duties of the family state, and thus render each department of woman's profession as much desired and respected as are the most honored professions of men" (Beecher and Stowe 1869, 17). At the center of the "woman's profession" is the commitment to the creation of a home that will promote growth. Such a home begins literally with the physical house itself. Such a house, the authors write, is "a house contrived for the express purpose of enabling every member of a family to labor with the hands for the common good, and by modes at once healthful, economical, and tasteful" (Beecher and Stowe 1869, 24). Beecher and Stowe wish to undermine the hierarchical relation between women and men while promoting the idea of growth as a standard in terms of which to organize a home place. At the same time, they achieve this goal by adopting a rigid separation between women's and men's roles and between internal, domestic affairs and the "public sphere" in which men's work occurs. The rigid structures to be imposed on the home, however, cut against the vision proposed by Child and reveal the operation of an attitude more closely related to the colonial attitude that dominated the social and political developments of the period.

The publication of the *Treatise on Domestic Economy, The American Woman's Home,* and related works in the 1840s and later supported some aspects of the program Child advocated in *The Frugal Housewife* and *The*

---

thought. Anna Julia Cooper, for example, brings together aspects of both in her work, especially her 1892 work *A Voice from the South* (1998). There are also strong points of contact both in places like Hampton Institute as well as the various missionary societies in the late nineteenth century. There are also much older historical connections between Native and African peoples. See Forbes 1993.

7. See Kathryn Kish Sklar's biography of Beecher (1973).

Mother's Book (not to mention *The First Settlers*), but they also undermined Child's program by undercutting the pluralism inherent in her view. By establishing a fixed set of duties for women and men and setting a standard of success framed entirely in Christian terms, Beecher and Stowe's work left an ambiguous relationship between women's empowerment and women's subservience. In the 1890s, however, mediated by the work of a new generation of women writers in the Reconstruction period including Louisa May Alcott, new activists emerged who began with the logic of home and transformed it again into an instrument of social change.

Alcott's narratives in particular provide a new ground for the logic of home and a renewed interest in devising a means for women to conceptualize their own circumstances in the context of a particular place. Narratives in this way could provide both a detailed description of a situation and the relations that make it up and provide resources for carrying the relations into a wider situation. In her novel *Work: A Story of Experience,* for example, Alcott presents the story of a woman's quest for a home against circumstances of poverty, exclusion, male domination, and civil war. In the end, the central character, Christie Devon, is able to construct a home place following in some detail the sorts of recommendations made by Child in her early fiction and in *The Mother's Book.* Christie almost literally learns all of the kinds of work available to women at the time and in so doing gains both alliances with other women of different racial, ethnic, and class backgrounds, and is able to establish a home in which these alliances with other women can flourish even in the absence of men. While the relations of Christie's life serve to indicate the sorts of relations that can be used to structure a better life for women at the end of the nineteenth century, the book itself, with its narrative structure focused on these relations, also offers a way to understand and act that will sustain diversity and promote the growth of wider communities.

Charlotte Perkins Gilman, born in 1860, a great granddaughter of Lyman Beecher and great niece of Catharine Beecher and Harriet Beecher Stowe, took up her great aunts' strategy of applying experimental science to the problems of human growth and development. In her seminal work, *Women and Economics* (1898), Gilman takes seriously the idea that human beings could only be understood in interaction with their environments.[8] Women and men, as organisms in particular envi-

8. Gilman and other thinkers in the last half of the nineteenth century often used Darwin's general idea of evolution as a way to frame and verify their discussions of social change. Those already working from the perspective of the logic of home had long admitted the role of environment and the need to find meaning in a changing world. The de-

ronments, developed different ways of interaction based on their distinct physiologies, differences in opportunity, and differences in expectations. Like Child, she adopts the idea of growth as the standard according to which interactions could be evaluated, and, like Child, maintains that it is the logic of home and the demands of growth that provide a framework for women's independence. Nearly repeating Child's position published seventy years earlier, Gilman says, "Granting squarely that it is the business of women to make the home life of the world true, healthful, and beautiful, the economically dependent woman does not do this, and never can. The economically independent woman can and will. As the family is by no means identical with marriage, so is the home by no means identical with either" (Gilman 1898, 220). Reacting against the separation between home and society defended by her great aunts, Gilman demands that home and society be viewed as continuous. To the extent they become separate, growth is blocked and women are driven to subservience (Gilman 1898, 222–223). Child, Sedgwick, and Alcott viewed the relations of home as providing a means for social transformation. The new circumstances at the end of the nineteenth century allowed Gilman to read the relation in the other direction, arguing that social transformation can make homes, the places of concrete interactions, also places of growth. Gilman's fiction, too, seems to owe much to the earlier work of Child and the other antebellum activist writers. Her story "The Yellow Wallpaper" is an excellent example of a narrative grounded in a place that serves to present both an instance of inquiry and an example of how one can examine the destruction of the relations that sustain a home.[9]

Jane Addams, also born in 1860, took up the logic of home as it emerged from the work of writers like Child and Alcott and from the abolitionist movement and made it the framework for a pragmatist social ethic. In her 1902 work *Democracy and Social Ethics,* Addams overtly adopts a logic of home where problems must be understood in terms of their circumstances and where solutions are to be found literally in the situation itself. Here Addams seems to recall the long-standing pragmatic commitments when she concludes that when men and women gain "a wider acquaintance with and participation in the life about them," they "slowly learn that life consists of processes as well as results, and

---

velopment of evolution theory in a sense provided an opportunity for the sort of analysis developed by Child to reach a wider and more sympathetic audience.

9. Hans Seigfried has written an excellent reinterpretation of "The Yellow Wallpaper" as an instance of Deweyan inquiry. Taken more broadly, the same analysis can make a case for the work as an examination of a breakdown of the fit relations of place.

that failure may come quite as easily from ignoring the adequacy of one's method as from selfish or ignoble aims" (Addams 1907, 6). Such a realization leads to a conception of democracy as a way of life that depends upon the coexistence of different people. "[D]iversified human experience and resultant sympathy," she says, "are the foundation and guarantee of Democracy" (Addams 1907, 7). Such diversity is not, however, a matter of abstract reflection, but rather the consequence of taking up the logic of place and home and attending to the relations of particular places. "We realize too," she continues, "that social perspectives and sanity of judgment come only from contact with social experience." The result of such an approach to understanding and action is not a universal set of rules. "No attempt is made to reach a conclusion, nor to offer advice beyond the assumption that the cure for the ills of Democracy is more Democracy,"[10] that is, the only response to the problems of one's place is a method that will find a solution in the place, its people, history, land, and interests.

For Addams, solutions to the problems faced by women, especially women in impoverished urban circumstances, cannot be imposed from without but rather require a restructuring of the circumstances, beginning from the resources available in the place. Such resources call on the material circumstances, but also upon the particular histories of the people and places, the interests of those involved, and the "outside" forces that often undermine the possibility of establishing interactions that will lead to growth. The standard within these situations that can be generalized is the idea that solutions will lead to new possibilities, and new experience. Her autobiography, *Twenty Years at Hull House,* published in 1910, can be understood as a series of place analyses that show both the possibilities of success and the possibilities of failure in attempting to address lived problems. Addams constantly resists an approach that would argue for a general solution to social problems and both advocates and models an approach that, like Child's narratives, takes up a particular situation, examines the active relations and the resources at hand, and presents what happens in that situation. The reader, it is clear, is not to attempt to apply her results unreflectively in new situations, but rather is to adopt her method, in this case, by living close to the problem and listening carefully to what is said and not said in the situation itself.[11]

When Addams co-founded Hull House with her friend Ellen Gates Starr in a poor immigrant neighborhood in Chicago, her work instanti-

---

10. Dewey uses this same phrase twenty-four years later in *The Public and Its Problems* (1926, 325, 327).
11. Also see Addams 1911 and Addams 1916.

ated the ideas carried in the tradition of Neolin and Sagoyewatha, Johnston Schoolcraft and John Ross. Meaning is, they said, a matter of place,
and the flourishing of the place, that is, making a home, will depend
upon establishing fit relations in the interactions of the place. Hull
House marked an attempt to establish such a concrete place. Hull House,
says Addams, "is an experimental effort to aid in the solution of the
social and industrial problems which are engendered by the modern
conditions of life in a great city" (Addams 1981, 98). But in taking up
the problems of a place, Hull House also becomes part of the place. "It
aims . . . to develop whatever of social life its neighborhood may afford,
to focus and give form to that life, to bring to bear upon it the results
of cultivation and training; but it receives in exchange for the music of
isolated voices the volume and strength of the chorus" (Addams 1981,
97). The response to the "precarious and uncertain" place of which Hull
House is a part is the institution of a logic of home as a process of social
inquiry.[12] By reflecting on the relations within the place, the people of
Hull House and its community are able to identify problems and adjust
circumstances in order to promote growth. As in Teedyuscung's analogy
of the cultivation of corn, Hull House and its community make a home
through placed and collective action.[13]

Dewey met Jane Addams in 1892 during a visit to the University of
Chicago shortly after Hull House opened. Dewey wrote to Addams about
their first meeting. "I cannot tell you how much good I got from my stay
at Hull House," he said. "My indebtedness to you for giving me an insight
into matters there is great. While I did not see much of any particular

12. Writing in 1898, Addams says, "the good we secure for ourselves is precarious and
uncertain, is floating in mid-air, until it is secured for all of us and incorporated into our
common life" (quoted in Addams 1981, 92). Mead is a particularly important figure in connecting the work of Addams and Hull House to both classical pragmatism and twentieth-
century sociology. See Deegan 1988.

13. The connections between the development of pragmatism in the early twentieth
century and the development of the so-called "Pan-Indian" movement of the early twentieth century has yet to be explored. The last decade of the nineteenth century and the first
two in the twentieth marked a rise of Native American activism alongside the black anti-
racist movement and feminism. Addams's Hull House was a focal point, bringing together
Native women activists, including Susan LaFlesche and Gertrude Bonin, with black activists, including W. E. B. Du Bois, and white philosophers, including Dewey, Royce, and Mead.
For Native American thought, Bonin, LaFlesche and Laura Cornelius Kellogg are particularly important though they have not yet been considered as part of the developing Native
philosophical tradition in the twentieth century. Also active at this time in the Native tradition were Arthur C. Parker, Francis LaFlesche (Susan's brother), Luther Standing Bear,
and D'Arcy McNickle, among others. Again, there are at present few studies of the work
of these Native thinkers and no work that considers them as part of a larger developing
philosophical tradition.

thing I think that I got a pretty good idea of the general spirit and method. Every day I stayed there only added to my conviction that you had taken the right way" (quoted in Davis 1973, 96–97). In their meeting, there is a sense in which the diverse sources of pragmatism were rejoined and together provided the catalyst and many of the key resources for the development of classical pragmatism. In the last decade of the nineteenth century, Dewey, Peirce, and James were able to combine the experimental and community-based science of Franklin, the social activism of the feminist pragmatists, and strands of European philosophy into an epistemology and ontology that begins in lived experience. In a sense, the commitments of the indigenous attitude became expressed in still another logic. Starting from the process of doubt and inquiry, in Peirce's terms, this logic joined with James's conception of a socially located self, bound by material conditions, physiology, habits, and the insights of others, and then joined with Dewey's expansion of experimental logic to become the logic of cultural naturalism. In each case, the formal philosophical development was framed over an attitude inherited in part from Native American thought as it emerged along the border with European America. That indigenous attitude already expected meaning to be found in interactions against a pluralist background, framed by community, and aimed toward growth.

In a way, Dewey had already been prepared to learn from Addams when he became the husband of Harriet Alice Chipman in 1886. In his life with Chipman he became part of the philosophical tradition that began in the work of Child and was alive in the work of Addams, Gilman, and Chipman herself. Chipman was born in Fenton, Michigan, then a border town between Native and European America. When she was still young, her parents died and her grandparents took her in. Her grandfather, Frederick Riggs, was described by Dewey's biographer as "a colorful, adventurous type, who had had a rich background of experience both in the West and Midwest. . . . He had had close associations with Indians in the West, and had sided with them in their attempts to get social justice from the white man" (Dykhuizen 1973, 53). Riggs had been adopted by the Chippewa nation, and, as is the case with most white intellectuals along the border, Chipman herself probably had opportunities to learn from Native people as well as from African Americans who had come north in the wake of the war.[14] It is possible that Dewey's own experience in the relatively diverse setting of Burlington, Vermont,

---

14. See Westbrook 1991, 34–36, and Jane Dewey's biography of her father in *The Philosophy of John Dewey* (1939, 20).

helped make him particularly responsive to Chipman's activism. In any case, Chipman is generally credited with providing Dewey the motive for transforming his academic interests in philosophy into an interest in making philosophy relevant to the real problems faced by the United States at the end of the nineteenth century.[15] As Jane Dewey concluded about Chipman, "[a]wakened by her grandparents to a critical attitude toward social conditions and injustices, she was undoubtedly largely responsible for the early widening of Dewey's philosophic interests from the commentative and classical to the field of contemporary life. Above all," she concludes, "things which had previously been matters of theory acquired through his contact with her a vital and direct human significance" (Jane Dewey 1939, 21).

In a syllabus for one of his courses in the winter of 1892, Dewey explained that the "business" of philosophy and science "is to reveal experience in its truth, its reality. They state what *is*" (Dewey 1969, 211). Philosophy from this perspective, like the history told by Mather and the story of progress told by Jefferson, was a process that transcended the particularities of experience, and sought, as Dewey put it, "the real whole."

By the following December, however, after his visit to Hull House and perhaps with the encouragement of Chipman and others, Dewey had reconstructed his own view of philosophy. In an article for the university newspaper entitled "Why Study Philosophy?" Dewey writes, "The philosopher . . . is a social being, and works out his ideas by expressing them, by trying them on others, by making them influence the actions of others" (Dewey 1893, 62–63). The impact of the work is not to state "what is" or "the real whole," but to engage the ways in which people understand and act. "[T]he ideas" that emerge from philosophy, he says, "come to live as a part of the common and unconscious intellectual life of men in general. They become the presupposed background, the unexpressed premises, the working (and therefore controlling) tools of thought and action." Such a view of philosophy necessarily displaces the transcendent perspective of the colonial attitude and comes to see philosophy as part of a place. In his 1927 address "Philosophy and Civilization," Dewey concludes, "The movement of time has revealed" that philosophy is part of culture. "Those who assert in the abstract definition of philosophy that it deals with eternal truth or reality, untouched by local time and place, are forced to admit that philosophy as a concrete existence is historical, having temporal passage and a diversity of local

---

15. Charlene Haddock Seigfried has traced these connections in some detail (1996).

habitations" (Dewey 1927, 4). Philosophy, like experience and meaning, is a matter of place, of "local habitations." In order to understand the process of making places meaningful, it is not a matter of searching for fixed principles or a viewpoint that will take one outside a place, but rather will involve the investigation of the relations and interactions of the place itself, that is, an investigation of place as home. "The world we have experienced becomes an integral part of the self that acts and is acted upon in further experience," Dewey writes in *Art as Experience*. "In their physical occurrence, things and events experienced pass and are gone. But something of their meaning and value is retained as an integral part of the self. Through habits formed in intercourse with the world, we also in-habit the world. It becomes a home and the home is part of our every experience" (Dewey 1934a, 109).

Even as Dewey's work took up a standpoint within the tradition emerging from Native resistance to Indian removal and its development through Child and American feminism, he also inherited the tradition of Franklin, both in his conception of science and in his conception of democratic communities. In his 1940 article "Presenting Thomas Jefferson," he affirms Jefferson's approach to science as the one developed by Franklin and displayed in Jefferson's regret "that chemists had not followed Franklin in directing science to something 'useful in private life'; with a hope that their science would be applied to 'brewing, making cider, fermentation and distillation generally, making bread, butter, cheese, soap, incubating eggs, etc.'" (Dewey 1940, 205). Lewis S. Feuer sees the connection between Dewey and Franklin as especially clear in the concluding words of the introductory essay in Dewey's collection *The Problems of Men*. As Dewey puts it in his introduction, the business of philosophy is "wholly with that part of the historic tradition called search for wisdom:—Namely, search for the ends and values that give direction to our collective human activities" (Dewey 1946, 161). Such a tradition does not hold that "grasp of eternal and universal Reality" is the best means for conducting this search. It rather endorses "the methods and conclusions of our best knowledge, that called scientific." As Feuer puts it, "Dewey thus placed himself in that tradition which from Thales and the Seven Hellenic Sages to Benjamin Franklin has indeed been concerned more with the problems of men's everyday and social existence rather than with the ultimate nature of existence generally" (Feuer 1989, xxx). Although Feuer identifies a different philosophical genealogy than the one I have discussed, it seems clear that Dewey inherited a conception of science developed, at least in part, along the border between Native and European America in the work of Franklin and Jefferson.

Dewey also inherited the legacy of Franklin's conception of democratic communities. In *Freedom and Culture,* Dewey discusses Jefferson's contributions to the idea and practice of democracy, and in so doing marks the aspects of Jefferson's views that are most like the ideas Franklin developed in his proposals recognizing the sovereignty of communities. "I could easily fill pages," Dewey writes, "from Thomas Jefferson in which he insists upon the necessity of a free press, general schooling and local neighborhood groups carrying on, through intimate meetings and discussions, the management of their own affairs, if political democracy was to be made secure" (Dewey 1939, 91). Even as Dewey criticizes Jefferson for his elitism and his commitment to the determinism found in the Deist ideas of "Nature and the plans of a benevolent and wise Creator," he affirms Jefferson's conception of placed communities as the key to developing a pluralist democracy.[16] Citing himself to illustrate the principle, Dewey writes, "Democracy must begin at home, and its home is the neighborly community" (Dewey 1939, 176).[17] This link between home and democracy follows the approach Jefferson advocated in the "development of local agencies of communication and cooperation, creating stable loyal attachments, to militate against the centrifugal forces of present culture, while at the same time they are of a kind to respond flexibly to the demands of the larger unseen and indefinite public." While Dewey owes much to the conception of democracy developed by Addams, it is also clear that he saw himself as one who had inherited his idea of democratic communities from late eighteenth-century American thought. In this case, Jefferson's view follows Franklin's long commitment to the idea of framing democracy in terms of places. When Dewey inherits this view of communities, he also inherits an attitude and a logic that can be linked to Native attempts to establish the peaceful coexistence of flourishing places. In short, Dewey's work brings together the traditions of Franklin and Child founded at the intersection of Native and European American thought and developed through the work of Teedyuscung and the Native Prophetic movement and the work of Johnston Schoolcraft and those who resisted Indian removal.

The "unvarnished tale" of the development of pragmatism provides an alternative way of understanding American intellectual history and classical pragmatism. It recasts American philosophy as the inheritance, on one hand, of the commitments of the indigenous attitude to the principles of interaction, pluralism, community, and growth. By making the

16. See Dewey's comments (1939, 108, 174, and 179). While, as I have argued, Jefferson grounded his views in the commitments Dewey mentions here, Franklin did not.
17. The quotation is from *The Public and Its Problems* (Dewey 1927, 368).

commitments explicit and taking note of their presence and absence within the wider American tradition, one also has a means to reassess that tradition and identify both its successes and failures. On the other hand, the tale is an account of the way the indigenous attitude and its commitments have been instantiated as ways of understanding and acting in the world. The practices of *wunnégin* and the logics of place and home provide a way of fostering both a flourishing American society and a diversity of distinct home places. Although lacking in the certainty and clarity of direction that was provided by the colonial attitude, these alternative approaches have a history of successes and failures that have nevertheless sustained differences in America even against brutal assault, coercion, starvation, and genocide. These ways of thinking, especially as they have sustained the living cultures and places of Native peoples, have proven their potential. The "unvarnished tale" of the ways this approach has emerged in the struggle for survival provides an invaluable starting point for new responses to the crises and possibilities of a new century.

The process of reconstructing American pragmatism is in a sense an effort from within the tradition—a kind of "American angle of vision," as McDermott calls it, that takes seriously the places from which American philosophy emerged.[18] From this standpoint, there are two further implications of the new "unvarnished tale." First, the history of American thought in general and pragmatism in particular becomes broader and deeper. The intellectual and historical resources available, the scope of the problems addressed, and the voices involved in the conversation radically multiply. From this perspective it is no longer a matter of course to set aside those who are not already recognized as part of the tradition. Instead, there develops an expectation that philosophy will actively seek out alternative points of view, moments of interaction and influence, and the "domestic details" that make situations concrete. As Dewey describes it, it is a philosophy that "forswears inquiry after absolute origins and absolute finalities in order to explore specific values and the specific conditions that generate them" (Dewey 1909, 10). But it also follows that such a practice of philosophy is not a retrospective one. It is forward-looking in response to the problems and concerns that challenge people and communities in their places even as it looks toward the ways in which places are connected. Such a practice of philosophy will, in a sense, call for new languages that can reconstruct places in ways that reveal points of contact and shared interests, while at the same time

18. See McDermott 1966.

reflecting the fundamental pluralism any such task will involve. McDermott describes this task well. "[W]e must," he says, "develop a new celebratory language, rooted in contemporary American experience, pluralistic in style and able to resonate creatively throughout the fabric of world culture" (McDermott 1976, 79).

Second, this "angle of vision" supports a renewed analysis of concrete problems in a way that takes seriously the interaction of the land and its inhabitants, the histories of a place, cultural practices and institutions, and the need for and possibility of growth. Philosophers will need to attend not just to the traditional texts and their contexts, but the interactions of those texts and the ways of thinking they demand, both within places and between them. Once pragmatism is taken up from the perspective of its own American history, it almost necessarily becomes like the prophetic pragmatism proposed by Cornel West. For West, the classical pragmatic tradition was not yet the philosophy of social transformation it could be because it lacked a sense of the tragic, a sense of the ways that evil is part of human experience. "Prophetic pragmatism," he says, "is a form of tragic thought in that it confronts candidly individual and collective experiences of evil in individuals and institutions—with very little expectation of ridding the world of all evil" (West 1989, 228). At the same time, he continues, prophetic pragmatism "is a kind of romanticism in that it holds many experiences of evil to be neither inevitable nor necessary but rather the results of human agency." The approach modeled in the process of reconstructing the Native roots of pragmatism can be seen as one version of prophetic pragmatism, because the evil of the American tradition is as much a part of its development as its hope for flourishing homes. By recognizing the complexity of the tradition and the diversity of its resources, histories, and aspirations, one is faced both with the failures of people to coexist and with moments of success. In this story, the heroes are often flawed, often incomplete, but at the same time the story recognizes their attempts, their commitments, and the lessons that might be relevant to new struggles.

In the end, we are returned to where the story began, faced with new problems of cultural conflict and the hope for a future in which diversity of all sorts can flourish. In an important way, the answers that were first proposed by Miantonomi when he welcomed Roger Williams may still provide the best response. John Mohawk, a Seneca writer and lecturer in social philosophy at the State University of New York at Buffalo, makes this point in his 1992 article "Looking for Columbus." "For 500 years we have seen a clashing and an intermixing of cultures," he says. For a long time the dominant response has been to advocate a "'melting pot', and yet that approach has failed to enrich this culture. . . . [I]nstead of requiring everybody to be the same, maybe we should learn to live with one another, and allow for a genuine multiplicity of cultures. We are living in a world in which difference is just a simple fact of life, but our collective thinking has yet to truly come to grips with this reality. This *has* to change." The change involves a change in attitude and the adoption of ways of understanding and acting in the world that recognize the importance of place and home. Mohawk continues, "A workable world mentality means that we are going to have to make peace with those who are different from us. We must also come together in the realization that social initiatives, social justice, and ecology have to go hand in hand." One alternative is for people to try to restore old philosophies, ways of thinking from another time and place. "Or," he asks, "should we look at other peoples' ways of thinking about the world and its societies, and decide anew how human priorities and human societies ought to be constructed? We need to give ourselves permission to trust our own thinking and not allow bureaucrats and crazed guys at the pulpit to do our thinking for us. And we need to take this kind of ideology and make it work for us on *the land*" (Mohawk 1992, 442–443). By learning the lessons of a way of thinking that is committed to the importance of interaction and pluralism, the necessity of community, and the value of growth, that is, by recovering the ways of understanding and acting indigenous to America, we also gain the possibility of a flourishing pluralist society.

REFERENCES

Adair, James. 1775. *The History of the American Indians.* London: Printed for
E. and C. Dilly.

Addams, Jane. 1907. *Democracy and Social Ethics.* New York: Macmillan.

——. 1911. *Newer Ideals of Peace.* New York: Macmillan.

——. 1912. "A Modern Lear." *Survey* 29: 131–137.

——. 1916. *The Long Road of Women's Memory.* New York: Macmillan.

——. 1981. *Twenty Years at Hull House.* New York: Signet Classic.

Alcott, Louisa May. 1977. *Work: A Story of Experience.* Introduction by Sarah
Elbert. New York: Schocken Books.

Amcs, William. 1979. *Technometry.* Translated with an introduction by Lee W.
Gibbs. Philadelphia: University of Pennsylvania Press.

Anderson, Paul Russell, and Max Harold Fisch. 1939. *Philosophy in America.*
New York: D. Appleton-Century Co.

Apess, William. 1992. *On Our Own Ground: The Complete Writings of William
Apess, a Pequot.* Edited and with an introduction by Barry O'Connell.
Amherst: University of Massachusetts Press.

Arens, W. 1979. *The Man-Eating Myth: Anthropology and Anthropophagy.* New
York: Oxford University Press.

Baily, Marilyn. 1973. "From Cincinnati, Ohio to Wilberforce, Canada: A Note
on Antebellum Colonization." *Journal of Negro History* 58: 427–440.

Bancroft, George. 1854. *Literary and Historical Miscellanies.* New York: Harper
& Brothers.

——. 1878. *History of the United States of America from the Discovery of the Continent.* 6 vols. Boston: Little, Brown and Co.

Barnum, Phineas T. 1854. *The Life of P. T. Barnum.* New York: Redfield.

Beare, Francis Wright. 1981. *The Gospel According to Matthew.* San Francisco:
Harper & Row.

Beauchamp, William M. 1907. *Civil, Religious, and Mourning Councils and Ceremonies of Adoption of the New York Indians.* New York State Museum and Science Service Bulletin, 113.

Beecher, Catharine E. 1850. *Treatise on Domestic Economy.* New York: Harper &
Brothers.

Beecher, Catharine E. and Harriet Beecher Stowe. 1869. *The American
Woman's Home.* New York: J. B. Ford and Co.

Bercovitch, Sacvan. 1978. *The American Jeremiad.* Madison: University of Wisconsin Press.

——. 1993. *The Rites of Assent: Transformations in the Symbolic Construction of
America.* New York: Routledge.

Bier, Jesse. 1970. "Weberism, Franklin, and the Transcendental Style." *The
New England Quarterly* 43: 179–192.

Bierhorst, John. 1995. *Mythology of the Lenape: Guide and Texts*. Tucson: University of Arizona Press.

Black Hawk. 1990. *Black Hawk: An Autobiography*. Edited by Donald Jackson. Urbana and Chicago: University of Illinois Press.

Blau, Joseph L. 1952. *Men and Movements in American Philosophy*. New York: Prentice-Hall.

Bourne, Randolph S. 1999. *War and the Intellectuals*. Edited with introduction by Carl Resek. Indianapolis: Hackett Publishing Co.

Bragdon, Kathleen Joan. 1996. *Native People of Southern New England, 1500–1650*. Norman: University of Oklahoma Press.

Brown, Herbert Ross. 1940. *The Sentimental Novel in America, 1789–1860*. Durham, N.C.: Duke University Press.

Bunyan, John. 1965. *The Pilgrim's Progress*. Edited by Roger Sharrock. New York: Penguin Books.

Burr, George Lincoln. 1914. *Narratives of the Witchcraft Cases: 1648–1706*. New York: Charles Scribner's Sons.

Calloway, Colin G. 1990. *The Western Abenakis of Vermont, 1600–1800*. Norman and London: University of Oklahoma Press.

Calvin, John. 1981. *Commentary on a Harmony of the Evangelists*. Volume Second. Translated by Rev. William Pringle. Grand Rapids, Michigan: Baker Book House.

Campbell, James. 1999. *Recovering Benjamin Franklin: An Exploration of a Life of Science and Service*. Chicago: Open Court.

Cass, Lewis. 1828. *Considerations on the Present State of the Indians, and Their Removal to the West of the Mississippi*. New York: Arno Press, 1975.

Cave, Alfred A. 1996. *The Pequot War*. Amherst: University of Massachusetts Press.

Chafe, Wallace L. 1967. *Seneca Morphology and Dictionary*. Washington, D.C.: Smithsonian Press.

Channing, William E. 1877. *The Works of William E. Channing, D. D.* Boston: American Unitarian Association.

Child, Lydia Maria. 1827. "The Indian Boy." *Juvenile Miscellany* 2: 28–31.

———. 1829. *The First Settlers of New England*. Boston: Printed for the Author.

———. 1831. *The Mother's Book*. 2nd ed. Boston: Carter and Hendee.

———. 1833. *An Appeal in Favor of That Class of Americans Called Africans*. Edited with an introduction by Carolyn L. Karcher. Amherst: University of Massachusetts Press, 1996.

———. 1841. "The Quadroons." In *Rediscoveries: American Short Stories by Women, 1832–1916*, ed. Barbara Solomon. New York: Mentor Books, 1994.

———. 1845. *Letters from New York, Second Series*. New York: C. S. Francis & Com.

———. 1855. *The Progress of Religious Ideas, through Successive Ages*. 3 vols. New York: C. S. Francis and Co.

———. 1972. *The American Frugal Housewife*. Edited with an introduction by Alice M. Geffen. New York: Harper and Row.

———. 1986. *Hobomok and Other Writings on Indians*. Edited with an introduction by Carolyn L. Karcher. New Brunswick, N.J.: Rutgers University Press.

———. 1997. *A Lydia Maria Child Reader*. Edited by Carolyn L. Karcher. Durham, N.C., and London: Duke University Press.

———. 1998. *Letters from New-York*. Edited by Bruce Mills. Athens and London: University of Georgia Press.

Churchill, Ward. 1993. *Struggle for the Land*. Monroe, Me.: Common Courage Press.

Cohen, Felix. 1952. "Americanizing the White Man." *The American Scholar* 21: 2, 177–191.

Cohen, I. Bernard. 1990. *Benjamin Franklin's Science*. Cambridge and London: Harvard University Press.

Cohen, Morris Raphael. 1962. *American Thought: A Critical Sketch*. New York: Collier Books.

Colden, Cadwallader. 1946. "An Introduction to the Study of Phylosophy Wrote in America for the Use of a Young Gentleman." In *American Philosophic Addresses: 1700–1900*, ed. Joseph L. Blau. New York: Columbia University Press.

Columbus, Christopher. 1988. *The Four Voyages of Columbus*. Translated by Cecil Jane. New York: Dover.

Converse, Harriet Maxwell. 1908. *Myths and Legends of the New York State Iroquois*. Education Department Bulletin, 437. Albany, N.Y.

Cooper, Anna Julia. 1998. *The Voice of Anna Julia Cooper*. Edited by Charles Lemert and Esme Bhan. Lanham, Md.: Rowman and Littlefield.

Cooper, James Fenimore. 1954. *The Leatherstocking Saga*. Edited by Allan Nevins. New York: Pantheon Books.

Cotton, John. 1830. "Cotton's Vocabulary of the Massachusetts (or Natick) Indian Language." In *Collections of the Massachusetts Historical Society*, vol. 2, 3rd Series, 147–255. Cambridge, Mass.: E. W. Metcalf and Co.

Curtin, Jeremiah, and J. N. B. Hewitt. 1918. *Seneca Fiction, Legends, and Myths*. Edited by J. N. B. Hewitt. Washington, D.C.: Government Printing Office.

Daniel, Stephen H. 1994. *The Philosophy of Jonathan Edwards: A Study in Divine Semiotics*. Bloomington and Indianapolis: Indiana University Press.

Davis, Allen F. 1973. *American Heroine: The Life and Legend of Jane Addams*. London: Oxford University Press.

Davis, Jack L. 1970. "Roger Williams among the Narragansett Indians." *The New England Quarterly* 43: 593–604.

Day, Gordon M. 1978. "Western Abenaki." In *Handbook of North American Indians*, vol. 15. Edited by Bruce Trigger. Washington, D.C.: Smithsonian Institution.

Deegan, Mary Jo. 1988. *Jane Addams and the Men of the Chicago School, 1892–1918*. New Brunswick, N.J., and Oxford: Transaction Books.

Deloria, Vine Jr. 1979. *The Metaphysics of Modern Existence*. San Francisco: Harper and Row.

———. 1994. *God Is Red: A Native View of Religion*. Golden, Colo.: Fulcrum Publishing.

———. 1995. *Red Earth, White Lies: Native Americans and the Myth of Scientific Fact*. New York: Scribner.

Densmore, Christopher. 1999. *Red Jacket: Iroquois Diplomat and Orator*. Syracuse: Syracuse University Press.

Dewey, Jane M. 1939. "Biography of John Dewey." In *The Philosophy of John Dewey*, ed. Paul Arthur Schilpp. Evanston, Ill., and Chicago: Northwestern University Press.

Dewey, John. 1893. "Why Study Philosophy?" In J. Boydston, *The Early Works, 1882–1898*, vol. 4. Carbondale: Southern Illinois University Press, 1969–1972.

——. 1905. "Philosophy and American National Life." In J. Boydston, *The Middle Works, 1899–1924*, vol. 3. Carbondale: Southern Illinois University Press, 1976–1983.

——. 1909. "The Influence of Darwin on Philosophy." In J. Boydston, *The Middle Works, 1899–1924*, vol. 4. Carbondale: Southern Illinois University Press, 1976–1983.

——. 1916. *Democracy and Education*. In J. Boydston, *The Middle Works, 1899–1924*, vol. 9. Carbondale: Southern Illinois University Press, 1976–1983.

——. 1922. "Pragmatic America." In J. Boydston, *The Middle Works, 1899–1924*, vol. 13. Carbondale: Southern Illinois University Press, 1976–1983.

——. 1925. *Experience and Nature*. In J. Boydston, *The Later Works: 1925–1953*, vol. 1. Carbondale: Southern Illinois University Press, 1981–1990.

——. 1925a. "The Development of American Pragmatism." In J. Boydston, *The Later Works: 1925–1953*, vol. 2. Carbondale: Southern Illinois University Press, 1981–1990.

——. 1926. *The Public and Its Problems*. In J. Boydston, *The Later Works: 1925–1953*, vol. 2. Carbondale: Southern Illinois University Press, 1981–1990.

——. 1927. "Foreword to Paul Radin's *Primitive Man as Philosopher*." In J. Boydston, *The Later Works: 1925–1953*, vol. 3. Carbondale: Southern Illinois University Press, 1981–1990.

——. 1929. *The Quest for Certainty*. In J. Boydston, *The Later Works: 1925–1953*, vol. 4. Carbondale: Southern Illinois University Press, 1981–1990.

——. 1931. "Context and Thought." In J. Boydston, *The Later Works: 1925–1953*, vol. 6. Carbondale: Southern Illinois University Press, 1981–1990.

——. 1932. *Ethics, Revised Edition*. In J. Boydston, *The Later Works: 1925–1953*, vol. 7. Carbondale: Southern Illinois University Press, 1981–1990.

——. 1934. "Philosophy." In J. Boydston, *The Later Works: 1925–1953*, vol. 8. Carbondale: Southern Illinois University Press, 1981–1990.

——. 1934a. *Art as Experience*. In J. Boydston, *The Later Works: 1925–1953*, vol. 10. Carbondale: Southern Illinois University Press, 1981–1990.

——. 1938. *Logic: The Theory of Inquiry*. In J. Boydston, *The Later Works: 1925–1953*, vol. 12. Carbondale: Southern Illinois University Press, 1981–1990.

——. 1938a. "Democracy and Education in the World Today." In J. Boydston, *The Later Works: 1925–1953*, vol. 13. Carbondale: Southern Illinois University Press, 1981–1990.

——. 1939. *Freedom and Culture*. In J. Boydston, *The Later Works: 1925–1953*, vol. 13. Carbondale: Southern Illinois University Press, 1981–1990.

——. 1940. "Presenting Thomas Jefferson." In J. Boydston, *The Later Works: 1925–1953*, vol. 14. Carbondale: Southern Illinois University Press, 1981–1990.

——. 1944. "Between Two Worlds." In J. Boydston, *The Later Works: 1925–1953*, vol. 17. Carbondale: Southern Illinois University Press, 1981–1990.

——. 1946. Introduction to *The Problems of Men*. In J. Boydston, *The Later Works: 1925–1953*, vol. 15. Carbondale: Southern Illinois University Press, 1981–1990.

————. 1948. *Reconstruction in Philosophy*. In J. Boydston, *The Later Works: 1925–1953*, vol. 12. Carbondale: Southern Illinois University Press, 1981–1990.

————. 1969. "Introduction to Philosophy: Syllabus of Course 5 Philosophical Department." In J. Boydston, *The Early Works, 1882–1898*, vol. 3. Carbondale: Southern Illinois University Press, 1969–1972.

Douglass, Frederick. 1984. *The Narrative and Selected Writings*. Edited with an introduction by Michael Meyer. New York: Modern Library.

Dowd, Gregory Evans. 1992. *A Spirited Resistance: The North American Indian Struggle for Unity, 1745–1815*. Baltimore: Johns Hopkins University Press.

Du Bois, W. E. B. 1989. *The Souls of Black Folk*. New York: Bantam Books.

Dykhuizen, George. 1973. *The Life and Mind of John Dewey*. Carbondale and Edwardsville: Southern Illinois University Press.

Eastman, Charles. 1911. *The Soul of An Indian*. Boston: Houghton Mifflin.

Eckstorm, Fannie Hardy. 1934. "The Attack on Norridgewock." *The New England Quarterly* 7: 341–378.

————. 1945. *Old John Neptune and Other Maine Indian Shamans*. Portland, Me.: Southworth-Anthoensen Press.

————. 1970. *The Penobscot Man*. Freeport, N.Y.: Books for Libraries Press.

Edwards, Jonathan. 1972. *The Great Awakening*. Edited by C. C. Goen. New Haven, Conn., and London: Yale University Press.

————. 1985. *The Life of David Brainerd*. Edited by Norman Pettit. New Haven, Conn.: Yale University Press.

————. 1989. *A History of the Work of Redemption*. Transcribed and edited by John F. Wilson. New Haven, Conn.: Yale University Press, 1989.

Eliot, John. 1904. *The Logic Primer*. Cleveland: Burrows Brothers Co.

Emerson, Ralph Waldo. 1909. *Journals of Ralph Waldo Emerson*, Vol. 1. Edited by Edward Waldo Emerson. Boston and New York: Houghton Mifflin Co.

————. 1929. *The Complete Writings of Ralph Waldo Emerson*. New York: W. H. Wise & Co.

————. 1939. *The Letters of Ralph Waldo Emerson*. Edited by Ralph L. Rusk. New York: Columbia University Press.

Erikson, Vincent O. 1978. "Maliseet-Passamaquoddy." In *Handbook of North American Indians*, vol. 15, ed. Bruce Trigger, 123–136. Washington, D.C.: Smithsonian Institution.

Evarts, Jeremiah. 1981. *Cherokee Removal: The "William Penn" Essays and Other Writings*. Edited, with an introduction, by Francis Paul Prucha. Knoxville: University of Tennessee Press.

Fay, Cornelius Ryan Jr. 1950. "An Essay Describing Colden's *The First Principles of Morality*." Master's thesis, Columbia University.

Fenton, William N. 1985. "Structure, Continuity, and Change in the Process of Iroquois Treaty Making." In Francis Jennings, William N. Fenton, Mary A. Druke, and David R. Miller, eds., *The History and Culture of Iroquois Diplomacy*. Syracuse: Syracuse University Press.

————. 1987. *The False Faces of the Iroquois*. Norman: University of Oklahoma Press.

Feuer, Lewis S. 1989. Introduction. In J. Boydston, *The Later Works: 1925–1953*, vol. 15. Carbondale: Southern Illinois University Press, 1981–1990.

Flower, Elizabeth, and Murray G. Murphey. 1977. *A History of Philosophy in America*. 2 vol. New York: Capricorn Books.

Foner, Eric, and Robert James Branham, eds. 1998. *Lift Every Voice: African American Oratory, 1787–1900.* Tuscaloosa and London: University of Alabama Press.

Forbes, Jack D. 1992. *Columbus and Other Cannibals: The Wétiko Disease of Exploitation, Imperialism and Terrorism.* Brooklyn, N.Y.: Autonomedia.

———. 1993. *Africans and Native Americans: The Language of Race and the Evolution of Red-Black Peoples.* Urbana and Chicago: University of Illinois Press.

Foster, Edward Halsey. 1974. *Catharine Maria Sedgwick.* New York: Twayne Publishers.

Foster, Michael K. 1985. "Another Look at the Function of Wampum in Iroquois-White Councils." In Francis Jennings, William N. Fenton, Mary A. Druke, and David R. Miller, eds., *The History and Culture of Iroquois Diplomacy.* Syracuse: Syracuse University Press.

Franklin, Benjamin. 1907. *The Writings of Benjamin Franklin.* Collected and edited by Albert Henry Smyth. New York: Haskell House Publishers, 1970.

———. 1959–. *The Papers of Benjamin Franklin.* 34 vols. Leonard W. Labaree, Editor; Whitfield J. Bell, Jr., Associate Editor. New Haven, Conn.: Yale University Press.

———. 1987. *Writings.* New York: Library of America.

Gardener, Lion. 1833. "Relation of the Pequot Warres." In *Collections of the Massachusetts Historical Society*, vol. 3, 3rd series. Cambridge, Mass.: E. W. Metcalf and Co.

Gaustad, Edwin S. 1991. *Liberty of Conscience: Roger Williams in America.* Grand Rapids, Mich.: W. B. Eerdmans.

Gilman, Charlotte Perkins. 1898. *Women and Economics.* Boston: Small, Maynard and Co.

Goddard, Ives. 1978. *Delaware Verbal Morphology: A Descriptive and Comparative Study.* New York: Garland.

Goddard, Ives, and Kathleen J. Bragdon. 1988. *Native Writings in Massachusett.* 2 vols. Philadelphia: American Philosophical Society.

Gookin, Daniel. 1970. *Historical Collections of the Indians in New England.* With notes by Jeffrey H. Fiske. [n.p.]: Towtaid.

Gould, Philip. 1996. *Covenant and Republic.* Cambridge: Cambridge University Press.

Grinde, Donald A., and Bruce E. Johansen. 1991. *Exemplar of Liberty: Native America and the Evolution of Democracy.* Los Angeles: American Indian Studies Center, University of California.

Grinde, Donald A. Jr. 1977. *The Iroquois and the Founding of the American Nation.* San Francisco: Indian Historian Press.

Hakluyt, Richard. 1877. *A Discourse concerning the Western Planting.* Edited by Charles Deane. Cambridge: Press of John Wilson and Son.

Hale, Horatio. 1883. *The Iroquois Book of Rites.* New York: AMS Press.

Handlin, Lilian. 1984. *George Bancroft: The Intellectual as Democrat.* New York: Harper and Row.

Harding, Vincent. 1991. *A Certain Magnificence: Lyman Beecher and the Transformation of American Protestantism, 1775–1863.* Brooklyn, N.Y.: Carlson Publishing.

Harvey, Oscar J. 1909–1930. *A History of Wilkes-Barré, Luzerne County, Pennsylvania.* 6 vols. Wilkes-Barré, Pa.: [Raeder Press].

Heckewelder, John. 1971. *History, Manners, and Customs of the Indian Nations.*

Philadelphia: Historical Society of Pennsylvania. Reprinted by Arno Press and the *New York Times*.

Hedges, William L. 1976. "From Franklin to Emerson." In *The Oldest Revolutionary: Essays on Benjamin Franklin,* ed. J. A. Leo Lemay. Philadelphia: University of Pennsylvania Press.

Hegel, Georg W. F. 1861. *Lectures on the Philosophy of History.* Translated by J. Sibree. London: H. G. Bohn.

——. 1975. *Lectures on the Philosophy of World History.* Translated by H. B. Nisbet. Cambridge: Cambridge University Press.

Heimert, Alan, and Perry Miller, ed. 1967. *The Great Awakening: Documents Illustrating the Crisis and Its Consequences.* Indianapolis and New York: Bobbs-Merrill Co.

Herder, Johann Gottfried. 1968. *Reflections on the Philosophy of the History of Mankind.* Abridged and with an introduction by Frank E. Manuel. Chicago: University of Chicago Press.

Hertzberg, Hazel W. 1971. *The Search for an American Indian Identity: Modern Pan-Indian Movements.* Syracuse: Syracuse University Press.

Hewitt, J. N. B. 1902. "Orenda and a Definition of Religion." *American Anthropologist* 4: 33–46.

——. 1903. "Iroquoian Cosmology." In *Twenty-First Annual Report of the Bureau of American Ethnology, 1899–1900.* Washington, D.C.: Government Printing Office.

——. 1928. "Iroquoian Cosmology—Second Part." In *Forty-Third Annual Report of the Bureau of American Ethnology, 1925–1926.* Washington, D.C.: Government Printing Office.

Howe, M. A. De Wolfe. 1908. *The Life and Letters of George Bancroft.* 2 vols. New York: Charles Scribner's Sons.

Howell, Wilbur Samuel. 1956. *Logic and Rhetoric in England, 1500–1700.* Princeton, N.J.: Princeton University Press.

Hsia, R. Po-Chia. 1988. *The Myth of Ritual Murder: Jews and Magic in Reformation Germany.* New Haven, Conn.: Yale University Press.

Jacobs, Harriet. 1987. *Incidents in the Life of a Slave Girl.* In *The Classic Slave Narratives,* edited with an introduction by Henry Louis Gates Jr. New York: Mentor Books.

James, William. 1902. *The Varieties of Religious Experience.* New York: Longmans, Green and Co.

——. 1950. *The Principles of Psychology.* 2 vols. New York: Dover.

——. 1956. *The Will to Believe.* New York: Dover.

——. 1967. *The Writings of William James.* Edited by J. J. McDermott. New York: Random House.

——. 1975. *Pragmatism: A New Name for Some Old Ways of Thinking & The Meaning of Truth: A Sequel to Pragmatism.* Cambridge, Mass.: Harvard University Press.

——. 1992. *Writings 1878–1899.* Edited by Gerald E. Myers. New York: Library of America.

——. 1996. *Some Problems of Philosophy.* Lincoln and London: University of Nebraska Press.

——. 1996a. *Essays in Radical Empiricism.* Lincoln and London: University of Nebraska Press.

Jefferson, Thomas. 1984. *Writings.* New York: Library of America.

Jennings, Francis, William N. Fenton, Mary A. Druke, and David R. Miller, eds. 1985. "Glossary of Figures of Speech in Iroquois Political Rhetoric." In Francis Jennings, William N. Fenton, Mary A. Druke, and David R. Miller, eds., *The History and Culture of Iroquois Diplomacy*. Syracuse: Syracuse University Press.

———. 1995. *The History and Culture of Iroquois Diplomacy*. Syracuse: Syracuse University Press.

Jensen, Joan. 1990. "Native American Women and Agriculture: A Seneca Case Study." In *Unequal Sisters: A Multicultural Reader in U.S. Women's History*, ed. Ellen Carol DuBois and Vicki L. Ruiz. New York: Routledge.

Johansen, Bruce E. 1982. *Forgotten Founders*. Harvard and Boston: Harvard Common Press.

———. 1998. *Debating Democracy: Native American Legacy of Freedom*. Sante Fe: Clear Light Publishers.

Johnson, Samuel. 1929. *Samuel Johnson, President of King's College: His Career and Writings*. Vol. II, ed. Herbert and Carol Schneider. New York: Columbia University Press.

Karcher, Carolyn L. 1994. *The First Woman in the Republic: A Cultural Biography of Lydia Maria Child*. Durham, N.C., and London: Duke University Press.

Karlsen, Carol F. 1987. *The Devil in the Shape of a Woman: Witchcraft in Colonial New England*. New York: Norton.

Kenny, James. 1913. "Journal of James Kenny, 1761–1763." *The Pennsylvania Magazine of History and Biography* 38, no.1.

Knowles, James D. 1834. *Memoir of Roger Williams, the Founder of Rhode-Island*. Boston: Lincoln, Edmands and Co.

LaFantasie, Glenn W. 1988. *The Correspondence of Roger Williams*. 2 vols. Providence, R.I.: Published for The Rhode Island Historical Society by Brown University Press/University Press of New England, Hanover and London.

Lambert, Frank. 1999. *Inventing the "Great Awakening."* Princeton, N.J.: Princeton University Press.

Landsman, Gail H. 1992. "The 'Other' as Political Symbol: Images of Indians in the Woman Suffrage Movement." *Ethnohistory* 39, no. 3 (Summer): 247–284.

Leland, Charles G. 1884. *The Algonquin Legends of New England*. Boston: Houghton, Mifflin and Co.

Lemay, J. A. Leo. 1993. "Rhetorical Strategies in 'Sinners in the Hands of an Angry God' and 'Narrative of the Late Massacres in Lancaster County.'" In *Benjamin Franklin, Jonathan Edwards, and the Representation of American Culture*, ed. Barbara Oberg and Harry S. Stout. New York and Oxford: Oxford University Press.

Lepore, Jill. 1998. *The Name of War: King Philip's War and the Origins of American Identity*. New York: Knopf.

Lincoln, Charles H. 1913. *Narratives of the Indian Wars: 1675–1699*. New York: Charles Scribner's Sons.

Lindsey, Donal F. 1995. *Indians at Hampton Institute, 1877–1923*. Urbana: University of Illinois Press.

Locke, John. 1955. *A Letter Concerning Toleration*. With an introduction by Patrick Romanell. Indianapolis: Library of the Liberal Arts.

———. 1959. *An Essay Concerning Human Understanding*. 2 vols. Collated and annotated by A. C. Fraser. New York: Dover.

Lovejoy, Arthur O. 1936. *The Great Chain of Being: A Study of the History of an Idea*. New York: Harper and Row.

——. 1963. *The Thirteen Pragmatisms and Other Essays*. Baltimore: Johns Hopkins University Press.

Mather, Cotton. 1691. *The Life of the Renowned John Eliot*. Boston: Benjamin Harris and John Allen.

——. 1966. *Bonifacius: An Essay upon the Good*. Edited by David Levin. Cambridge, Mass.: Belknap Press of Harvard University Press.

——. 1967. *Magnalia Christi Americana*. 2 vols. New York: Russell & Russell.

——. 1977. *Magnalia Christi Americana*. Edited by Kenneth B. Murdock. Cambridge, Mass.: Belknap Press of Harvard University Press.

——. 1994. *The Christian Philosopher*. Edited with an introduction and notes by Winton U. Solberg. Urbana: University of Illinois Press.

Mather, Increase. 1986. *Departing Glory: Eight Jeremiads*. Delmar, N.Y.: Scholars' Facsimiles & Reprints.

McCosh, James. 1887. *Realistic Philosophy Defended in a Philosophic Series*. London: Macmillan.

McDermott, John J. 1966. *The American Angle of Vision. Cross Currents*, Winter and Fall, 1965.

——. 1976. *The Culture of Experience: Philosophical Essays in the American Grain*. New York: New York University Press.

McKenney, Thomas Loraine. 1827. *Sketches of a Tour to the Lakes*. Baltimore: F. Lucas, Jun'r.

Meek, Ronald. 1976. *Social Science and the Ignoble Savage*. Cambridge and New York: Cambridge University Press.

Miller, Perry. 1939. *The New England Mind: The Seventeenth Century*. New York: Macmillan.

——. 1953. *Roger Williams: His Contribution to the American Tradition*. Indianapolis: Bobbs Merrill.

——. 1953a. *The New England Mind: From Colony to Province*. Cambridge, Mass.: Harvard University Press.

——. 1956. *Errand into the Wilderness*. Cambridge, Mass.: Belknap Press of Harvard University Press.

Mills, Bruce. 1994. *Cultural Reformations: Lydia Maria Child and the Literature of Reform*. Athens and London: University of Georgia Press.

Mohawk, John. 1992. "Looking for Columbus: Thoughts on the Past, Present and Future of Humanity." In *The State of Native America: Genocide, Colonization, and Resistance*, ed. M. Annete Jaimes. Boston: South End Press.

Morgan, Edmund S. 1967. *Roger Williams: The Church and State*. New York: Harcourt, Brace & World.

Morton, Thomas. 1972. *New English Canaan; or, New Canaan*. New York: Arno Press.

Mulford, Carla. 1993. "*Caritas* and Capital: Franklin's 'Narrative of the Late Massacres.'" In *Reappraising Benjamin Franklin: A Bicentennial Perspective*, ed. J. A. Leo Lemay. Newark: University of Delaware Press.

Mumford, Lewis. 1926. *The Golden Day: A Study in American Experience and Culture*. New York: Boni and Liveright.

Newton, Isaac. 1931. *Opticks; or, A Treatise of the Reflections, Refractions, Inflections and Colours of Light*. 4th ed. London: G. Bell & Sons.

Nye, Russell B. 1964. *George Bancroft*. New York: Washington Square Press.

Parker, Arthur C. 1968. *The Constitution of the Iroquois in Parker on the Iroquois.* Edited by William N. Fenton. Syracuse: Syracuse University Press.

——. 1989. *Seneca Myths and Folk Tales.* Lincoln and London: University of Nebraska Press.

Parkman, Francis. 1962. *The Conspiracy of Pontiac.* New York: Collier Books.

Parrington, Vernon L. 1927. *Main Currents in American Thought.* 2 vols. New York: Harcourt, Brace, and Co.

Peirce, Charles Sanders. 1955. *Philosophical Writings of Peirce.* Edited by Justus Buchler. New York: Dover.

——. 1992. *The Essential Peirce.* Vol. 1, ed. Nathan Houser and Christian Kloesel. Bloomington and Indianapolis: Indiana University Press.

——. 1998. *The Essential Peirce.* Vol. 2, ed. the Peirce Edition Project. Bloomington and Indianapolis: Indiana University Press.

Porter, Noah. 1894. *History of Philosophy,* by Friedrich Uberweg. Vol. 2. Translated by George S. Morris. New York: Charles Scribner's Sons.

Pratt, Scott L. 1996. "The Influence of the Iroquois on Early American Philosophy." *Transactions of the Charles S. Peirce Society* 32, no. 2 (Spring).

——. 1997. "'A Sailor in a Storm': Dewey on the Meaning of Language." *Transactions of the Charles S. Peirce Society* 33, no. 4 (Fall).

——. 1997a. "Native American Thought and the Origins of Pragmatism." *Ayaangwaamizin: The International Journal of Indigenous Philosophy* 1, no. 1.

——. 1998. "Ceremony and Rationality in the Haudenosaunee Tradition." In *Theorizing Multiculturalism: A Guide to the Current Debate,* ed. Cynthia Willett, 401–421. Malden, Mass.: Blackwell Publishing.

——. 2001. "The Given Land: Black Hawk's Conception of Place." *Philosophy and Geography* 4:1, 109–125.

Pratt, Scott L., and John Ryder, eds. Forthcoming. *The Philosophy of Cadwallader Colden.* Buffalo, N.Y.: Humanity Books.

Pulsifer, David. 1859. *Records of the Colony of New Plymouth in New England.* Vol. 1. Boston: William White.

Radin, Paul. 1957. *Primitive Man as Philosopher.* 2nd ed. New York: Dover.

——. 1990. *The Winnebago Tribe.* Lincoln and London: University of Nebraska Press.

Ramus, Peter. 1969. *The Logike of The Moste Excellent Philosopher P. Ramus Martyr.* Translated by Roland MacIlmaine, edited by Catherine M. Dunn. Northridge, Calif.: San Fernando Valley State College.

Randall, John Herman. 1958. *Nature and Historical Experience: Essays in Naturalism and in The Theory of History.* New York: Columbia University Press.

Riley, I. Woodbridge. 1907. *American Philosophy: The Early Schools.* New York: Dodd, Mead, and Co.

Rogin, Michael Paul. 1975. *Fathers and Children: Andrew Jackson and the Subjugation of the American Indian.* New York: Vintage Books.

Rosenthal, Sandra B. 1994. *Charles Peirce's Pragmatic Pluralism.* Albany: State University of New York Press.

Ross, John. 1985. *The Papers of Chief John Ross.* 2 vols. Edited and with an introduction by Gary E. Moulton. Norman: University of Oklahoma Press.

Russell, Bertrand. 1919. "Professor Dewey's 'Essays in Experimental Logic.'" In *Dewey and his Critics: Essays from the Journal of Philosophy,* ed. Sidney Morganbesser. New York: Journal of Philosophy, 1977.

——. 1939. "Dewey's New 'Logic.'" In *The Philosophy of John Dewey*, ed. Paul Arthur Schilpp. Evanston, Ill., and Chicago: Northwestern University Press.

——. 1945. *A History of Western Philosophy, and Its Connection with Political and Social Circumstances from the Earliest Times to the Present Day*. New York: Simon and Schuster.

Salisbury, Neal. 1982. *Manitou and Providence: Indians, Europeans, and the Making of New England, 1500–1643*. New York: Oxford University Press.

Santayana, George. 1912. "The Genteel Tradition in American Philosophy." In *The Development of American Philosophy: A Book of Readings*, ed. Walter G. Muelder, Laurence Sears, and Anne V. Schlabach. New York: Houghton Mifflin Co, 1960.

Satz, Ronald N. 1975. *American Indian Policy in the Jacksonian Era*. Lincoln: University of Nebraska Press.

Sayre, Robert F. 1977. *Thoreau and the American Indians*. Princeton, N.J.: Princeton University Press.

Schneider, Herbert W. 1946. *A History of American Philosophy*. New York: Columbia University Press.

Schoolcraft, Henry Rowe. 1856. *The Myth of Hiawatha, and Other Oral Legends, Mythologic and Allegoric, of the North American Indians*. Philadelphia: J. B. Lippincott & Co.

——. 1962. *The Literary Voyager, or, Muzzeniegun*. Edited with an introduction by Philip P. Mason. East Lansing: Michigan State University Press.

Sedgwick, Catharine Maria. 1850. *The Irish Girl and Other Tales*. London: Kent & Richards.

——. 1969. *Redwood: A Tale*. New York: Garrett Press.

——. 1987. *Hope Leslie; or, Early Times in the Massachusetts*. Edited with an introduction by Mary Kelley. New Brunswick, N.J., and London: Rutgers University Press.

Seigfried, Charlene Haddock. 1990. *William James's Radical Reconstruction of Philosophy*. Albany: State University of New York Press.

——. 1996. *Pragmatism and Feminism*. Chicago and London: University of Chicago Press.

Shakespeare, William. 1959. *The Merchant of Venice*. Edited by Brents Stirling. Baltimore: Penguin Books.

Sheehan, Bernard W. 1973. *The Seeds of Extinction: Jeffersonian Philanthropy and the American Indian*. New York: W. W. Norton & Co.

Shoerer, C. E. 1962. "Indian Tales of C. C. Trowbridge: The Star Woman." *Midwest Folklore* 12: 17–23.

Simmons, William S. 1986. *Spirit of the New England Tribes: Indian History and Folklore, 1620–1984*. Hanover, N.H., and London: University Press of New England.

Sklar, Kathryn Kish. 1973. *Catharine Beecher: A Study in American Domesticity*. New Haven, Conn., and London: Yale University Press.

Smith, Erminnie A. 1883. "Myths of the Iroquois." In *Second Annual Report of the Bureau of Ethnology: 1880–81*. Washington, D.C.: Government Printing Office.

Smith, John E. 1963. *The Spirit of American Philosophy*. London: Oxford University Press.

——. 1992. *America's Philosophical Vision*. Chicago: University of Chicago Press.

Smith, Samuel Stanhope. 1995. *An Essay on the Causes of Complexion and Figure in the Human Species.* Introduction by Paul B. Wood. Bristol, England: Thoemmes Press.

Snow, Dean R. 1978. "Eastern Abenaki." In *Handbook of North American Indians,* vol. 15, ed. Bruce Trigger. Washington, D.C.: Smithsonian Institution.

Solomon, Barbara H., ed. 1994. *Rediscoveries: American Short Stories by Women, 1832–1916.* New York: Mentor Books.

Speck, Frank G. 1935. "Penobscot Tales and Religious Beliefs." *The Journal of American Folklore* 48: 187.

———. 1940. *Penobscot Man; The Life History of a Forest Tribe in Maine.* Philadelphia: University of Pennsylvania Press.

St. John de Crèvecoeur, J. Hector. 1981. *Letters from an American Farmer.* Edited by Albert E. Stone. New York: Penguin Books.

Stannard, David E. 1992. *American Holocaust: Columbus and the Conquest of the New World.* New York: Oxford University Press.

Stevens, Frank E. 1903. *The Black Hawk War.* Chicago: Frank E. Stevens.

Stone, William L. 1866. *The Life and Times of Sa-Go-Ye-Wat-Ha, or Red Jacket.* Albany, N.Y.: J. Munsell.

Stuhr, John. 1997. *Genealogical Pragmatism: Philosophy, Experience, and Community.* Albany: State University of New York Press.

Teicher, Morton I. 1960. "Windigo Psychosis." In *Proceedings of the 1960 Annual Spring Meeting of the American Ethnological Society,* ed. Verne Ray. Seattle: American Ethnological Society.

Thayer, H. S. 1981. *Meaning and Action.* Indianapolis: Hackett Publishing.

Thoreau, Henry David. 1966. *The Maine Woods.* New York: Thomas Y. Crowell Co.

Tocqueville, Alexis de. 1969. *Democracy in America.* Edited by J. P. Mayer. Translated by George Lawrence. New York: Harper and Row.

Tompkins, Jane. 1985. *Sensational Designs: The Cultural Work of American Fiction 1790–1860.* New York: Oxford University Press.

Tooker, Elizabeth. 1988. "The United States Constitution and the Iroquois League." *Ethnohistory* 35, no. 4.

Trowbridge, Charles C. 1939. *Shawnese Traditions.* Edited by Vernon Kinietz and Erminie W. Voegelin. Museum of Anthropology Occasional Contributions, no. 9. Ann Arbor: University of Michigan Press.

Trumbull, James Hammond. 1903. *Natick Dictionary.* Washington, D.C.: Government Printing Office.

Tuana, Nancy. 1993. *The Less Noble Sex: Scientific, Religious, and Philosophical Conceptions of Woman's Nature.* Bloomington: Indiana University Press.

Turner, Frederick Jackson. 1996. *The Frontier in American History.* New York: Dover.

Van Doren, Carl, and Julian P. Boyd, eds. 1938. *Indian Treaties Printed by Benjamin Franklin, 1736–1762.* Philadelphia: Historical Society of Pennsylvania.

Van Doren, Carl. 1938. *Benjamin Franklin.* New York: Viking Press.

Vespucci, Amerigo. 1895. *The Letters of Amerigo Vespucci and Other Documents Illustrative of his Career.* Translated with an introduction by Clements R. Markham. London: Hakluyt Society.

Vetromile, Eugene. 1866. *The Abnakis and Their History.* New York: James B. Kirber.

Voegelin, C. F. 1945. "Delaware Texts." *International Journal of American Linguistics* 9: 105–119.

Wagner, Sally Roesch. 1992. "The Iroquois Influence on Women's Rights." In *Indian Roots of American Democracy*, edited with an introduction by José Barreiro. Ithaca, N.Y.: Akwe:kon Press, Cornell University.

Wallace, Anthony F. C. 1990. *King of the Delawares: Teedyuscung, 1700–1763*. Syracuse: Syracuse University Press.

Wallace, Paul A. W. 1945. *Conrad Weiser, 1696–1760: Friend of Colonist and Mohawk*. Philadelphia: University of Pennsylvania Press; London: Oxford University Press.

———. 1994. *The Iroquois Book of Life: The White Roots of Peace*. Sante Fe, N.M..: Clear Light Publishers.

Wallis, Wilson D., and Ruth Sawtell Wallis. 1955. *The Micmac Indians of Eastern Canada*. Minneapolis: University of Minnesota Press.

Weatherford, Jack. 1988. *Indian Givers: How the Indians of the Americas Transformed the World*. New York: Fawcett Columbine.

Welter, Barbara. 1966. "The Cult of True Womanhood: 1820–1860." *American Quarterly* 18: 151–174.

West, Cornel. 1989. *The American Evasion of Philosophy: A Genealogy of Pragmatism*. Madison: University of Wisconsin Press.

Westbrook, Robert B. 1991. *John Dewey and American Democracy*. Ithaca, N.Y., and London: Cornell University Press.

White, Morton. 1972. *Science and Sentiment in America: Philosophical Thought from Jonathan Edwards to John Dewey*. London: Oxford University Press.

White, Richard. 1991. *The Middle Ground: Indians, Empires, and Republics in the Great Lakes Region, 1650–1815*. Cambridge and New York: Cambridge University Press.

Williams, Roger. 1848. *The Bloudy Tenent of Persecution for Cause of Conscience Discussed and Mr. Cotton's Letter Examined and Answered*. Edited for the Hanserd Knollys Society by Edward Bean Underhill. London: Haddon.

———. 1866–1874. *Publications of the Narragansett Club*. 6 vols. Providence, R.I.

———. 1963. *The Complete Writings of Roger Williams*. Vol. 7. Edited by Perry Miller. New York: Russell & Russell.

———. 1973. *A Key into the Language of America*. Edited with a critical introduction, notes, and commentary by John J. Teunissen and Evelyn J. Hinz. Detroit: Wayne State University Press.

Williams, Selma R. 1981. *Divine Rebel: The Life of Anne Marbury Hutchinson*. New York: Holt, Rinehart and Winston.

Winthrop, John. 1996. *The Journal of John Winthrop, 1630–1649*. Edited by Richard S. Dunn, James Savage, and Laetitia Yeandle. Cambridge, Mass.: Belknap Press of Harvard University Press.

Wright, Frances. 1829. *Course of Popular Lectures*. New York: Office of the Free Enquirer.

Wollstonecraft, Mary. 1975. *A Vindication of the Rights of Woman*. Edited by Carol H. Poston. New York: Norton.

Zwarg, Christina. 1995. *Feminist Conversations: Fuller, Emerson, and the Play of Reading*. Ithaca, N.Y., and London: Cornell University Press.

INDEX

SCOTT L. PRATT is Associate Professor of Philosophy and head of the Philosophy Department at the University of Oregon. He received his B.A. in philosophy from Beloit College (Wisconsin) and his Ph.D. from the University of Minnesota. He teaches American Philosophy and the history of Modern European Philosophy, and is co-editor of *American Philosophies: An Anthology* and *The Philosophical Writings of Cadwallader Colden.*